*George Plasketes*

# Images of Elvis Presley in American Culture, 1977-1997
## *The Mystery Terrain*

*Pre-publication
REVIEWS,
COMMENTARIES,
EVALUATIONS . . .*

"What could be left to say about Elvis? Well, consider, as George Plasketes does, this question: Does the New England Patriot football emblem resemble the King? If so, is it intentional? E-worship is by now an accepted fact of American culture, but just how ubiquitous E-iconography has become is this entertaining study's subject. Comprehensive, well documented, possessed of a fine bibliography and filmography/videography, the book is a pleasure for fan and critic alike. Presleyphiles will revel in it, of course, and Presley-phobes (e.g., Spike Lee, whom Plasketes cites for whining, 'I wish [Elvis had] never died . . . so I wouldn't have to hear about him every single day') will derive perverse pleasure as Plasketes helps legitimate their worst fears. A special treat needs mention: the discography, composed of songs about Elvis, from Adrenalin A. O. D.'s 'Velvet Elvis' to Frank Zappa's 'Elvis Has Just Left the Building.' Elvis-intensive collections, take this hunka-hunka burnin' read."

***Booklist***

" **I**f the King himself is the heavenly engineer on the Mystery Train, George Plasketes, in *Images of Elvis Presley in American Culture, 1977-1997: The Mystery Terrain*, is a more than able earthly conductor. Plasketes admits that when he was young he was among those who 'never loved Elvis.' He too, however, has become a victim of the contemporary 'Elvirus,' mainly through a fascination with the seemingly infinite manifestations of Elvis veneration that permeate every corner of American culture, from obscure punk rock rantings to Al Gore's only half-joking claim that Bill Clinton may be the King of Rock and Roll reincarnated. There are hundreds of examples of Elvisiana in the book, each of them detailed by Plasketes in a lively style that is scholarly, amused, or appalled, sometimes all at once.

Like any good train conductor, Plasketes keeps the cars organized and the train running on time. The huge number of examples are organized into logical chapters–records, literature, drama, film, etc.–and individual items are described not only by content but by theme and in relation to one another. The trip is both fun and in-depth and the book is by far the most thorough analysis of the ongoing Elvis phenomenon yet published. If Plasketes never brings us to the exact meaning of why Elvis remains so central to American culture, it is because, as he himself demonstrates, the subject itself has almost as many meanings as there are black velvet Elvis paintings.

Elvis fans and students of American culture will all want to climb aboard this *Mystery Terrain*. The Elvis sightings are frequent, funny, and full of insights."

**Jack Nachbar, PhD**
*Professor of Popular Culture,*
*Bowling Green State University,*
*Ohio*

" **D**r. George Plasketes thoroughly examines the sociocultural impact of Elvis since his death twenty years ago in *Images of Elvis Presley in American Culture, 1977-1997: The Mystery Terrain*. The author investigates Elvis 'citings . . . not sightings' in music, books, theater, art, sports, television, film, and ultimately, our political culture as well. Even though we all probably take the pervasiveness of Elvis for granted, readers are likely to be surprised at just how ubiquitous Elvis really is in contemporary America today.

Plasketes is successful with his book on a number of fronts. He voluminously catalogues his topic,

*More pre-publication*
*REVIEWS, COMMENTARIES, EVALUATIONS . . .*

and is discerning in his analysis of Elvis as a malleable signpost who is regularly employed by musicians, filmmakers, television producers, fine artists, sports figures, even the U.S. Postal Service and President Clinton, all to their own ends. Plasketes is obviously having fun with his subject as he explores Elvis's 'mystery terrain' in a kind of stream of consciousness writing style that entertains as well as illuminates. This book is not only a must-read for Elvis aficionados, but for anyone seriously interested in popular music, the mass media and society, and cultural studies."

**Dr. Gary Edgerton**
*Professor and Chair
of the Communication
and Theatre Arts Department,
Old Dominion University;
President of the American
Culture Association*

" **I** n his compilation of 'Elvis citings' 1977-1997, Plasketes has created an encyclopedic reference of use not only to students of the Presley phenomenon, but to the study of the popular culture of these two decades.

For any who persist in viewing Elvis as somehow peripheral, reading *Images of Elvis Presley* will allow them not only to know but to feel his centrality to American culture.

What King Arthur was to the Tudor English or the BVM was to nineteenth-century Catholics, Elvis is to postmodern Americans–only there is so much more evidence of it.

This is a good book. I like it, and an *incredible* amount of work went into it, work I won't have to do when I have to track down an Elvis reference–a task facing anyone doing contemporary cultural studies."

**Dennis Hall, PhD**
*Editor,* Studies in Popular Culture;
*Professor of English,
University of Louisville,
Kentucky*

" **G** eorge Plasketes has drafted a thoughtful afterlife biography of American popular culture's primary musical icon, Elvis Presley. This freewheeling overview explores motifs, messages, metaphors, memorabilia, and the many, many mysteries surrounding Elvis beyond his August 16, 1977 demise. Plasketes is literate, but irreverent; he is also analytical, but humorous. The explosion of the Presley myth and the commercialization of everything Elvis are fodder for the author's sociological pursuit. Whether a paean to performing greatness or a plague to the international image of American society, Plasketes documents the burgeoning movement that propelled the dead Elvis toward greater fame and fortune than the mortal rocker could either imagine or attain.

The breadth of Plasketes' perspective on the continuing Elvis phenomenon exceeds that of all previous scholarly investigators. The author's rich background in both contemporary music studies and American popular culture research enables him to provide stunning insights into the entity of Elvis, the empire of Graceland, and the enormous commercial enterprise of current Presley commodities, from RCA record re-issues to Memphis-based 'We Love Elvis' license plates. Plasketes plumbs the ongoing cultural obsession with 'The King' and concludes that the best (or worst) is yet to come. This book is a treasure trove of adoring excess, of fan euphoria, and of the eternal Elvis."

**B. Lee Cooper, PhD**
*Provost and Vice President
for Academic Affairs,
The University of Great Falls,
Great Falls, MT*

"George Plasketes' rather unconventional resource book will be a boon to Elvis scholars and Elfans alike, as well as a highly entertaining read for the great unwashed. It is not at all what you would expect from a reference book.

The writing is clever, witty, intelligent, and enthusiastic, but never over-the-top. Plasketes has not (yet) lost himself to the severe identity crisis that afflicts so many Presley accolytes. His admirable restraint allows him to present a tremendous amount of information on the appearance of Elvis images in music, print, visual art, sports(!), politics, film, theater, and television. However, his reserve is tempered by a real affection for The King and his rather loony subjects. The constant wordplay is inspired by the pop culture jargon surrounding Elvis and the writing snaps and pops along like an old 45 played at 78. Whether biography or portrait, appearance or apparition, in the studio or on the silver screen, Plasketes treats it all with fondness, wonder, and a sly wink in his whirlwind chronicle of the Presley phenomenon."

**Remy Miller, MFA**
*Assistant Professor,
Memphis College of Art*

# Images of Elvis Presley in American Culture, 1977-1997
## *The Mystery Terrain*

# HAWORTH Popular Culture
## Frank W. Hoffmann, PhD and B. Lee Cooper, PhD
### Senior Editors

New, Recent, and Forthcoming Titles:

*Arts & Entertainment Fads* by Frank W. Hoffmann and William G. Bailey

*Sports & Recreation Fads* by Frank W. Hoffmann and William G. Bailey

*Mind & Society Fads* by Frank W. Hoffmann and William G. Bailey

*Fashion & Merchandising Fads* by Frank W. Hoffmann and William G. Bailey

*Chocolate Fads, Folklore, and Fantasies: 1000+ Chunks of Chocolate Information* by Linda K. Fuller

*The Popular Song Reader: A Sampler of Well-Known Twentieth Century Songs* by William Studwell

*Great Awakenings: Popular Religion and Popular Culture* by Marshall W. Fishwick

*The Christmas Carol Reader* by William Studwell

*Media-Mediated Relationships: Straight and Gay, Mainstream and Alternative Perspectives* by Linda K. Fuller

*The National and Religious Song Reader: Patriotic, Traditional, and Sacred Songs from Around the World* by William E. Studwell

*Rock Music in American Popular Culture: Rock 'n' Roll Resources* by B. Lee Cooper and Wayne S. Haney

*Rock Music in American Popular Culture II: More Rock 'n' Roll Resources* by B. Lee Cooper and Wayne S. Haney

*The Americana Song Reader* by William E. Studwell

*Images of Elvis Presley in American Culture, 1977-1997: The Mystery Terrain* by George Plasketes

# Images of Elvis Presley in American Culture, 1977-1997
## *The Mystery Terrain*

George Plasketes

The Haworth Press
New York • London

Cover design by Donna M. Brooks.

The Haworth Press, Inc., 10 Alice Street, Binghamton, NY 13904-1580

**Library of Congress Cataloging-in-Publication Data**

Plasketes, George.
  Images of Elvis Presley in American culture, 1977-1997 : the mystery terrain / George Plasketes.
      p.    cm.
  Includes bibliographical references, discography, filmography, videography, television programs, and index.
  ISBN 1-56024-910-2 (alk. paper).
  1. Presley, Elvis, 1935-1977–Influence. 2. Popular culture–United States–History–20th century.  I. Title.
ML420.P96P59  1997
782.42166′092–dc20                                                              96-32995
                                                                                    CIP
                                                                                    MN

for

julie grace
flow, river of my soul

and

anaïs and rivers


"we're happy living on the B-side of life"

# ABOUT THE AUTHOR

**George Plasketes, PhD,** is Associate Professor of Radio, Television, and Film in the Department of Communication at Auburn University in Alabama where he teaches such courses as Popular Culture and Mass Communication and Scriptwriting. He is a member of the Popular Culture and American Culture Associations, and is an Advisory and Discography Editor for *Popular Music and Society.* Dr. Plasketes' articles on music, the mass media, and popular culture have been published in various journals and anthologies.

# CONTENTS

# Acknowledgments

There is a line from William McCranor Henderson's obsessive Elvis impersonator novel, *Stark Raving Elvis*, that has had a peculiar haunting effect on me as I have sifted and sorted through the Elvis clutter during this writing odyssey. Tad, one of the characters, scoffs at an Elvis wanna-be, "Just what the world needs, another Elvis Presley." The sneering sentiment is certainly not one of the more memorable, perceptive, or humorous lines about Elvis I have come across, but I have somehow managed to paraphrase it into a sense of personal Presley paranoia. Though many of the fine folks in the following "without whom" understandably may have been thinking it, they were at least considerate enough *not* to echo Tad's skepticism by saying to me, "Just what the world needs, another Elvis Presley *book*." I appreciate it.

*It Takes a Village (People)*. If it takes a village to raise a child, the same might also be said of writing this book. Though an awkward, but perhaps appropriate starting point, I should hail the King himself for being a source of such a rich cultural text. So, Elvis, if indeed you are out there somewhere, as many believe you are, I just want to say thank you, thank you very much.

Obviously, undertaking this project would not have been possible without the countless impressions and expressions of artists, musicians, performers, writers, poets, filmmakers, comedians, creators, and others who have responded to and represented Elvis Presley in some form or fashion. It has been a privilege and pleasure compiling and interpreting your works in these pages.

The many critics, historians, and observers who have previously written about Elvis have provided a foundation for what I have presented here. It should be apparent from the number of times they are cited in this text that I have found the works of Dave Marsh and Greil Marcus to be particularly insightful and inspiring. And just as the reflections of my many Presley predecessors have shaped this work, I can only hope that what I have presented in these pages might contribute in some small way to others who will no doubt continue to probe the Elvis Presley myth.

Many other "village people" came through with Elvis insights, books, photos, scripts, interviews, stories, tidbits, fragments, articles, clippings, names, dates, places, quotes, leads, and puzzle pieces: Ace Atkins, Margaret Joffre at Pedal Power, Wildman Steve, Rob Brantley, Lee Gaither, John Fortenberry, Jay Henton, Bill Schurk, Jonathan Lavan at World Tattoo, Bill and Virg Kolar, Doug Hartzell at the Halsted Theater, Terry Spencer, Stephanie Pierce at Where's the Art?, David "Gumbie" Sheppard, Steve Kalbaugh at Tulane University Sports Information, USPS Postmaster Terry Dozier in Opelika, Alabama, Lynn Miller, Mary Smiley, Vernon Chadwick, and Beth Wilborn. The Humanities Reference staff at the Ralph B. Draughton Library in Auburn (especially Glenn Anderson), and various bookstore clerks were kind enough to provide and verify bibliographic information. To borrow from the legendary Sam and Dave tune, "You didn't have to but you did, and I thank you."

No one was a greater Presley provider than Greg Metcalf. This project might have been completed much, much sooner were it not for Greg's constant stream of references, subreferences, and cross-references, via phone conversations, faxes, and packages in the mail. Greg had an uncanny knack for coming across a citation just as I was finishing a relevant chapter. I must confess that as the manuscript drew closer to completion, I was reluctant to open Greg's letters for fear they contained another Elvis reference that I would have to insert. These pages would be fewer and the collection of citings severely lacking without Greg's thoughtful vigilance and contributions.

I am very grateful to the following individuals and organizations for promptly and willingly responding to my annoying faxes, panicky phone calls, and urgent letters seeking permission to reprint or reproduce materials: John Crawford, Rob Rogers, Natasha Cooper and United Media; Peter London and Avon Books; Laurie Lesher at St. Martin's Press; Mike Nicholson and Mellow Mushroom; Susan Jimison and *Weekly World News*; Jay Allen Sanford, Revolutionary Comics, and Re-Visionary Press; John Smelzer and NFL Properties; Paul Sacksman and *Musician*; El Vez, Stella; Rich Shupe, The Residents and Cryptic Corporation; Todd Schorr, John Berkey, Dennis Van

Keersblick, Shane Swank, and Geoff Bevington, who was especially supportive. I appreciate your generosity; your images of Elvis really enhance this volume.

Many other friends and colleagues have provided personal and professional support, resources, and encouragement, both directly and indirectly: Remy Miller, Gary Burns, Robert Thompson, Roger Myrick, Dennis Hall, Ron Shapiro, Jim Dees, Rachel and Duane Gamache, Ben Shell and the staff at the Auburn University Film Lab, the Department of Communication, especially Pat Manos for her administrative assistance, and department heads Margaret Fitch-Hauser and Mary Helen Brown. Despite these difficult economic days for higher learning, my department and the College of Liberal Arts were able to provide funding for manuscript preparation (although I'm not sure they knew the contributions were in the name of Elvis).

And thanks to anybody else who at some point during the process of writing this book asked how it was going. Although your casual inquiry usually caused great anxiety, I really appreciated your interest.

*Every Day I Write the Book.* The seeds of this project were sown, unknowingly, many moons ago, in the form of an article I wrote on images of Elvis in popular music. Jerome Stern, the editor of *Studies in Popular Culture,* was tremendously encouraging. His initial positive response had a baptismal effect that has lingered as the Elvis references have accumulated over the years into this book. Jerome, wherever you are in The Afterlife, thanks.

Lee Cooper graciously took the time to carefully review a draft of the project proposal. He directed me to The Haworth Press and the Popular Culture Series Senior Editors, Frank Hoffmann and Bill Bailey, who were receptive to the concept.

I appreciate the opportunity, the confidence, and patience from everyone at The Haworth Press Book Division. From beginning to end, everyone I have worked with has been enthusiastic about the project. It meant a lot that they understood what I was trying to accomplish in scope, style, and structure. I appreciate the creative latitude they allowed, and their commitment, compromise, and guidance along the way. Bill Palmer, Managing Editor, has been very supportive, not to mention unreasonably understanding every time I asked for an annual, semiannual, or quarterly deadline extension. (He subtley prodded me by putting me on hold each time I called and cueing up the Kinks' "Tired of Waiting.") Susan Gibson was always available to answer questions, respond to anxieties, and assist in negotiations for titles, subtitles, words, pages, and photos as the manuscript traveled through the various stages of the production process. Peg Marr performed miracles with this manuscript. I am very thankful for Peg's diligent editorial scrutiny, her careful attention to detail, her tolerance for my carelessness, language liberties, stylistic quirks, and her concern for my annoying affection for alliteration. Thanks to Dawn Krisko, who gave such careful attention to the final stages of production, as well as to the index, and to Production Manager Patricia Brown who supervised the project from the first stages until the book hit the presses. All apologies, appreciation, and admiration to the entire administrative, editorial, and production staffs because I know this manuscript was much to deal with at every level.

*Blinding Me with Science.* I might still be stubbornly scribbling all this stuff hieroglyphically in pencil on pink and yellow legal pads, hopelessly hitchhiking on the backroads of the Information Superhighway, were it not for several people who reminded me that it is the 1990s and I didn't have to feel guilty about turning my back on my turntable several years ago; there is no quota on technological uses and gratifications. If not for the guidance of my computer whiz, Emmett Winn, with fine tuning, software, and hardware from colleague Jim Weaver, losing my high-tech virginity would have been much more traumatic. (But, please, don't push e-mail on me just yet; let us enjoy our recent household upgrade from rotary to touch-tone phone—a Pink Princess—for a while.) In addition, I'm very grateful for the great deal on a computer upgrade from Paul and René Williams. And I know Steven Williams has been my patron saint, hovering over my shoulder and holding my hand to make sure I pushed the correct keys.

*Gurus, Methods, Teachers.* Since I might be already sounding like a recipient on an awards show ceremony, I might now drift into a version of the "The More You Know" public service announcements, by recognizing some of the many individuals who have marked my academic time line. Will Norton and Denise Trauth were catalysts or co-conspirators for my mecca to study at Bowling Green. Jack Nachbar, Chris Geist, Ray Browne, Don Callen, and Dawn Glanz were among those whom I had the special opportunity to study under and interact with. I owe a lot to the late, great R. Serge Denisoff, who was very supportive and provided many opportunities to write. And I couldn't have had a better mentor all of these years than Gary Edgerton. All of these individuals tried to teach me all they know; the only problem was they know too much and I have a short attention span (too much TV?). But what I have managed to retain from them has significantly shaped my critical view. It has been a challenge and privilege learning from them. I would not be doing what I do, nor have been capable of pulling off this project without their guidance and collective casual brilliance.

*Ironic/Through Your Hands/Slow Turning.* One of the many great John Hiatt lyrics that has penetrated my spirit is "it will come through your hands." I find it ironic that in the process of writing a book I've learned that words mean nothing. And "isn't it ironic . . . don't you think?" that while writing how "it's good to be King," I discovered that it's not good to be King, rather good to just be. While that may sound like some 30-second inspiration from a Calvin Klein cologne commercial, there are two sacred sources who have prevented me from being trapped in my own history, my back pages. My heavenly wife, Julie, and healing guide, Judy Vercher, have graced my chronology with their wisdom, and blessed my being with keys to inner work, a sense of self, clarity, wholeness, and sublime redemption. Life and love will never be the same. To borrow from another Hiatt hymn, "It's a new light, new day, new place . . . just listening to old voices with a new ear." It has come through my hands because of the illumination from their inner lights. It moved me, it shook me, and I'm still shaking now. I will never let go; I will never forget. As another Hiatt chorus closes, "It's been a slow turning, from the inside out. Not fade away."

*Bring the Family.* Maybe it's just me, but I think there is a subtle seductive selfishness to writing a book. You think this old world stops spinning, while everyone is waiting and wondering about your words, which in the big picture aren't really worth that much. But life goes on, mostly daily. And so does death, birth, and rebirth. At the heart of it all lies family, who provide, among other things, roots and wings. It has taken me 40 years to learn to fly; fly away home. In the process of taking off and landing, taking off and crash landing, there has always been faith in, and of, the family: my parents Charles and Rita; as well as Laura, Lynette, Dave, Tyler, Chandler, and Alexa; and the Williams—Rodger and Joan, Rodger P., Sherry, Rodg, Justin, Steven,

David, Margaret, Lindsay, Sarah, Kate, Paul, René, Elliot, Sophia, Nancy, Todd, Peter, Shaye, and Maggie. Thanks for the nest.

*There's No Place Like Home.* More specifically and intimately, our children, Anaïs and Rivers, provide daily beauty, wonder, and inspiration. When she wasn't dancing, Anaïs routinely passed along detailed Elvis references that she came across while reading or watching television (mostly Nickelodeon, of course). It always meant so much when she asked, "Daddy, did you get any work done on your book?" Rivers, I'm proud to say, at age five is already among those who "never loved Elvis." Even though I tried to sway him by relating Elvis comparisons to two of his favorite things—Indians and saints ("people in heaven")—Elvis was not a part of Rivers' precocious and multicultural world (and another world view). To him, the guy is still "dumb Elvis." Thanks to you both for keeping me going. There is no place like home.

*Amazing Grace/Inarticulate Speech of the Heart.* I could spend every moment of every day for the rest of my life searching for the words, images, songs, scenes, meanings, or metaphors that could capture what my partner for life, Julie Grace, has meant to me during the tortures of writing this book, and as my constant, caring, colorful companion during our 17-year journey together on this broad highway and in the tunnel of love. I try, but nothing comes close. Any expression becomes an inarticulate speech of the heart. "I'm a soul in wonder," and Julie, my saving grace, my amazing grace, my Grace Land. You'll never know, dear. . . .

*George Plasketes*
*Opelika-Auburn*

# Introduction

# Endless Elvistas

## POST-PRESLEY PRELUDE: A LITANY

Eventually everybody has to die, except Elvis.

> —humorist Dave Barry

The guy [Elvis] has been busier after he died than when he was alive.

> —comedian Dennis Miller

I wish he [Elvis] never died myself, so I wouldn't have to hear about him every single day.

> —filmmaker Spike Lee, *Spin* (October 1990)

I'll keep right on managing him.

> —Colonel Tom Parker, on being asked what he would do now that Elvis is dead (1977)

I knew no escape from the King . . . while E's presence was daily extruded into our lives, it unavoidabled that we be baptized in his flood, however unwillingly.

> —Isabel Bonney, character in *Elvissey* (1993)

He [Elvis] is the "Big Bang," and the universe he detonated is still expanding, the pieces are still flying.

> —Greil Marcus, *Dead Elvis* (1991)

Elvis's disappearing body is like a flashing event-horizon at the edge of the black hole that is America today.

–Arthur Kroker, *Panic Encyclopedia* (1989)

I don't know what a nervous breakdown is supposed to feel like, but I think I'm having one. Everyone in the world is startin' to look like Elvis Presley.

–Jimmy Buffet, "Are You Ready for Freddy?"
in *Tales from Margaritaville* (1989)

Elvis is everywhere.

–Mojo Nixon and Skid Roper song (1976)

Elvis . . . The world will never be the same.

–bumper sticker

I think that Elvis Presley will never be solved.

–Nick Tosches, *Country* (1978)

## THE ELVIS ENCORE:
## CULTURAL CONVERGENCES

America is a Kingdom, its cultural landscape a mystery terrain of endless Elvistas. During the post-Presley parting period of the past 20 years, the modes, motifs, messages, meanings, meditations, metaphors, memorabilia, and mystery surrounding Elvis Presley's life, death, and myth have multiplied and been magnified. The asterisk many placed by his August 16, 1977 death marked the beginning of his afterlife biography. Since then, the King has been exhumed, exalted and exiled, exploited and exhausted into an elusive, expanding, exploding, enduring event that is enigmatic and epic–the Elvis Encore.

John Lennon stated that "before Elvis, there was nothing." And after Elvis? The Presley presence permeates American culture and subculture like a pulse and plague. It is a polysemous polymythic totem. Through mass meditation or mass media attention, images of Elvis—from black velvet and blue suede, to pink and pastel, to vinyl, solid gold, rhinestone or 100 percent cotton—consume and captivate our consciousness and imagination like no other.

Elvis's likeness—whether jailhouse or jumpsuit, junk or junkie, punk or parody, Cadillac or coffin—is pressed, placed, preserved, and packaged in plastic and on postage stamps; credit cards, checks, and currency; art and artifact; greeting cards and cologne ("For all the King's men"). Businesses, boulevards, and babies bear and borrow his name, a revered and registered trademark. There are waves of UFO-like sightings and legions of impersonators. Airlines have offered discount fares for look-alikes on Elvis holidays in January and August. His omnipresence hauntingly hovers, from a King-connected constellation "rock star" in the heavens (Sellers, 1993), to highway horizons on billboards, to the depths of Ruby Falls, 1,100 feet inside Lookout Mountain in Chattanooga, Tennessee, where "Elvis '75" is magic-markered onto the side panel of a utility light. Whether read as the handiwork of a graffiti-crazed guide, bored tourist, evidence from an Elvisitation 20 years ago or a more current clue, such signposts, symbols, and sightings solicit some response, be it smile, smirk or suspicion, scorn or celebration.

References surface in obscure, international, and interplanetary settings. Consider "Citizen Arcane," Dennis Miller's wry observation that ABC news correspondent Sam Donaldson's hairline looks like the cove where Elvis got married in *Blue Hawaii*; or that within the 325,000-stone blanket covering Atlanta's Centennial Olympic park there is a brick with the inscription "Elvis Presley: 1935-?" When evidence of life on Mars generated enthusiastic interest in missions to colonize the Red Planet, *Newsweek's* Kim Stanley Robinson could not resist a reference to the frequent tabloidian space case Elvis: "The initial crossing to Mars will be made for a greater number of reasons, some of them solid (to see if there really are fossil bacteria there), some of them not (to look for Elvis)" (September 23, 1996, p. 59).

An excessive enterprise, empire, and entity, Elvis appears on memorabilia and merchandise, in roadside relics and Graceland's gift shops; at fast food chains, in front yard flea markets and backyard shrines;

World Wide Web sites in cyberspace and sporting events; at parties and parades; or as part of promotions, protests, and pranks. In 1991, at Carleton College, a small liberal arts school in the southern Minnesota town of Northfield, a group named RAISE–Replace All Institutional Symbols with Elvis–kidnapped an American flag and unfurled one bearing the King. They demanded that school President Stephen R. Lewis perform an Elvis impersonation. Lewis obliged the demands with a rendition of "Hound Dog" at a council meeting.

Another president has also been a notable Presley participant and persona. In 1992, Elvis was a "running mate" of sorts for then-Arkansas governor Bill Clinton and his successful campaign to win the White House. One month after taking the Oval Office oath, an inconspicuous tidbit from an Elfan in Little Rock appeared in the "Letters" page of *Musician* magazine (March, 1993, p. 10) (see Figure 1).[1] It was one of many fanciful fragments of fusion to follow framing Bill Clinton as King of the country. And althouth Elvis was not an "issue" when Clinton was re-elected in 1996, the President's second term set up the possibility of playful parallels with Elvis's dichotomous career.

The mass media and popular arts have been prolific purveyors of the pervasive and perpetual myth. A Presley prism, they reflect and disseminate Elvis images throughout American culture via tabloids, talk shows, advertisements (Figure 2), situation comedies, songs, radio formats, films, videos, musicals, paintings, performances, portraits,

FIGURE 1

# *ELVIS SIGHTING*

Thank you so much for your issue on Elvis (Oct. '92).
You know I'm a fan and an amateur musician
so I'll enjoy your magazine.

*Bill Clinton*
*Little Rock, AR*

Source: *Musician* magazine, March, 1993.

plays, poems, and puns ("Love Meat Tender"), needlepoint, quilt, short stories, cartoons, comic strips, graffiti (Wright, 1996), ballet, books, newspapers, and magazines. The accumulation of these expressions might best be captured in one of the final frames of John Crawford's eight-panel cartoon, "*Baboon Dooley Rock Critic Consults the Deity!*" A divine voice from the heavens reveals the "the Great Secret of Existence" to Baboon, that the "universe is one big Elvis Presley" (Figure 3).

## ELVISYNERGY: MIXING METAPHORS

This collective cultural obsession might be analogous with what novelist Jack Womack calls an "Elvissey," that is, "an eternal search for the home with the King" (1993: 262). Collectively we have become a congregation of post-Presley expressionists and impressionists, endlessly exploring Elvis's life, death, and afterlife, in words and images, sights and sounds, allegories and metaphors, litany and language, parallels and parables, quotes, comments and comparisons, until the story dissipates further into myth.

In William Price Fox's novel, *Dixiana Moon* (1981), two travelers driving through the South hear an old Elvis tune on the radio. "Wonder what he was like," says the young New Yorker. "He wasn't like anyone," replies the old Southerner. "You start trying to compare Elvis to something and you can forget it . . . all you can do is sort of point at it when you see it going by, and maybe listen for the ricochet."

There is foresight in this fictional fragment. We still wonder, continually compare, point, listen and look, juxtaposing Elvis with everything and everyone. The roster of richochets is endless. Elvis is not only the King, but has been widely recast, reconsidered, and reconstructed as the Queen, the Fisher King, Burger King, King of Kings, King of Comedy, and King Kong. A clown, clone, cartoon character, Cajun and Kennedy; athlete and addict; drug and drag; Dean and Dylan; Air Jordan and Jordanaires. He is Seinfeld, Springsteen, and the Statue of Liberty; landmark, legend, lyric, and Lazarus; vampire, Venus, Valentino, and Virgin Mary; Pelvis, Melvis, Hellvis, and Hitler; high priest, pauper, prince, politician and president; patriot and pioneer; prima donna, Madonna, Mona Lisa, and Marilyn; bigot and burger

FIGURE 2. Images of Elvis appear in advertisements.

Source: Mike Nicholson, Mellow Mushroom, Atlanta, GA.

FIGURE 3. An answer to the question: What is the Great Secret of Existence?

Source: John Crawford, 1988.

(topped with peanut butter and bacon on restaurant chain Ruby Tuesday's menu); mascot, messiah, and murderer; demon, deity, and Disney; ghost, god, glutton, and gimmick; saint, sinner, savior, sucubus, and siren; Bigfoot, Buddha, Beavis and Butthead; beauty, beast and burden; Pez, pet, prophet, and profit.

In Greil Marcus's view, "we are the ricochet" (1991, p. 39). Marcus, along with Dave Marsh and Peter Guralnick, comprise a trinity of obsessive critical observers and biographers who have provided the most perceptive Presley perspectives in print. Marcus foresaw the Elvis fixation more than 20 years ago, calling it a "helpless commitment." In "Presliad: Fanfare," in his classic, *Mystery Train: Images of America in Rock 'n' Roll Music* (1982; first published in 1975), he writes, "Elvis proves then that the myth of supremacy for which his audience will settle cannot contain him; he is, these moments show, far greater than that."

Years later, in *Dead Elvis: Chronicle of a Cultural Obsession* (1991), he places Elvis's "permanent ubiquity" and "infinite circularity" in a Big Bang context:

> When he died, the event was a kind of explosion that went off silently, in minds and hearts; out of that explosion came many fragments, edging slowly into the light, taking shape, changing shape again and again as the years went on. (p. viii)

Over the years, Elvis has proved Marcus to be prophetic; he cannot be contained. The supreme Elvis myth has evolved into a boundless form described by Manny Farber as "termite art." "It's as if the present day Elvis wants most of all to devour the culture that for so long has fed off him," assesses Marcus (1991, p. 182).

Julie Wilson's cartoon-like rendering, "Connect the Elvis Dots," a placemat/handbill for Trixie's Manhattan restaurant provides another fitting metaphor to the mix (Figure 4). Presley points crisscrossing and connecting the cultural landscape is highly appropriate description. Overweight and overwrought, Elvis is the embodiment of duality. The Presley polarity, conveniently illustrated in the 1992 Elvis stamp election, embraces both feminine and masculine, good and evil, heaven and hell, young and old, faith and doubt, rich and poor, comic and tragic, black and white, life and death, mirror and mirage,

FIGURE 4. Placemat/handbill for Trixie's Manhattan Restaurant.

whisper and shout, primitive and profound, mainstream and fringe, sacred and sexual, unique and universal, convention and invention.

In addition, Elvis represents an alliterative list of royalty and ripoff, grunge and gospel, the glamourous and grotesque, fact and fiction, the hysterical and historical, the iconic and ironic. He is vision and voice; kitsch, catechism and contagion; time and space; prophecy, parody, paradox and paranormal; fetish and fashion; corpse and corporation; rhetoric, rumor, ritual and religion; occupation and preoccupation; genre, generation and gender; the cosmic, concrete, coincidence, complex, and contradictory; demographic and the democratic. Connect the Elvis dots.

A similar puzzling metaphor might be extracted from a sitcom episode of *Full House* (ABC), as Uncle Jesse, an aspiring rock and roller, supervises his twin sons who are close to completing their Elvis jigsaw puzzle, which is missing only one piece—the left sideburn.

Mixing metaphors may provide some method and meaning to the mystery. Yet it is Elvis himself who remains the all-inclusive metaphor, the lodestar of American culture, with a mystic knack for showing up everywhere.

## *ELVISOLOGY: CONTEMPLATING THE KING*

In his Elvis obituary, late great rock critic Lester Bangs wrote, "I can guarantee you one thing, we will never agree on anything as we agreed on Elvis." (1977) Yet, we continue to struggle with the essence of his life and death. "The End" is an unresolved point along the Elvis Time Line, as well as our collective cultural chronology. We travel between points, early and late, looking for clues and closure, endlessly entangled in dead and/or alive discussions and dialogue, debating Elvis's demise. The myth and mystery only becomes more muddled (Figures 5, 6, and 7).

Many suggest that Elvis's royal ruination began long before the pills and parody period of the 1960s and 1970s. The usual suspects or accomplices include his mother Gladys, the adoring fans, Dr. Nick, and Colonel Parker, whom producer Phil Spector was convinced hypnotized Elvis. Rock purist and historian Charlie Gillett believes the downfall began when Elvis signed with RCA, which resulted in "production line" rock and roll. To Dave Marsh, it was the "employee mentality" of submission that did Elvis in. He also points to Presley paranoia in suggesting the possibility of a government plot to protect a conservative 1950s America from the pelvis. Patsy Guy Hammontree points to the "isolation . . . insulation from reality . . . and vast abyss between his way of life and the way of life of others" (1985, p. 90). There were television producers insisting on "waist-up" only shots, or the humiliating, carnivalesque appearance on *The Steve Allen Show* in 1956, when a tuxedoed Elvis was stripped of his significance as he serenaded a hound dog. John Lennon blamed the Army. Novelists symbolically cite the haircut,

FIGURE 5

FIGURE 6

FIGURE 7. Evidence of the continuing debate of whether or not Elvis is truly dead.

Source: *Weekly World News*, June 15, 1993. Reprinted by permission.

jumpsuit, or inherent pitfalls of rising from poverty to fame. One might even dig deep in mythology to compare Elvis's wound of "too much too soon" with the Fisher King's search for the Holy Grail. Others joke that the cholesterol-crammed diet that included deep-fried peanut butter and banana sandwiches was the culprit. And for those who refuse to accept that the King is gone, there are enough imaginative, conspiratorial "Elvis alive" theories for an Oliver Stone film.

Participation in the Elvis universe, whether accidental or intentional, formal or informal, as activist, observer, or interpreter, is no longer the exclusive domain of die hard Elfans. Artists, writers, performers, musicians, and scholars are among those who have been "baptized into his flood" with their Presley pursuits.

In addition to Graceland gatherings and annual Impersonator conventions, there are other formal assemblies dedicated to the study of this cultural phenomenon, from kindergarten classes to college campuses to international conferences that convene to contemplate the King.

Predictably, children are a source of pure Presley perspectives and portraits, whether expressed in Art Linkletter-like, *Kids Say the Darndest Things* comments, or artistic renderings, such as those our daughter, Anaïs, provided at ages three and seven (Photo 8). Unable to find the tiny Elvis in the gold lamé suit among gold records, pink Cadillacs, and music notes floating in a souvenir wand, our five-year-old son, Rivers, innocently provided an ideal tabloid lead, "Elvis hides good. I bet if he played hide-and-seek no one would ever find him." More advanced third grade perceptions of Elvis are that " 'He was the guy who sang with his brothers Theodore and Simon'—a Chipmunk," or "he only comes out at night" (Marcus, 1991, p. v).

Elvisology is not limited to elementary inquiry; it has become a serious subject for scholarly symposiums and higher learning. Among institutions offering courses on the King are The Smithsonian and the University of Iowa, where Professor Peter Nazareth's "Elvis as Anthology" is part of the English and African-American World Studies curriculum. At the University of Mississippi, Vernon Chadwick teaches an English course titled "Blue Hawaii: The Polynesian Novels and Hawaiian Movies of Melville and Elvis." In April 1994, EducArts, a nonprofit organization dedicated to interdisciplinary education, sponsored a symposium, *Icons of Popular Culture I: Elvis and Marilyn*, at the Georgetown University campus. In August 1995, the University of Mississippi, host of yearly seminars on native son William Faulkner, held an International Conference, *In Search of Elvis* (Chadwick, 1997). Oxford, Mississippi Mayor John Leslie echoed a common dissentiment when he vetoed a $7,000 town grant for the gathering, saying he did not see the academic merit particularly within a community "that prides (and markets) itself on the high-cultural status of William Faulkner" (Chadwick, 1997, p. 261). "Elvis is beneath the dignity of the university and beneath the dignity of the city," said the Oxford mayor during an interview that aired during an ABC Nightly News segment. He was overruled by the Board of Aldermen. "We see this as broadening the areas of Southern culture," countered conference codirector William Ferris. "What we're doing is raising an academ-

FIGURE 8. A Child's Perspective.

A

B

ic recognition of not only Elvis but popular culture in general . . . because of the power that these things have in our lives."

## *THE ELVIRUS*

There is a line in an episode of *Wings* (NBC) that complements Isabel Bonney's comment in *Elvissey* about "unwilling baptism" into Elvis's flood. Brian pages through an old yearbook, and casually comments on one of his classmates, "Such a nice guy in high school, who'd have thought he'd grow up to be so obsessed with Elvis." Both remarks characterize what has become a shared experience among many post-Presley expressionists and explorers. They describe their personal and professional Elvislution or Elvishood as an unavoidable or accidental attraction. Irresistible and inevitable, the involvement is contagious, an Elvirus they unsuspectingly contracted while their resistance was low.

It is interesting that many cultural interpreters relate their Elvis encounters with caution. They are quick to qualify their interest in Elvis as a serious subject, often preceding any discussion of their Presley probe or portrayal—be it a play, portrait, poem, painting, or performance—with a disclaimer-like statement that echoes the Wonder Stuff album title, *Never Loved Elvis*.

Count me among those who "never loved Elvis" but nonetheless became an accidental tourist traveling across the cultural Kingdom. I was born in 1955, around the time Elvis's career was just taking off. The King, and his music, meant nothing to me, even when I became passionately aware of rock and roll ten years after. It wasn't until the late 1980s that I became "baptized in his flood." It was then my wife and I casually noticed a steady stream of songs with Elvis references in popular music, particularly along what was at the time, the obscure alternative axis. As I proceeded to compile an extensive discography, symptoms of the Elvirus slowly surfaced. I could feel myself being drawn further into the flood, swimming in the mystery of history. It was a black hole. An X-File. Marcus was right; it *is* a helpless commitment. And so was Isabel Bonney; there *is* no escape.

My heightened awareness, or fanciful fascination, became a sixth sense; an Elvis antenna with automatic fine tuning. I began to listen and look for the ricochets, just as the Southern gentleman said in *Dixiana Moon*. In some instances, my mind was so programmed for Presley pieces, the ricochet radar's reception proved deceptive. A Young Fresh Fellows song, "Mr. Salamander's Review," caught my attention on the car radio. I was convinced the song was yet another alternative rant demystifying the King: ". . . with his broken brain that pours shit from his mouth like rain from a drain . . . worshiped by all . . . with his leer at the ready and the food spewing pout of his mouth like confetti I just love to be near him . . ." However, when I looked up the lyrics, I was surprised to discover that my Presley programming had provided a misperception. What I interpreted as "Here's a picture of Elvis" was actually "He's a picture of *eloquence* . . . He's a picture of *elegance*." *I* had become the ricochet. My sound-alike substitution of "Elvis" for "eloquence" and "elegance" magnified some broader cultural responses to Elvis, particularly the sightings phenomenon. The illusory, distorted view that has become a tabloid trademark is poignantly expressed in the postcard designed by Kevin Pope depicting an aerial view from 300 feet up of barely decipherable Elvis serenading whales from an island shoreline. He is merely a dot in the distance, a grain of sand.

## *ELVISIANA: CITINGS, SIGHTSEEING, AND SOLVING THE PRESLEY PUZZLE*

This book is not about Elvis sightings, rather Elvis citings, and sightseeing. It is about images and imagination. It is a composite of America's cultural Kingdom—a collection, collage, and chronicle with critical commentary that connects the dots, the fragments of fallout, the pieces of the Presley puzzle that have been scattered throughout music, religion, literature, theater, art, sports, television, film, and politics since 1977.

Exploring Elvisiana is an endless task of gathering, managing, and interpreting a mass of material. The research and writing process itself became analogous with the metaphors I was mixing, as I found myself constantly arranging and rearranging the puzzle pieces into patterns and connecting the dots. The best I could hope for was to provide a substantial survey and a sense of order to the overlapping, overflowing collection of chaos. While categorization was possible, a comprehensive, conclusive composite was out of the question. I was well aware that I would not have the fantastic fortune of Jesse's sons on *Full House,* who found the final piece–the missing left sideburn–to complete their Elvis jigsaw puzzle. There is not now, nor ever will be, a complete Elvis. The search continues.

My interdisciplinary approach might be loosely compared to the time travelers John and Isabel Bonney as they "reresearched the construct of E" for their mission in *Elvissey.* The couple "daily monitored, drenching ourselves in image"; and were "doubleprepped . . . classed in linguistics, sociobservation, popular artifacts, cultural anticipation, historical processes. . ." (Womack, 1993, p. 54).

I consciously avoided a search of the information superhighway that would furnish every available source on the subject. The decision, I might add, should not be interpreted as a trendy tribute to the Unabomber manifesto by one of his low-tech disciples. While my procedural preference for primitive-like "participant observation" might suggest slacker, rather than scholarly sensibility, such high-tech scrutiny would have proved methodologically maddening, and expanded the parameters of the project to be even more consuming than it has been for the past eight years. Swimming in the mystery of history is one thing; drowning in it is another. The Elvis flood is fathomless.

Relying on an Elvisian "sixth sense" may appear awkwardly and arbitrarily aligned along the archeological and anthropological axis. Yet, the Presley proof is in the pages. The accumulation of references, subreferences, and cross-references cited within this text is testament to the extent of how "Elvis's presence is daily extruded into our lives" (Womack, 1993, p. 62). The results of this "backroad" route are not as random as they are *representative* of the variety and vastness of Elvis images that have permeated American culture during his active afterlife.

During an August 27, 1993, *Nightline* (ABC), discussion about American and United Nations' efforts to catch an elusive Somali warlord, Admiral Jonathan Howe dismissed a question about specifics by saying, "I said from the beginning I wouldn't be detailing every Elvis sighting."

Neither will I. I have no pretentions of solving the mythical Presley Puzzle. My aim is to provide pieces and patterns, to identify and interpret Elvis images and issues, to find and fit fragments, and maybe connect some dots. Of these, there are many.

Each chapter is essentially both a piece and puzzle within itself, with its own point of view, be it defined by generation, genre, gender, occupation, class, race, region, or religion. Connected, the sections collectively comprise a more complex conundrum. Familiar figures (Vernon, Gladys, Jesse Garon, The Colonel, Jesus, Richard Nixon, Marilyn Monroe, Impersonators), events (birth, death, Army, television appearances, shooting out TV screens), prevalent patterns and recurring themes (fame, vilification, deification, demystification, commercialization, sightings), settings (Tupelo, Memphis, Hollywood, Las Vegas), sayings ("Elvis has left the building," "Thank you; thankyouverymuch"), artifacts and conventions (souvenirs, jumpsuit, sideburns, pink Cadillac, fat jokes, lip curl), emerge in the various expressions, which commonly convey simultaneous homage and critique and contain clues to our individual and collective cultural identity.

The tour of the terrain begins with the most concrete part of the Elvis legacy—music. A significant sampling of songs about Elvis or with Elvis references—from mainstream pop to alternative to obscure underground—establishes themes and motifs, particularly deification, which can be traced throughout all of popular culture. Also emerging is a separatist, or countermythology, revealed in the strikingly divergent views toward Elvis and his music among older and younger, and black and white musicians.

The Elvis literary landscape is no longer limited to telltale biographies, many which border on fiction. Elvis cookbooks, encyclopedias, photo collections, and travel guides are among the stream of materials in print. A variety of fictional and factual forms and fragments provide a fascinating focal point, as writers provide Elvis narratives in novels, short stories, poems, children's books, and subliterary modes such as comic books. The scope of these historical revisions includes science fiction fantasy, mystery, and romance, with several authors probing the darker side of Elvis's "gladoration" of his mother.

In theater, playwrights Ellen Byron and Terry Spencer echo Laura Kalpakian's point of view in her novel, *Graced Land,* as all three writers furnish a female point of view on Elvis adulation and encounters through the struggles of the central characters of their stories.

Art and sports offer two unlikely settings for Elvis. Although he is not commonly identified with the aesthetic and athletic, an increasing number of Elvis images have managed to (dis)grace gallery and grandstand, from portraits to playoffs.

Television and film provide a panoramic view. Like literature, mass media portrayals and presentations contain an abundance of Elvis images and references. The Elvis expanse not only embraces every genre and subgenre, but represents social class, character types, ages, races, religions, regions, settings, and professions as well.

This expedition concludes, for now, with the coronation of the King as traced through the 1992 Presleydential elections involving the White House and Post Office, with political and postal Presley parallels demonstrating demographics and democracy, and power and imagination at work.

## *RUNAWAY TRAIN OF THOUGHT*

There are many characterizations and comparisons that have been used to try to capture Elvis Presley's essence during the past 20 years–Second Coming or Encore; Empire and Kingdom; Elvissey, Elvirus, Elvisynergy; a puzzle, prism, or plague; Big Bang, black hole, or universe; collage or kaleidoscope; fragments of fallout, a flood or flashing event-horizon; ricochets or dots. As I have meditated on the mystery, mixing many metaphors and messages in search of one with the most meaning, I arrive at *the mystery terrain.*

"Mystery Train"–based on the Carter Family's 1930 song "Worried Man Blues," and written and recorded by Little Junior Parker, along with Sam Phillips in 1953–has been synonymous with Elvis Presley since he recorded the signature Sun Studio song in 1955. "Elvis *owns* the song," proclaims Dave Marsh, who ranks the train traveling tune twelfth on his list of the 1,001 greatest singles ever made (1989). Poet David Wojahn, independent filmmaker Jim Jarmusch, and critic Greil Marcus are among those cultural interpreters who have appropriated the song title for their Presley-prevalent projects.

The train image certainly is an appropriate analogy as Elvis images roll across the cultural landscape, connecting all points and destinations in his Kingdom. And, if we accept, as film critic Roger Ebert (1993, p. 443) suggests, "mystery train" as the "two most evocative words in the language," then it follows in the metaphorical equation that Elvis Presley stands not only as the most evocative word in the language, but the most fertile, meaningful image in, and of, American culture.

Yet the song, and the train, like most Elvis analogies, are lacking. He may own the song, but Elvis cannot be confined to its three minutes, even if it is "sixteen coaches long." Over the years, the mystery train has become a runaway train *and* train of thought, rolling replete with Elvis representations, revisions, ricochets, reflections, responses, references, repetition, and resonance. Not only the song, but the train, its track, travelers, and their thoughts are all Presley possessions. By the mid-1990s, the train has been transformed into terrain.

The mystery remains. It will never be solved, just as Nick Tosches prophesized 20 years ago. And of course we respond; it is a helpless commitment. Fans, impersonators, observers, artists, writers, musicians, critics, athletes, politicians, performers, scholars, accidental tourists—train travelers all—still wonder, compare, create, probe, pursue, point, listen, and look across the mystery terrain. The Elvistas are endless.

## NOTE

1. According to *Musician* publisher Paul Sacksman, a fixture of the quality publication for 17 years, President Clinton's letter is authentic, but should not conjure up images of the Commander in Chief and the Secret Service jogging to the newsstand to pick up a copy of the publication. Aware of the President's well-published fondness for the King, the editors sent a copy of the October 1992 "Elvis issue," to him. Clinton soon responded with the letter of appreciation to the editors. Sacksman proudly adds that the exchange was not the magazine's only presidential encounter during its 20-year history. The other also featured the signature of a Democrat. In the late 1970s, *Musician* received a check from President Jimmy Carter to renew daughter Amy's subscription to the magazine.

Chapter 1

# The King Is Gone
# but He's Not Forgotten

The story shrinks, then, down to the size of your favorite song, whatever it is—down to the size of whatever mystery it contains, whatever it was that made you like it then, and like it now.

—Greil Marcus, *Dead Elvis* (1991:203)

Even though the Elvisian myth has often overshadowed his music during the Elvis A.D. era, Presley purists persist that music is the most concrete and comprehensive body of evidence Elvis left us. The point is well taken, as the King's musical vault appears to be a bottomless boxed set. By 1992, the quantity had become so overwhelming and incomprehensible that RCA Records chose to use comparisons rather than numbers to tally the sales of Elvis recordings as they marketed the five-CD, *Complete 1950s Masters* collection. The information released by the label resembled those Elfactoids pondered upon by Screamin' Jay Hawkins hotel night manager character in Jim Jarmusch's film *Mystery Train* (1989): "It would take 13,800 years to play all the records sold by the King, and if stacked, they would reach a height of 523 miles, higher than any space shuttle has flown and 1,956 times higher than the Empire State Building."

The breadth of the Elvis discography could also be seen and heard a few years earlier around the time of the sightings frenzy. While radio stations were offering huge cash awards—"a King's

Parts of this chapter appeared in a very different form in "The King Is Gone but Not Forgotten: Songs Responding to the Life, Death, and Myth of Elvis Presley in the 1980s," *Studies in Popular Culture*, XII(1), pp. 58-74.

ransom"–for anyone who could bring in Elvis, other opportunistic programmers mined the music into all-Elvis formats.[1] In August 1988, with "Heartbreak Hotel" pronouncing its arrival, Cincinnati's WCVG-AM unveiled its new format and station slogan–"Elvis all the time." The move was financially fueled, as the station was in last place in the ratings, with "nowhere to go but up," according to general manager John Stolz. The unusual format change prompted a phenomenal response, including more than 600 phone calls from listeners and world media, with a *CBS This Morning* live broadcast from the station among the coverage. The novel one-artist approach ran its course in less than a year, and WCVG became the Business Radio Network, without appropriating the Elvis *Take Care of Business (TCB)* logo as its slogan. WHOS in Decatur, Alabama underwent a similar short-lived experiment, converting from gospel to an all-Elvis format, which for six months generated more media attention than listenership.

While the Presley recording archive represents an endless sound source, another Elvis-related music collection has accumulated over the years. Since 1956, songs about Elvis have been released every year in 35 different countries. The collection, totaling more than 1,000–an impressive number considering the closest are the Beatles, who have had 400 songs written about them–includes tributes, parodies, songs with reference to Elvis and his songs, cut-ins of songs, imitations, and cover versions (Banney, 1987).

During the past 20 years, the spectrum of musicians who have recorded songs about Elvis Presley has expanded beyond the Country and Western genre to include a range that spans popular artists such as Paul Simon, Billy Joel, U2, and Bruce Springsteen, to fringe dwellers such as Mr. Bonus, Pink Lincolns, Dead Milkmen, and Wall of Voodoo. For the most part, the musician's aims appear to be less motivated by commercial concerns than others who have capitalized on Elvis. Granted, the mere mention of Elvis in any song is likely to attract avid fans and collectors and increase sales. And even though Paul Simon's *Graceland* (1986) was a commercial and critical success, the attention the record received can be attributed more to the use of South African music and musicians than the song "Graceland."

Although Elvis songs have been numerous, the majority remain obscure album tracks, appear as B-sides to hit singles, or have been found primarily on what was until the early 1990s, a limited exposure axis of college/alternative radio, which has since evolved into the mainstream of the music market.[2]

The songwriting styles range from dark, novel, reverent, humorous, and ridicule, in their responses to the Elvistory. There is considerable repetition of certain themes and images in these songs, which cannot only be found in the motif itself, but can be traced in the recurring themes *within* the motif. Among the common references are fame, fortune, sightings, drugs, fat jokes, impersonators, Graceland, Cadillacs, songs, stories, souvenirs, and events. Familiar figures, from Jesus to Marilyn Monroe, are among those frequently juxtaposed with Elvis.

Whether originating from the mainstream or fringe, these songs are valuable responses as the artists offer simultaneous homage, critique, and interpretations of the life, death, and myth of Elvis Presley. In examining a representative sampling of these songs, five broad thematic categories emerge that are also prevalent in Elvis representations throughout American culture: (1) deification; (2) vilification; (3) iconization; (4) commercialization; and (5) demystification.[3] In addition, dissidents defined by race and generation who dismiss Elvis with a countermythology can be traced throughout the musical responses in these overlapping categories. The lingering racial resentment that has shadowed Elvis since the 1950s resurfaces in several songs. More striking are the divergent views of Elvis between the younger and older musicians. While Elvis has been frequently placed within the context of the African-American community and its heritage in situation comedies and other cultural fare, the clear-cut division along generational lines in response to Elvis is more apparent in music than anywhere else in the cultural arena.

## *PRESLEYTERIAN DEIFICATION: THE KING AND KING OF KINGS*

And unless you understand that Elvis Presley was more than anything a spiritual leader of our generation, there's really no way to assess his importance, much less the meaning of his music he created.

—Dave Marsh, "How Great Thou Art"
*Elvis Presley obituary* (1977)

Spirituality and the deification of Elvis continue to be among the most thriving dimensions of the Presley myth. The pious parallels are pervasive, with fragments of both traditional and non-traditional religions widely represented. The Elvis Lives phenomenon is but one manifestation of religious activity surrounding Elvis. The messianic movement includes a following of fanatics, true believers worshiping a deity, and spiritual and supernatural implications of conversion, resurrection, prophecy, and a second coming. The fundamental Presleyterian doctrine is that "Elvis" is an anagram for "Lives."

Every year, an estimated 12 million faithful make the pilgrimage, a Memphis mansion mecca through the gates of Graceland. Elvis Presley International Tribute Week marks an annual August holy week of candlelight vigils, cross-shaped floral arrangements, and weeping worshipers. Souvenirs and sweat-stained scarves are anointed sacred saintly relics. Elfan rooms, houses, and gardens are transformed into shrines and altars. Impersonators are high priests "in the image of Elvis," disciples disseminating a musical gospel. Random taggers graffiti spray-paint proclamations such as "Elvis is the answer." In Portland, Oregon, there is a 24-hour coin-operated art installation entitled *Church of Elvis*, where Elvisitors may engage in wedding ceremonies, confessions, and catechisms before the *Miracle of Spinning Elvises*. There have also been whispers of a clandestine Church of Elvis gathering in Fort Wayne, Indiana, and another congregation located in Manhattan's Lower East Side. Another denomination, The First Presleyterian Church of Elvis the Divine, meets weekly on the Internet, a gospel and lobbying group which suggests putting jobless people to work building Elvis shrines.

While the Elvisian religious attributes have become magnified since his death, they have always been present. "Forget saying that Elvis is a religion now. He was from the beginning," writes Patsy Guy Hammontree, author of the seminal reference work, *Elvis: A Bio-Bibliography* (1985). Elvis's early performances transcended music and sexual energy. The effect was frequently described in "religious experience" terms—the hot flash ecstasy of conversion, cleansing, redemption, revelation, and the kind of weeping joy often associated with Baptist revivals.

Deification soon followed. In the mid-1950s, Sam Phillips straddled the fine line between blasphemy and truth when he made

Elvis-Christ comparisons, declaring their births as the two most important events in American history. Even Elvis himself contributed his own "chosen one" notions as he got more deeply involved in the mystic and supernatural.

These items, activities, and the rampant Elfanatacism do not necessarily constitute a solid theological foundation upon which to build a religion in the "traditional" sense. There are numerous fragments of faiths which can be found in the Presleyterian devotion: the Catholic traditions of rituals, relics, and icons; Scientology's cosmic mixture of dramatized science fiction, personal revelation and healing, personality, and enthusiastic publications filled with fantasy; and Southern Baptist roots, although some argue that Southerners have greater difficulty reconciling the Elvis God with their own church and religion than other denominations and regions do. Numerology has also fueled the fervor of true believers, with "new (age) math" equations such as: the month, day, and year of Elvis's death (8/16/77) add up to 2001, as do the day he was born (8), the day he died (16), his age at death (42), and the year of his birth (1935).

Whether catechism or coincidence, the Christ comparisons continue. Among the book-length explorations of Elvis's divinity are Ted Harrison's *Cult of the King* (1992) and Jack D. Malley and Warren Vaughn's *Elvis: The Messiah* (1993). Peter Stromberg's (1990) essay places Elvis fundamentalism within the context of consumerism, Marxism, and commodity mysticism. Chet Flippo (1989) lists some of the more peculiar Presleyterian connections. For example, the Hebrew word "el" means "God," and the Latin translation for "vis" is "power." Each of Elvis's three primary homes contain "el" in its name–Tupelo, Graceland, Bel Air. The long-time music writer also points out that the "2001: A Space Odyssey" theme used by Elvis as his introductory fanfare late in his career is music taken from Richard Strauss' tone poem *Also sprach Zarathustra*, which is based on a work by Nietzsche portraying the struggle of a mortal man to become a godlike superman. The comparisons have become so ingrained into our cultural consciousness that The Church Ad Project, a nonprofit company in Eagan, Minnesota that designs advertisements for local churches, places Elvis and Jesus alongside each other in one of its ads. "Unfortunately, there seems to be a little confusion about which one of them actually rose from the dead," states the copy above pictures of the two messiahs.

Without question, much of the foundation of Elvis worship is based upon the cult of personality. Uniting opposites is part of the essence of any religion, whether organized, church, sect, or cult. And Elvis blurred distinctions not only between musical forms, but races and social classes as well. In the process, a personal culture of fans faithfully surrendered in the name of Elvis, and have remained passionately devoted to him. Such fanaticism, is, in the words of sociologist Eric Hoffer, "a malady of the soul and a miraculous instrument of resurrection" (1951). And, it is a movement too wide-spread to be ignored.

Songwriters have certainly not ignored the Elvis Christ, as lyrics expressing this theme have accumulated into a significant collection over the years. In varying ways, from dark and novel, to sacrile-gious and ironic, to reverent and celebratory, many artists acknowl-edge Elvis as a religious figure or spiritual leader, and at the same time, comment on the deification itself.

## HEAVEN OR LAS VEGAS:
## THE JESUS, MARY, AND ELVIS CHAIN

It's a good thing Jesus died when he did because if he hadn't, he'd have ended up like Elvis.

–comedian/actor Dennis Leary

Elvis called God every morning,
then left the phone off the hook

–Bono, *"Elvis: American David"* (1994)

Perhaps one of the most haunting images of Elvis Presley in American culture can be found in the Presley family monument in the Meditation Gardens at Graceland. A giant marble statue of Jesus with outstretched arms stands in front of a cross. While the proph-et's pose is familiar, the memorial contains a wickedly surreal juxta-position. The "Presley" inscribed in the statue's base beneath

Christ can be read as a twisted suggestion that Jesus's last name is "Presley." (The full page of the statue in Chet Flippo's *Graceland: The Living Legacy of Elvis Presley* (1993) is equally striking in its strange spirituality.)

This depiction is mirrored elsewhere. In his thirty-first, and final, feature film, *Change of Habit* (1970), Elvis plays a young doctor working in a ghetto clinic. Mary Tyler Moore, playing one of a trio of plainclothes nuns who have been sent to aid the doctor's cause, falls in love with him. During one scene, Elvis stands radiantly at a chapel altar, singing a hymn while the smitten sister looks on. The camera follows her eyes from Elvis' face to Christ's on the cross, cutting back and forth several times. The final shot of the nun's perplexed face suggests that for her there may be no difference between the two men.

Dave Marsh sees this scene as surpassing John Lennon's ambiguous "We're bigger than Jesus" remark for its arrogance. And in many of our eyes there isn't much difference either. This confusing view and inability to distinguish between Elvis and Jesus also surfaces in music as several songwriters present a similar juxtaposition of the twin saviors.

The character in Adrenalin A.O.D.'s "Velvet Elvis" (1987), covets the Elvis portrait nailed to an expensive hotel room wall for a place in their collection, "right next to the fuzzy Jesus Christ."

The two popular figures go from velvet to video, again appearing alongside each other in the third video from Tom Petty's *Wildflowers* (1994) album, "It's Good To Be King." In the narrative's closing sequence, an image of a junkyard Jesus statue in a trailer park follows a close-up shot of an Elvis Impersonator.

Don Henley's, "If Dirt Were Dollars" (1989), is a musical replica of the scene from *Change of Habit* that also wryly comments on Elvis deification. The song's narrator is not sure if it was Jesus, or maybe Elvis, he saw on the plane while flying back from Lubbock. "You know they kinda look the same," concludes the passenger. Written around the peak of the Elvis sightings season, Henley's intentions here are not so much to exalt or deify as they are to respond to American culture's morbid curiosity and obsessive nature. Although the songs may be recognized as religious reflectors, they also reveal a negative nature of our cultural condition.

"There's a very large spiritual gap in this country," he explains. "People are so hungry for a miracle, there've been more sightings of Jesus and Elvis than Bigfoot or the Loch Ness Monster" (Marcus, 1991, p. 180).

The solo flying Eagle, known for crankiness, offers further perspective on the song in an October, 1989, interview in *Musician*:

> Look at this Elvis-is-alive phenomenon; that is the sickest thing I've ever seen. That's why I make the comparison with Elvis and Jesus. That's a part of the American psyche I don't understand; that's what I think is dark, that offends every sense of propriety and dignity that I have. Yesterday Geraldo Rivera was digging up poor Marilyn Monroe again, speculating on whether she was murdered. I say let people die with dignity. It's an amazing thing that you can make more money dead than alive in this country. (Flanagan, 1989, p. 61)

Graham Parker expresses similar "miraculous" cynicism in "Weeping Statues" (1991), a song which associates Elvis with religious figures, signs, miracles, unsolved mysteries, and unexplained phenomena. According to Parker's pointed perspective, events such as weeping statues, Elvis sightings, visitations, and lightning striking, "rip apart the fabric of our daily lives." Parker is not among the true believers. Like Henley, he demystifies the sightings and fanaticism with a reminder of the King's frequent fast food chain appearances during the 1980s. "But statues only weep for some, and Elvis just shows up when he's hungry," stings Parker.

"Weeping Statues" draws in the original Madonna–the Virgin Mary–with Jesus and Elvis to form a religious revision of the holy family. Parker echoes Jim Greer's irreverent observation in *Spin*'s fifth anniversary issue (April, 1990) that Elvis "made more personal appearances than any dead person other than the Virgin Mary" (Greer, 1990, p. 46).

Greer's comment connecting the competing cultural couple on comeback tours contains more substance than what lies on the surface of the flippant phrase. The visiting Virgin is a percusor to the contemporary Elvisitations. For centuries, people have flocked to the locations where Mary is said to have appeared. Astonished worshipers return with miraculous accounts of healing, weeping statues, images in the clouds, rosaries, and rainbows. Ironically, the frequency of reported Mary apparitions increased sharply during the late 1970s and through the 1980s, a period which coincides with the wave of Elvis sightings. Advocates claim there have never been so many widespread unusual sightings and occurrences involving Mary as have been reported during the past 20 years, perhaps reinforcing Henley's view of a the existence of a significant "spiritual gap."

There are obvious Presley parallels in the enduring Marian movement. The most renowned apparition sites represent sacred grounds for the respective followers, from Medjugorje to Memphis, Guadalupe to Graceland, Lourdes to Las Vegas, Fatima to Tupelo. The events have spawned a Virgin Mary network of true believers. Like the Elvis underground, the Marians have established an "organization" that includes dozens of prayer groups, publications, seminars, and offices such as the Marian Center in Delray Beach, Florida, that spread the word of Mary's appearances and her messages.

In addition to the annual pilgrimages to sacred sites, testimonies of miracle and wonder, and devout followers clinging to anointed artifacts and relics, other dimensions of the Marian movement's strong current of activity and worship, such as souvenir statuettes, shrines, festivals, and gatherings, also resemble prominent features of the Elvis contagion.[4]

Musical expressions of Elvis sacralization and religiosity are far reaching. The promotional card for the underground band, Elvis Hitler's *Disgraceland* LP (1988), which explains that a religious experience was the foundation for the group's existence and iconoclastic spirit:

> like Saul on the road to Damascus, James Hitler saw a brilliant flash of light that compelled him to change his name and the direction of his life's path. Backed by the life savings he had earned a truck driver, bowling alley janitor, and apprentice butcher, James became Elvis and a legend was born of the two greatest overnight sensations of the 20th century.

While name change is a common practice following such a conversion, the name "Elvis" is unlikely. Consistent with the names of many religious leaders, the utterance "Elvis" is among a select few names in American culture which predominantly signifies the image of just one person.

Willie Nile also places Elvis with biblical characters (Moses and Abraham) in his playful tune, "Everybody Needs a Hammer" (1991). And while Alannah Myles sings the praises of Elvisism as the "new religion" in her hit, "Black Velvet" (1989), the Christ and King comparisons are more common. Wall of Voodoo's "Elvis Bought Dora a Cadillac" (1987) is the story of Dora, a waitress who Elvis tipped with a brand new 1957 Cadillac. Twenty years later when he died, Dora parked the car in her drive, surrounded it with plastic statues, lights, and stands, and called the front yard shrine "Presley Land." Greedy developers eventually force her to sell the house so they could tear it down and replace it with a used car lot. The song's chorus views the social class and generous deeds of Elvis and Christ as analogous: "And the Gods I loved were poor white trash/One was making wine at Canaan, the other tipping waitresses Cadillacs."

Similarly, Mr. Bonus, in "Elvis What Happened?" (1986), suggests parallels with the lives of other spiritual leaders and their missions to teach others: "you showed us how to live and then you died." The helpless groans drowning in grating electric guitar chords of Death Ride '69's "Elvis Christ" (1988) utter: "Elvis Christ, rising again/Elvis, there's just one thing I need/Save me." The album's sleeve featured a bearded Elvis wearing a crown of thorns and a robe. In "Velvet Elvis" (1987), Adrenalin A.O.D. covets the Elvis portrait nailed to expensive hotel room wall for a place in their collection, "right next to the fuzzy Jesus Christ."

Other underground groups substitute Elvis's name where "God" is more commonly used. In "Going to Graceland" (1987), the Dead Milkmen proclaim "E Pluribus Elvis," perhaps suggesting that the opposite sides of the coins and currency should bear Elvis's image and the inscription, "In Elvis we trust." The issuance of the Elvis credit cards and postage stamps are manifestations of this thought. And both the Vandals, in "Elvis Decanter" (1988), and Bruce Springsteen, in "57 Channels (and Nothin' On)" (1992) curse, "In the name of Elvis. . . ."

Mojo Nixon and Skid Roper became cult stars with their clever underground hit, "Elvis Is Everywhere" (1987), a novelty song that salutes the gaudy Presley pervasiveness in mock fundamentalist fashion. The duo sees a little bit of Elvis in everybody (your mom, the young, old, fat, skinny, white, black, brown, blue) and everywhere (jeans, cheeseburgers, Nutty Buddys, unexplained phenomena). In addition to pointing to Elvis's omnipresence, Nixon and Roper warn of the evil opposite of Elvis—the anti-Elvis (Michael J. Fox, because he has no Elvis in him); and cry out for Elvis to "heal and save/Make me born again in the perfect light." Following a mock interview in *Spin* (October, 1988) in which the duo communicates with the King via Ouija Board, the magazine's editors began to "ghostwrite" a "Dear Elvis" advice column which appeared in the monthly music publication until May 1994 (Bordowitz, 1988, p. 2).

The late Frank Zappa also playfully combines heavenly visions of Elvis with he's-still-alive notions in "Elvis Has Just Left the Building" (1988). According to Zappa, after Elvis "left the building, he climbed the heavenly stair and is up there with Jesus in the big purple chair, making him laugh. And Jesus isn't the only one amused: "The angels all love him/He brings them relief/With droplets of moisture from his handkerchief." The only problem is that the Elvis faithful on earth love him, too. They want him back, and a tug of war for the King's soul ensues. Zappa prayerfully urges, "Jesus, let him come back/We don't want Elvis dead/So take down the foil from his hotel retreat/And bring back the King for the man in the street." The hotel hideout image also appears in a Gary Larson cartoon depicting Elvis and exiled *Satanic Verses* author Salmman Rushdie peeking through their room blinds.

In contrast, Sonic Youth's Karen Carpenter tribute, "Tunic (Song for Karen)," (1990) provides a more reverent vision of rock and roll heaven and its singing saints such as Elvis and Janis Joplin. One of the most significant music subcultures offers its own afterlife vision. Following the 1995 death of Grateful Dad, Jerry Garcia, Deadheads and Elfans together could find comfort in the bumpersticker message, "Jerry's not dead, he's just hangin' with Elvis."

Even before the "Elvis Is Alive" wave, resurrection has been a recurring image in Elvis Presley tribute songs. Greg Copeland "thinks the King is back in town" in "At the Warfield" (1982), a song that suggestively plays word association with Elvis's life. The parable mentions burning away, contracts, control, crowds, ambitions, prisoners, and illusion. Copeland also expresses casual indifferences to the "cause of death" controversy: "died from dope or a heart attack/ they both turn out the same." In "Twilight's Last Gleaming" (1986), Nixon and Roper "wanna resurrect the King . . . hear him sing again . . . see Elvis's ghost alive on a black velvet painting." Likewise, Warren Zevon's dark meditation, "Jesus Mentioned" (1982), includes sacred and secular adoration, necrophilia, and drug use. Zevon turns a ghoul- ish idea into an act of devotion as he heads to Memphis thinking about the King: "Can't you just imagine/Digging up the King/Begging him to sing/About those heavenly mansions/Jesus mentioned/He went walking on the water . . . With his pills."

Despite the black humor, Zevon isn't detached. The song's title evokes thoughts of Elvis's final days and final moments. Why had he reportedly been reading *The Face of Jesus*, about the Shroud of Turin? What were the last words he gasped? And we don't have to imagine the rest of what Zevon sings about; many of the Elvis faithful have either refused to bury him or repeatedly dug him up since 1977. Yet the brilliance in Zevon's meditation lies in its ability to hauntingly tap into our imaginations—the one clear moment envisioning Elvis still being alive and the what-if? possibility; the whispering suspicion dur- ing the Graceland tour upon being informed by the guides that visita- tion to the upstairs and kitchen is prohibited; or the dark curiosity to see the bathroom were he died. Pagan Kennedy's "Elvis' Bathroom" (Ebersole and Peabody, 1994, pp. 154-169) and Lawrence Bloch's "The Burglar Who Dropped in on Elvis" (Sammon, 1994, pp. 72-86) further explore the allure of the mansion's upstairs rooms, which nobody can visit. For the many who have struggled with accepting Elvis's death, the thoughts of resurrection represent hope that he will sing again, even if, as one author suggests, it is at his own funeral (Marcus, 1987, p. 64).

Others view Graceland, Memphis, and Tupelo as holy lands. Aus- tralian rocker Nick Cave's "Tupelo," the lead cut on his conceptual/ mystical Deep South LP *The Firstborn Is Dead* (1985), is a biblical adaptation of a John Lee Hooker blues tune. Cave's "beginning of time" narrative combines parable with nursery rhyme. There is black rain, and nature is suspended "Until the King is born! In Tupelo!"[5]

The Talking Heads' "Cities" (1979), and the Mekons' "Mem- phis, Egypt" (1989), from *The Mekons Rock 'n' Roll* album which features antiblack velvet paintings on its covers, place Elvis's Tennessee home in the context of the ancient gods. The songs conjure images of Memphis' architectural companion to Graceland, the city's civic center, or King's tomb, built in the shape of a pyramid. Marc Cohn's Grammy-winning hit, "Walking in Memphis" (1994), relates a born-again experience. He puts on his blue suede shoes and heads to the land of Delta Blues, to Beale Street and Union Avenue where he sees the ghost of Elvis and follows him up to the gates of Graceland, where he walks right through unnoticed. "Boy, you got a prayer in Memphis," whispers the ghost. And when someone asks the visitor, "Are you a Christian, child?", he proclaims, "I am tonight!", as the song builds to a gospel chorus.

The Blue Nile's poignant "God Bless You Kid" (1996) is a beautiful association of personal emptiness with the desolate mood of past-Elvis Memphis: "I drive all over town/to the bars without need/It feels like Memphis/after Elvis/There's nothing going on."

Delusions, dreams, and destiny are often entangled in Graceland visits. Blind faith becomes delusion in Richard Thompson's, "From Galway to Graceland" (1993), the sad saga of a woman who journeys from the west coast of Ireland to west Tennessee to be with the King. Believing she "wears the King's ring," the fan sits at his gravesite day after day until closing time when she is dragged away by authorities.

Billy Joel, John Hiatt, and Paul Simon also view Graceland in religious terms. Riding down "Elvis Presley Boulevard," the B-side to Joel's hit, "Allentown" (1982), is an observation of a mission-like line of people holding a vigil. In the crowd are losers, nameless, hopeless, lonely, and crying faithful. "Step on the shoes and I'll see you in hell," warns the narrator. The song appears to be an account of learning about Elvis's death and the accompanying disbelief, confusion, and frustration. Once again, the savior analogy is made: "And I saw that silent mansion/And I knew I was lost/ They were selling plastic souvenirs of Elvis on the cross." Tired of all the ugly rumors and unable to face the truth, the narrator smashes his car to pieces and "says goodbye to youth." Yet he finds salvation and enduring comfort in the silent mansion, where "nobody's home but the light is always on."

Hiatt, too, sees the light from the mansion on the hill and becomes a faithful follower in "Riding with the King" (1983): "He's on a mission of mercy to the new frontier/He's gonna check us all out of here/I never saw his face but I saw the light/Tonight everybody's getting their angel wings/Don't you know we're riding with the King?"

Simon's "Graceland" (1986) is a glorious symbol of redemption for "poorboys and pilgrims with families," and the song's narrator who is running from a broken relationship. For reasons he cannot explain, some part of him wants to see Graceland. He stands at the gates of the impenetrable mansion because he has "reason to believe we all shall be received" there. In Simon's biographical documentary, *Paul Simon: Born at the Right Time* (1992), which aired on public television, Simon explains that "Graceland" is not based on personal experience, nor was he writing specifically about Elvis and his mansion:

> I was singing those lyrics before I'd ever been to Graceland. In fact, I went to Graceland when I finally gave up thinking that I was going to change what the song was about. Because I desperately did not want to write a song called "Graceland" on a South African-based album. But it just wouldn't go away, so finally I said, 'Well, obviously I'm into this song, so I better go to Graceland.' I'd never even been there!
>
> But when I got to Graceland, I really could feel relaxed in the fact that the song had nothing to do with Elvis Presley or Graceland. It had to do with finding a metaphorical Graceland; a state of grace; a state of acceptance.

### IN HIS IMAGE:
### ELVIS IN-PERSON NATION

Two mirrors make infinity . . .
I'll sculpt you 'til you breathe.

—Robin Hitchcock, "Queen Elvis"
© *1990 EMI Virgin (BMI)*

Among the most active and visible members of the Presleyterian congregation are the Elvis Impersonators, disciples who spread the musical gospel according to Elvis. These "chosen few" (thousand) represent a denomination unto itself. During a 1989 small club performance, singer/producer T-Bone Burnett offered a wry per-spective on the growing flock of Elvii: "In 1977 when Elvis Presley died, there were 41 Elvis Impersonators in the world. This year, 12 years after his death, there are about 47,000. By the year 2000, one out of every three people in the world will be Elvis Impersonators."

Although the U.S. Census Bureau does not as of yet officially tabulate statistics on the number of Elvis Impersonators, it appears that Burnett's calculations are playfully exaggerated. Nonetheless, the King clones represent a significant following. In music, the imitative expression has been manifest in look-alikes, sound-alikes, and songs about being "one with Elvis."

Elvis Impersonation is an equal opportunity enterprise, with per-formers ranging from the lesbian Elvis Herselvis, to "The Mexican Elvis," El Vez, who claims to be the love child of Elvis and Charo. This south-of-the-border sensation's shtick reinterprets Elvis hits in a Mexican context, often with mock social commentary. Thus, "That's Alright Mama" becomes "Esta Bien Mamacita." The B-side of the novel 45 features "En El Barrio" ("In the Ghetto"), an urban tale that has the young man joining a gang because "there's one thing he can't stand is to join a mariachi band." The singer also incorporates surreal snippets of Traffic and the Beatles midway through the song. The green vinyl single, "Maria's the Name (of His Latest Flame)," features The Elvettes—Gladysita, Priscilita, Lisa Marie—rephrasing the Strangeloves' "I Want Candy" into "We want El Vez." The picture sleeve is multilayered with meaning as it blends the roots iconography of the *Elvis Presley* LP with the Clash's *London Calling*, right down to the backside depiction of El Vez about to smash his acoustic guitar. The borrowed images are ambiguous. Is El Vez paying homage to or rebelling against, (or both) the original rockers? Similarly, *Graciasland* mirrors Paul Si-mon's *Graceland* album design (Figure 1.1).

Another Impersonator who has attracted significant attention as a novelty act has been Tortelvis, the lead singer for Dread Zeppelin. The band has charted considerable smileage on *Un-Led-Ed* (1990) and *5,000,000\** (1991) by covering Led Zeppelin songs with an Elvis Impersonator over reggae rhythms and dubbed production accents. The recordings, viewed suspiciously by some as mere com-mercial exploitation, are thoroughly postmodern Presley that get the

FIGURE 1.1. Promotional poster for Graciasland.

Source: El Vez.

Led out by welding "Heartbreaker" and "Heartbreak Hotel" together, and running "Black Dog" into "Hound Dog."

Several other cover projects provide a less novel, imitative sense of homage to the King than El Vez and Tortelvis. Among the multi-artist tributes are *New Musical Express's The Last Temptation of Elvis* (1990),[6] which transforms Elvis's B-movie tunes into B-side covers; *It's Now or Never* (1994), an all-star salute from an October 1994 commemoration; and the *Honeymoon in Vegas* (1992) soundtrack featuring a diverse assembly of artists interpreting Elvis's songs.

The most interesting and conceptual of the Elvis cover/tribute presentations is the Residents' *The King and Eye* (1989), a stage show and soundtrack (Figure 1.2). The Elvis volume was part of the avant garde band's *American Composer Series*, a projected 16-year undertaking. The pre-King compilations included *George and James* (1984), which matches a side each of George Gershwin and James Brown; and *Stars and Hank Forever* (1986), which juxtaposes Hank Williams and John Philip Sousa marches. On *The King and Eye*, 16 vintage Elvis songs are given a complete Residential minimalist overhaul. Through the perspective of a father telling his children fables about a long dead king and his songs, and a poignant string of narrative interludes–"The Baby King"–the work hints at a darker side of the Elvis mystique and questions the spiritual nature of his reign. "[The record] incisively portrays Elvis's life and work as a misguided abandonment of innocence in favor of a sad yet comedic Oedipal journey," writes Jim Green (Robbins, 1991, p. 550).

A less intentional Presley personification is identifiable in artists such as Chris Isaak, Bruce Springsteen, Steve Earle, and k.d. lang, among others. Isaak's hair and vocal stylings draw immediate early-Elvis comparisons. His crooning "Blue Moon" at the all-star Elvis tribute concert in October 1994 in Memphis, and on the spin-off album *It's Now or Never* (1994), was high-note haunting, with Isaak's voice drifting in and out of Elvis and Roy Orbison. A "Go To Your Room" profile of Isaak on *Naked Cafe*, VH-1's version of *Entertainment Tonight*, reveals a commemorative Presley plate hanging on the wall in the singer's apartment. During the segment, Isaak bears a striking resemblance to actor Kurt Russell, who ironically starred as Elvis in the highly rated made-for-television movie *Elvis* (1979).

FIGURE 1.2. Album cover from the Residents.

Source: The Cryptic Corporation.

Bruce Springsteen's admiration for Elvis is well documented, from his biography, *Glory Days* (Marsh, 1987), to novelist Tama Janowitz's short story, "You and the Boss" (1985). In Janowitz's fantasy, she replaces Springsteen's wife and is pregnant with their baby. Bruce decides he's going to call the kid "Elvis," even if it is a girl. (The real-life Boss and E-Street wife, singer Patty Scialfa, have three children, Evan James, Jessica Rae, and Sam.) The Elvis in Springsteen was apparent during a backstage interview after he received a Golden Globe Award for his soundtrack song, "The Streets of Philadelphia." The scene was reminiscent of an early

Elvis press conference. The softspoken superstar, dressed semiformally without a tie at the black tie affair, mirrored young Elvis's humble boy presence and "aw shucks" awkwardness in the media spotlight.

Nashville outlaw Steve Earle offers an eerie glimpse of what Elvis might look like today if he were (barely) alive. His performance before inmates at the Cold Creek Correctional Facility in Henning, Tennessee, which aired on an MTV special in August 1996, was *Jailhouse (Country) Rock* revisited and unplugged. In sunglasses and sideburns, the overweight, sweating Earle conveyed a Presley-on-parole presence. The connection was further magnified by Earle's long struggles with drug abuse and rehabilitation.

Gender-bending Canadian country singer k.d. lang embodies Elvis's androgyny. Whereas El Vez is characterized as an Elvis/Charo hybrid, lang represents an archetypal offspring of Elvis and Barbara Streisand or Judy Garland. "Elvis is alive–and she's beautiful," proclaimed Madonna, after meeting lang backstage at a concert (Bennetts, 1993).

Robin Hitchcock also recognizes the androgynous Elvis, making a drag association in "Queen Elvis" (1990), a poignant song about sexual identity. Ironically, another familiar Presley name–Priscilla–appears in the same context in the movie, *The Adventures of Priscilla, Queen of the Desert* (1994).

Virtually every musical genre features its Elvis look-alike. In 1994, when Gregorian chants charted at the top of the music market, a CNN entertainment segment on the trend included a glimpse of the trademark Elvis sideburns peeking out from beneath a hooded monk. The monastic existence provided an ideal setting for Elvis-is-alive theorists to ponder.

A number of songs consider "being one with the King" on various levels. R.E.M.'s surreal tribute to the late Andy Kauffman, "Man in the Moon" (1992), wonders if the comedian who imitated Elvis as part of his act is "goofin' on Elvis" in the afterlife. Lead singer Michael Stipe himself attempts an Elvisian, "Hey baby," throughout the song, and mimics Elvis's hand gyrations while walking along a desert highway in the song's video.

Numerous songs relate the sad sagas and broken dreams of Elvis wanna-bes. The narrator in Jason and the Scorchers' "Broken

Whiskey Glass" (1984) criticizes the false pursuits of a partner, who "went to Memphis to find yourself/Read every Elvis book on the shelf/Even popped a pill or two." He moralizes that consulting Elvis's life story as a how-to manual is not the answer: "White soul heroes are made more than legend's trashy dreams."

In "Money Fall Out the Sky" (1982) by the New York post-punk band, Cool It Reba, the singer recognizes the consequences, but nonetheless wants to do everything like Elvis–live, drive, sleep, walk, take drugs, make love, and go to hell.

Carnival Art's "Little Elvis" (1992) is also a tale of a boy who "lives on velvet songs" and dreams of being Elvis. "Everywhere he goes he sings, Like Presley I'll be King." The reality is that his dream is only a "rumor he could fly"; he will never "build his own Graceland."

Kirsty MacColl offers a lighter view of an Elvis acolyte in her novelty song "There's a Guy Works Down the Chip Shop (Swears He's Elvis)" (1993). A U.K. Top 20 hit in the early 1980s, it foreshadowed the sightings phenomenon and conjured low-budget images of Elvis's film roles.

### *ELVIS, WHAT HAPPENED? VILIFICATION, CURSING, AND BETRAYAL*

It was like he (Elvis Presley) came along and whispered a dream in everybody's ear and then we dreamed it.

–Bruce Springsteen

Must be hard being a king.

–Forest Gump, reflecting on Elvis

Elvis Presley's ugly demise can be interpreted as a betrayal. "He was supposed to be around much longer, as a sort of national treasure to be shared," writes Dave Marsh in his Elvis obituary. Every element of the rock and roll dream was his–wealth, genius, inspiration, adulation. He had it all and he blew it, betraying his own talents and the faith everyone placed in him. He was not who he said he was; he became the antithesis of our dreams. What was possibility ended in ruin. Death made Elvis ordinary and left his followers furious. For many, the man who was godlike became godforsaken.

While most musicians, particularly the older wave who grew up listening to Elvis's music and experienced his liberating impact, display a sense of reverence and homage in their songs about him, they also offer a critique. They curse what happened to Elvis and the culture for destroying him, and they curse Elvis for failing his gifts and letting it happen. (Marcus, 1987). In their collective criticism, these songs present a recurrent narrative in American popular culture–the artist as victim of his/her own weakness, and the artist as victim of a demanding, materialist culture.

Creedence Clearwater Revival founder John Fogerty remembers the dream and the impact, but also laments the loss in "Big Train (from Memphis)" (1985): "Like no one before, He let out a roar/ And I got to tag along/Each night I went to bed with a song in my head/And the dream was a song/But I'm tellin' you, when that Memphis train came through/This old world was not the same/Big train from Memphis/gone, gone, gone."

Both Zevon ("He went walking on the water with his pills") and Hiatt ("Up to that mansion on a hill where you can get your prescription filled") curse the drug use; and to Joel, Elvis Presley Boulevard represents a "one way, dead-end street." Their cursing isn't self-righteous; Zevon's and Hiatt's own personal struggles with alcohol and drugs have been well documented in the rock press. While there is no doubt an underlying awareness that they, too, could have died the way Elvis did, this generation of artist appears to write with an appreciation for of Elvis's lasting influence on their music.

Another Elvis–Costello–writes about the "fine idea at the time" that is "now a brilliant mistake" in "Brilliant Mistake" (1986). Though the songs are biographically based, with Costello juxtaposing his experiences with his father's disappointing career as a jazz musician, the references to drugs, behind-the-scenes manipulators, and adoring fans fit the Presley story as well: "He thought he was the King of America/But it was just a boulevard of broken dreams/A trick they do with mirrors and chemicals/The words of love in whispers/And the axe of love in screams."

Costello's arrival on the music scene as an angry young man in 1977 coincided with Elvis's departure and the emergence of punk. From the beginning, Costello has been aware, if not self-conscious, of his namesake, and at times has himself contributed to the King, as well as King Kong comparisons (Robbins, 1989, p. 150). On the cover of his debut album, *My Aim Is True* (1977), Costello looks like Buddy Holly in a Presley punk pose, with "Elvis is King" spelled out in the squares of the black-and-white checkerboard background. (The phrase apparently got lost in the format-shrinking process as the letters are not visible on the compact disc cover graphics.) Among the testy tunes on *Goodbye Cruel World* (1984) are "Sour Milk-Cow Blues," an update of Presley's "Milk Cow Boogie;" and "Worthless Thing," which attacks the "grave robbers from Memphis, Las Vegas body snatchers, and vintage Elvis Presley wine." "It's about the disproportionate importance placed on rock and roll, particularly in America," Costello explains. "It's about the Elvis Presley industry, all that bloody nonsense, how it's all blown up." (Flanagan, 1987, p. 254).

Costello invites further Elvis comparisons with *King of America* (1986), from the album's title, the cover portrait of a crowned Costello, a sound which drifts between the Band and latter-day Elvis, and further lyrical probing. In addition to the opening declaration, "He thought he was the King of America" in "Brilliant Mistake," the album's lead track, Costello writes about the dubious embrace of celebrity and fame in "Suit of Lights," and the crown of the king of fools and the accompanying mockery in "I'll Wear It Proudly." Another nine years later, the print ad for Costello's *Kojak Variety* (1995) contains a peculiarly self-conscious Presley inference by specifying: "featuring extensive liner notes by Elvis C" as if to alleviate any Kingly confusion.

Other songwriters view the Presley demise within the context of broken dreams, the music business, and rock stardom. Robbie Robertson's "American Roulette" (1987) examines three of our most prevalent and enduring cultural icons—James Dean, Elvis, and Marilyn Monroe—and how they staked their lives on the system. His prayerful plea places some blame on those who worked behind the scenes: "Take that boy and put him in a mansion/Paint the windows black/Give him all the women that he wants/Put a monkey on his back/All of your so-called friends/Take you where the sidewalk ends/Can't sleep at night/Lord please save his soul/He was the King of rock and roll."

Together, Elvis and Marilyn Monroe represent the King and Queen, god and goddess of American popular culture. Perhaps the richest exploration of these intersecting icons can be found in the collection of essays and accompanying art exhibition, *Elvis + Marilyn: 2 X Immortal* (1994). Their connection has also been a popular subject in song. Former Jefferson Airplane member Marty Balin's "Elvis and Marilyn" (1981) is a tantalizing fantasy about the two together as a couple. The song contrasts their celebretized lives in alternating verses, then finds common ground: both "spent their nights alone" and were "kept under lock and key." The chorus at once expresses wishful thinking, wonder and regret about Elvis and Marilyn meeting and falling in love.

Transvision Vamp offers a more rebellious than hopefully romantic view, listing Elvis, Marilyn, JFK, Madonna, Jackie O, and Billy the Kidd among the cast of pop culture figures who were "Born To Be Sold" (1988).

On "Lay Down Your Weary Tune Again" (1995), Steve Forbert replaces visions of Romeo and Juliet with Elvis and Marilyn while courting a small town southern sweetheart. She is the "drugstore daddy's flesh an' blood/Like Marilyn Monroe" and he "can't cop his [Elvis's] grin."

One of the darker meditations on Elvis and Marilyn is T-Bone Burnett's "After All These Years" (1983). According to Burnett's explanation during a live show, the song was originally titled "Song for the Coroner." And even though it was based on the three exhumations of Monroe's body, the song "ended up being about Elvis." Opening with, "I heard you saw her again last evening," Burnett's morbid curiosity poses a series of questions relevant to both Elvis and Marilyn: "Does she still look the same after all these years? Will they uncover her terrible secret and untangle the mystery of her life? Could she still drive you crazy by the look in her face? Was she still a scandal, still a disgrace? Still as helpless and full of fears? Still as provocative, compelling . . . Was she still as late after all these years?"

The Replacements' "Bastards of Young" (1985) mentions Elvis as a "son of no one." The song's composer, Paul Westerberg, shares Robertson's views on dreams unfulfilled: "What a mess on the ladder of success/Where you take one step and miss the whole first rung." Where Robertson sees celebrities as "spinning their wheels out of desperation," Westerberg claims they are "the ones who love us least."

In the shadowy image of "Elvis Presley and America" (1984), U2's Bono curses the music business and those who controlled Elvis. The song, recorded in one take, remains vague. Bono explains:

> I felt as if these people had put a straitjacket on Elvis Presley. [He was] unsure of himself intellectually, when he should have been sure of himself. He was dragging himself down. "And the rain beats down/And the rain keeps coming down"–all those images. "And you should feel sentimental/But you don't care if what you share is what is in your heart." All these lines are coming out. I believe the essence of any performer is gut instinct–"and you love though no one told you to/You know but no one told you how." Because it's all you, it's instinct. That's what Elvis Presley's about. And yet the music business tries to make you explain yourself and your actions and reactions. And Elvis couldn't and he felt he should have been able to. And I think that tore at him and it shouldn't have because he was better than all those people. (Flanagan, 1987, p. 452)

Bono further demonstrates his compassionate comprehension of the Elvis story in "Elvis: American David," (DePaoli, 1994) a meditative stream of Presley pieces that forms a beautiful biographical and mythical narrative.

Neil Young also examines the transience of rock stardom in "My My, Hey Hey (Out of the Blue)" and its electric companion, Hey Hey, My My (Into the Black) (1979). Many assumed that the song was immortalizing Elvis because the line, "the King is gone but he's not forgotten." However, Young states unambiguously in the next line, "This is a story of a Johnny Rotten." Young is paying tribute to a type of character, to those artists from Elvis to Johnny

Rotten who have "gone and can never come back." He recognizes the fleeting nature of rock stardom and the tendency of an artist to maintain a false image for an entire career. It is this determination to avoid a stage image and "resist the rust" which is the theme of the song (Rogan, 1989, pp. 151-152). The line, "It's better to burn out than it is to rust," clearly spans rock's "died too soon" spectrum, from Elvis to Kurt Cobain. (Cobain quoted the lines in his suicide note; Young responded with "Sleeps with Angels" in 1994.) Young's burn out or rust treatise is insightful:

> The essence of the rock and roll spirit, to me, is that it's better to burn out than it is to sort of decay off into infinity. (Crowe, 1982)
>
> Rust implies you're not using anything, that you're sitting there and letting the elements eat you. Burning up means you're cruising through the elements so fucking fast that you're actually burning, and your circuits, instead of corroding, are fucking disintegrating. You're going so fast you're actually fucking the elements, becoming one with the elements, turning to gas. That's why it's better to burn out. (Glen, 1988, p. 40)

The view shifts from rust, to "dust never sleeps," in Graham Parker's "Museum Piece" (1991). Although Parker lists Elvis P. and Jerry Lee among those museum artifacts he does not want to end up like, he simultaneously defends the "old guys" from the youthful arrogance of bands.

Cursing can also be heard from the younger wave of performers. Mr. Bonus (Peter Holsapple) scrutinizes Elvis's life for answers to the questions so many have asked, "Elvis, What Happened?" But the song's narrator knows the answer, and who is to blame: "What happened was you died/You showed us how to live and then you died/And it was not a pretty sight." The song expresses a strong sense of betrayal—"And you made us feel like fools/For believin' what we say/Like how you loved religion/And how you loved your maw"—and cursing—"And then you died, you stupid ass/And left it all behind." Though the most intense criticism is directed at Elvis, Holsapple also curses others. The litany includes Dr. Nick ("that evil prick/for all that thorazine"), Colonel Parker ("catering to Elvis' whims and making things look clean/You let him be your Teddy Bear/And he made you Frankenstein"), Elvis's dad ("he seemed to egg you on"), the commercialization ("but thanks to RCA we still get pieces of the pie"), and the fans ("adoration was a burden and the public a rape"). The song presents the dichotomy between adoration and cursing, between faith and doubt: "When we read that Goldman book/And we think we misread you." Like Simon's character and many others, Mr. Bonus remains devoted and will "still visit Graceland whenever he's in town." But the lingering hurt from the betrayal surfaces again in the song's last lines: "Only wish you were around/To see the look on all the faces when they say/Elvis, what happened?"

Bruce Springsteen also mourns Elvis's unnecessary death. "To me he was as big as the country itself, as big as the whole dream. He just embodied the essence of it and he was in mortal combat with the thing. It was horrible and, at the same time, it was fantastic. Nothing will ever take the place of that guy," said Springsteen in *Rolling Stone* ("Elvis," *Rolling Stone*, September 22, 1979, pp. 37-59). According to Boss biographer Dave Marsh, the memory of Elvis Presley seemed to exhaust Springsteen; he brooded for years about the useless way Elvis allowed his life to decompose. Many of Springsteen's thoughts are concisely expressed in "Johnny Bye Bye" (1984), the B-side of the single, "I'm on Fire." To open the song, Springsteen borrows lines from Chuck Berry's "Bye Bye Johnny," which capture the romantic promise of rock and roll dreams of stardom, and then twist them into a tragedy: "She drew out all her money from the Southern Trust/Put her little boy on the Greyhound bus/Leaving Memphis with a guitar in his hand/With a one-way ticket to the Promised Land." In the ensuing verses, the mythic romance of the Elvis legend is replayed, including a beautiful vision of the funeral procession itself. But in the end, the song turns its gaze unflinchingly on the ugly fact: "They found him slumped up against the drain/With a whole lotta trouble runnin' through his veins/Bye bye Johnny, Johnny Bye Bye/You didn't have to die/You didn't have to die." The emotional moan and repetition of the final line emphasizes the unnecessary death. The prophecy of the Promised Land with guitar in hand in "Bye Bye Johnny" becomes an epitaph in "Johnny Bye Bye." And the dream that Elvis whispered in everyone's ears became a deafening fact of ruin. Must be hard being a King.

## SACRED STUFF:
## STORIES, SOUVENIRS, AND SONGS

During a *Designing Women* episode set in a diner outside Grace-land, one character remarks, "Aw, everybody's got an Elvis story." Whether fact or fiction; reverent, gaudy, or mocking accounts; the memory of an Elvis serenade or the news of his death, most of us have had some Elvis experience, response, or at least an awareness of his cultural presence. Objects or incidents associated with Elvis become meaningful or glorified, the way objects or incidents associated with saints become holy. Elvis stories, souvenirs, and songs have been transformed into the sacred as permanent images, artifacts, icons, and myth narratives in the American consciousness.

The primary Presley portrait medium–velvet–is the fabric of choice among many songwriters, and a particularly popular referent with the underground.[7] Aztec Two Step (1986), Weird Al Yankovic (1988), Adrenalin A.O.D. (1987), and Peter Holsapple (this time for the Pink Lincolns) (1987) are among those with "Velvet Elvis" song title credits; Alannah Myles ("Black Velvet") and the Ringling Sisters ("Velvet Crush" (1990)) also provide velvet variations; and the Enigma Records roster includes a band named Velvet Elvis.

Just as Adrenalin A.O.D.'s character checked into a hotel room with a "Velvet Elvis" nailed to the wall, The Pink Lincolns, prov-ing that there is more than one portrait in circulation, find a black velvet King while sifting through rummage at a sale on some old lady's lawn. Tacky as the portraits might be, both the hotel guest and bargain hunter are determined to take them home as center-pieces for their lava-lamp shrines; one would be placed in a bed-room next to the fuzzy Jesus Christ, the other over the television in a room with naugahyde chairs, beaded curtains in the doorway, and Sangria bottles with candles dripping wax. "I will pay any price," says the hotel guest, who vows to take better care of the painting than the maids who have not vacuumed Elvis's fuzzy face. And the Pink Lincolns' character delights in the thought of being the first on the block to own a "Velvet Elvis," and how jealous everyone will be of the prize possession. However, the experience becomes a moral dilemma for the lucky, but broke, bargain hunter, who is less willing to pay for the portrait than the hotel guest, so he steals it and outruns the old lady.

Having a velvet Elvis in his den is a "life-changing experience" for Weird Al (1988). The proud owner assesses the masterpiece's value ("not worth much dough"), aesthetic quality ("means more to me than some old Rembrandt or Van Gogh"), authenticity ("he's no Velvet Imitator"), and function ("big enough to cover the hole in the wall").

Mojo Nixon and Skid Roper want to see "Elvis's ghost alive on a black velvet painting" in "Twilight's Last Gleaming" (1986); while Tom Petty's wryly reverent velvet view in "It's Good To Be King" urges "give 'em a smile."

Other Elvis icons and artifacts such as Cadillacs and souvenir decanters are also the subject of songs. Although Bruce Springsteen's "Pink Cadillac" (1984) may be a classic cruising tune and ideal Mary Kay cosmetic anthem, it certainly conjures images of the King's fleet. Faint foreshadowing of the film *True Romance*, John Hiatt's "Tennessee Plates" (1988) is the tale about a restless California fugitive and a Nevada hitchhiker who arrive at the gates of Graceland where they find what they are looking for: "There must've been a dozen of 'em parked in that garage/No Lincolns, Dodges, or Japanese models or makes/Just pretty, pretty Cadillacs with Tennessee plates." The couple rationalizes their crime, "Elvis wouldn't care; hell, he gave 'em to his friends."

"Elvis Decanter" (1988) is the Vandals' story of a broken relationship, the result of a decanter full of whiskey in the image of the King. The unselfish girlfriend "put a little away everyday" until she could buy her boyfriend the $130 decanter she saw gathering dust inside the liquor store. His friends told him not to break the seal to assure the collectable value, but he couldn't resist and "that King of rock got lighter everyday." Soon it was half empty and he was half as close to his girlfriend; and when he drank the rest he drank their love in two. A commemorative Elvis decanter also appears on the back cover art of Richard Thompson's *Mirror Blue* (1994) record. The ceramic Elvis head hovers over broken pieces of a statue of Thompson lying on gold lamé.

In addition to being the subject of songs and album art, Elvis memorabilia is a popular artifact among musicians. Tom Petty and the Heartbreakers and their road crew use "The Best of Elvis" deck when playing cards to pass the time while traveling across the country on their tour bus. In a *Rolling Stone* (November 25, 1993) interview, singer Art Garfunkel mentions how proud he is of the birthday gift he has for his former partner Paul Simon–a magic wand filled with little stars, hearts, gold records, music notes, a pink Cadillac. The object is to find the tiny gold lamé Elvis floating inside (Dunn, 1993).

For every story about an Elvis souvenir, there is another about an Elvis song. Many express a female point of view. Celtic singer Katell Keinig recalls how her initial songwriting experience involved Elvis. "The first song I wrote, when I was ten, was about the death of Elvis," she says. "Except I called him Emily, and she died of tuberculosis" (Chaplin, 1994).

The Ringling Sisters' "Velvet Crush" conveys part of the female frenzy and Presley puberty that has been a part of the Elvis myth from its inception. Like the character CeBe in the film *Out of the Blue* (1980), the Elvis idolator in the song desires to be, and be with, Elvis. She wears his name on a necklace, relishes his moves and learns his steps. And, as she listens to his music on the floor, her "love festered behind a closed door."

Two songs are sex and violence Elvisian echoes of Lou Reed's "The Day John Kennedy Died" (1982). In the Odds' "Wendy Under the Stars" (1990), a 17-year-old loses his virginity to a 32-year old woman the night Elvis died. Elvis's departing spirit is a "succubus and an angel who enters the two bodies, guides them, seals the act with his presence." (Marcus, 1991, p. 199) Like the Vandals' decanter disaster, Elvis is a factor in another couple's breakup in Syd Straw's "Listening to Elvis" (1985), a combination when-Elvis-died/favorite-Elvis-song saga. In an ironic twist of fate, it is "their song"–"Don't Be Cruel"–and Elvis' death, which led to the lovers' tragic separation: "Fevers ran high/We got into a fight when Elvis died/He ran out to some bar in town/Some big-mouth drunk was makin' jokes puttin' Elvis down/My baby gave him fair warnin' everybody said/But when he sang 'Don't Be Cruel', baby lost his cool and shot him dead/." With Elvis gone, and her baby hiding out in Mexico, the narrator is left sad and alone listening to Elvis with "Don't Be Cruel" her only remaining connection with her two true loves.

Elvis's comforting presence in such lonesome tonight scenarios is common. Saint Etienne's gentle "Hobart Paving" (1993) contains a sad and beautiful analogy in the verse, "Rain falls, Like Elvis tears;" Willie Nile "hears Elvis" in "Heart of Wonder" (1992); and an Elvis song provides salvation in the Del Lords' "Saint Jake" (1986). With prospects dim and his wallet light in Fun City on a Saturday night, the song's storyteller returns home to turn on the radio. "I'm flippin' through the stations getting depressed/When suddenly . . . Elvis." He is saved as the sound of Elvis's voice soothes his pain and loneliness as no other music could. Elvis's musical memory accompanies a rite of passage in the Eurythmics' dirge-like "Angel" (1989). "I believed in you," repeats singer Annie Lennox in a funeral farewell, "like Elvis Presley singing psalms on Sunday," and in another verse, "singing 'Viva Las Vegas'."

The Los Angeles Punk band X presents an Elvis experience that is less "down home," with a much sharper edge. "Back 2 the Base" (1981) is a brutally unrestrained account of a psychotic bus rider screaming curses at the King: "Presley's been dead, the body means nothing/Man in the back says Presley sucked dicks with a picture of Lil' Stevie over his head/I'm in the back with a hole in my throat." Eventually everyone runs from the bus "screaming about Presley." Interestingly, this is one of the rare instances when "Presley" is used as a reference rather than "Elvis" or "The King." In light of our deification and signification of Elvis, using "Presley" to identify Elvis sounds powerfully demeaning and impersonal. Despite its tone, Greil Marcus considers "Back 2 the Base" likely the best song ever written about Elvis. He writes, "It was, as Tom Carson wrote, 'about how culture shapes lives—as indiscriminately as water shapes wood.' It was, in other words, the first song about Elvis' place in the American unconsciousness" (Marcus, 1982, p. 287).

### REMOTE (GUN) CONTROL:
### WHAT'S THE FREQUENCY, ELVIS?

R.E.M.'s hit single, "What's the Frequency, Kenneth?" (1995), is based on a 1986 incident involving CBS anchor Dan Rather, when he was attacked by a stranger who repeated that question over and over. "It remains the premiere unsolved American surrealist act of the twentieth century," says Michael Stipe. "It's a misunderstanding that was scarily random, media hyped, and just plain bizarre." Stipe's characterization of the Rather incident contains a peculiarly striking parallel to Elvis's frequent practice of shooting out television screens with a pistol years earlier.

Elvis's committing telecide on the broadcast image of Robert Goulet as he sang "Camelot" on *The Carol Burnett Show* in 1968 has gathered mythic significance similar to his visit with Richard Nixon in the Oval Office. Human Radio mentions both Elvents in the adventurous "buddy song" "Me and Elvis" (1990): "[We] never worried about the cops/He flashed that badge he got from Nixon/Every time we got stopped." And when they watched TV until late, "We would never change the channel/We'd use Elvis's .38."

With typical underground irreverence, the Chillbumps, an unsigned Southeastern band, mockingly depict Elvis's TV target practice on a handbill promoting one of their performances. In the illustration, pills are scattered on the floor as a caricatured Elvis squats above the toilet and fires a gun at a television set.

Less obscure are Bob Dylan's "TV Talkin' Song" (1990) and Bruce Springsteen's "57 Channels (and Nothin On)" (1992), which treat Elvis as a role model and justify such "television violence." When Dylan overhears people sharing views about "different gods" and the evil effects of television, he believes the answer lies with another god whose aim is truth: "Sometimes you gotta do like Elvis did and shoot the damn thing out."

As its title implies, Springsteen's song is a channel-surfing lament. Inspired by Elvis, the dissatisfied cable subscriber literally takes matters into his own hands (upgrading the firepower from a .38 caliber to a .44 magnum) and declares holy war on his television. "And in the blessed name of Elvis well I just let it blast/'Til my TV lay in pieces there at my feet." War is hell.

Numerous songs place Elvis in different mass-mediated channels. In "I Saw It on T.V." (1985), John Fogerty's list of televisual memories includes *Howdy Doody*, JFK's assassination, the Beatles, and "Hound Dog Man's" appearance on *The Ed Sullivan Show*. Also in a historical vein, only "wireless," Van Morrison's youthful recollection, "In the Days Before Rock 'N' Roll" (1990), recalls being down on his knees trying to tune the radio knobs to receive Elvis, Fats, Jerry Lee, and other rock and blues pioneers.

Dire Straits and conceptual artist Laurie Anderson's preferred mode of communication with the King is the telephone. Their songs "Calling Elvis" (1991), a home alone scenario with a pedestrian listing of Elvis hits throughout, and "Hiawatha" (1989) modify Steven Spielberg's extraterrestrial (E.T.) catchphrase into "E.P. Phone Home." Anderson dials Memphis from the mythical shores of Gitche Gumee. The operator knows who she is calling "and he's not home/He's been away/But you can hear him on the air waves/ He's howlin' at the moon." And if Elvis was there, he would not want to talk; "Keep those cards and letters coming/And please don't call again." With Elvis unavailable, Anderson resorts to her long distance circle of friends and family that includes Captain Midnight, Geronimo, Little Nancy, Marilyn, and John F. In Marcus's dissection of the song, it is Elvis "who by the force of his personality has given all these old symbols their resonance; they are reflections of him" (Marcus, 1991, pp. 199-200).

### NEVER LOVED ELVIS, OR IT'S GOOD TO BE KING?

Here's my main problem: Elvis just doesn't mean jack-shit to me. Growing up in the '70s, I was always confusing him with Evel Knievel, who in any case was more famous and dressed sort of the same and had better material. Elvis–that's the guy who jumped over Snake River Canyon, right?

–Jim Greer, *Spin* (August, 1994, p. 77)

If Elvis was the sort of indispensable cultural pioneer who made the kind of map we can trust, what does it mean when pioneers of a later generation have to willfully torch the map?

–Dave Marsh (1992, p. xi)

Demystification frequently accompanies most popular myths as they evolve. Since his death in 1977, the Elvis Presley myth has simultaneously expanded and been diminished or dismissed in various cultural corners. Among the most notable attempts to diminish the complexity of Elvis's meaning is the countermythology presented in Albert Goldman's *Elvis* biography (1981), which opposes the view that Elvis was a cultural pioneer and his story the embodiment of a route to the American dream.

Willie Nile, Elvis Costello, and the Popinjays are among those who respond to such graverobbing journalism and posthumous exploitation. "Someone's gonna write a book about you/No matter if anything in it is true/. . . talk to everybody that you ever knew/draw their own picture," sings Nile in "Don't Die" (1991). He cautions victims such as Elvis, Hemingway, John Belushi, Joan Crawford, and John Lennon, another Goldman subject. "They're gonna try to make a million dollars off your bones." In "Suit of Lights" (1985), Costello metaphorically addresses the spotlight of resurrection scrutiny: "And they pulled him out of the cold, cold ground/And put him in a suit of lights." And in the Popinjays' "Vote Elvis" (1992), the voice repeatedly laments, "What will you do to me now?" (The song is actually about an eccentric Parliament candidate who ran on the platform that listening to Elvis records could heat the planet.)

Like the various accounts which present another side of Elvis, many songs are a part of the demystification process as they portray Elvis as a racist, junkie, fraud, and failure, among other things, and emphasize the commercial sprawl surrounding his name. Such critiques commonly originate from the younger generation of musicians, the underground, and the African-American community. In contrast, the older generation of artists, even in their cursing and criticism of the King's demise, display a scnse of reverence and debt to Elvis. While the younger wave's treatment of Elvis may appear a less knowledgeable, or immature response, it is understandable and legitimate. There is a constant revolutionary impulse in art for each generation to declare itself as vital and sincere and the previous one as dead and corrupt. To much of the younger generation, Elvis is the old god. Their tendency is to identify Elvis late in his career or after his death. The Elvis they grew up with, know, and recognize, was a bloated, addicted, wealthy, self-parody, and registered trademark, not someone whose presence represented liberation, possibility, excitement, and new modes of expression, as he did early in his career.

Two photographs from record liner notes illustrate the great divide. The predominant Presley view of indifference among the younger generation of musicians may be best captured in The Wonder Stuff's album title, *Never Loved Elvis* (1991), the phrase extracted from a lyric in their song "Mission Drive." Presumably more than a marketing ploy, the anti-Elvis theme can be traced from the bell-bottom jumpsuit that is part of the cover's collage, to Andy Catlin's photograph on the inner sleeve which portrays the band standing inside a store, surrounded by wall-to-wall Elvis memorabilia. They are clearly not gathered to pay homage or to buy souvenirs; the setting becomes a backdrop for an anti-Elvis statement, as one band member casually lifts his hand to cover his huge "never loved Elvis" yawn.

At the opposite end of the Presley polarity is Lindsey Buckingham, the production genius behind Fleetwood Mac. A photo on the inside of his second solo record, *Out of the Cradle* (1992), shows Buckingham, guitar in hand, seated at the console of his recording studio. Among the strewn microphone chords, reels, instruments, and electronic equipment that clutter the space is a velvet portrait of Elvis propped up against a chair. In contrast to The Wonder Stuff's boredom in the presence of the King, reverence rules Buckingham's personal palace. It is as if Elvis is a patron studio saint and Buckingham engages in a duet with him.

Tom Petty's "It's Good to Be King" song title provides an antithesis to the Wonder Stuff's "Never Loved Elvis." Petty joins Buckingham, Springsteen, and other allies of the King whose lives were shaped by Elvis's music and presence. "I think I was about eleven years old when I first became aware of rock," explains Petty. "I went home and traded my Wham-O slingshot for a box of Elvis records that this kid got off his older sister. And that, sort of, ruined my life, I suppose." Petty's boyhood friend's sister may be the "good girl" he sings about in "Free Fallin'" (1989); she loves her Mama, Jesus, horses, America, her boyfriend, and "she's crazy 'bout Elvis." She is also a kindred spirit with "Maria, from Nashville, with a suitcase in her hand, (who) wants to meet a boy who looks like Elvis," in the Counting Crows "Round Here" (1993).

Petty further demonstrated his reverence when he declined to appear at the 1994 all-star sixtieth birthday salute to Elvis in Memphis, calling the gathering "a hokey affair." "If anyone's been tributed to death, it's Elvis," says Petty. "Maybe the idea was to illustrate that the man was one of the great artists of all time, a fact blurred when he became such a huge, mythical part of culture. But tributes are a delicate matter, because you can actually disgrace the artist by paying tribute" (Gunderson, 1994b, p. 1D).

The conflicting Elvis mythologies become a point-counterpoint narrative in songs. For every unhallowed punk entry, such as the Butthole Surfers' "Revenge of Anus Parsley" (1983) or the Nightingales' eerie "previously unreleased diary entries" in "Elvis, the Last Ten Days" (1981), there is a song which offers a more appreciative and venerating view of the King.

## *RESURRECTION, ROYALTY, AND RIPOFF*

Commercialization and the "still alive" phenomenon are two primary components of the Elvis countermythology. "Elvis is Dead" (1988) is the Forgotten Rebels' brief response to Elvis's death. To them, he's a "big fat goof." And the millions of mourners are not the faithful or pilgrims Billy Joel and Paul Simon saw lining the Boulevard and standing at Graceland's gates; to the Forgotton Rebels, they are simply "assholes." They, too, want to dig up the King, but their plan is to "steal his body for ransom and leave his hypodermics where his body lays."

Numerous songs honor the Zevon lyric—"imagine digging up the King"—and demystify Elvis by responding to the dead-or-alive debate. Graham Parker's "Loverman" (1995) is a "things I could do for you" monologue of an obsessive character trying to impress a woman. In a final desperate attempt to attract her, he says, "Did I tell you last night I found Elvis hangin' in my closet?" The line does not impress; "it looks like you're bored."

Nixon and Roper want to "cut through all this tabloid jive" in their "Elvis is Everywhere" sequel song, "(619) 239-KING" (1989), an "E-phone" number (a percusor to e-mail?) anyone can call with information as to Elvis's whereabouts. Familiar faces (Dr. Nick), themes (the give anything desire to hear Elvis sing again), and theories (lives on an island with Marilyn Monroe) appear throughout. Elvis's return is conditional; this time he must "do it right"—no Vegas or movies, "just leather, black and tight." Nixon's ultimate dream, before Michael

Jackson stole his dream girl in 1994, was to get Lisa Marie to marry him so he can call his father-in-law "great Big Daddy." The Jackson-Presley split up in 1996 rekindles his hopes.

Also aligning at the novelty end of the underground axis is Pink Slip Daddy. They don't believe the King is dead or what the radio says; they've seen a guy all over town and there's no mistaking him–dark glasses, black pointed shoes, knows every song. It's the "Elvis Zombie" (1988), who "Comes out of cracks about twelve o'clock/Lookin' real greasy with his lip curled up/Hot and nasty and ready to rock/But he don't come out 'til he hears the sound/Make way for the Elvis Zombie/Walkin' and talkin' just like the King/Looks so cute when he do that hip-shake-thing."

In contrast, the critically acclaimed bar band from the late 1970s, Joe Gruschecky and the Iron City Houserockers, describe a sympathetic ghostly Elvis encounter in the middle of the night on "Talking to the King" (1992). The afterlife has done Elvis some good; he is keeping clean, and has dropped some weight. Although hindsight has provided perspective, he still sits alone on his throne, missing a place to sing. He may be a wiser King, but there is sadness and regret in his tone as he answers the night visitor's questions. He cautions: "You better be careful or you'll lose everything/It ain't no fun to be King/You should be glad nobody knows your name/Sometimes I think I sold my soul to become the King of rock and roll."

In "Elvis in Paraguay" (1986), the Generic Blue Band provides a new death hoax theory: "An albino Negro gospel singer with Elvis's race/Was loaded with prescriptions and died in his place." And Elvis–"It broke his heart to see Nixon fail, the pot head demons, the Holy Grail"–is hiding out, unknown to Priscilla, Lisa Marie, and The Colonel. "He's hoping the Russians will blow the place away/So he can come back rockin' from Paraguay." The band also prophesies the King's apocalyptic return, when "every hotel in Vegas will be his to buy and sell, and the only folk not destroyed are Wayne Newton, The Kid, and Pink Floyd." The song's international flavor is similar to the Leroi Brothers' "Elvis in the Army (1985), a lighthearted response to "our boy Elvis's" tour of duty overseas. The crew cut King is cast as a world leader pretend, representing America in a conflict with Kruschev over the Berlin Wall. When told not to mess with his new wall, diplomat Elvis laughs at Kruschev, calls him "fat boy," and threatens to knock the wall to kingdom come.

Loudon Wainwright also foresees Elvis being back for the millennium. "Happy Birthday Elvis" (1993) contains the witty folkie's musings on the "Elvis alive" phenomenon, including the cassette recordings, tabloid abductions, sightings, and conspiracy plots. Wainwright suspects that "Down in that bunker beneath Graceland/ The King sits on his throne."

Among Elvis enterprises and excesses, Graceland is a glaring focal point for dissenters. The Elvis Hitler instru-metals "Disgraceland" (1988) and "Elvis Ripoff Theme" suggest a more appropriate title and anthem for the Kingdom. In "Elvis Incorporated" (1987), Sons of Ishmael expands on Transvision Vamp's "Born To Be Sold" cynicism. Not only does the Canadian band criticize Elvis ("overweight, payroll your only concern, you rusted fast, self-parody set in fast"), they blame the American system as well: "He's a business you created/He's been run down by prostitution, a big American institution/His merchandise sold like crazy while he became fat and lazy."

The dB's express indifference in "Rendezvous" (1984). To them, eating ribs in Memphis is more fulfilling than a visit to Graceland: "Counting all his rings/Taking Care of Business/Heh, Heh, doesn't mean a thing."

The Dead Milkmen's irreverent, "Going to Graceland" (1987) is a divergence from Paul Simon's vision of the mansion as a symbol of redemption. The view on this visit is vintage Beavis and Butthead; a field trip to a stand-in-line, royalty reaping rip-off. "We better watch our language or the guards will beat us up," cautions the narrator, who nonetheless remains enthused, but not because of the collections or historic rooms. To him, the tours represent, among other things, a chance to: "see the bucket Elvis Presley kicked; go to his grave and try not to smile; cut loose, abuse tourists, act real stupid, try to pick up girls, have a wild time, make some cheap jokes and buy cheaper souvenirs (If this were Disneyland I'd buy a pair of Elvis ears)." A line from the song may be representative of the scornful view of Elvis shared by much of the younger generation of musicians and others who have adopted and offered a countermythology: "When my time comes/That's how I want to go/Stoned and fat and wealthy/And sitting on the bowl."

## EL DISS:
## PUBLIC ENEMY NUMBER ONE

African-American musicians are not so divided along generational lines in their responses toward Elvis. Many of the older performers, scarred by white exploitation of black musical forms during the 1950s, remain resentful. Ray Charles is but one example. During an interview with NBC's Bob Costas in July 1991, Charles was visibly uncomfortable when asked to assess Elvis's influence in rock and roll. Nonetheless, the elder rhythm and blues spokesperson could not resist the knowledgeable Costas's bait, and proceeded to diminish the King's importance as a rock pioneer.

The hurt felt by the older artists has sustained, and evolved into a more hostile expression among some of the finest contemporary black musicians, many whom disdain any worth Elvis might possess at all. To Elvis biographer Dave Marsh, that widespread dismissal may be "the greatest Elvis-related tragedy of all" (1992, pp. x-xi). Marsh is sympathetic, not single-minded. It is obvious from his writings that Marsh, a Motown native, has been one of the most musically diverse and politically correct music critics during the past 25 years. Yet, black artists widely refute his advocacy of Elvis as "a figure of integration," insisting that the Mississippi white boy "was nothing but a Klansman in blue suede shoes."

Public Enemy and Living Colour provide two of the more notable raps on the King. In "Fight the Power" (1989), the theme song played during the opening titles and closing credits of Spike Lee's film, *Do The Right Thing*, hip-hop leader Chuck D disses the King: "Elvis was a hero/But he never meant shit to me you see/Straight up racist that sucker was/Simple and plain."

Living Colour's Vernon Reid is equally pissed. "Elvis is Dead" (1990) is a post-funk demystification of the fanatic deification and commercial exploitation of Elvis. "A Black man taught him how to sing/And then he was crowned king . . . Now the masses are his slave . . . yes, even from the grave," spew the lyrics. The song reflects the belief that the mythification of Elvis is part of white music industry's attempt to wrest rock and roll's commercial potential away from its black originators. "Part of it is who defines things," remarks Reid about the issue. "It's not enough for the powers that be to love Elvis, for him to be *their* king of rock and roll. Elvis has to be the king of rock and roll for everybody. And that is something I cannot swallow."

Reid's resentment lingers contagiously. At a New York City show in September 1994, funk bassist Me'Shell NdegéOcello, in a bit of a funk herself, scornfully proclaimed, "If Elvis is King, then who the fuck is James Brown–God?"

Such generational and racial countermythology has become so deeply ingrained that Michael Jackson's "To the real King" dedication in his *HIStory* (1995) anthology, presumably a humble passing of his King of Pop crown to producer Berry Gordy, was also read by a few critics as another El-diss, a subtle or unintentional slight of his "temporary" father-in-law.

### EXILED OR EXALTED:
### LONG LIVE THE KING . . .

It's every generation throw a hero up the pop chart.

—Paul Simon, "The Boy in the Bubble"
© *1986 Paul Simon (BMI)*

In the four-month period following Elvis Presley's death in 1977, more than 200 records about him were released worldwide; another 100 followed in 1978. Though the number has leveled off since the initial posthumous period's pace, songs about Elvis continue to be a tangible manifestation of Elvis culture into the mid-1990s.[8]

The prevalence of songs originating from the underground or alternative music axis is an indication that generations will likely continue to respond to Elvis and his myth. Songwriters both young and old, black and white, male and female, will remain divided in their views, offering a simultaneous musical homage and critique. Some will shrug or yawn with indifference, "Never loved Elvis;" while others will proclaim, "It's good to be King." Some will mock and curse Presley as a fact of ruin, a bloated, addicted, registered trademark. Others will exalt him as The King, a godlike, inspirational, scepter of possibility. Bands, such as the New York-based Sons of Elvis, will even use his name (in vain?); while others, such as the Rolling Stones, will revere his image, as they did by paying homage in the stage tableau backdrop of their 1994 *Voodoo Lounge Tour*. Like the rest of us, songwriters and musicians will continue to dig up the King, beg him to sing, put him in a suit of lights, ask "What happened?", and be among those who visit Graceland, sometimes for reasons we cannot explain.

A fitting metaphor for this endless song cycle surfaces in a caged hamster vision of Elvis in the Beat-poet-like lyrics of the Blue Aeroplanes' "Colour Me" (1991): "Elvis sings 'Love Me Tender'/Runs his wheel/We all get younger."

## NOTES

1. Among the stations sponsoring challenges in "Bring Elvis In" was WEBF in Westport, Connecticut, which reportedly received 500 calls weekly for nearly a month following its million-dollar bounty. WKRC in Cincinnati, Ohio, KKEX in Portland, Oregon, WDAF in Kansas City, Missouri, and WTVN in Columbus, Ohio raised the stakes to $2 million for its listeners. Nashville's WWHY topped out at $100 million for anyone who could deliver Elvis by midnight, August 16, the anniversary of his death. No prize money was claimed at any radio station across the country.

2. Focusing primarily on popular and underground artists limits the number of songs, yet illustrates the repetition and use of the Elvis motif in contemporary music. Similar Elvis exaltation that emphasizes the "hillbilly heaven" tradition can be found throughout Country and Western music. The C & W style is more straightforward and sentimental compared with the elaborate hyperbole and metaphor used by popular and underground artists.

3. Earlier, and less extensive versions of the material presented in this chapter include, "The King is Gone But Not Forgotten: Songs Responding to the Life, Death and Myth of Elvis Presley in the 1980s," *Studies in Popular Culture*, XII:1, 1989:58-75; and "Long Live the Ling: An Annotated Discography of Elvis Presley as a Motif in Popular Music in the 1980s," *OneTwoThreeFour*, Number 9, Autumn 1990:77-87.

4. A sampling of events and Marian activities includes: In April in southern Florida, a particularly popular location for Marian interest, thousands travel to a parish in Palm Beach County to venerate a crowned, jeweled statue of Our Lady of Fatima, built to resemble the figure children in Portugal reportedly saw in 1917. In September, there is an annual Festival of Our Lady of Charity, which Cuban Catholics celebrate with a Mary statue at a local park. Joseph Januszkiewicz of Marlboro Township, New Jersey began seeing the Virgin Mary in the blue spruce trees in his back yard in 1990. When the news of the "appearance" spread through the Marian network, thousands of pilgrims traveled to the sacred sighting

location. In Lubbock, Texas, the annual Festival of the Assumption attracts an average of 12,000 followers. In 1988, many in the crowd said they saw the faces of Mary and Jesus in the clouds. In the words of Don Henley, "Or maybe it was Elvis, you know they kinda look the same."

5. Check out Greil Marcus's insightful discussion of this song in *Dead Elvis* (1991:122-123).

6. Greil Marcus treats this compilation as a comprehensive climax of his cultural chronicle, *Dead Elvis*, pp. 201-203.

7. Songs with popular culture referents are common along the college music/ alternative axis. The perception of greater tolerance of irreverent views on the radio programming formats and the popularity of the novel variations of these songs may encourage such commentary and demystification in the songwriting.

8. Checking the flow chart, Banney's (1987: xii and xiii) 1980s numbers indicate a total of 201 Elvis tributes and novelties released from 1980 through 1987. The yearly totals, beginning in 1980 are: 39, 38, 24, 22, 14, 32, 21, 11.

# Chapter 2

# Presley Pulp Fiction:
# Swimming in the Mystery of History

History is so unbearable it must be dignified with story.

—Laura Kalpakian, *Graced Land*

Once you get into this great stream of history you can't get out.

—Richard Nixon

Since his death, the stream of printed material on the life, death, and myth of Elvis Presley has been continuous. Virtually everyone who has ever been associated with Elvis in some way, real or imagined, from distant cousins, housekeepers, and hairdressers, to cooks and karate instructors, has provided a written account of their Elvis experience. "Outsiders" such as historians, music critics, cultural observers, and opportunistic biographers have also contributed their interpretations of the story. What has accumulated on the book "shelvis" is an extensive and diverse catalog that extends beyond biographies to include cholesterol crammed cookbooks (Butler, 1993; McKeon, Gevirtz, and Bandy, 1992), photo journals, travel guides, encyclopedias of trivia and memorabilia (Stern and Stern, 1987; Worth and Tamerius, 1990), and various other Presley parodies, parables, and paperbacks. In addition, Elvis's name has also been appropriated into catchy book titles. Humorist Lewis Grizzard's *Elvis Is Dead and I'm Not Feeling So Good Myself* (1984), Colin MacEnroe's *Lose Weight Through Great Sex with Celebrities the Elvis Way* (1992), and Kinky Friedman's *Elvis, Jesus, and Coca-Cola* (1993) are among examples. This King collection in print could fill a wing of many reading centers, if not constitute a library in itself.

Writers of fiction have also been among those contemporary cultural creators who have interpreted the Elvis story. Whether writing romance, mystery, science fiction, or fantasy, authors have used Elvis's life and legacy as a theme, basis, and backdrop for their narratives. While many of the Presley biographies are arguably borderline "fiction," Elvis is widely represented in conventional fictional forms such as novels, short stories, poems, children's stories and even subliterary modes such as comic books. The fascination with Elvis as a subject among the literari is evident in the number of anthologies that began appearing in the early 1990s: *The Elvis Reader: Texts and Sources on the King of Rock and Roll* (Quain, 1992); *Elvis Rising: Stories on the King* (Sloan and Pierce, 1993) (Figure 2.1); *Mondo Elvis* (Ebersole and Peabody, 1994); and *The King Is Dead: Tales of Elvis Postmortem* (Sannon, 1994).

No matter the literary mode, the Elvis authors are swimming in the mystery of history. Their historical revision quests yield an abundance of images–power and persona, porch and pill, uniforms, hair, a yo-yo, flashlight, telephone, serpent, king, evangelist, magician, homicidal maniac–as they revise, re-examine, and retell the Elvis Presley story.

## *PILL AND PORCH*

Laura Kalpakian's *Graced Land* (1992) contains is a familiar story of Elvis devotion, salvation, and conversion. However, the novel contains several distinct attributes which set it apart from other Elfanatic narratives, among them, the setting (a Southern California desert burg, St. Elmo, in 1982), social class distinctions, and a woman's voice and view of Elvis expressed through the characters.

Emily Shaw, a recent USC grad who would trade her high-class future for a tender present, is a social worker whose caseload includes "Elvis fruitcakes," including *Graced Land's* central character, Joyce "Rejoice" Jackson.

Joyce is a welfare mother whose "unusual attachment to Elvis" is evident in her daughters (Priscilla, Lisa Marie), dog (Colonel), and an immaculately kept, open-air chapel honoring The King on her front porch.

The shrine is to Joyce what the jumpsuit or other artifacts are to other Elfans–a source of power and strength. Though deeply personal,

FIGURE 2.1. One of several anthologies of Elvis literature.

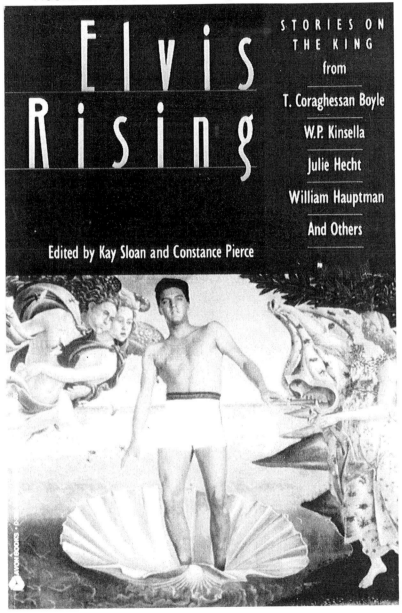

Source: Avon books. Reprinted by permission.

Joyce's memorial resembles other Elvis shrines as it is created from a familiar primitive palette of materials and memorabilia: American and Confederate flags, plastic daisies, satin rosettas, pictures in quilted black frames, ribbons and streamers, hundreds of tiny twinkling Christmas lights, hand-lettered signs proclaiming Elvis's greatness nailed to the trellis.

The front porch is holy ground. When the new paperboy unknowingly delivers the *Herald* to the shrine, rather than the backdoor, Lisa scolds him for his irreverence, and threatens to call the police. When he flips his cigarette butt into the gutter and says, "Oh piss off and take Elvis with you," the ironic image is one of young punk Presley.

The neighborhood landmark is both a roadside attraction and distraction, referred to by curious visitors and passersby as "Heartbreak Hotel." To Large Marge Mason, Social Service's "institutional asshole," Joyce's shrine is a low-class publicity stunt, and Elvis "poor white trash" and a "hip-swinging, drug-addicted degenerate." The antagonist is determined to keep Elvis and his fruitcake followers in their rightful place at the lowest rung of the social ladder. When Marge senses her caseworker Emily is being sympathetic, and possibly "converted," she warns the sorority sophisticate, "it's unbecoming on an educated person."

The shrine is not a gimmick to Joyce, but a genuine devotion that dates back to the 1950s when she was a teenager. It was then she began taking the pill—the Elvis Pill—a rhythm method, mystical medication from an unheard melody. Kalpakian's passage describing the experience derived from the pill suggests both the divine and the sensual:

> You could take an Elvis pill anywhere. Invoke an Elvis song and perform upon it a sort of musical communion: eyes closed, a strong intake of breath, the song pressed into a wafery round, sweet, hard, fragile as the coating on a Jordan almond—laid up against the roof of the mouth, neither sucking nor insisting, just her tongue pressing gently, firmly, till she could feel the music dissolve, the volume diminishing into her blood, rising up through her bones. The Elvis Pill allowed Joyce not simply to hear the music, but to have it. (p. 97)

Throughout Joyce's life, the Elvis Pill provides the only effective medication for her worldly struggles. When her husband leaves her (on the same day Elvis dies) Elvis becomes her salvation. Elvis's music, keeping his shrine, carrying on his work, helping others in his name resuscitate her daily life.

Unlike many Elfanatics, Joyce can distinguish between Elvis and Jesus. Yet, she recognizes similarities in both saviors, notably their shared suffering and humanity. Joyce drifts helplessly into a tearful evangelical state as she delivers a sympathetic sermonette to Emily about Elvis's demise:

> Oh it's terrible what they say. Don't they understand? Drugs were part of his punishment. They were part of his suffering. No one could save him from the suffering. No one. He sang himself to death because he loved us, all of us—as much as we loved him. He died for us.
>
> The drugs only prove he was human, born to suffer like the rest of us. We're all born to die and sin and suffer. The drugs were a disgrace, of course they were! Didn't Jesus suffer disgrace? Wasn't the cross a humiliation? The crown of thorns? There's no disgrace in his suffering. There's only his humanity. (p. 22)

Joyce's devotion to Elvis provides an interesting contrast to other fictional portrayals, particularly when comparing gender views. For example, Byron Bluford in *Stark Raving Elvis* (Henderson, 1984) is from the same social class as Joyce and possesses a Presley passion comparable to hers, yet their motivations and missions are clearly different. Byron's worship is rooted in a quest for power; he wants to be Elvis. Joyce's devotion is more pure and honorable; her power derives from compassion. When Emily asks her what she wants to do with her life, Joyce replies, "I'd like to carry on Elvis's work." Joyce does not mean as an Elvis Impersonator, or a music and movie star. "That wasn't his work, that was his job," she corrects Emily. Joyce identifies with Elvis's humanity, goodness, and generosity. She wants to serve in his name, frequenting halfway houses, delivering goods and clothes to the needy: "Here, Elvis Presley wants you to have this coat."

The spiritual connection is further revealed in Joyce's metaphorical interpretation of Elvis's death.

He didn't exactly die, he passed through time like it was a
sieve. He left off his suffering flesh. His spirit just passed
through that sieve like steam, no different than water heated up
turns to steam and gets free of the kettle and passes through
air, invisible so you can't see it, but you can feel it. (p. 75)

The image of Elvis as savior crystallizes in the story's final scene.
Joyce and her ex-husband are reunited in the hospital following his
near fatal motorcycle accident. As he lies in unconscious in the ICU
with Joyce at his side, once again it is the Elvis Pill–the unheard
melody of Elvis's voice–that resonates deeply, serenading and sooth-
ing Joyce's spirit, a saving grace for the lost and the found.


## *I AM ELVIS:*
## *CASES OF MISTAKEN IDENTITY*

Just as they have been represented in art, film, television, and
theater, Elvis Impersonators have been widely captured in words
and images on the printed page. The imitators are an automatic
entry into opportunistic humor/parody paperback such as Christopher Fowler's alter-ego trip guidebook, *How to Impersonate Famous People* (1984). Photographers have compiled portraits of the
clones into bound biographical collections such as *The King and I:
A Little Gallery of Elvis Impersonators* (Pritikin, 1992), and the
boldly titled, *I Am Elvis: A Guide to Elvis Impersonators* (1991).

In addition, Impersonators have been central and supporting characters, a basis and backdrop for numerous fictional narratives. Singer
Jimmy Buffet's bestselling collection of "fictional facts and factual
fiction," *Tales from Margaritaville* (1989), includes "Are You Ready
for Freddy?," a brief account of wandering into an Elvis convention on
the outskirts of Philadelphia. The Impersonators are intertwined with
the Village Irregulars, Uptown and Downtown Judies, a missing documentary film, and mob murder in Kinky Friedman's New York Tex-
Mex mystery *Elvis, Jesus, and Coca-Cola*.

Though Stephen Mooser's *Elvis Is Back and He's in the Sixth
Grade* (1994) may be more playful and innocent than other sordid
sagas about being Elvis, there is delusional grandeur of childlike
proportions in the story for young readers. "It's funny. But some-

times I actually think I am Elvis. It's like my destiny or something," says Eldon Grant before performing at his junior high talent show.

Mississippi Gulf Coast artist Steve Shepard counters the "I am Elvis" approach in his colorfully illustrated kid/adult book, *Elvis Hornbill: International Business Bird* (1991). The story incorporates an "I am not Elvis" inversion through a parental/pet conflict.

While in West Africa, the narrator and his wife adopt a baby bird and name him after Elvis Presley because he sings so well. Dad encourages his adopted hornbill/son to be a rock star rather than pursue a more conventional adult-approved profession. But the Presley pet rebels. The bird's interests are in accounting and economics, not music. This Elvis prefers business suits, briefcases and bank notes to sequined jackets, guitars, and eighth notes. While Mom allows Elvis to make up his own mind, Dad cannot understand why his "son" wastes his talents on "no-good business" and "frivolous finance." He hopes it is a stage Elvis will grow out of. Ironically, the exotic bird's preference for money makes him just as worthy of the Presley name and legend as does music.

## DRESSED TO KILL: LORD BYRON, "AN AUTOMATIC GOD"

Being the King is about the hardest thing a man could do– almost impossible.

–Byron "Blue Suede" Bluford

Along with P. K. Kluge's *Biggest Elvis* (1996), a tale of a trio of Philippine-based Elvi–"Baby," the callow, naive 1950s version; "Dude," a punk movie star; and "Biggest," a wandering academic bored with teaching–perhaps the most extensive and excessive fictional treatment of Elvis Impersonation can be found in William McCranor Henderson's *Stark Raving Elvis* (1984), a redneck to riches to ruin fable of Byron "Blue Suede" Bluford, a dime-store God pursuing his Cadillac dreams of being Elvis. Byron's quest begins at an assembly line in Portland, Maine and leads to Hoot Night competition at beer and motor oil, swinging pool cue stick local roadhouse dives, to a climax in Las Vegas at the colossal Battle of the Elvises. The novel's premise may be best captured by Dave Marsh, who writes in *The First Rock and Roll Confidential* (1985), "Find out why we all want to be rock stars–and how lucky it is that we aren't."

The familiar Presley parallels emerge–prescriptions, a penis named "The Little Prince," pistols shooting out annoying TV sets, and plenty of parasites. The supporting cast of caricatures features familiar faces as well: the controlling and calculating Colonel Frank Bruno; Rockin' Doc and his bag o' drugs; the nymphomaniacal Elvis Woman; body-guards "Screech" and "Earthquake" who resemble the characters from *Raising Arizona*, a pair of drifting desperado Elvis hobbyists who once had a scheme to steal his body and keep it in their garage; and Estelle, psychic tailor to the stars. While the seductresses and scaven-gers surround Byron and spoon-feed his blurred vision, Wendy Wayne, an aspiring Joni Mitchell folkie, hopelessly stands by her man as he drifts in an out of the seemingly possessed Presley persona.

This white trash saga intertwines the cosmetic lip curl surgery, Lady Clairol hair color, wholesale scarves world of Elvis Imperson-ation with the more complex psychospiritual realm of obsession and power. Byron's journey is an Elvis allegory, replete with religious imagery, allusions, and subtexts that explore the duality of existence–young and old, good and evil, truth and lies, lost and found, fantasy and reality, emptiness and fulfillment–all within a rock and roll, American Dream backdrop.

Byron is presented as a "chosen one." When he fatefully meets the King in his dressing room following a show in 1976, Elvis gives Byron his pearl-handled .22. Byron has an "Amazing Grace" out-look on the exchange; he "found" what Elvis "lost." He was receiv-ing potency from the suffering King and the full force of his earthly mission. He is to inherit the throne. "One day there's gonna be a hole in the sky where Elvis Presley used to be and I've got to be pre-pared," says Byron. Despite scoffing skeptics, the consumed Byron views Elvis's death as a sign that the path is cleared for him to follow in his divine footsteps.

Byron's evolution from Prince to King to Lord and back to Byron provides a study of identity and power, illusion and confusion, and the interconnectedness between the physical, spiritual, and psychological. Henderson often provides a reflective narrative, posing a universal curiosity–"How the hell could you make a life out of being Elvis?

What could you do with it that wasn't just a gag?"—then probes for answers through his subject.

Distinctions emerge. On a pure level of performance, impersonating Elvis is a routine, an expression that in itself is a how-to manual. The physical attributes such as costume, gesture, and gyration are obvious; it's the inner dimension accompanying the act—the sense of identity and power—that distinguishes between Elvis as a way of life and Elvis as a life.

Like many impersonators, Byron believed that being Elvis meant being somebody; it was an achievement, a distinction. His only struggle was which Elvis to be, a dilemma that was fictional foreshadowing of the 1992 Stamp Election. Byron preferred the edgy Elvis, the punky, pure highwire artist full of risk and rebellion to the safe, homogenized, tired old dude dressed like Liberace.

Routinely reminded that Elvis himself bombed in Vegas doing "early Elvis" in the 1950s, Byron responded with the resentment of a prophet whose message was being rejected. "They don't want to see a greaser in a zoot suit, they want to see God." His sleazy entourage structures a religious regimen of watching Elvis performances as if they were instructional videotapes. Byron diligently reviews and trains, weaving the choreography, karate, sweeps, runs, and kneeling sequences into larger patterns, until its final form—The Routine. The new, mature, magnetic Elvis emerges from Byron's cocoon in splendor, rationalizing that with Elvis dead, late was just as "historical" as early. "It's like a heart transplant. The parts of me that weren't Elvis had to go so they wouldn't reject the heart," explains Byron.

The heart image is recurring. One night Byron dreams he is hanging around Graceland when someone comes out and says that Elvis is inside with his heart pulled out. "I'm gonna eat that goddam heart," reacts Byron. He enters a dark room where Elvis is laid out in his coffin. His heart, sizzling like a steak, sits on a plate beside him. Byron sits down with some A-1 steak sauce, starts carving and eating. Elvis rises up like a vampire, and Byron is trapped, unable to do anything but chew.[1]

Though obvious, the heart and dream appropriately characterize Byron's total transformation. He has crossed the fine line, going from "in the image of" Elvis to a state of total being and oneness with the King. For Byron, there is no other way. He no longer considers himself an impersonator, rather an "authentic practitioner, an illusionist." All the others are impostors, wind-ups, assholes, bootlegs, freaks, and rhinestone retards. To Byron there is no room in the world for two Elvises:

> You either *are* Elvis or you're an imposter. If you're the King, you sit on a throne; if you're a fake you get dumped in the alley. And when the King dies, there's only one possible man to replace him. It's that simple. I'm that man. I'm not faking anything. I'm just swimming in the river of history. I used to imitate Elvis. Now I am Elvis. (p. 94)

Others who observe King Byron place the familiar behavior in a religious context. "I've seen 'em like that. They get carried away," says Big Elmo, Byron's toughest competition for the throne. "It ain't an act anymore. They think they been resurrected." And bartender Eddie delivers a sermonette:

> Guys like him get so involved in emulating a monster like Elvis Presley that their own personality disappears. They think they're kind of a hero like Johnny Appleseed, but it's all haywire . . . crack brains running around thinking the great spirit has descended on them and now they're semi-divine, with a cosmic role to fulfill. With [Byron] it's Elvis. It might as well be Napoleon or Jesus Christ. He's a nut. He's not normal up there . . . (p. 150)

Such delusional cases of "mistaken identity" are commonplace among the legions of Elvii.[2] To Henderson, the Elvis identity is about power, and the central source is *not* represented by the gun, songs, or even the heart. It's the jumpsuit. More than a cream cheese costume with spangles and four-inch fringe, the jumpsuit, inspired by Inca/Aztec warrior costumes, takes on mythic significance as a life force, very much the same way Sailor's jacket does in *Wild at Heart* (Gifford, 1990). To Byron, there is danger woven into its design. Elvis's image stuck to his jumpsuit, as if it had melted and hardened, slowly possessing and squeezing the life out of his fattened, suffering flesh.

The jumpsuit embraces a dual nature as a central point of contention and conversion for Byron. The strangling second skin is both sacred and sinister, savior and serpent, splendor and salvation. "I'm small time because I don't wear a fucking jumpsuit," says Byron, resentful of the Vegas attitude that "early Elvis ain't Elvis."

The suit becomes the apple and Las Vegas the Garden of Eden in this allegory. "That's the secret," explains Colonel Bruno, tempting Byron to wear the forbidden suit. "Once you put it on in this town, you don't have to tell them who you are; they know. You're starting at the top. You're a God. An automatic God."

Following the Battle of Elvises at the Roman Gardens, an Armageddon of Impersonators competing for an authentic Elvis jumpsuit, distraught runner-up Byron takes the four finalists hostage. His madness and heart are about to explode when Byron has a sudden realization—"the goddam jumpsuit." Like an animal chewing off its foot to escape a trap, Byron frantically tears the suit away and shreds it, "a flayed mess of old skin."

Like a soul's lingering departure from a body in the moments following death, Elvis's spirit remains in Byron. As he looks in the mirror, mourning his crumbling dream, Byron's fearful face still reflects Elvis—pathetic and puffy, asking directions, seeking knowledge, unsure of the owner, the strain from pushing too hard at the edge of youth.

And once again, Henderson entangles the now familiar images of the heart, serpent, and jumpsuit in a passage that not only summarizes Byron's sorrowful journey, but offers an interpretation of Elvis's demise as well:

> The dead boy had flashed so bright, made such a strong run at being a man and lost it. Manhood had risen up and smothered the King, like a snake from inside his guts, twisting his heart into silence, all the while whispering to him, a white jewel-studded serpent of death, telling him he was still the world's boy. (p. 210)

In this gospel according to Henderson, the sinister suit is the forbidden fruit Byron could not resist wearing. It is temptation made sin, signifying among other things, loss of innocence, purity, and perhaps soul. The jumpsuit is Elvis's sin, as well as Byron's. It is what separates "early Elvis" from "late," young from old, and ultimately life from death. Byron could not resist the whispers of power it held. He was not content being one of the Elvis godhead's imitating angels, he wanted to be an "automatic God."

Amidst the chaos following the competition, the judges reconsider and declare Byron King. He returns to the Roman Gardens dressed in his prize for one final appearance before "his people." "Here he is. I'm wearing him. And it's itchin' me to death," declares Byron before ceremoniously stripping the second skin, tearing it apart like some sacrificial heart and casting its pieces to the frenzied fans.

This final Act of Elvis reflects the dual nature of the jumpsuit—the death and birth cycle, a blessing and curse, the evil Elvis exorcised and the savior dying for Byron's sin. Either way, it marked the end of Byron's journey, the awakening from a rock and roll nightmare, the completed but unfulfilled spiritual mission. The quest had come full circle.

The Neil Young "better to burn out" hypothesis arises in the moral of the story. There is the lingering implication that Byron's dream was no more excessive, inevitable, and delusionary than Elvis's and Elvis's no more than Joplin's or Hendrix's or Morrison's or Rotten's or Cobain's; and theirs perhaps no more than the local bands playing the club circuit with hopes of trying to break on through to the other side. What lurks in *Stark Raving Elvis* is the notion that rock's deepest spirit, the energy that links the needs and fantasies of artists and fans, the worshippers and worshipped, is basically corrupt. Like the musical martyrs, dreamers, and burnouts who preceded him, Byron had to find his ending, good or bad.

Henderson's messianic metaphor used to describe Byron's state might also be a meditation on Elvis's spirit of relief in death in August 1977: "His role was played out. He floated above it all. Over it. Free of it. He felt light and perfect. Naked like a baby with no name. No past. He was brand new."

### EARLY ELVISLUTION:
### "THE EMPLOYEE MENTALITY"

Elvis died the day he went into the army.

—John Lennon

Whereas Henderson's novel attributes Elvis's demise to the jumpsuit, another "uniform" suggestively signals the beginning of the end in Mark Childress's *Tender* (1990). The novel, one of the more mainstream pieces of Elvis fiction, explores early Elvis parallels through the character Leroy Kirby, a poor white boy from Tupelo. The bio-blueprint traces Leroy's meteoric rise to rock and roll stardom from his birth in 1935 until 1958 when he was drafted into the Army. This Presley parenthesis spans the same time frame used in the Elvis television series on ABC in 1989.

Leroy's (the name means "king" or "royalty") fictional footsteps follow the Elvis chronology conspicuously close: a twin brother Jessie stillborn at birth, and his haunting memory; an overprotective Mama whom Leroy loves better than anybody; a manipulating manager; truck driving for Crown Electric; Memphis recording sessions; television appearances, movies, mania, and a Memphis mansion named Hopeville. The setting captures the social and cultural climate of the times, its racial barriers and rock's formative stages with youthful rebellion, screaming teenagers, fearful parents, and a rattled establishment.

Other period pieces use racial and generational distinctions as their focal points. For example, Alice Walker's short story, "Nineteen Fifty-Five" (1981), is an Elvis parable about a white singer who records a black blues song, becomes famous, feels guilty, and dies young, alone and helpless.[3] In another Walker novel, *The Temple of My Familiar* (1990), Ola, an African dramatist, says that Elvis and Johnny Cash are Indians (which helps explain Elvis's clothing tastes–buckskin, fringe, silver). According to Ola, foreigners recognize the Native American qualities immediately; but Americans do not. Ola elaborates by using Elvis as a metaphor in a play he is writing: "That in him white Americans found a reason to express their longing and appreciation for the repressed Native American and black parts of themselves. Those non-European qualities they have within them are all around them, but which they've been trained from birth to deny" (pp. 188-189). Jan Marino's novel for young readers, *The Day Elvis Came to Town* (1991), is framed within the small-town segregated-South setting in 1964. Though the title's substitution of Elvis for the more familiar and festive coming-to-town connections such as Santa Claus and the circus, the atmosphere is hardly playful. Marino crowds in nearly every imaginable social and soap opera subplot into the story's convoluted story line. The central character is Wanda Sue Dohr, an adoring teenage Elfan, who must surrender her attic bedroom to a boarder, Mercedes Washington, a black jazz singer who claims to know Elvis. Elvis is cast in his familiar role as symbolic savior for Wanda Sue. Having the chance to see her idol becomes more than an obsession, but an inner source of strength that helps her cope with the many adolescent and family worries surrounding her, in much the same way Rejoice Jackson does in Kalpakian's *Graced Land.*

Childress' point of view in *Tender* is more faithfully biographical within this sociocultural mileau. He provides details that most other accounts of Elvis's life–both fictional and nonfictional–have left the reader wondering what Elvis's Mama, and others, whispered in his ear. "If you look at the biographies of Elvis, his childhood is covered in two or three pages," says Childress, a native Alabamian who admits to being a Beatles baby, not an Elvis idolater. "It's like he was born, went to school, had a mama and daddy, and then became a star."

Childress's minutiae of Leroy's childhood and adolescent struggles– the innocence and insecurity, parental and peer pressure, acceptance and rejection, crushes and locker-room bullies–provides a compelling portrait of Elvis's formative youth, the claustrophobic lifestyle of stardom, and the sadness of achievement.

*Tender* is not a divergent period portrayal between early and late Elvis, rather a pre-Elvis-lution exposition. Though not as tortured as stark-raving Byron in his quest to be King, duality is present as "opposites" tear at, and shape Leroy's identity. Leroy is the good boy and bad boy; poor boy and rich boy; Mama's boy and big boy; white boy moved by gospel and blues on WDIA, the Mother Station of Negroes; the pretty boy more interested in hairstyles, makeup, and clothes than sports. Leroy is Camille Paglia's (1990) Elvis and Andy Warhol's silkscreen Elvis: vulnerable, androgynous, disguised.

Leroy's physical transformation during his trips to the beauty salon and clothing store provide an insightful character study of the cosmetic creation and concerns of early Elvis. Rather than a conventional haircut at Mr. Beebe's Barber Shop, 16-year-old Leroy goes to Mary Jane's Beauty Salon to replace his dirty blond top with a wavy blue-black look to set off his bedroom eyes–a pompadour, full and tall, steel-finished sides and burns, tapered to a DA at the neck–"a duck's ass . . . a Cadillac fin"–like cool Tony Curtis in the magazine page he keeps folded up in his pants pocket.

From there, he finds cool cat clothes to complement his "truly successful hair" and go-to-hell snarl, visiting Irving Brothers, the pride of Beale Street, "where colored people buy their Saturday night outfits, and famous hillbilly singers their spangled shirts." Leroy is fascinated with the racks ranging from slick, slinky, and sequins to trousers in lightning, leather or fur.

Like Byron's jumpsuit, Leroy's hair takes on mythic Samson-like significance as a source of secretive power. It is a ritualistic obsession. When the color begins to fade, Leroy colors the sacred strands one shade at a time until the jet-black blue, and his power, is restored. He oils it down with Robinson's Brite-Shine because it gleams better than Brylcreem or Vitalis. He uses Max Factor Blue Mystery eye shadow because it goes with his hair and brings out his Valentino eyes more dramatically than Maybelline Mystic Brown.

It is that power and persona that both thrills and frightens Leroy, and those around him. Each day, afraid to wonder how, why, and what was happening to him so quickly, Leroy repeats a prayer: "Don't let it end. Don't let it end."

In Childress' narrative, the demise of early Elvis is not so much a physical death as it is a ruination in the form of loss of innocence, freedom, and dignity. Leroys' induction into the Army in *Tender's* conclusion implies that his military service is more than a mere interruption in the chronology, but a contributing factor, if not a point to be marked as the downfall.

Leroy/Elvis's compliance with his draft notice, and refusal of special preference as an entertainer (Muhammed Ali provides a similar case) was consistent with his character. A product of 1950s passivity, Leroy/Elvis did as he was told. He was a rebel by instinct rather than choice. That rebellion seldom conflicted with the "good boy" in him, and though reluctant, he would serve his country. "I have to, everybody is watching," says an image-conscious Leroy.

Dave Marsh (1992) characterizes Elvis's dilemma as an "employee mentality," something Elvis would never escape. Everyone was his boss. "His own needs and desires were, if not entirely subordinate, beside the point," writes Marsh.

The ruination process began long before Elvis received his draft notice. Control, conformity, and authority were well established in Elvis's life by a parade of bosses. The hierarchal community began with obedience to his mother and expanded to Colonel Parker's manipulative management; movie studio moguls with B-grade film scripts; television censors ordering waist-up only camera shots; variety show hosts insisting on a hound dog serenade in a tuxedo; preachers in pulpits persecuting the pelvic Presley; song publishers; record companies like RCA and their production line rock and roll; and adoring fans. The accumulation of submission took its toll.

Marsh provides a compassionate and lyrical view of Elvis's entrapment:

> Picture Elvis imprisoned, locked inside dark, somber, massive walls. On a beautifully moonlit evening, he brazenly slips over the wall, snapping free easily. And as he stops—for just an *instant*—to drink his new freedom, to savor how simple it had been, to gape in awe at the prospect stretched out before him, he hesitates a moment too long, and as he turns for one last glance at the walls that no longer encircle him, new fences are already going up around him. Elvis had more space now, but had lost the totality of freedom he had known for one moment. Now, he seemed to be free only from a distance; up close, he was obviously trapped. (p. 131)

Marsh's images conjure up the mythical Fisher King, the young prince wounded in his generative region by an arrow that can neither be driven through nor pulled out. He is trapped, unable to live or die, freely or fully.

The Army as a point of ruination or death for Elvis may in part be magnified because "John Lennon said so" or because God and country represented a higher level of authority. Lennon's draft death view translates into a loss of honor to Marsh. "The government's intention in drafting Elvis was to rob him of everything—not just fame, but also his wealth and whatever new dignity he had acquired," writes Marsh. The critic goes as far to suggest that Private Presley was a plot designed by the government, hoping that a tour of duty would "eliminate Elvis's unholy arrogance." And by the time Elvis was released in 1960, the adolescent girls would outgrow their hip-shaking obsession.

Childress's fiction further suggests through Leroy that the Army might not have been the only boss to plot against Elvis in 1958.

Drafted and distraught, Leroy imagines he sees the long shadow of his manager Sam Sanders (a colonel criss-cross to Kentucky Fried Chicken?) behind the draft disaster. It was part of his master plan; Sanders had been fretting about Leroy's image and exposure. "And what better cure for 'overexposure' than two years of Private 2nd class Leroy Kirby, U.S. Army," says the sly Sanders, sensing his secret scheme is a success.

The two years of Elvis's service were filled with dramatic change, both personally and professionally. On August 14, 1958, five months after he entered the Army, Elvis's mother, Gladys, died. Near the end of his tour, he met Priscilla Beaulieu in West Germany and eventually married her. When he returned in 1960, his fans remained but a lot had changed in music. Potential heirs to his throne–Chuck Berry, Little Richard, and Jerry Lee Lewis–missed their opportunities due in large part to various scandals involving the IRS, Mann Act, and 13-year-old cousins. Ritchie Valens and Buddy Holly were killed in a plane crash. While rock and roll remained controversial, many ballad singers began to gain popularity on the charts. The Colonel responded by repositioning and reshaping Elvis's image for his Army afterlife. When he returned to civilian, Elvis's "unholy arrogance" was gone; the "employee mentality" remained.

During this transition, the hair which had been so vital to the Elvis persona maintains its mythic significance. In *Tender*, Leroy's hair clearly defines a beginning and an end–a life and death cycle that originates in Leroy's imagination and desires; is brought to life in a Mary Jane's beauty Salon; is nurtured by Leroy; then tragically lies on the floor, a pile of clippings to be swept up and burned by an anonymous Army private to keep away from souvenir hunters following The Haircut.

Just before he is to leave for the Army, Leroy stands before a mirror. He thinks he hears the whispers of his dead mother and brother. "They say hair and fingernails keep growing after you die," writes Childress, presumably a thought in Leroy's head. And it is the hair that stands as the image which lingers as a turning point, if not death knell. Employee Elvis's defining ducktail that was shorn by one of his bosses–the establishment–never did grow back.

## THAT'S ALL RIGHT . . . THROW MAMA
## FROM THE MYSTERY TRAIN

What was it his mother told him? That he was just as good as
anybody? Or did she whisper, late at night when no one else
was there to hear, that her boy could never lose?

—Greil Marcus, *Mystery Train*

Do a song about your mother. It worked for Elvis.

—Noah's advice to Shirley
as she prepares for a talent show
*Second Noah* (ABC, 1996)

Elaine Dundy's *Elvis and Gladys* (1985) and clinical psychologist Peter Witmer's complex twinning case study *The Inner Elvis:
A Psychological Biography of Elvis Aaron Presley* (1996) might be
viewed as biographical bookends for the collection of nonfictional
works that explore the Presley lineage. Elvis's family members,
particularly mother Gladys and stillborn twin brother Jesse Garon,
have been favorite fictional focuses as well. Gerald Duff's *That's
All Right Mama: The Unauthorized Life of Elvis's Twin* (1995)
imagines what would have happened if Jesse Garon had actually
lived. Climbing on, or hanging from another imaginative branch of
the family tree is *Return to Sender: The Secret Son of Elvis Presley*
(1996), a mystery novel by Les and Sue Fox. The plot's preposterous Presley premise is that Elvis secretly arranged to have a son
through the world's first in vitro fertilization. An unsuspecting in-
fertile couple is selected for the procedure and in 1977 they give
birth to a boy who only Elvis and his lawyer know is actually the
King's son. Released with a publicity campaign calling for a national search for "the secret son of Elvis," the thickly plotted novel's
elements are familiar–an unsolved Memphis murder, tabloids, sex,
religion, intrigue, and Elvis as a deeply troubled superstar driven to
the extremes by the pressure of fame.

In *Elvis Presleydream Calls His Mother After The Ed Sullivan
Show* (1992), Samuel Charters is among those who wonders what
Gladys Presley whispered to her son. The sparse and graceful novel

by the former director of Folkways Records in the Smithsonian Institute magnifies an Elvis moment following a memorable, if not monumental Presley performance through Elvis's rotary-dialed routine of ringing mother Gladys long distance.

Elvis's infamous waist-up appearance results in a predominantly "below the waist" point of view, from the book's clever cover design featuring a series of panels with Elvis waist down dance poses; to a Robert Browning quote about the lustful Pan, god of wild nature from Greek mythology; to Charters' imaginative narrative.

The extended monologue fits like an operator's headset; the reader eavesdrops on every line as Elvis runs up the bill with rambling recollections and reflections on rock and roll, the road, relationships, who he is, his insecurities, dreams, and fears. And although he is talking to his Mama (Charters uses "Momma" in the text), he is preoccupied with sex, readily recalling the groupie who followed him across the country but could not make love to him because "he was an ocean to drown in." She needed "a calmer place to get her feet wet." And while he innocently views his performances as "having fun for the kids" and "using what God gives me to use," his shaking "makes them think about what's already in their minds . . . telling everybody's secrets."

The tone captures the hushed nuances, the urgency and introspection of a late-night phone call as it further explores the emotionally incestuous nature of the Presley mother-son relationship and the good boy/bad boy tug-of-war. Though Gladys does not have any lines in the novel, her caring and controlling character is easily decipherable in Elvis's monologue.

As the boys in the band party in and out of Elvis's hotel room with lingering female fans, a distracted Elvis assures Mama he is alone, while he gently coaxes a woman to be his evening companion. Whether out of consideration for his mother's feelings, fear, or both, Elvis's tone gives the impression he is holding back. He measures his words; he cannot say what is on his mind, or tell Mama about the girl in his room. He lies to her, saying "it's the boys." It's his blind spot, a shadow, the employee mentality. He wants to be one of the boys, talk the way they do, do the things they do, if only Mama will approve. As a result, there is an occasional trace of resentment in his words.

This struggle is apparent from the opening exchange. After Elvis boasts about "the best part" of him that could not be seen on television during his performance, it is clear by his response that it's not all right with Mama. Elvis's shameful reply–"Alright Momma, I won't do it again"–is an eerie echo of a Norman Bates fearstruck "forgive me" plea to his domineering mother. (Gary Larson plays with the *Psycho* premise in one of his *The Far Side* [1988] cartoons. The drawing depicts three silhouette figures in the second-floor window at the Bates Motel. It is Norman introducing a "new house-guest" to Mother. The caption beneath reads, "What really happened to Elvis.")

The tension between the two teeters. "Did you ever think, Momma, that maybe what I need when I'm on the road is a girl of my own to travel with?" he asks when she offers to join his tour. When she finally learns of Elvis's companion, Gladys orders her son to describe his "date" so she can give her approval or disapproval.

Yet the good boy pampers Mama, telling her about the Hollywood screen test he will get for her so she can be together with her son in a movie. The screenplay he has in mind is his own idea about a boy and his mother running away together and coming back to each other after a girl takes the boy away from Jesus and turns his thoughts to sin. One senses that the working title, "The Lord's Singing Spirits," could easily evolve into a darker "Throw Momma from The Mystery Train" revision similar to the mamacide scene in Jack Womack's *Elvissey* (1993). Sinister son Elvis "suffocates" his mother by placing the telephone under his pillow so she will not hear him "get acquainted" with the girl in his room.

Not only is fear apparent in Elvis's relationship with his mother, but with his own future. Uncertainty weighs as heavily as Gladys. While he is aware and awed by his own impact, and understands every father's fears that he is bad for their daughters, Elvis has a blind spot. He does not recognize just how "far in" he is. Yet, he senses something about to devour him, repeatedly referring to his career as "this crazy thing I'm doing."

As Elvis shares his dreams, several images emerge as foreshadowing and metaphors for the consuming lifestyle of fame. Lines such as "What's eating got to do with the way I sing?" and "If rock and roll loses out I can always do some other kind of singing" are prophetic. Elvis saying he "really feels like a yo-yo, just going up and down," provides a particularly striking image. "I get all wound up . . . then I let it all out . . . I got to come back up the string, a little bit at a time, and sometimes I can feel my arms getting tired when I pull myself up," says the world-weary 21-year-old.

He envisions himself evolving into a trinity comprised of a king, magician, and evangelist, outfitted in capes and spangles, playing with an orchestra rather than a combo. And since kings always carry something in their hands, Elvis would carry a flashlight. While the image is laughable, it becomes a metaphor for the blinding, lonely light of fame. Several times during the conversation he drifts into mentioning how he is on stage in darkness and can never see who is "out there." During one performance, he did not even realize the police had moved the screaming crowd leaving the first 20 rows empty. Or, that a gig at a Louisiana dive was actually a Ku Klux Klan gathering, a situation reminiscent of a scene from *The Blues Brothers* when Jake and Elwood pose as the Good Ol' Boys. Sensing the crowd's restlessness with "the nigger shit" he is singing, Elvis and the boys try "The Star Spangled Banner." However, repeated renditions of "Dixie" are the only tune to soothe the hostile crowd.

While his evangelical dream is a vision of worldly, "now we're going to pray" power, Elvis's King/magician fantasy is an image fitting for Disney animation. He envisions coming out on stage, opening his mouth to sing and a bird comes out instead of words. "I could have a whole string of birds like that, all different colors, and I could make the audience guess what song I was singing by the colors of the birds," Elvis explains.

While these royal and religious visions come true for Elvis, his only "real" dream is an impossible one. He tells Mama he wants to be simple again, "maybe get a truck and drive around doing electrician jobs and nobody would say anything about who I was or how I was wearing my hair."

This fantasy is a common referent. Among others, Michael Barson presents it in his rock and roll playful poster/postcard collection *Rip It Up* (1989). On the message side of a "Tommy Sands vs. Belafonte and Elvis" illustration, Barson's caption summarizes their three careers. "Elvis had a few hits, was drafted, then returned to driving a truck for Crown Electric in Memphis and was never heard from again."

While Elvis indeed "took his dreams more seriously than most ever dare, and he had the nerve to chase them down" (Marcus, 1982, p. 160) his simple dream is elusive, if not impossible. It is Elvis's blind spot. He does not see how his stardom has eclipsed his simplicity. Elvis is trapped. He cannot be one of the boys. Or get his old job back, or be normal instead of being famous. He does not understand that there is no return from splendor for him.

While rambling to his Mama, he relates an encounter with another groupie, who asked him if he "feels any different from me." Elvis does not know. "I can't tell you if I'm any different," he says. Elvis's real dream is analogous to his leap off the stage trying to escape the blinding light, only to find himself alone among empty seats surrounded by darkness.

## ELVIS'S EXCELLENT ADVENTURES

Elvis's experimental, accidental, or excellent adventures with scientists, government agents, or teenage time travelers on historical revision quests have not been limited to the comic and dramatic narratives of film and television. Such science fiction fantasies have also been popular in literature. These playful Presley presentations have proven to be particularly popular in subliterary forms such as comic books, whose heroes were inspirational to Elvis early in his career.

Gary Panter's depraved *Invasion of the Elvis Zombies* (1984) is considered by many to be the finest work of Elvis comic-strip cartoon art. In drive-in horror movie fashion, Panter's panels chronicle an outbreak of flesh-eating Elvis zombies that terrorize a small town before the local law can destroy them with a barrage of bullets and fire. The last page of the allegorical work features "a Mississippi Godzilla, rising out of a burning Safeway supermarket, immortal, undead" (Marcus, 1991, pp. 114-116).

Revolutionary Comics' Ayn Rand-inspired *Elvis Shrugged* (McCray and Garcia, 1993) is a three-part pop culture epic. The parody's diverse cast includes Spike Lee, Michael Jackson, Sinéad O'Conner, Frank Zappa, Bono, Stephen Sondheim, Philip Glass, and a cybernetic, Schwarzenegger-like Sinatra. Part two's cover features Elvis in King-

Kong fashion atop the New York City skyline, clutching Madonna in one palm and crushing an airplane in another (Figure 2.2). The closing image of the trilogy unites the King and Queen in holy Blue Hawaiian matrimony: "And in the end, there was only the sea and the sky and Madonna and Elvis Presley."

Two other Revolutionary series devoted to Elvis are more biographical in nature: *The Elvis Presley Experience* (Shapiro and McCray, 1992) a seven-part biographical journey through the soul of the King, from crib to casket to Christhood, as observed by Elvis himself in eternity; and *The Secret Files* (McCray, 1992), two issues concentrating on "The Fringe Years" late in his career.

A. J. Jacobs and Eric White spoof the comparisons in *The Two Kings* messianic and religious: *Jesus, Elvis* (1993). The litany of one-liners (Jesus was a carpenter/Elvis majored in woodshop; Jesus walked on water/Elvis surfed.) does not wear as well as the illustrations, such as the cover portrait of Elvis with a frosted-doughnut halo. In *An Alphabet of Sweets* (DeSaulniers, 1996), artist Nancy Gardner Thomas also provides a culinary illustration—the King of Kiwi in black pompadour and white spangled jumpsuit singing, "don't step on my brown suede fruit."

Elvisian theology and fantasy have been expanded into longer narrative forms. One such futuristic fragment can be found floating as a forbidden tune in Margaret Atwood's *The Handmaid's Tale* (1986). Unaware of the song's origins, a slave in the Republic of Gilead (formerly the U.S.A.) sings to herself the "I feel so lonely, baby" verses from "Heartbreak Hotel."

Jack Womack's *Elvissey* (1993) is a novel of Elvis past and future shock. In this science fiction fantasy with a road movie spirit and Capra-esque qualities, hindsight and foresight criss cross, creating a surreal atmosphere in which a second coming and a second Elvis oddly merge between parallel worlds.

*Elvissey*'s premise echoes Douglas Adams' *Mostly Harmless* (1992), in which Elvis is willingly abducted by aliens in a UFO, and swished off to another galaxy where he cruises in an ugly pink spaceship. In what is perhaps the most fitting "endless Elvis" metaphor, or prophecy, Elvis remains as the only surviving being from earth following its destruction.

FIGURE 2.2. Elvis comic book series.

Source: ©   Revolutionary Comics, 1994.

The cross-time godhead abduction in *Elvissey* is described by William Gibson, author of *Neuromancer* (1984), as "one of the flat out, weirdest Fisher King inversions yet perpetrated in American literature." A continuation of Womack's sequence of novels—*Ambient* (1987), *Terraplane* (1988), and *Heathern* (1990)—*Elvissey* is set in New York, and centered around the corporate monolith, Dryco, which dominates what remains of public and private life in the twenty-first century.

Longtime Dryco employees, Isabel Bonney, and her husband, John, are assigned to the Elvis Project. Their mission is to travel through a time portal into the unfamiliar "shadow world" of the twentieth century to retrieve the young, unknown Elvis from 1950s Memphis to serve as a manipulable idol for their Age's chiliastic masses and the Church of E.

Womack first introduced the Church of E in *Ambient*. Three novels later, it had split, divided, and resplit into playful perpetuity. For example, there were the Prearmyites, whose fundamental musicological doctrine held that the recording act is an impenetrable firewall between singer and hearer, and that rhythms of Elvis' songs were irreconcilably tainted once accompanied by drums. Among the "hundred dozen" other denominations were the Hosts of Memphis, the Shaken, Rattled, and Rolled, River Jordanaires, Gracelandians, Vegassenes, Gladyseans, the C of E Now or Never, the Redeemed Believers in Our Master's Voice, and the Church of the True Assumption of His Burning Love. The Jesseans pronounced the dead baby to be their messiah, and were thus excommunicated by all the other sects of the C of E.

According to the story's narrator, "Elvii congregants outnumbered and outshouted those who followed Godness." Her descriptions of the other-world Elvii worshipers bear a striking resemblance to real world Elfanatics:

> locusts, a harmless, even funful, swarming, proselyting, suffocating mass . . . praying for, talking about, listening to and posing as the King for days on end . . . Dialoguing with them became, inevitably, monologuing. Elvii understood no referents but E, and all else existed but to be measured against his greatness or found lacking. That *they* believed didn't satisfy;

to their eyes all should want him as desperately, and to the exclusion of everything else. (p. 42)

A typical worship service, or Elcon, was a massive gathering that might feature an organist banging out "Big Hunk O' Love" and other hymns; an altar with a revolving statue of E with microphone, tinted glasses, and jumpsuit with high collar and cape; a wall in the background with a colorgraph (other-world stained glass) of E shaking hands with Nixon; and a closing blessing and dismissal from the minister, "Like E, let us leave the building."

Each sect believed their King and their doctrine true. The only universal given was that The King would return. Dryco recognized this mass Elvulnerability, and thus, enacted its plan to deliver a savior from the other world's counterpart.

The Bonneys were not among their world's true believers. They rejected Elvis's divinity. The couple remained among the unconverted even after "drenching themselves in [Elvis] images" to prepare for their mission. They found in his essence a mystery barely theological. Only when Elvis sang did Isabel and John detect a "religious glow," as if he "dropped into the studio from another world." In those special moments, a dual nature emerged, making it difficult to determine if Elvis was "possessed" or "infiltrated by the Holy Spirit."

Isabel's account of their "back to the future" training contains several metaphorical images of Elvis. She relates that never in either print or image did the same Elvis twice appear, implying a continuous and multifaceted metamorphosis and snowflake similarities. A more common religious analogy emerges as she describes their unavoidable involvement with Elvis as a baptism.

Other cultural and commercial critiques slip into the dialogue. As the Bonneys prepare to depart through the tear in the atmosphere's curtain, known as The Window, in their 1953 Hudson Hornet, a friend instructs them, "Don't bring back souvenirs; nostalgia's worse than any drug."

Upon their arrival in the first week of May, 1954, the time travelers find an Elvis who is far from heavenly. The 18-year old is a sullen, gun-toting, white trash bigot who likes science fiction, and, like Kevin Kline's character in the film, *A Fish Called Wanda*, doesn't like to be called "stupid." A punk wearing mascara, Elvis is in his attempted-sneer stage. The best that the boy can manage of his eventual trademark defiant gesture is puckered lips, no doubt similar to the unrefined imitation snarls worn by novice impersonators.

This Elvis is also homicidal. Upon entering the Presley pre-Graceland residence at 462 Alabama Avenue, the Bonneys find Gladys lying down in what appears to be a red apron. It is blood. Elvis has just killed his mother because she did not want to listen to the Hank Williams record he bought her for Mother's Day. The gift initiated an disagreement over which musical style Elvis should pursue. Gladys wanted her son to sing country, but Elvis "hated that shit" and preferred the blues, but nobody wanted to hear that. They argued; she slapped Elvis and told him he was no good like his father, so Elvis shot her. "Nothin' I ever did was right, hear her tell it," says the remorseless son.

Here, Elvis is not as much Jesse Garon's evil twin as he is Norman Bates'. The mamacide is an extreme, but perversely refreshing twist of the usual Elvis Gladoration and gun fascination. However, the "Throw Momma from the Mystery Train" scenario is not that uniquely bizarre. The mother-son dynamics in *Elvissey* are only a shade darker than those present in *Elvis Calls His Mother*. The difference lies at some point (blank) between a long distance phone call and a bullet. The authors have given birth to twin sons. Charters' 1956 version is ticking just like Womack's 1954 tightly wound replica. Both boys resent Mama's nagging. Elvis's terse tone over the phone with his mother suggests a similarly strained relationship as that in *Elvissey*. There is a sense that boiling just beneath the sideburned surface, the possibility exists for perilous consequences. Perhaps it is only the long distance separation that saves the one mother from the tragic fate of the other. Of the twin Elvises, one son let his finger do the walking, while the other let his trigger finger do the talking.

Southern voice Barry Hannah also probes the deeper, darker recesses of the Elvis-Gladys connection in "Mother Mouth," a very short essay from his collection *Bats Out of Hell* (1993). Affectionately referred to in segments of the writer's community as "the Jerry Lee Lewis of literature," Hannah focuses on Gladys' burning fixation for her son. She is addressing Vernon in what is perhaps an imagined monologue in her head. Gladys' fevered delusion is a simultaneously scornful and sensual expression. The image is that of a wife telling her husband that she is leaving him for another man—their son—while masturbating to her own words.

"Today, Vernon, I noticed Elvis was getting hairy," begins Gladys. "Finding that, my tongue got hot all the way down to my heart to which it was attached. There was no keeping off the temperature or the rump rump noise of my want in my person."

Gladys' malevolence toward her husband matches the obsessive attraction to her son. "The Philco is all we could afford after you wrote the extra zero on that check and left us for three years in jail," she mercilessly reminds Vernon. The bitterness lingers from his transgression. To her, Vernon is "a disgrace, with no say in the family." There is the sense that she would like to continue to punish him by making love to Elvis in front of him. Her "oneness" is clearly with her son, and not her husband.

She projects reciprocating emotions on her son, claiming that every one of his songs "will be about me," and that nobody will ever see love in Elvis' eye for any woman "because it will only be me, and our music together."

Gladys also prayerfully ponders her own destiny beyond death, and considers how her survivors will respond. She predicts Vernon "jail trash, will be back venaling around like a rodent with an evangelist hairdo," and warns that "the money will always be bad." Gladys believes she will spend eternity together with her son. Her disparate vision of Elvis is synergized with surreal, spiritual and sexual imagery. She prophetically envisions her boy,

> coiled and wrapped and weird inside and out, leaping in flight wild with Tupelo space clothes on him, doing movements that are trying to climb the ladder to heaven where his mama is . . . and he is making those thrown-out grabbing postures and sweating like with my fluid all over him, becoming a mass, just a groping mass, on the rope—up, up, me waiting for him. (p. 154)

The meditation climaxes with her saying, "Because there ain't anything like Mama Nooky."

Elvis's murder of his mother in *Elvissey* is no lapse into temporary insanity. This Presley is paranoid and panicked. His excellent adventure veers off the map into a cross-world road trip that travels similar psychoscenic routes as the films *Wild at Heart*, *Kalifornia*, and *Natural-Born Killers*. (Interestingly, in the Oliver Stone celebrity serials killer saga, an infatuated fan compares the hedonistic honeymooners, Mickey and Mallory Knox, to "all the great figures from the states . . . Elvis, Jack Kerouac, (James) Dean." Elvis first turns the tables on his abductors. After assaulting John, Elvis binds and gags him and stuffs him in the back seat. He makes physical advances to Isabel. And after they cross the border into Mississippi, Elvis kills two more people at a restaurant over $3.98 worth of chicken, peach pies, and colas. Elvis is a unique fugitive; he is wanted for multiple murders in his own world, and wanted as savior in another.

Their arrival in the alternate cosmos shifts the perspective to a biographical bird's-eye point of view that is at once *Back to the Future* and Capra's *It's a Wonderful Life*. Like numerous other Elvis narratives which use this hovering hindsight, the hero unknowingly catches a glimpse of his personal chronology, from the prediscovery state to being Elvis then to late-Elvis and beyond.

*Elvissey*'s tangled time-line is as playful as it is inventive. The biographical tinkering and crystal ball perspective are often amusing when compared to actual accounts of Elvis's life. When Elvis sees his cosmic counterpart for the first time, appearing "like a big ol' hog ready for market," he is confounded.

"As he is, so you'll be," says a Dryco official in a sanctifying tone to Elvis.

"I don't look like that," replies a puzzled Elvis.

"You will," answers the authority.

Elvis is just as appalled at the trademark King costume. He refuses to wear a "sissy suit." "I like clothes as much as the next guy, but not that shit. This's 'bout as sorry as it comes." Isabel agrees. "Not even Elvis had ever looked so ridiculous. They clowned you."

Dryco's strategies for "The Anointed" have other-world roots as they reflect the familiar Colonel Parker control–"let people see him as *we* want"–and maximum marketing–"full shopability while retaining Elvisceral heritage." Among the corporate designs for personifying and programming their captive is a universal image of Elvis which contains all races within it.

Yet the young Elvis is just as unhappy in the other world as he eventually was in his own. "Just stand there and let them love you," a Dryco instructs. But Elvis resists the savior status, and is reluctant to be a messiah figure even in metaphor.

The climactic scene when all the C of E sects gather for the second coming, or Elvissey, is filled with Vegas-style fanfare and Elvis impersonator imagery. The congregation of Interpreters, as they are called, stand chatting, comparing leg and hip wiggles, studying karate gestures, running ringed fingers over each other's scarves, headshaking to demonstrate proper hair-flopping methods, radaring the room to see who might emerge as the most real. The assembly is the same multinecklaced crowd in *Honeymoon in Vegas*, *Stark Raving Elvis*, and Buffet's short story "Are You Ready for Freddy?"

In Douglas Adams' *Mostly Harmless*, the important distinction between "A King" and "The King" is deep-space doctrine. "Everyone in the universe knows who *the* King is." Adam's fictional galaxy may have been more advanced than Womack's alternate universe. Ironically, the real Elvis–the 18-year-old American who would become The King–is mocked and rejected as an imposter when presented to the Elvissey in an obvious parallel to the crucifixion of Christ by the Romans.

Though familiar, Womack's grand themes surrounding Elvis– loss of grace, humanity's longing for charismatic figures, the possibility of redemption–are carefully orchestrated. They develop beyond their beginnings in *Ambient* where old-man Dryden of the Dryco founding family recounts when he once met E, and concludes, "had Jesus been real, and if he'd been in the same situation as E, he'd have done it all the same way." The narrator carries his thought one step farther. "And vice versa, I supposed, picturing E in that jumpsuit, crucified."

That particular image, and an accompanying sense of ascension and descension, become an all-encompassing theme that continues throughout the *Elvissey* journey. The trade paperback cover depicts the different world duality with twin Elvis images, alternating a 29-cent Elvis USA postage stamp (not the actual one) with one issued by Dryco, a two-dollar seal with a haloed, jumpsuited Elvis in crucifixion pose. (The cover images were painted by Minnesota illustrator John Berkey, who also designed the "Vegas Elvis" candidate for the 1992 Elvis stamp collection. Figure 2.3). The novel's very first line about "craving ascension and dreaming of descension" reads like a caption for the cover illustration, only it confuses rather than clarifies. While the words and images combine as a thesis statement that foreshadows the sequence of events that lies ahead in the pages, they also create an ambiguous metaphor in motion. The symbolic dichotomies and locations may be clear–two lives, perhaps two gods, situated or traveling between two places, two worlds, two separate spheres, maybe heaven and hell, or life and the afterlife–but the direction and final destination are uncertain. Is Elvis taking off or landing? "Leaving the building" or arriving? Is Elvis looking downward to where he is coming from or where he is going to? Is he descending from above to a realm below, or ascending the stairway to join his Mama in eternity? Either direction, ascension and descension represent metaphorical marks on the Elvis time line that reflect the simultaneous mythmaking and mythbreaking processes which have characterized his life and afterlife.

## *ELVERSES*

Literary presentations of Elvis have not been limited to narratives and novels. *Mystery Train* (1990) is David Wojahn's "sequence" of 35 rock-and-roll-related poems. The poet straddles the fictional fence with works which are inspired by various histories, biographies, decades of music, and "sometimes based on wholly invented incidents." The chronological collection, both compelling and quirky, juxtaposes peculiar perceptions with a wide cross section of familiar faces and events from the rock era–assassinations and funerals, tatoos and tours, tribesmen and Trashmen, lounges and living rooms, the White House and Wax Museum, trains–both "C" and Mystery, and Deltas, the Mississippi and Mekong.

Six of Wojahn's poems are "Elverses," which, when strung together, provide a demystifying biographical narrative. "W.C.W. Watching Presley's Second Appearance on *The Ed Sullivan Show*, Mercy Hospital, Newark, 1956," is a cantankerous tale of a hospital

FIGURE 2.3. Is Elvis leaving or arriving?

Source: Courtesy John Berkey.

patient. The use of "Presley" in the title, rather than the more common first-name basis, foreshadows the contemptuous lines to follow. The surly speaker—perhaps poet William Carlos Williams or a Wojahn family member?—is a "a goddam hostage" to the institution's smells. He is midthought, stalled between a window and TV screen. Neither view is pleasing and the tone is terminal, cranky, and elderly. He scoffs at the kids outside getting juiced on the cheapest wine beside a blazing junk heap, and the "pomped-up kid" who preens on the TV screen "tells us 'Don't Be Cruel.'" "Kid, forget it. You don't know a thing about cruelty, yet," ends the poem.

"The Assassination of Robert Goulet as Performed by Elvis Presley: Memphis, 1968" and "Nixon Names Elvis Honorary Federal Narcotics Agent at Oval Office Ceremony, 1973" provide rather pathetic Presley partner-in-crime portraits—the King, ARVN Commander, and Commander in Chief—with a palette of power, politics, and Presley obsessions. Wojahn's prosaic account of the infamous shootout is a "Memphis Meets Saigon" version juxtaposing an Elvent with a world event. Prefacing the poem is the Elvis quote—"That jerk's got no heart"—a comment, which along with Elvis's .38 caliber, was aimed at Goulet singing on television. After the Boys at the Mansion change the blown fuses, *The Carol Burnett Show* is replaced by satellite footage of the Tet Offensive. The channel change is striking, going from an exploded TV tube in the King's Graceland three-TV-den to bodies strewn along Ky's palace fences in Saigon.

Though the twin television executions—Goulet's and a boy's head blown apart—represent vicarious violence through televisual transmissions, one act contains much more meaning. The horrifying reality of Vietnam shocks Elvis's excess into perspective. His macho act of insecurity and firearm fascination suddenly dissipate into a self-indulgent triviality. Both the King and the ARVN colonel are cowards. Their postexecution poses—Elvis toying with his pearl-handled beauty and the soldier smoking a cigarette before their fallen victims lingers, along with the quote that precedes the poem, "That jerk's got no heart."

Like the Goulet assassination, Elvis's meeting with Richard Nixon became a mythical Elvent. In December 1970, Elvis arrived unannounced at the White House seeking permission to see the

President. Earlier, Elvis had written a note to Nixon from his Washington, DC hotel, introducing himself, expressing his love and concern for the country, and volunteering his services as a Federal Agent at large to assist, in of all things, the antidrug campaign.

The note is a curious correspondence. It is barely legible, with a rough-draft resemblance to a cover letter for a job application. Elvis considers himself to be uniquely "qualified" for such a position. He writes with a psychotic citizen sensibility:

> I have done an in-depth study on drug abuse and Communist brain washing techniques . . . I am right in the middle of the whole thing. The Drug Culture. The Hippie Elements. The SDS. Black Panthers etc. do not consider me their enemy or as they call it The Establishment. I call it America and I love it. I will be here for as long as it takes to get the credentials of a Federal Agent. (Worth and Tamerius, p. 141)

As with any Elvent, there are various versions. Some suggest Elvis's intentions were not so much as a Tennessee volunteer or patriot, but as an avid collector seeking to obtain a narcotics badge and credentials to add to his impressive personal collection. When Deputy U.S. Narcotics Director John Finlander refused the King's request, Elvis went straight to the top.

By any account, the visit is a testimony to Elvis's power, popularity, and peculiarity. Consider that Elvis shows up at the White House gates, virtually unannounced, accompanied by two members of the Memphis mafia, and he is carrying a weapon—a commemorative World War II Colt .45 pistol encased in a wooden box. Once inside, Elvis not only gets the badge and credentials, but Presidential souvenirs and memorabilia for himself.

Wojahn's shift of the date of "Mr. Presley goes to Washington" from 1970 to 1973 provides a political subtext. The historical revision places the Elvisitation within a series of notable Nixonian events from 1973, among them the Watergate hearings, the removal of U.S. troops from Cambodia (an invasion Nixon initiated in 1970), and his disclosure that he paid less than $1,000 in taxes in 1970 and 1971.

The poem again probes the darker corners and ironies beneath the surface of the mythical meeting, offering an alternative caption to the Oval Office photograph of the two icons shaking hands that has been one of the most popular and permanent Presley images disseminated throughout American Culture. The late model Elvis here is hardly conscious, politically or otherwise, and he is leering. "The King is thinking Tricia's got nice tits," is the poem's ominous opening. Elvis, "his mind a blur of dexies and reds," drifts into reminisces about the President's daughter's wedding—Grace Slick spiking the punch, the Erlichman's dancing the Funky Chicken, the Turtles' musical schlock. His handshake with Nixon is a whisper, a devil's deal of denial—"I am not a prescription junkie" and "I am not a crook" gripped together.

The phrase—"but scored with an M.D.'s prescription"—further highlights the widespread denial of Elvis's condition. While Wojahn chooses illegal drug jargon such as "score," faithful followers will forever cling to the terms "legal" and "prescription" and choose "heart attack" rather than "drug overdose." The familiar "company line" rationalization even surfaces in Nixon's recollection of meeting with Elvis. The former President claimed Elvis's "flash was covering up the junk," but Elvis never used illegal drugs, only those prescribed by his physician.

When Elvis politely explains the TCB hieroglyphic on his ring, the motto seems strangely appropriate for Nixon. It is as if Elvis is a newly appointed cabinet member offering the President valuable advice, whether about Watergate or taxes. "Taking Care of Business with a Flash" echoes "The jerk's got no heart," as both quotes punctuate the partner in crime and power portraits.

Wojahn moves from the political to spiritual realm in "Elvis Moves a Small Cloud: The Desert Near Las Vegas, 1976." Among Elvis's excesses was an interest in religion and mysticism. Encouraged by his hairdresser, Larry Geller, to read books on the occult, esoteric healing, and Eastern religions, Elvis reportedly became so immersed in the subjects that he believed himself to be a "chosen one" who possessed special spiritual powers such as healing the sick and communing with nature.

Wojahn provides an account of "His Highness reading again" and demonstrating his powers to his bodyguards and hangers-on. Elvis orders his limo to stop, gets out, and "aims a finger at Nevada's only cloud." "Lo! Behold! Now watch that fucker *move!*"

As with all of Wojahn's Presley poems, the view is distressing;

Elvis in delusional decline one year before his death. Wojahn fore-shadows the King's Christ complex in the Nixon poem: "Grace Slick named her baby *God*, a moniker, He (Elvis) thinks, almost as good as *Elvis Aaron*." Wojahn foreshadows the King's Christ con-fusion in the Nixon poem. In his critical comparison of Wojahn's account of the desert incident with Ian McEwan's novel, *The Inno-cent* (1990), in which "an unknown singer creates an irreversible event," Greil Marcus accurately characterizes Elvis as "pathetic–didn't he know how many *lives* he'd moved" (1991, p. 190).

Elvis probably had no clue, if a passage from the biography, *If I Can Dream* (Geller and Spector, 1989), is accurate. Elvis begins a conversation with guru Geller:

> Think back when I had that experience in the desert. Didn't only see Jesus' picture in the clouds–Jesus literally exploded in me. Larry, it was me. I was Christ . . . I thought I might be him. I really thought I was singled out, not only to be Elvis, but ah . . . (p. 88)

Geller calmly replies, "Elvis, are you trying to say you thought you were Jesus Christ?" Elvis, with visible relief, grinned.

Wojahn's two remaining Presley poems are set at Graceland during the 1980s, and provide divergent visitor's views of the Mem-phis mansion and myth. "At Graceland with a Six-Year-Old, 1985" echoes the bored-child view of Paul Simon's "Graceland." Young Josh, like most kids his age, would probably prefer Disney's King-dom to Elvis's. The kitsch and Cadillacs, gold records and grave-site, are meaningless. The only worthwhile attractions are Elvis's private jet with Lisa Marie's name enlarged on the side, and the living room wall of mirrors where the boy makes faces.

"Pharaoh's Palace (Memphis 1988)," the thirty-fifth and final poem of the *Mystery Train* sequence, is a lengthy observation of Graceland's extravagant interiors and exteriors, as well as the Labor Day weekend crowd.

The atmosphere is carnivalesque white trash, from the mass min-gling of mourners gathered at gravesite to a tour guide wearing an incongruous eye patch. Some of the faces are the familiar "poor-boys and pilgrims waiting to be received," only here many are cast into cameos reminiscent of darkly directed scenes from David Lynch films.

Clearly, the tour has not converted the narrator into a faithful follower. Wojahn's demystifying view of the previous five Presley poems comes full circle. He challenges the doctrine—"Above us the shuttered room where the overdose took place, although the guards claim heart attack."

Just as W.C.W. scoffed at early Elvis from his hospital bed, there is doubt and disillusion in the visitor's view. "The Pharaoh, he claimed, of rock and roll." Elvis's lifestyle and excesses trigger resentful reflections, of "how his crooked Greek physician shot him up," and how he "dispatched his private jet from Memphis to Las Vegas . . . to ferry back peanut butter and jelly sandwiches from some skid row deli he remembered . . . But he was a *nice boy*, always . . ."

The final verses depict a stark shift in setting to a stop off the highway home from Graceland at a kudzu-covered barn and collapsed house. A path leads to a family plot where a "hornet's nest patching a single marker proclaiming no name, only HERE US O LORD IN R SORROW."

The images of excess and exaltation beside the simple and solitary are striking in their desperateness. Yet, beneath the surface of their contrast lie similarities that connect both locales. The masses, memorabilia, mirrors, movies, tacky decor, and TV sets in infinite recession smother the mansion in excess and adulation, just as the clinging kudzu suffocates the fallen rural shack. Both places are visions of decay.

And the unrefined inscription on the primitive marker surrounded only by insects is analogous to the millions who pass by the dazzling eternal flame at the Presley family plot and read a similarly clumsy, but sincere epitaph, "the wretched poem Daddy Vernon wrote," cited by Wojahn in both Graceland visits.

The phrase, "Proclaiming no name" is curious in its suggestion of anonymity. That loss of identity appears in all six Elvis-related poems, as Wojahn for the most part avoids referring to Elvis by his name. Instead, the substitutions—"this kid, E.P., King, His Highness, Pharaoh, the shut-in, and he"—convey an impersonal, irreverent tone.

The rustic passage provides fitting closure, not only for the "Pharaoh's Palace" tour, but the other Elverses, the entire *Mystery Train* sequence, and the various fictional narratives which have retold the Elvistory. The "two lane headed home" signifies a return to roots via roads outside Memphis—Highway 78 to Tupelo, or Highway 61 to the Mississippi Delta—reminders of the historical, mythical journey to the Promised Land, rock and roll dreams, and dead ends.

## NOTES

1. The darkness and fun of this dream is reminiscent of the "Elvis Echoes" Greil Marcus sprinkles throughout the "Presliad" in his *Mystery Train: Images of America in Rock and Roll Music* (1982).

2. This view echoes, among others, Nicholas Cage's observations and interactions with Elvis Impersonators during the filming of *Honeymoon in Vegas* (see film chapter). In a similar situation, Dennis Quaid reportedly got "too far into his role" as Jerry Lee Lewis during the filming of the Killer's bio, *Great Balls of Fire*, and at times believed he was Lewis. In an unusual life-imitating-literature twist, William McRanor (Henderson) followed his fictional character's lead and eventually became an official Elvis impersonator. He discussed his participant observation, training, and transformation from English teacher and writer into Elvis during a panel presentation at the Popular Culture/American Culture Association in the South conference in October 1996 in Savannah, Georgia. McCranor's experience will be documented in a forthcoming book.

3. In *Dead Elvis* (1991:36-37), Greil Marcus argues that Walker "bluntly dismisses" Elvis in her story, which is based on Elvis, Willie Mae Thornton, and "Hound Dog," a song Thornton was the first to record even though she did not write it.

# Chapter 3

# Hopeless Necromantics:
# It's a Wonderful Afterlife

Better to chase after a dead man than a live one . . .

—Bev, *Graceland*

If Elvis visits you and nobody else sees him . . . was he really
there?

—Trudy, *Christmas with Elvis*

Many of the Elvis themes and narratives on printed pages come
to life in off-beat and off-Broadway productions on local, regional,
and national theater stages. Cloak-and-dagger mysteries with espio-
nage and secret agents have been transformed into jumpsuit-and-
microphone "who dunnits?" involving Elvis impersonators on the
dinner theater in the round circuit. At fringe performance outlets,
productions such as *A Whole Lotta*, a free-form Elfest at Ka Boom!
Comedy Club in Chicago, is representative of the more experimental, conceptual, and even celebratory approaches that combine performance, music, art, tribute, food, and drink (Figure 3.1).

And, not to be upstaged by the Buddy Holly touring musical tribute
revue, Elvis countered with multimedia musical extravaganzas such as
*Elvis: A Rockin' Remembrance*, with three giant screens, elaborate sets
and costumes, a large cast of singers and dancers, and 49 hit songs;
and *Elvis: A Musical Celebration*, with three Elvises of varying ages
which toured 25 cities across the country during the late 1980s.

On a less spectacular scale, *Him*, (1995) a flaky spoof on pop
religion through Elvis, played at New York's Public Theater in

FIGURE 3.1. Advertisement for Elvis celebration at Ka Boom! Comedy Club in Chicago.

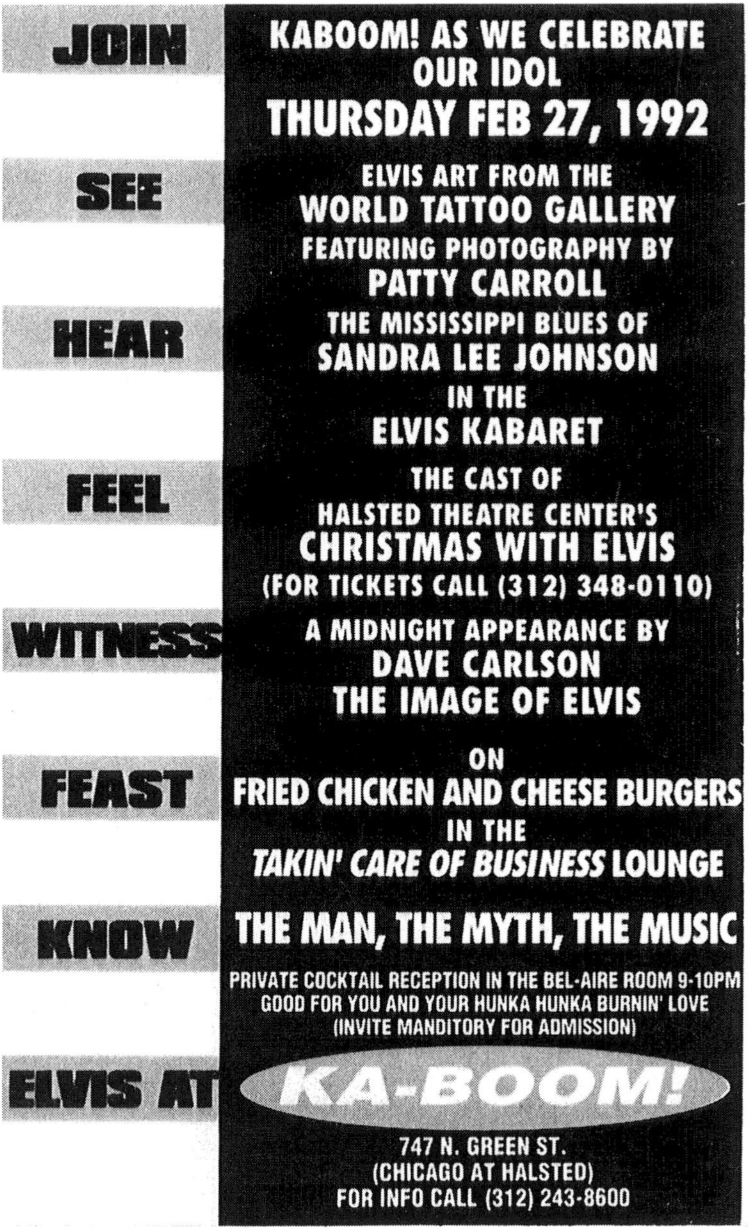

1995. Actor Christopher Walken wrote and starred in the play, which follows Elvis as he loafs around in Limbo, a halfway house of the Hereafter haunted by Elvis look-alikes, including his still-born brother. Elvis takes his final bow in beefy drag in a truckstop waitress uniform.

Whether gyrations, jailhouse jive, or jumpsuit gestures, elements of dance have always been part of Elvis's routines. Although ballet might appear to be a gracefully incompatible form of Presley performance, Elvis's blue suedes are transformed into toe shoes in *Blue Suede Shoes*, an 80-minute ballet set to Elvis music which premiered at the Cleveland State Theater in May 1995.

And *Lend Me a Tenor*, Ken Ludwig's breakneck Broadway farce about a young Midwesterner's attempt to impersonate a famous Italian opera singer, is a premise easily adapted into, or derivative of, a "Love Me Tender" scenario involving Elvis Impersonators.

Two plays, in particular, stand out in their portrayals of Elvis and our posthumous responses to him. In *Graceland* and *Christmas with Elvis* (1989), award-winning playwrights Ellen Byron and Terry Spencer provide women's perspectives on Elvis with voices that complement Laura Kalpakian's *Graced Land* novel. These views are particularly beneficial when considering how throughout his career, Elvis was surrounded, pursued, and adored by women of all ages. From screaming teenagers to worshiping blue-haired bouffants, Elvis was the powerful embodiment of song, sexuality, and spirituality.

The central characters of these plays—Bev, Rootie, Trudy—join Kalpakian's Rejoice and Emily scattered at various points along the relationship spectrum. The range includes divorced and not coping; separated but hoping to reconcile; unhappily married but coping; trying to save a marriage from ending in divorce; and engaged with doubts. Burning love does not exist in this struggling sisterhood, as each experiences some degree of marital and male misery. Though not an exclusive Southern sensibility, this menagerie of characters and connections combine to create a composite one might expect in a Beth Henley play, a contemporary country song, a *Designing Women* or *Grace Under Fire* sitcom episode, or television talk show panel. Emerging as a common thread in these tender tales is Elvis, who is cast in roles ranging from companion, counselor, and comforter to matchmaker, savior and Santa, ghost and god, to "Mr. Right" and "Mr. Typical."

## BRIGADOON:
### *WAITING AT THE PEARLY GATES*

Ellen Byron's *Graceland* involves a squatter's rights, sacred struggle between devoted female fans determined to be the very first visitor to set foot in the doors of Elvis's hallowed Memphis mansion. The tone and characterization, at times, echo Richard Thompson's "From Galway to Graceland," the song about a woman who travels across the sea to Memphis because she believes she is married to Elvis. Bev Davis, 42, is a generous, overweight, polyester Dolly Parton-type from Wilmington, Delaware, and Rootie Mallard is a skinny, simple, 22-year-old from Lafayette, Louisiana. The generational, physical, and regional distinctions between the two women intersect at the gates of Graceland, where the two jockey for the first-in-line honor, three days before its official opening on June 7, 1982.

Both are worthy of christening the Presley Palace. Bev has paid her Elfan dues, "loving him with the purest and truest love possible since I was fifteen." As if interviewing for a job, she explains her qualifications, often using profanity for emphasis. Like Rejoice, she has dedicated her life to preserving the memory of the King. Instead of the porch shrine of Rejoice Jackson, Bev has turned her basement into a memorial. She threw out her kid's pool table in order to make room for her collection of records, pictures, a sweat-stained scarf ('72 Vegas edition), and every liquor bottle made into an Elvis statue. Her Elvita also includes an experience list of "firsts"–first to enter the Meditation Gardens, museum, and gravesite, as well as touch the statue.

Although Bev's needlepoint depicting Elvis on a map of the world might suggest otherwise, her fanatic worship has its limits. Like Rejoice, Bev can distinguish between deities. When an awe-struck Rootie is moved to kneel before the mansion, Bev instructs, "You should only kneel for God, Honey."

Rootie represents what Bev must have been like 20 years earlier–naive and enthusiastic. "I have to get to him, she bubbles. "Get to him? Are you crazy? He's dead," replies Bev. Rootie rationalizes,

"I know that. But I'm gonna make him come back. If you love somebody enough, you can."

As "proof," Rootie cites the movie *Brigadoon*, in which "Gene Kelly made a whole village come back just because he loved the girl so much." Though naive, Rootie's comments and analogy certainly capture the postmortem fervor of Elfanatics, particularly those diehards who embrace a similar correlation between love and resurrection.

While Bev may be caring, her motherly instincts toward Rootie also have their generational limits. "Why don't you just chase after one of those teenage idol types and leave this to the people who really care? What could you possibly know?" questions Bev.

Rootie surprises Bev with what she knows as the two engage in a rapid-fire round of Trivial Pursuit, the Elvis Edition. As Rootie rattles off names, dates, places, and songs, and facts as if a crazed contestant on *Jeopardy!* locked in the Elvis column during the lightning round. Though Bev's skepticism diminishes somewhat, Rootie's performance is not enough to convince her that a change of the guard at the gates is in order. Bev refuses to surrender her first-in-line position to the young fan.

The gap between the two women narrows further when they learn they have other things in common besides Elvis, most notably, marriages to uncaring husbands. It is this common shaky ground of struggling marriages, more than the distinction of being the first to enter the mansion, that have fatefully brought Bev and Rootie to Memphis. They are among Paul Simon's "poorboys and pilgrims with reason to believe they shall be received at Graceland."

According to Bev, Elvis saved her marriage. Again, parallels to Rejoice Jackson emerge. Just as Rejoice took "Elvis pills" to help cope with her problems, Bev relies on "Elvis daydreams." And when her truck-driving husband is gone for most of the month, Bev listens to Elvis records, dusts her statues, and plans the memorial room. Unbeknown to her husband, Ty, Bev enjoys a secret marriage to Elvis. "That's why I had to come here today," explains Bev. "I had to show my love and gratitude to the most important man in my life–Elvis."

Rootie hopes to find similar salvation. While Bev was falling in love with Elvis when she was 15, Rootie married her brother's best friend, Weebo. Like Bev's husband, Ty, Weebo is usually away. When he is not driving his Frito-Lay delivery truck, he prefers drinking and playing with the boys to being with Rootie. He is a control-ling, demeaning chauvinist who batters Rootie's self-esteem. When Rootie learns that Bev made the Elvis needlepoint herself, Rootie responds, "I can't believe it. Weebo says that the only things a woman should make are dinner, the beds, and out."

Rootie's situation is a dead end, figuratively and literally. Her Memphis mansion mecca is a mission with deep personal and spiri-tual significance. She seeks strength and salvation from the two good men in her life, who unfortunately are in the afterlife–Elvis and her brother Beau, who was killed in Vietnam. Rootie explains,

> Elvis was the most important person in Beau's life . . . So since Beau's birthday is also the very first day Elvis's house is open, I figured that if I were the first person inside, everything would all come together, and I'd get a sign from the Heavens, and Weebo would see me on TV and be real sorry about what he done, and everything would be all taken care of.

Despite Bev's attempt to diminish Rootie's expectations of a miracle from the two dead men, the young woman clings to her *Brigadoon* belief that "some things are more powerful than death even."

Bev's determination to remain first in line does not suffocate her goodness. All along, she listens carefully; Rootie's situation strikes a familiar chord. Bev knows from experience that "Elvis works in mysterious ways." And just as he saved her marriage, this could be Rootie's opportunity for relationship redemption. Realizing this, the elderly Elfan compassionately relinquishes her spot to Rootie. "Tell Beau and Elvis I send all my love," says Bev.

The touching moment produces a symbolic generational "pass-ing of the Presley torch." Just moments earlier Bev sternly re-minded Rootie that both Beau and Elvis were dead. Bev's sudden "approval" of Rootie's blind faith suggests her recognition that *what* Rootie believes may not be as important as the *act* of believing itself, and that with Elvis, all things are possible.

Bev appears as a guardian angel figure, who, though stubborn throughout her assignment, has completed her preordained task and earns her wings. Pouring a celebratory shot into a Dixie cup, she sings an Elvis song, folds up her chair, pauses for a farewell to the mansion, and slowly exits. The soft serenade provides fitting closure as a comforting hymn.

*Graceland's* closing is reminiscent of final scenes of other dramatic presentations involving Elvis. For example, in an episode of *Homicide: Life on the Street* (NBC), Detective Bolander (Ned Beatty) mutters "Love Me Tender" to himself while drowning his sorrows at a bar over the end of his 23-year marriage. More melodramatic than musical, Rita Mae Brown's made-for-TV-movie adaptation of Kalpakian's *Graced Land*, *The Woman Who Loved Elvis* (1993), shows Rejoice (Roseanne Arnold) at her husband's hospital bedside following his life-threatening motorcycle accident. Clutching his hand, she appears to squeeze life into him. As his hand responds to her touch with the first signs of recovery, the camera slowly zooms in on Rejoice's Elvis ring, an obvious life force inference.

Although these elements of hope and despair, religiosity, and possibility are overused melodramatic and musical conventions, they nonetheless remain effective within narratives as they blend the unique and universal, the simple and powerful, and the human condition as it relates to Elvis.

## *NOËL, NOELVIS: BLUE CHRISTMAS*

Just as *Brigadoon* subtly frames much of Byron's *Graceland*, another movie provides a similar backdrop for Terry Spencer's campy *Christmas with Elvis*.[1] In the play's opening scene, thirty-something Trudy Davis switches on the television set in her dismal apartment on Chicago's North Side on Christmas Eve. Predictably, the holiday favorite, *It's a Wonderful Life*, appears on the screen.

The Capra classic provides an appropriate parallel to Trudy's tribulations. Like Jimmy Stewart's character George Bailey, Trudy must reach a crisis and discover things about herself before becoming empowered to change the course of her life.

Much like the women in *Graced Land* and *Graceland*, Trudy's dilemma involves male misery, fear, and low self-esteem. Her night before Christmas, which also happens to be her wedding anniversary, begins with a phone call from her ex-husband, Harlan, who appears to belong to the same insensitive fraternity as Ty and

Weebo. The strikingly similar self-esteem-battering tendencies are apparent as Trudy hovers near her answering machine, eavesdropping on Harlan's message that he is remarrying "someone with problems similar to yours." "Go out," he advises. "You're never going to meet Mr. Right sitting in your apartment, Trudy."

Seeking solace, Trudy puts on a record–Elvis's "Are You Lonesome Tonight?"–an obvious choice, and sits on the couch with her bottle of Evian water. As she painfully converses with the lyrics, Elvis appears before her in smoke and thunder. Startled, but not "afraid of a man who looks like Dolly Parton threw up on him," she cannot decide if it is a dream, singing telegram, joke, or "new slant on that tree falling in the forest thing." Trudy is further shaken when she realizes that she fits the composite profile of "The Type" for Elvis sightings–sad, lonely, crazy, unfulfilled.

What follows is not the standard Elvis encounter. Before the night is over, the neurotic, pitiable recluse and the gluttonous ghost together confront loneliness and anxiety, life, death, food, music, fame, and addiction. Their debauched "date" is appropriately characterized by one critic as "Mr. Ominous meets Ms. Omniphobia."

*It's a Wonderful Afterlife* might be a more fitting subtitle for Spencer's play. Fifteen years have not changed Elvis much. The "old habits die hard" adage applies as the King's deathstyle mirrors his lifestyle. "Late Elvis" he remains, characteristically caricatured, an obsessive, narcissistic, self-destructive pleasure seeker. Acting like the Federal Drug Agent he always wanted to be, he frantically searches Trudy's apartment for drugs and alcohol. When not on his search and seizure operation, he takes advantage of Trudy's vulnerability by trying to seduce her. In addition, he has developed a postmortem preference for drinking and Domino's; he orders a case of Jack Daniels, a six pack of Bud, a case of Myers rum, and diet Coke to wash down the ten pizzas he calls out for.

Although Elvis has not lightened up on the weight scales, death has lightened up his outlook. Spencer's King has a refreshing sense of humor, which is apparent in his first exchange with Trudy:


**Trudy:** My God!
**Elvis:**  Nah, although people have confused us before.

**Trudy:** No. No. No. No. This can't be happening. Too unbeliev-
able.
**Elvis:** Nah, Hendrix would be unbelievable. I seem to keep
poppin' up all over the place.
**Trudy:** Why?
**Elvis:** That's what I'd like to know.

Death has been a liberating experience for Elvis and a "condition" which allows him to explore excesses without consequences.
Frustrated because there is no booze and only Motrin number 6 in
Trudy's apartment, Elvis drinks rubbing alcohol. "What's it gonna
do, kill me? Make me deader?" he asks a shocked Trudy.

Spencer's "Elvis" is a perversely professional version of Elvis,
the monthly advice columnist who wrote for *Spin* magazine for four
years. Here, he appears to have advanced to the next level of amateur psychology and comedy, albeit a primitive, instinctive one.

Elvis's "patient" Trudy is a fretting, borderline bulimic prone to
anxiety attacks. Trudy's existence is not Elvian, rather Evian, as in
water—"no calories, no color, no kick." She is a *Friends* flunkie.
Since her divorce, Trudy has not dated, danced, or done anything
with anyone. She clings to the careful, always-in-control end of the
continuum rather than the carefree, out-of-control end where Elvis
aligns. Their contrasting outlooks spark an evening of discussion
that drifts between a lively debate and the confessional conversation
of a therapy session.

Elvis listens attentively, withstanding Trudy's repugnant remarks
about his pleasure-seeking "sickness, wretched excess, and performance masturbation." Although Elvis does not relate specifically to
her eating disorder, he draws upon his own "minor problems" to
frame his responses. When Trudy explains that she "doesn't want
to want things," Elvis defends his way of life, offering no apologies. Their dialogue often echoes lines from the necrophiliac cult
film *Harold and Maude*.

**Elvis:** You might be afraid of dying, but honey, you're afraid of
living even more.
**Trudy:** Just because to me life's more bearable if we have some
degree of control over it instead of just going into excessive urges.

**Elvis:** Urges, excessive or not, is what life is all about. Feeling as much as you can as often as you can, with whoever you can . . . whenever you can.

Their session does not focus exclusively on the risk-to-rewards ratio of their lifestyles, but more significantly on self-esteem. Elvis is sincere about teaching Trudy about loving herself. Despite their divergent views, Trudy is comfortable and trusting enough to reveal things to Elvis which she had never confessed to anyone, including her "real" analysts.

Elvis also reveals a secret, which perhaps is a key to the Presley myth, music, and his unique ability to connect with people. When Trudy wonders what so many others have–"how a man who never met me could say such personal things to me"–Elvis explains that he was never singing to Trudy, or anyone else, for that matter. "I was singing to me . . . in a way that I wished somebody else would sing to me. Loving myself in a way that everybody needs to be loved," explains Elvis.

Trudy's personal communication and connection with the King through his music is certainly not unique. The power of Elvis's songs is a universal truth and mystery that has been probed and portrayed, experienced and expressed in countless real-life testimonies, fictional archetypes, songs, poems, and dramatic presentations. To many, music is the essence of the myth.

This particular scene and the discussion of Elvis's music represents the playwright Spencer's Elvis "experience," and her own attempt to solve the Presley Puzzle. She explains:

A few years ago I was sitting at Ed Debevic's with my preschool daughter, her friend, and her friend's mother when an Elvis record came on the jukebox. "I never really liked Elvis until I got divorced," the woman told me. "But ever since then, whenever I hear Elvis sing, I feel like he's singing just to me."

I couldn't stop thinking about her statement. I went out and bought some Elvis records. I listened to them constantly. I didn't know what it was but I heard it too. A longing. A love. A haunting transcendence.

Interestingly, Laura Kalpakian's experience mirrors Spencer's, as her novel *Graced Land* was not inspired by her lifelong devotion to Elvis. It was only after she invested in the King that she understood, and became a convert in the process:

> When I began [*Graced Land*], I was not an Elvis fan. I got the idea from the house, a shrine, like the one in the novel. The idea became so powerful that I had to put every project aside. In May 1990, I went to the store and bought everything of his [Elvis's] I could find. I put on the headphones. I waited for the downbeat and I wrote the book. I wrote it to the music. The novel was written with the zeal of a convert.

Elvis's revelation provides an insight into his own myth, as well as a moment of self-discovery for Trudy, similar to the "meaning of life" moment experienced by Emily Shaw through Elvis and Rejoice in *Graced Land*. The scene also marks a turning point, or climax, for the evening, as their discourse advances to intercourse. Trudy, still wrestling with her fears while listening to a seductive medley of Presley persuasion, consents, only after realizing that she has stumbled across the ultimate safe sex. "When you died, there was no AIDS. Yes!" she proclaims orgasmically.

Before the evening ends, Elvis shifts from savior to Santa. While the role may represent one of the few he was not cast in during his movie career, Elvis as Santa is rather fitting within the play's holiday setting, as well as the overweight, generous, and other physical and personality parallels.

Santa Elvis provides "gifts" to exchange in the play's closing scene. The predictable present for Trudy is a potential partner for Trudy—Detective Fort, who arrives at her apartment to investigate after the Domino's delivery boy blows Elvis's cover and a frenzied crowd assembles outside chanting "Elvis!"

Fort represents a unique law enforcement professional, a forerunner to FBI agents Mulder and Scully on *The X-Files*. He is an Elvis Ghostbuster, a contemplative cop and psychologist who "specializes" in Elvis sightings. Though admittedly motivated by curiosity as much as anything, Fort is not the typical tabloid Elvis sightseer. He is well versed in the Presley mythology. His view of Elvis's death as betrayal echoes the sentiments of the deepest Presley ponderers–Marcus, Marsh, and Guralnick. From years of looking for Elvis clues, he has formulated many of his own theories about Elvis apparitions. One view of the ghost is as a guardian angel. "I think he shows himself to people who need to see him . . . Elvis moves in mysterious ways," he explains. "Some people see him and other people just benefit somehow from his existence . . . even now."

Fort offers a profile of the pizza delivery boy to build his case– 16 years old, parents divorced, bright but only a C-student, nonathlete, working Christmas Eve. "Does that sound like a happy kid to you?" he asks. "But after the kids at his school read about him and see the $500 tip he scored from The King, he's going to experience a lot of limelight for a while."

Fort represents a glimmer of hope in a woman's world filled with typical male losers like the three stooges–Weebo, Harlan, and Ty. While Fort may be a likely candidate to replace Robert Stack on *Unsolved Mysteries* or other camcorder cop shows, he may be more reminiscent of Harvey Keitels' compassionate cop in *Thelma and Louise*. Or, he would be an ideal Presley partner to patrol the precinct with Ned Beatty's Detective Bolander in *Homicide*. Fort and Bolander represent the type of potentially compatible partners Kalpakian's, Spencer's, and Byron's "Elvis women" might scan singles ads in the classified section of *Blue Suede News* for.

Fort, 38 and never married, also receives his gift from Santa Elvis. "I've spent years investigating people who've received things, gifts, mementos, from Elvis," he explains to Trudy. "But coming here, meeting you, I feel like I got my first personal gift from the King."

### ELVISITATIONS:
### "JUST HUMAN, I GUESS"

*Christmas with Elvis* provides an engaging postmortem view of Elvis. Spencer insightfully probes the myth, imagining how Elvis, like us, might look back on his life and wonder. The King's hindsight offers no apologies and no regrets for how he lived. However, even in death it is not quite clear to him why he continues to be an object of worldly worship and obsession. Whether a moment of false modesty or actual awareness, Elvis is self-conscious of his own deification and the inevitable Christ comparisons. "You know, Jesus is dead and tonight nearly everybody I know is waiting for him to come back. So why does everybody get so bent out of shape when they see me?" he wonders in a slightly tortured tone.

Hearing Elvis ask the same questions about himself that others have asked is an intriguing inversion. In between his analyzing and philosophizing, Elvis seeks some understanding for and about himself, and others. He has not been listening to his own teachings. Like a disciple who has absorbed the wisdom of the philosopher whose feet she sits at, Trudy attempts to provide some clarity for Elvis with a simple lesson about love.

> You're a symbol to them, to me. You know what you wanted and you got it. And, as you told me, despite your problems and the drawbacks to loving you, you enjoyed being you. So if you could do it, love yourself, maybe we can love ourselves, problems and all.

Elvis and Trudy's Christmas Eve two-step is a 12-step commentary appropriate for the 1980s era of "R and R"–rehabilitation and recovery. As the generational mental mantra has shifted from "I'm Okay, You're Okay," to "I'm dysfunctional, you're codependent," Elvis advocates a vogue psychoview that says it is okay to laugh, to have fun, and to push the limits a little. "The real addiction is a need for what isn't. A diversion from what is, what we are, what we can be, can't be. And that's just human, I guess," Elvis explains to Trudy.

Elvis's "just human, I guess" response may reflect a casually indifferent attitude or a convenient rationalization for many problems. Yet the phrase also embodies an overlooked view in Elvis's godly case. Images of Elvis tend to clutter at opposite extremes of the spectrum. At one end is the adulation, at the other, demystification. In between, there is a largely neglected area of simply being human.

*Christmas with Elvis* focuses on the essence and humanness beneath the various Elvis images and ideals commonly presented. The Elvis/Christ connection is a convenient crisscross worth considering. It might not be a stretch to compare Spencer's treatment of Elvis to filmmaker Martin Scorsese's portrayal of Jesus in *The Last Temptation of Christ*. Both explore their characters' struggles to make choices, their flaws and failures, their moments of doubt and faith; all common, human qualities that are largely lost in the emphasis on the godliness of these two men.

Spencer neither deifies nor crucifies; making her King more accessible. Elvis is a reluctant savior who is not only human, but very male. The feminine mystique and androgyny accentuated in other portrayals are not a part of this Elvis. He never misrepresents his identity to Trudy, making it clear that he is actually more of a "Mr. Typical" than a "Mr. Right." When Trudy demands, "What do you want?" Elvis has another "I guess" response:

> Well, I'd like to rest in peace but since that just doesn't seem to be in the cards for me, I'll take heartfelt worship, complete admiration, total surrender, and as much Jack Daniels as you can pour. Same as any man, I guess.

By most biographical accounts, the image of Elvis as a "Mr. Right" or ideal mate is merely fantasy. In her seminal and scholarly *Elvis Presley: A Bio-Bibliography* (1985), Patsy Guy Hammontree examines some of the expectations and conditions attached to Elvis and Priscilla's marriage, a blissless situation which resembles the fictional struggles of other "Elvis women." Hammontree writes:

> Elvis wanted Priscilla to live in a romantic vacuum. He viewed himself as married when he was with Priscilla, but he saw himself as being beyond the conditions of marriage when he was in the world at large. He behaved accordingly. (p. 78)

According to the biographer, Priscilla compared her life with Elvis to being in a cocoon. She frequently spoke of boredom and how Elvis controlled her life and lifestyle, choosing her clothes, make up, hairstyles, and activities.

In attempting to put the Presley's relationship into perspective, Hammontree proposes another view of Elvis which turns out to be consistent with many fictional portrayals. "Elvis quite possibly saw himself as her protector and guardian more than he really felt himself to be her husband," writes Hammontree.

And it may be one of Trudy's lines spoken to Elvis in *Christmas with Elvis* which captures the universality of women's struggles, whether Priscilla Presley, or the character types created by Kalpakian, Byron, and Spencer. "You think it was hard for you to live up to everybody's expectations! Try being a woman," Trudy challenges Elvis.

The women in *Christmas with Elvis, Graceland*, and *Graced Land* represent extensions of their creators, exploring and experiencing Elvis's "haunting transcendence," whether through an Elvis pill, song, or visit. This intimate communication contains meanings and messages, both personal and universal, about gender and generation, strength and self-discovery, sexuality and spirituality, longing and love.

In considering the scope of her own play, Terry Spencer also captures the essence of her fellow women writers' works about Elvis:

> *Christmas with Elvis* is not about Elvis. It's about Trudy. It's about all women—our desires for love, pressures, needs, and aversions to conforming, fears of rejection, anger and self-blame and irony . . . I think we all could use a little visit from the King every now and then.

## NOTE

1. I am grateful to author Terry Spencer for providing the script of *Christmas with Elvis* and for discussing the play and her Elvis experience with me. Ditto to director Doug Hartzell at the Halsted Theatre Center in Chicago for contributing materials such as programs, reviews, and fliers.

# Chapter 4

# Absence Makes the Art Grow Fonder: Pop, Primitive, and Postmodern Presley

For Elvis there was no escape in art, since his original triumph was his artlessness.

—Peter Guralnick,
*Country Music* (December 1977)

One of the drawings in Dan Piraro's second collection of cartoons, *Too Bizarro* (1988), depicts a scene at a museum of art. The atmosphere within the flat, black-and-white single frame is formal. In the background, a man and a woman, who is wearing a fur, study a painting. The gallery guide, appearing more like a uniformed guard on duty, stands solemn and straight, hands folded in front. In casual contrast before him is a visitor who appears suspiciously out of place, as if an obvious answer to a "what's wrong with this picture?" question. The museum misfit, outfitted in flared trousers, pointed shoes, sideburns, and glasses, asks, "Which way to the Elvis paintings?"

The high art "intruder's" innocent inquiry resounds in the space's hushed formality. Had Piraro expanded the scene into a multiple-paneled storyboard, the result might resemble the "When E.F. Hutton talks, people listen" commercial. We might see the couple in the background, with noses upturned and shocking stares, react in disbelief and disgust at such a profane utterance within the gallery walls. The unflinching guide might diplomatically explain to the Elvis patron there are no "Presleys" in the permanent collection or on display, and then kindly escort him out.

Piraro's cartoon offers a perspective on "Elvis's artlessness" and his accompanying struggle for acceptance in the art world. No matter how skilled the creator, or sincere the intention, Elvis images in art have not been taken seriously and are frequently met with widespread elite rejection.

Most Presley portraits are unable to transcend the black velvet anaesthetic. Instead, they are dismissed as kitsch, pop, and schlock, with low class, no class, and white-trash collector appeal. Culturally, the Presley parameters are limited, with "acceptable displays" including junk shops, personal shrines, trailer parks, discount chains, and roadside flea markets. We are not as comfortable seeing Elvis's image in a gallery, art museum, or other space where fine art is exhibited. To many, such "artlessness" is unthinkable and inappropriate; and to others it is laughable.

## *POP AND PORTRAITURE:*
## *"ANDY, ARE YOU GOOFIN' ON ELVIS?"*

At the same time Elvis's movements began shaking 1950s America, a major art movement was also developing. That movement would eventually draw Elvis into being more "aesthetically acceptable." Artists began to reappraise the academic approach to painting. Many renounced the standard visual cliche that seemed void of context due to overfamiliarity. Instead, they turned to new sources for subject matter, and in the process, introduced a more formal radicalism outside the tradition of figurative realism. The movement signaled a dramatic shift in outlook, and a transformation of values that made formerly scorned and banal themes "admissible" in high art. A new vernacular of images, artifacts, and motifs drawn from commercial and popular culture and nostalgic Americana began to establish itself as a provocative new current, one which represented a sharp opposition to subjective preoccupations and idealism.

What emerged in the late 1950s and into the early years of the following decade became known as Pop Art, a trend that would change the look of modern American painting for years, and draw Elvis's image into artistic "acceptability."

Pop Artists such as Robert Rauschenberg, Jim Dine, Claus Oldenburg, Red Grooms, Jasper Johns, Tom Wesselman, Jones Rosenquist, Robert Indiana, Roy Lichtenstein, and Andy Warhol viewed popular culture as an endless source of subject matter, rather than as an evil to be confronted or avoided.

Using reproductions, commercial illustrations, comic strips, cartoons, collage, and ordinary mass-produced objects, their work represented an original and irreverent parody of material culture, and conveyed an anti-art intensity and sensibility.

As the movement diffused and developed into the 1960s, new spatial and communication ideas infiltrated art through process-oriented media such as film and television, "happenings," and other events which pushed technical and aesthetic frontiers, presenting unexpected creative opportunities which changed the focus of traditional painting, portraiture, and the figurative approach.[1]

Not only did the advent of Elvis and Pop Art coincide, both might be viewed as characteristically compatible. As subject matter, Elvis embodied an appropriate, if not ideal, model for an artistic movement which emphasized commercialism, consumerism, popular culture, and repetition that was often unnecessary and exhaustive. In turn, Pop Art provided a suitable stylistic vehicle to transport Elvis images into the elite domain of the fine arts. In 1964, Pop Art's most recognizable artist, Andy Warhol, portrayed America's most recognizable figure, Elvis, in silkscreened lithographs, *Elvis I* (the more familiar portrait, in color on acrylic) and *Elvis II* (on aluminum).

Warhol's pictures of soup cans, celebrities, and dollar bills refuse nearly all redeeming links to traditions of high pictorial seriousness. Frustrated critics struggling to decipher deeper meaning beneath the surface of his work speculated that Warhol was, among other things, a social commentator who used commercial devices to explore the mediocrity, manipulation, and exploititiveness of popular culture. Some viewed his work as the closest contemporary invocation of Canadian media theorist Marshall McLuhan's declaration "the medium is the message."

Despite the blankness, passivity, and plastic nature of his art, Warhol operates in the sphere of cultural myth and parable, often confronting the notion of cultural exhaustion through his control of the celebrity portrait. Warhol did not create images as much as he sought ready-made shimmering subjects. His aim, in part, was to intensify that allure. In addition to his well-known portraits of Elvis, Marilyn Monroe, Jackie Kennedy, and Jimmy Carter, his *The Myth*

*Series* (1981) included other pop culture figures–Dracula, Howdy
Doody, Superman, Santa Claus, The Shadow, Uncle Sam, The
Wicked Witch of the West (from *The Wizard of Oz*), Mammy,
Mickey Mouse, and The Star. From hero to eternity.

Consistent with his other work, Warhol's Presley print may be
considered shallow and vague. At the same time, the dual dueling
depictions of identical Elvii are at once ambiguous, laden with prophetic possibilities, and represent a stylistic metaphor for Elvis. The
pistol-packing punk Presleys mirrored side-by-side reflect a Frank and
Jesse James (perhaps Elvis and twin brother Jesse?) Siamese outlaw
persona. This design evolves full circle 30 years later during the 1992
Elvis Stamp Election when two Elvis images also appear next to each
other as contrasting candidates on posters, postcards, and ballots.

While the duality, repetition, and commentary on commercialism
may be evident, a critique which appeared in *Newsweek* (Orth, August
29, 1977) shortly after Elvis's death offers another view of the portrait:

> If you look closely at Elvis as Pop Artist Andy Warhol did . . .
> you saw an almost androgynous softness and passivity in his
> punk-hood persona. Elvis and his revolution were vulnerabil-
> ity disguised in bravado. (Orth, p. 48)

In her insightful essay, "Elvis, or the Ironies of a Southern Identity," Linda Ray Pratt (1979) further acknowledges Elvis's androgynous aura:

> The sexuality he projected was complicated because it com-
> bined characteristics and appeals traditionally associated with
> both males and females. On one hand, he projected masculine
> aggression and an image of abandoned pleasure, illicit thrills,
> back-alley liasons and on the other hand, a quality of tender-
> ness, vulnerability, and romantic emotion. Andy Warhol cap-
> tured something of this diversified stance with a gun in his
> hand but with the face softened in tone and line. The image
> made Elvis the perfect lover by combining the most appealing
> of male and female characterists and satisfying both the physi-
> cal desire for sensual excitement and the emotional need for
> loving tenderness. (p. 47)

Camille Paglia (1990) is also among those who looks closely at Elvis and recognizes an epicene quality in his archetypal beauty. In her cultural critique, *Sexual Personae*, Paglia views Elvis's face with Apollo, the Delphic Charioteer, and other distinct, youthful images of ancient Greece:

> . . . high brow, strong straight nose, girlishly fleshy cheeks, full petulant mouth, and short upper lip. It's in the face of Elvis Presley, Lord Byron, and Bronzino's glossy Mannerist Blue Boy. Freud saw the androgyny in the Greek adolescent: "Among the Greeks, where the most manly men were found among inverts, it is quite obvious that it was not the masculine characters of the boy which kindled the love of man; it was his physical resemblance to woman as well as his feminine psychic qualities, such as shyness, demureness, and the need for instruction and help." (p. 115)

Paglia expands the Elvis comparisons to Lord Byron, George Villiers, and the First Duke of Buckingham, all whom she characterizes "revolutionary men of beauty" and "dangerous men of notorious charisma." (p. 165) Probing beneath the surface, she identifies an "internal self-impairment," which may be analogous to "vulnerability disguised as bravado." Of Elvis and Byron she writes "their energy and beauty together are burning, godlike, destructive . . . tremendous physical energy was oddly fused with internal disorder, a revolt of the organism" (p. 362).

The film/comic strip repeats, or grid compositions, became a Warhol trademark. The year before he completed the Elvis lithographs, Warhol drew the *Mona Lisa* into his realm of reproduction. The da Vinci masterpiece, one of the most popular portraits in art history, has appeared in the works of numerous other artists, among them Duchamp, Rauschenberg, Wesselman, Johns, and Arneson, whose portrayal places the model with George Washington in *George and Mona in the Baths of Colona* (1976). Warhol's *Mona Lisa: 30 Are Better Than One* (1963) depicts five rows of six Mona Lisas in each. The images are scattered, not serial, with complete color changes. Some are tilted and two details of the paintings are added in frames. The result is a restless composition which celebrates the Mona Lisa's status as a cliche of twienth century art.

The title and repetition of the portrait contains a strange connection, as if a visual paraphrase of the album cover of the Elvis gold volume, *50,000,000 Elvis Fans Can't Be Wrong* that features multiple images of Elvis in his gold lamé suit. Considering the timing of the volume's releases–December 1959, reissued in stereo in 1962–and Warhol's attention to popular culture, the album cover's connection with his Mona Lisa is a possibility. The identical Elvii in gold lamé design continues to be appropriated. *Rolling Stone* (March 24, 1994) uses it in Colorform fashion on a Beavis and Butthead cover.

The mechanical reproduction that is characteristic of Warhol and Pop Art is in itself a fitting stylistic metaphor for Elvis. More than any image or icon in American popular culture, Elvis is the embodiment of repetition to the point of exhaustion. Elvis, expanded, if not exploded, the Warhol prophecy of 15 minutes of fame to 15 years, and going on forever. Clive James's in-depth chronicle, *Fame in the 20th Century*, reaffirmed the King's "most famous of the famous" status as Elvis was the Public Broadcast series lead image. And in January 1993, the endless rows of Elvis images on endless sheets of stamps rolling off the postal services production line presses were Warholian prophecy fulfilled, a homage to repetition, cultural cliché and the grid compositions from 30 years earlier.

The fascination with celebrity can be traced into the 1970s in other portraits, among them Lloyd Ziff's *Judy Garland* (1970), Antonio's *James Dean* (1976), Cooley's *Einstein* (1977), and Linda Stokes's *Marilyn Monroe* (1979). Yet no figure from American popular culture was as frequent a subject as Elvis. While he remained an idol, if not perpetual model for velvet, his image became widely portrayed on canvas, paper, and virtually every other medium and material.

Roger G. Taylor compiles over 100 Elvis portraits, along with quotes and anecdotes, in *Elvis in Art* (1987). The collection was gathered from representations on billboards, magazine covers, illustrations, record sleeves, caricatures, cartoons, drawings, movie posters, photographs, prints, and paintings.

In general, the representations reflect Pop's mechanical methodology and detached aestheticism. The Presley portraits are quite literal. They feature clean, sharp lines and pure color. A posterlike, airbrush, commercial quality is more prevalent in the works than abstraction or expressionism. Many of the artists and illustrators appear to treat Elvis as Warhol approached his subjects, with the attitude of the "uncommitted observer," which thwarts a sense of emotional identification.

Todd Schorr's *Impersonating Elvis* (1978) "masks" the emotional blankness and Pop repetition (Figure 4.1). Everyone in his composition wears an Elvis face. A jumpsuited impersonator splits on stage in a late-Elvis guise before rows of young Elvii, who have replaced screaming teenagers in the audience. The cultlike clones, in colorful collared shirts, are wearing masks that express innocence. The young Elvii fixated in the front four rows are an eerie cross between Ozzie and Harriet Nelson's boys and the Lost Boys, while the impersonator on stage conjures images of Yul Brynner's programmed villain in the futuristic science fiction/horror film, *Westworld*.

Schorr's use of the mask becomes a focal point that invites multiple interpretations. The effect is at once theatric, hypnotic, and robotic. Masks were common attributes of deities from the most

FIGURE 4.1. Todd Schorr's *Impersonating Elvis,* 1978.

primitive times; people literally impersonated their divinities by wearing masks. The disguises in the painting are not ornate or decorative. The simple, almost subtle string-tie style suggests classical Tragedy/Comedy theatrical masks featured in ancient sacred drama, where actors and members of the chorus were not expected to display emotions on their own faces. Japanese *nō* plays have a similar convention, using either masks or heavy makeup.

From a Presley point of view, is Schorr providing a cultural commentary on the widespread adoption of Elvis's identity? Is the artist perhaps ridiculing the artifice of impersonators, who seldom include masks as part of their costume anyway? Is he borrowing the repetitive motif from Warhol's grid compositions and replacing Campbells' soup cans with another consumer product—Elvis? Ironically, Schorr's composition was a reflection of Jimmy Ellis, a masked Elvis alter ego named "Orion," who surfaced around the same time period as the painting, the year following Elvis's death.

### *PRIMITIVE PRESLEY*

Pop artists have not been the only portrayers of Elvis. As folk and primitive art has been increasingly drawn into the cultural mainstream during the 1980s, images of Elvis followed in these "untrained" veins as well. Among the more notable, and representative renderings of Elvis in these styles are those appearing in the works of two Georgia artists, the Reverend Howard Finster and Joni Mabe.

One of America's preeminent folk artists, the octogenarian Finster became a popular figure not only in galleries, but among rock stars such as David Byrne and Michael Stipe. The Reverend painted album covers for the Talking Heads' *Little Creatures* (1985) and R.E.M.'s *Reckoning* (1984). And the video for R.E.M.'s "Radio Free Europe" was shot in Paradise Garden, Finster's junk collection outside his home in Somerville, Georgia.

Like many primitive/folk artists, Finster's source of inspiration is rooted in religion. He is a self-proclaimed "man of visions." In 1976, at age 60, when painting a bicycle in his shop, Finster saw a face in a smudge of paint on his fingers, and has been a painter ever since.

There is a childlike exuberance, down-home whimsy, and otherworldliness in the bright blue skies, smile-face-clouds, stick figure angels, and block-letter proverbs that characterize Finster's "holy art." His haunting hero portraits include the familiar faces of Jesus, John F.Kennedy, Martin Luther King, Eli Whitney, and Elvis.

Finster's *Elvis at 3* (1986) is a colorful interpretation of the famous photograph of 'lil El as a tyke, his hands in the pockets of his overalls. Finster, recognizing "three" as a numeric symbol of absolute divinity, writes, "Elvis at three, is an angel to me." Reproduced cutouts of the image, many with wings bestowed upon the Elvis boy, are among Finster's most popular works in collections and galleries all over the world.

The Athens-based Mabe picks up where Pop Art left off in the 1960s. A cultural curator, Mabe fancily chronicles icons, images, fetishes, and phenomena, many of which were assembled in 1988 by Nexus Press into *Joni Mabe's Museum Book*, billed as "The First Museum in Book Form Which Features Some Of The Greatest . . . Elvis, Jesus, Loretta Lynn, etc. And 3 Of The Worst . . . Hitler, The Klan, and Satan." A *Classic Postcard Book* followed in 1992.

Mabe is particularly obsessed with Elvis. "Elvis became the vehicle through which I played out my notions about America, the South, sex, religion, death, and whatever else took my fancy," explains Mabe. Her eye for Presley particles has resulted in "Elvis environments," noisy collages such as *I Could Have Saved Elvis If I Had Been Born Earlier, But I Was Born in 1957*, and *The Travelling Panoramic Encyclopedia of Everything Elvis*, a roving museum and coffeetable book (1996) of Elvis relics and oddities which boast such items as the rocker's toenail clippings and "the wart I bought that he had removed in '58." Her most recent Elvisian endeavor is to renovate her great-grandmother's house in Cornelia, Georgia into the world's first Elvis bed-and-breakfast museum.

Mabe clearly demonstrates her preference for the popular culture palette, or "Glop Art," as one critic describes her creations (Cameron, 1989). Yet what sets Mabe's work apart from Pop Art is that she deals with emotion that wanders into sentimentality, superstition, sexuality, and spirituality.

*Love Letter to Elvis* (1983) is a giant, handwritten Valentine with a border of snapshots of the bare-breasted artist rubbing up against a ceramic Elvis bust. "You could've discovered that sex and religion could be brought together in your feelings for me," writes the mesmerized Mabe, consumed with longing for "just one caress to remind me that you really were a man and not a god." Mabe closes with a confession, that she is carrying Elvis's child. "The last imitator I fucked was carrying your sacred seed. Please send money."

In the same spirit, Mabe's other found-object installations include *I Wanted To Have Elvis's Baby But Jesus Said It Was a Sin* and *The Official Elvis Prayer Rug*, a garish glittered five-color litho, complete with evangelical chain-letter instructions. "Pass your Elvis Prayer Rug to another lost soul and buy another for yourself."

Like many Presley impressionists and expressionists, Mabe sees Jesus and Elvis as being similar. "Both are worshipped, are very passionate, and emanate a sense of helplessness."

Mabe also avoids the sin of condescension toward Elvis and her method. Many artists who tap the rich vein of kitsch also have an "Of course, I'm actually above all of this ball fringe, black velvet, and sequins" attitude. "Mabe manages to coolly bridge the gap between being an actual participant in, and a distant observer of cultural dementia," writes Dan Cameron (1989).

## KITSCH AND CATECHISM:
## THOROUGHLY POSTMODERN PRESLEY

By the 1990s, Elvis's image expanded well beyond Pop and Primitive into the postmodern realm, appearing more frequently in galleries as part of exhibits, permanent fixtures, and features.

In August 1992, the creations of numerous artists and architects were linked into an 18-hole miniature golf art exhibit, *Putt Modernism*, at Artist's Space, an alternative gallery in TriBeCa, New York. Installations ranged from serious social commentaries on war (Mel Chin's reconstruction of the allegedly civilian bunker bombed in Baghdad), racism, and the politics of AIDS (Chris Clarke's *White House* made from empty AZT bottles with white neon that glows red when the ball drops in the hole), the plight of the homeless, and country club elitism to playful pavilions, 12-foot inflatable figures, golf ball towers, animated electric rabbits covered with Cheez Doodles dangling from the ceiling, and other follies.

Amidst the exhibit's round of sociopolitical constructions and architectural kitsch is Greg Amenoff's *King's Hole*, which explores

Elvis's life through a series of sand traps. The hazards include "Truck Driver," "Vegas," "Drugs," "Lose Control," and "Die." Amenoff's time line is familiar, if not worn, with no new revelations or answers to the question, "Elvis, what happened?" Nonetheless, the miniature golf setting, with its cutout cartoon obstacles and astro-turf slice of middle America summer nights is a novel and suitable setting for Elvis's image.

Amenoff's work became the signature piece, "the Presley par" of *Putt Modernism* as it began to tour. In December 1993, when the exhibit was featured on the arts and leisure magazine show, *CBS Sunday Morning*, the producers used Amenoff's piece in the still shots introducing and closing the segment.

In addition to touring with *Putt Modernism,* Elvis is a permanent fixture at Stephanie Pierce's Where's the Art?, a unique 24-hour, coin-operated gallery of "art for the smart" in Portland, Oregon.

The series of 3- $\times$ 4-foot interactive window displays includes such minipanoramas as *The World's Cheapest Psychic, Santa Rama,* and *The Church of Elvis,* which features three separate mira-cles–flesh, direct dial, and spinning Elvises (Figure 4.2).

Pierce, who has been creating coin-operated art since the mid-1980s, did not set out to pay homage to, critique, or exploit Elvis's image with her installation. The concept for *The Church of Elvis* evolved out of the artist's notion to explore the concept of worship, particularly in relation to organized religion and consumerism. "I wanted a church that worshiped styrofoam and plastic, and a confes-sional-like money machine where you get a prize for repentance," explains Pierce.[2]

While Elvis is a natural for such subject matter, his inclusion in the dogma is, in Pierce's view, "accidental." Two teenagers who were admirers of Pierce's window works suggested she do "an Elvis" for her gallery. Pierce initially resisted the idea. Not only was she not an Elvis fan, she considered the King passé. "I was reluctant, but the more I thought of it the more perfect it was for what I was trying to express," said Pierce. "It completed my trilogy–plastic, styrofoam, and Elvis. All three interchangeable, ubiquitous, and indestructible."

Pierce built the *Church of Elvis* out of her usual materials–found objects, Goodwill remnants, and dime-store grab bags. An old *Jeopar-dy!* game board, spinning pictures of Elvis, sacred cans, guardian

FIGURE 4.2. The caption for this display reads: "This is the sacred symbol of the 24-Hour Church of Elvis. Please study it carefully. It appears on our T-Shirts, Calendars, Bumper Stickers, Refrigerator Magnets, etc.—wherever The Truth needs to be displayed. Whenever you see it, please think of food or sex. Thank you."

Source: Courtesy Stephanie Pierce.

angels, a nun, motorcycle cop, Mountie, fly, Shriner, and Ninja Turtles are assembled on the panel. And, consistent with the vending machine motif, "churchgoers" receive a handmade prize for their quarter deposit and interaction. The piece places Elvis in a 1990s context with automatic teller machines and instant gratification. "It's convenient, cheap, and you get a prize at the end," says Pierce.

Pierce estimates the *Church of Elvis* tithing to average "maybe $70 worth of quarters" per week. Although that amount is less than what *The World's Cheapest Psychic* earns, the Elvis concept "translates really fast" to window patrons and to Pierce.

With that recognition comes widespread assumption that *The Church of Elvis* was designed as a publicity stunt or gallery gimmick, which strikes a resentful chord with Pierce.

> It gets all the publicity, and it really doesn't have as much to do with Elvis. There's more than just Elvis there. It's not based on liking Elvis. Art itself doesn't have much to do with Elvis. I was sick of Elvis even before I made *Church of Elvis*. I didn't set out to exploit his name or do it for publicity. But instead, its become the only thing anyone ever wants to talk about. Not my art, or the cultural phenomenon of a 24-hour coin-operated gallery. You create a monster.

Although the Elvis myth may overshadow Pierce's artistic vision, she also acknowledges that *Church of Elvis* "saved my store," as it evolved into a conceptual and commercial cornerstone of the space. Pierce's entrepreneurial efforts resemble Joni Mabe's merchandise. The *Where's the Art?* mail-order catalog is a mini-Graceland filled with official *Church of Elvis*abilia. The In-the-name-of Elvis collection ranges from "conventional" souvenir items such as buttons, stickers, magnets, calendars, and keychains, to the unusual—toaster covers, X-ray, glow-in-the-dark sperm samples ("The loveseed of the King; now you can grow your own Elvis"); to the sacramental and spiritual—rosary, usher's wings and perfect attendance pins, prayer rugs, a talisman amulet (with secret chant), wedding kit, d-lux shroud, Book of Elvis, sacred Elvis detector, and a plastic chalice coffee cup.

## *ART FOR ELVISSAKE*

One of the best representative assemblages of contemporary Elvis art is exhibited annually, since 1990, in Chicago at World Tattoo Gallery's *All-Elvis Art Show Extravaganza*.

The idea for the exhibit was playfully conceived by World Tattoo co-owners Jonathan Lavan and Tony Fitzpatrick, and Windy City radio personality Buzz Kilman. Admittedly founded, in part, on a "why not?" whim, there was also economic impetus. "The show was a lark that just kind of snowballed, which is usually how our best shows end up working," explains Lavan. "It's so hard for art galleries to stay open these days. Many closed after having been open 30 years. We've been unconventional in our approach, and one reason is to stay open."[3]

While the founding group does not consider themselves die-hard Elvis aficionados, they are a cumulative Elvis observer, creator, and collector. "I'm interested in why certain things affect people in certain ways," explains Lavan. "And I'm fascinated with the way Elvis affects people in so many extremely different ways." Fitzpatrick has written poems about Elvis, and his art, which has been exhibited nationally, and includes Elvis renderings such as *Memphis Tattoo King*. Kilman owns what the *Guinness Book of World Records* lists as "the world's largest Elvis on velvet," David Zwierz's 9′ × 9′ *Velvis*.

Part of World Tattoo's "unconventional approach" is to do theme shows that are capable of attracting attention. Exhibits that preceded the *All-Elvis Art Show* include *Sexuality and Religion* and *Thrift Store Parts*, featuring "art under $25."

On Thanksgiving Eve, 1990, six months after World Tattoo opened, the first annual *All Elvis Art Show* premiered, with works as far away as London on display in the gallery's 6,200 square feet of space. Billed as "a King-sized exhibition," on a promotional poster that featured the Mona Lisa with magic-markered Elvis hair and sideburns, the opening's night club atmosphere included Elvis impersonators, a band performing Elvis Vegas-style pop, and a cover charge. Lavan considered the caliber of the show "not what it might have been, but good; and it was a *great* event. We got people looking at art that night who might not have otherwise entered an art gallery."

The gallery director considered the show a success; attendance was impressive and many pieces were sold. Although the response, in general, was favorable, there were some dissenters among the patrons. Many of the hard-core Elfans found some of the art offensive, particularly *The Singing Toilet*. The "sculpture," a collaboration between Marcus May and Dino Eliopulos, is an actual porcelain commode covered with glitter and lights. An accompanying audiotape plays the verse, "sitting home all alone/you know I can't be found." The Impersonators were insulted that the president of their Chicago chapter blacklisted World Tattoo.

While the situation did not come close to reaching the magnitude of other contemporary controversies in the art community–Jesse Helms arch-conservative crusades, Robert Mappelthorpe's photograph exhibits, and the subsequent debates over taste, censorship and National Endowment for the Arts and Humanities funding–*The Singing Toilet* dispute was further proof that Elvis's image was capable of striking a chord, even in places where he was not taken seriously.

According to Lavan, the gallery gradually "took themselves more seriously," received more notoriety, both locally and nationally, and established a stable of regular artists. Some of that growth was evident as the second annual *All-Elvis Art Show Extravaganza* opened in the "Love Me Tender" atmosphere of Valentine's Day 1992 (Figures 4.3-4.6). The show featured 50 artists, more than 100 pieces of art, and attracted a wider audience. "Last year, it was mainly people who were obsessed with Elvis and people who were obsessed with the people who were obsessed with Elvis," said Lavan. "This year it was much more mainstream and mixed clientele."

The show also represented an even wider cross section of styles that transcended the convenient kitsch and memorabiliart categories. "There is some kitschy. If you're dealing with Elvis, you're dealing with kitsch anyway," says Lavan, resigned to the inevitable. "But the caliber of the work is excellent." The representations include photographs, sculpture, paintings, prints, comic panels and caricatures, computer animation, plates and pottery, illustrations, and installations in styles ranging from pop and primitive, impressionist and expressionist, to real and surreal, pointillist and pointless, abstract and white trash. Collectively, the show simultaneously reveals obsessiveness and playfulness.

The exhibit features familiar Elvis images and themes. Portraits offer both 1950s and jumpsuit Elversions in glitter, oil, crayon, airbrush, and velvet. Along with Dave Zwierz's huge *Velvis*, among the more stri-King portrayals are Tim Anderson's oils and Tim McWilliam's Seurat-style acrylic pointillist Presley, *Elvis II*.

FIGURES 4.3 - 4.6. Displays from the second annual All-Elvis Art Show Extravaganza 1992.

FIGURE 4.3

FIGURE 4.4

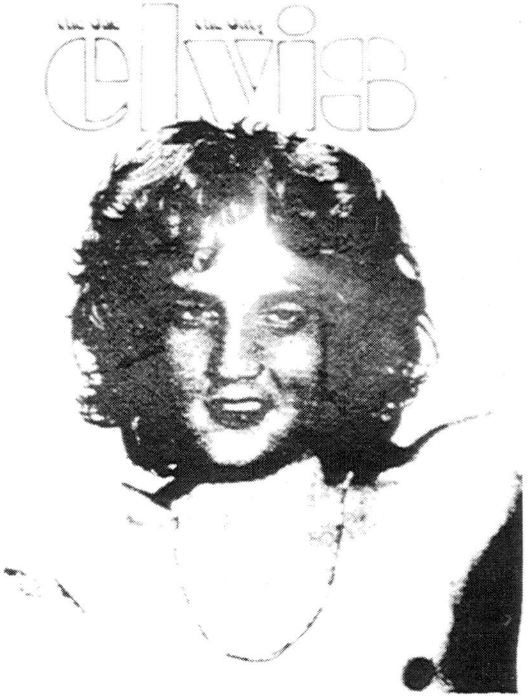

FIGURE 4.6

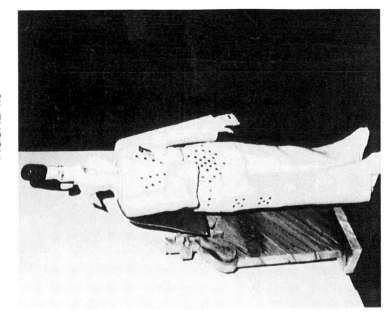

FIGURE 4.5

Sources: Photo 4.3: Courtesy Jonathan Lavan; Photo 4.4: © Geoff Bevington; Photo 4.5: "Elvis is the Boss; Brice is just an employee" by Shane Swank; Photo 4.6: "Elvistein" by Dennis Van Keersblick.

*133*

Photographic portraits, though not of Elvis himself, are also well represented in the works of Katherine Gann and Patty Carroll, who present different photo series of local Chicago Elvis Impersonators. (Jane Fisher's *"Jay" Elvis* and *The Wonder of You* also capture Impersonators in oil portraits.) Photographing Elvis Impersonators has become a noticeable trend, with the fashionable subject conveniently packaged into books. In December 1993, Atlanta's Gallery V displayed *Elvis: That's The Way It Is Now*, 25 photo portraits by Marion Rhodes. Having previously used Vietnam veterans and nursing home residents as subjects, Rhodes viewed the Elvis project as a way of exploring "why so many people, and it's growing exponentially, are interested in emulating and living in the shadow of someone who has been dead a long time."

Primitive and folk veins also run throughout the show. Joanna Neff's beautifully detailed handmade dolls *"Dodger" and Her Grandson* place Elvis at the train station bench before leaving for the Army. Kay Burlingham's *Once in a Lifetime* quilt provides one of the exhibit's surprisingly few images of Graceland, a bird's-eye view of the grounds and room layouts in blueprint fashion with Elvis hovering above. The quilt's companion piece is an eerie memorial pillow, *Mama Liked the Roses*.

The obsessions, memorabiliart, and kitsch often associated with Elvis are predictably prevalent. Crucifixes and pink Cadillacs are among the artifacts hanging from the outside panels of Anton Witek's box shrine, *Elvis, Not*. Inside sits an Elvis bust, painted black with red lips, draped with Mardi Gras beads and surrounded by wallpaper of Elvis trading cards.

Rob Thomas's *Slide Show II–The Elvis Chronicles* features 270 tiny pieces of cutout phrases and images of Elvis and his life. The fragments are designed to look like photographic slides and are arranged into 18 rows with 15 "slides" each. The repetition and size of the composition provide a glimpse of Elvis stamp collecting.

Julie Wishmeyer appears to be competing with Joni Mabe and Stephanie Pierce for Queen of Elvis Kitsch. Wishmeyer's display is the exhibit's gift shop, a small-scale replica to the souvenir stands that line Elvis Presley Boulevard outside the Gates of Graceland that includes seven different styles of sunglasses, shrines, clocks, a suitcase of memories, bookends, books, frames, guitars, and a table.

Religious imagery, artifacts, and motifs, which mock and deify, appear throughout the exhibit in shrines, crucifixes, vigil candles, angels, sculpted shrouds, and even titles such as *No Matter How Hard They Prayed, the Sun Sessions Were Over*, and *Elvis Plato Superstar Contemplating God and a Man with a Chainsaw*.

Charice Mericle's *Elvis Angel–1956 Retrospective* depicts a winged and haloed King in a robe grafittied with drawings of guitars, carrots, buildings, buses, crowns, a TV set, and fragmented phrases such as "toast of the town," "sad eyes," and "they have no heart." The oil on wood cutout hangs next to Alan E. Lieb's striking, but simple vinyl collage on acrylic, *Elvis Versus the Five Fingers of Satan*. A red hand emerges from a black background, about to seize young innocent Elvis who is gazing upward as he sings.

Doug Huston's *The Resurrection of Jesse Garon* depicts the baptismal rite. The computer-generated graphic shows an Elvis mannequin in black, propped up on an inflatable Elvis doll emerging out of a river.

In *Elvis in the Garden*, Sal Scolara adapts a circa-1960s lighted, lace gold metal frame surrounding a religious hologram into a scene with Elvis in Gethsemane. Duality, power, and betrayal are apparent. Elvis appears to be cast as a Judas or Pontius Pilate figure. In the right foreground, a cutout image of a young smiling Elvis wears a collaged crown of coral on his head. Hovering to his left, a Pan-like, demon creature caresses a glass ball which contains a scorpion relic while the 3-D Jesus prays in the background.

"Anatomy," ranging from the obese to the skeletal to the gross, is another prevalent motif in the exhibit. Steve Gorman's untitled cibachrome photograph resembles a kitchen wallpaper pattern. The "love meat tender" design features a heavyset Elvis in the center over a square background of vertical lines. A border of little pictures of different cuts of red meat frames the composition.

In medical illustrator fashion, Mary Baranchik's, *The Pelvis*, provides three skeletal views—front, side, and rear. Among the fragments of the colorfully detailed collage are guitars, frets, flowers, birds, butterflies, and human figures with gold Gustav Klimt-like patterns on a black background.

Philip Kalinowski provides a "body in tune" perspective with *Elvis' Song Title Anatomy*. The illustrative piece is a visual dissection of Elvis songs which mention some body part in the lyrics.

Other anatomical works might be considered "decompositions," as many artists take a no-skin-and-bones approach by focusing on deterioration. Charlie Athenas' interactive computer animation reveals what Elvis would look like if alive today. When activated, a time-lapse progression on the screen shows Elvis' features peeling away to his "current state"–a skull with a bat flying out of his eye socket. Likewise, *Stripped of Flesh*, by Rick Therio, shows a skinless, zombie-like Elvis with eyes, teeth, and hair, singing in his jumpsuit with upturned collar.

Visitors to the Elvis exhibit were greeted by Kevin Matthews' *Just Let Me Alone*, one of the show's centerpieces located just inside the main door. Matthews could have easily titled his piece, *Skelvis*, as it features a lifesize skeleton in tattered costume. A pink scarf dangles from the neck, and the cape is charred, perhaps suggesting burnout. A few strands of hair remain on the top of the skull, and only one dark lens remains in the sunglasses. The ghoulish pose actually resembles a Michael Jackson stance, making the piece even more layered, considering the title and the King of Pop's controversies and public and tabloid scrutiny.

Behind Matthews' figure, skeletons cling to palm trees in Grateful Dead fashion on the side panels of *It Was a Mirage*, an installation collaboration by Marilyn Houlberg and James Thorrick. The title offers a rather compelling perspective on Elvis's life and afterlife, while the piece itself features tinsel, stars, evergreens, sand, colored flood lights and a mirror in which Elvis's image is projected into. Intermittently, E.P. does E.T. as his heart lights up in red.

Lavan also designated cloning and comic corners. Dino Eliopulos and Marcus May, the creators of *The Singing Toilet* from the 1991 exhibit, returned with another mechanical masterpiece, *I'm Cloning Elvis*. When activated, the galvanized steel tube makes kitchen sink disposal-like sounds. A look inside the viewfinder slot reveals fetal figures in various stages of incubation spinning into clones and forming little sideburns.

The exhibit also reflected the widespread treatment of Elvis as a universal and interchangeable cultural component, as many artists juxtapose or substitute Elvis's image with an array of popular culture icons and figures. The cast includes famous rock stars, models, religious and political leaders, cartoon characters, toys, and famous art masterpieces.

Jim Morrison's image from the Door's *The One, The Only* is transformed into Elvis in Geoff Bevington's silkscreen, *Elvis Morrison*, just as comic artist Shane Swank sets the rock record straight with his eight-foot parody of Bruce Springsteen's *Born in the U.S.A.*, *Elvis is the Boss, Bruce is Just an Employee*.

Charlie Athenas works in a similar comic vein, using computer graphics to create a cartoon-like Elvis storyboard romantically linking Elvis with various women. In *Elvis and Elle in Hell*, the panel depicts an Elvis clone and supposed Elle MacPherson in a spaceship eloping to their honeymoon hideaway on Venus. In another episode, *Elvis and Betty Tie the Knot*, Elvis finds the missing 1950s pinup queen Betty Page while hunting for bear in the Ozarks.

*Elvis Gumby*, a father and son collaboration in tempera between Tom and Mars Billings, features dancing pills, and a sideburned clay Gumby aiming a gun at television sets. On occasion, similar Elvis/Gumby jaded comparisons have been directed at the Tulane University mascot.

Gary Dobry also toys with Elvis's image, substituting it for the Mattel boxing robots with Elvis in *Rock 'em, Sock 'em Elvis*, while Dennis Van Keersblick uses a carved broomstick to create his own monster in jumpsuit, *Elvistein*, standing in a Third Reich attention pose in front of a headstone.

Worship and fantasy merge in Charice Mericle's *American Icon*. Three crosses sit atop a metal frame which surrounds a drawing of Elvis wearing Mickey Mouse ears.

The exhibit features a fanfare of familiar figures alongside Elvis. Kirk Smith attaches actual rocks, rolls, and vinyl records to pictures of Elvis and Martin Luther King in his star-spangled wall sculpture, *Kings of Rock and Roll*. Reverend King is also depicted as a molecule in Bruce Tapola's *Defective Flow Chart*, a DNA model that includes Mother Theresa, Ghandi, and Elvis in the center, painted acrylic over a found painting of a kneeling couple embracing.

In *Hunka Hunka Flying Elvis*, Peter Jensen places Elvis alongside Jackie Kennedy in the fateful Dallas motorcade in November 1963. The bizarre historical revision shows blood exploding from

Elvis's head with Jackie in her pink suit smiling. A farewell message written vertically on the black border side reads:

> O' Jackie baby, I know I done you wrong by messin' 'round with those Hollywood whores. But when you enter those Pearly Gates, I'll be waitin' in my Solid Gold Cadillac and will cruise through heaven forever. I love you too much, Baby! The King.

Jensen's dark portrayal of the intersecting Elvis-Kennedy mythologies connects with a popular T-shirt design which states "Elvis Shot Kennedy."

Although one of Elvis's most popular partners in portrait, Marilyn Monroe, was not represented in the World Tattoo show, the touring exhibition, *Elvis + Marilyn: 2 × Immortal*, contains an equally eclectic representation of contemporary artistic visions of the iconic couple. The exhibition's colorful, conceptual, companion catalog complements the various images with insightful, anecdotal commentary from each contributing artist, and a collection of critical essays on the twin myths (DePaoli, 1994).

Several famous works of art are also acknowledged in the World Tattoo extravaganza. Like the Elvenus cover design of *Elvis Rising* in *Blue Hawaiian* surfer pose in a sea shell flanked by angels (see Photo 2.1), James Mesple pays homage of sorts to Boticelli with *Venus Mourning Elvis, Tormented by Cupid, Comforted by Apollo.*

Michelangelo figures from the Sistine Chapel appear in Jethro Kamberos' *When You Are Dead You Are Made for Life.* The comic-like scene is a re-creation of the creation. A robed figure from the clouds reaches down and hands a lightning bolt to the driver of a 1950s Cadillac convertible as a curtain unfolds. Other random floating images in the composition include Elvis's head inside a sun shape, Andy Warhol with a camera, cartoon space explorers, rockets, and Daffy Duck playing bongos.

It is fitting that the most famous Elvis art piece, Andy Warhol's *Elvis*, is represented in the show. Kirk Smith adapts Warhol's red clothed gunslinger into an A-shaped wall sculpture entitled, *Rock It, I'm All Shook Up.*

And one of the most famous portraits, *The Mona Lisa*, receives an Elvis face-lift from Doug Huston. The artist interchanges the two most prominent facial features of the icons–Elvis wears the model's trace of a smile, while Mona's expression becomes the singer's upturned lip snarl.

## THE AESTHETICIZATION OF THE ANAESTHETIC: "SERIOUS" OR "SO-CALLED" ART?

Elvis's presence in such masterpieces, or even within and upon the walls of galleries and museums frequently raises high culture questions of "serious art," let alone art at all. Does Elvis in art represent the aestheticization of the anaesthetic?

Joni Mabe's Elvis works are in celebrity collections (David Lynch, Jay Leno, Roseanne Arnold) and exhibited nationally and internationally. *The Church of Elvis* is the cornerstone of Stephanie Pierce's Where's the Art? gallery. And World Tattoo's annual Elvis exhibits are among the Chicago gallery's most popular and successful shows. Yet, the question and stigma lingers—how serious can an artist be if he or she is using Elvis as a subject?

Pierce is not a believer in fine art, but considers herself a member of what she refers to as the school of "so-called art." She laments that many do not take her "so-called art" seriously. Ironically, it is Elvis who is a blessing and a curse. Despite national exposure in *Rolling Stone's* "Random Notes," Jack Barth's *Roadside Elvis* (1991), various travel guides, and television shows, the Portland area press has largely ignored Where's the Art? during its ten-year existence. "I can't get art critics to cover the gallery; they refuse," says Pierce. "When they did come, they never wrote anything. One critic acted offended, and said 'What kind of way is that to present art—like a supermarket!'"

Lavan's view is more philosophical than resentful. He admits that Elvis art would "probably not be accepted at a more 'conventional' art space" than his World Tattoo gallery. He is aware, however, of Elvis's "place" in art, the skeptical high brow and receptive audiences, and the continuing struggle for serious acceptance. "If you're involved in the arts, you've got to be willing to look at all sides," says Lavan.

Elfans and obsessives are not the only groups attached to Elvis art. Within World Tattoo's clientele are a subgroup of collectors Lavan refers to as "art eccentrics," a fast-growing group of patrons drawn to novelties, Americana, and the "outsider" or "untrained" art of the primitive modes:

> They're interested in what makes America what it is, and Elvis is definitely a part of that. Sure, some of the patrons are into Elvis, but they have a certain amount of sophistication. They don't take things too seriously, which is what we're trying to do as a gallery. We want to create really good shows, and at the same time, stay as far away from the pretentiousness as possible. There's too much of that in the art business. The Elvis show is an example of us not taking ourselves too seriously, but examining something in our culture worth examining.

Lavan believes that although many may not consider Elvis "serious art," that does not diminish the quality of the artistic merit of the work and its creators.

> Just because someone uses Elvis as a subject doesn't mean the artist lacks vision, isn't passionate, creative, or unskilled. Over 100 people viewed the Elvis show, which in itself says something about the interest. I don't know how seriously they took it; that's hard to determine. The work that's meant to be taken seriously is. Other work isn't. But I certainly consider much of the work in the Elvis show to be "fine art."

### *"WHICH WAY TO THE ELVIS PAINTINGS?"*

Elvis's inclusion and intrusion in the art world continues, often in mysterious ways. In a "Shouts and Murmurs" essay entitled, "All Shook Up," in the February 1994 issue of *The New Yorker*, Bobbi Ann Mason juxtaposes Elvis with Edvard Munch's masterpiece, *The Scream*. Mason's essay was inspired by the number of "*Scream* sightings" since the 1893 painting was stolen from the National Art Museum in Norway. The author humorously details the inanimate encounter between the 18-inch inflatable *Scream, Jr.* she received as a gift from a friend, and her ceramic Elvis collectible in singing Las Vegas pose. "Now the King of Rock and Roll and the official spokesperson of angst stand face to face, their mouths hanging open," writes Mason. "It is as if they were meeting down at the end of Lonely Street, one block over from Valhalla." The collectible confrontation, described by Mason as "timeless, yet full of moment," is captured in a photo which accompanies the essay.

Intersecting at similar commercial and novel avenues, students at the Savannah College of Art and Design in Georgia broke the record for the world's largest painting with a 77,000 square-foot replica of an Elvis Presley stamp. The students, working around the clock for one week, painted a smiley-face pin on the King's lapel, a reference to the second-largest painting in the world.

Elvis also surfaces as another standard for "artlessness" in an episode of *Murphy Brown* (CBS), with Murphy engaging in a roundtable discussion about art and taste during a public television forum. Though none of the pretentious panelists are comfortable defining art, they differentiate between what *is* and *is not* "art." Following her outspoken participation as a guardian for elite cultural values, Murphy receives a mock token of appreciation—a Velvet Elvis portrait. "It's not even real velvet," states reporter Murphy, objecting to the fraudulent gift.

Elvis also reigns among the "tacky treasures" of the *More Bad Art* exhibit at the Museum of Bad Art in Dedham, Massachusetts. *USA Today*'s "Lifeline" column (November 26, 1996, p. 1D) printed a color reproduction of Bonnie Daly's painting, *Pablo Presley*, alongside a brief blurb about the exhibit, charity auction, and an accompanying book by Tom Stankowicz (1996) (Vigoda, 1996). While Byron's piece was likely featured due to Elvis's recognizability and promotional power, it also further reinforces his cultural designation as "Poster Child for Bad Art."

Elvis may not travel the high road, or even be widely embraced in art circles. He remains an outcast, or at best, on the fringe; his image synonymous with velvet and easily dismissed as kitsch or memorabiliart that is more conveniently heaped upon the "so-called art" junkpile, rather than displayed in museums and galleries.

One of the purest perspectives on the ongoing Elvis art discussion was spoken during the opening of the *2nd Annual All-Elvis Art Exhibit* at World Tattoo. Upon viewing the show, one visitor offered this concise critique: "Gosh, Elvis is so much more fun dead than he was alive."

The wry observation is poignant in its simplicity. It not only characterizes the Elvis exhibit, but summarizes the subtext of Dan Piraro's cartoon, the *Murphy Brown* "That's Not Art!" episode, and the impressions and expressions of the many artists whose Elvis works have appeared in galleries across the country, from Where's The Art? to World Tattoo to *Elvis + Marilyn* touring and beyond.

The anonymous voice in the gallery crowd could have belonged to Piraro's cartoon character who innocently asks, "Which way to the Elvis paintings?" Both are expressions of casual indifference, if not imperviousness, to aesthetic babble, gallery taste-test talk, and high culture seriousness. The simple response and acknowledgement of the "fun" in Elvis captures, in part, Elvis's active afterlife in American culture, *including* the sacred world of art.

## NOTES

1. Pop Art and its ability to preserve, transmit, and disseminate precise images, can be linked with what Daniel Boorstin called "The Graphic Revolution," a period which dates to 1873 with the development of dry plate photography, and continued until the arrival of commercial television in the late 1940s. Increased media saturation resulted in a cultural evolution into the information age and a collective consciousness that viewed culture in general far less seriously. In the transformation, the line separating popular culture from elite culture blurred. The two merge as the entire spectrum of culture absorbs and reflects some aspects of popular culture. Thanks, Julie Grace, for the art history insights and guidance through this chapter.

2. Many thanks to Stephanie Pierce for her willingness to discuss her art and the gallery with me over the phone.

3. This section of the chapter would not exist without the special efforts of some folks in Chicago. Bill and Virg Kolar provided photographs of the art in the 2nd Annual Extravaganza; and World Tattoo's Jonathan Lavan, not only enthusiastically discussed art and Elvis with me via long distance; but sent posters and exhibition materials; *and*, as if that was not enough, he supplied a personal tour and gallery talk of the entire exhibit on videotape. Many, many thanks.

## Chapter 5

# Unfit for a King:
# Jocks and Jokes, Jumpshots
# and Jumpsuits, Fans and Phantoms

Every year, in the midst of another mid-August melt in Memphis, there is a five-kilometer run that is part of the annual activities and ceremonies during Elvis Presley International Tribute Week. Though The Elvis Memorial Race may not attract a wave of serious runners who might prefer the prestige of the New York, Boston, Chicago, or Atlanta Peachtree Marathons, crossing the finish line at the Gates of Graceland does contain a degree of mythical appeal for participants.

There is also an undeniable subtext of ridicule. The notion of honoring Elvis with any type of athletic event is striking, ironic, and even absurd. While we have culturally expressed numerous Elvis fantasies, jogging is undoubtedly not among the more common. If there is one sporting image of Elvis that perhaps is more easily envisioned, it is that of a professional wrestler. One might mockingly suggest Elvis possessed all the necessary tools—the personality, heavyweight physique, costume, and colorful manager—to star on the World Wrestling Federation circuit.

Understandably, sports has been one of the few places in the American cultural landscape that has remained relatively immune from the pervasiveness of the Presley myth. Though sparse, Elvis representations and references have surprisingly surfaced in a variety of professional and amateur sports settings, with some of the world's greatest athletes and athletic events creating an Elvis sports spectrum which spans, among other things, the peculiar, predictable, promotional, hysterical, and historical.

## ELVIS'S SPORTING LIFE:
## HEAVYWEIGHT PRETENDER

Perhaps the paucity of Presley pieces in sports should not be surprising. Sports is a virtually nonexistent dimension of the Presley myth; thus, there are few reference points to build upon or integrate into an athletic context. More a fan than a participant during his life, Elvis has seldom been viewed in athletic terms. Despite the energy, instinct, and physical abilities he displayed while performing on stage, screen, and supposed sexcapades, Elvis's persona often projected a punk more than a jock; and more feminine tenderness than machismo. And the older, sweating, bloated Elvis invited "wider than the wide world of sports" comparisons, the antithesis of athleticism.

In most biographical accounts, there are only scattered mentions of Elvis's interest and involvement in sports. He is perhaps most closely associated with karate, his longtime hobby, and football, reportedly his favorite sport. Sources vary as to whether Elvis himself participated on the Humes High School football team in Memphis from 1948-1953. One version is that he played during his sophomore year; another states as a junior; and still another asserts that Elvis quit the team after several practices because his coach, Rube Boyer Jr., did not like the length of his hair. In an interview in Jerry Hopkins' *Elvis: A Biography* (1971), perhaps the best factual source on his life, Elvis says he played in several games.

Elvis also took part in pickup games in the Hollywood studio lots during shooting breaks on his film sets. And in the tradition of the Kennedy Clan scrimmaging on the White House lawn, Elvis organized friends and celebrities into teams for football games on the Graceland grounds, with hired referees for the contests.

An avid fan, Elvis enjoyed being quizzed on football facts, players, and trivia. His favorite professional team was the Cleveland Browns. And in 1974, the only year of the World Football League's existence, Elvis faithfully attended all the home games of his city's franchise, the Memphis Southmen.

## ELVIS DON'T LIKE FOOTBALL?

Elvis postmortem association with football has been kept alive largely by former National Football League head coach Jerry Glanville, who perhaps ranks as the biggest Elvis "advocate" in sports. One need only look as far as the title of Glanville's autobiography, *Elvis Don't Like Football* (1990), for evidence. A Harley-Davidson riding coach with a renegade reputation, Glanville personifies Elvis's sneering punk. His teams were marked by an aggressive style of play, taunting and flaunting. Over the years, Glanville's us-against-the-world attitude alienated many opposing, as well as his own, coaches and players.

On the sidelines, Glanville's appearance suggested a greater allegiance to Johnny Cash than Elvis. But his all-black attire was an intimidating fashion statement that conveyed his intended bad-ass image more than a bell-bottomed, rhinestone-studded jumpsuit could. And although his players had a propensity for show-boating, none were capable or courageous enough to integrate a recognizable Elvis routine into their gyrating end-zone celebrations following touchdowns.

Glanville's Elvis devotion became well known in August 1988, during the peak of the Elvis sighting season. Then coach of the Houston Oilers, he left a ticket for Elvis for his team's exhibition game in Memphis versus the New England Patriots. The pass, left at the will-call under "The King," was unclaimed. "I heard he's living in Michigan or Minnesota," commented the coach. "I don't care how much weight he's gained, we still love him."

Glanville's ticket routine triggered a trend which trickled through sports. Major league baseball pitcher Greg Swindell leaves tickets for country singer Garth Brooks whenever and wherever he pitches. "Certainly Swindell has a better chance of seeing his idol than . . . Glanville," observe Mel Antonen and Rod Beaton in their *USA Today* "Behind the Seams" column on baseball's odd and offbeat (1993).

Glanville interrupted his ritual on December 5, 1993, when he returned to Houston for a game with his new team, the Atlanta Falcons, a unit so unpredictable it was frequently referred to as "The Mystery Train." After the head coach admitted he had not set aside his customary free tickets for Elvis, NBC's *NFL Live* studio

host, Jim Lampley, consoled, "Worry not; Elvis has the best satellite dish of them all."

Glanville became widely recognized by the media, players, fellow
coaches, and fans as *the* Elfan of the NFL. A December 1991 CBS
*NFL Today* pregame profile featured race car enthusiast Glanville
speeding around a track, wearing his crash helmet with "Elvis
Lives" written on back. Following the segment, hip host Pat O'Brien
missed the obvious *Spinout* or "No Room to Rhumba in a Sports
Car" connections, but did comment, "Keep doing that Jerry, and you
*will* see Elvis."

That same season before their game against the Washington Red-
skins, the Atlanta coach questioned the legality of his opponents'
blocking tactics. Washington offensive line coach Jim Hanifan responded, "It sounds to me like he's a crybaby. I thought he was a
cowboy. Elvis wouldn't be proud of him."

And when the Falcons played the Saints in the New Orleans
Superdome, November 28, 1991, a CBS camera shot showed a fan
holding up a sign declaring, "Elvis is a Saints fan." Though the
message could be read as a rock and roll heaven reference, it presumably was suggesting Elvis's loyalty was not with Glanville's team.

On January 5, 1992, during an NFL playoff game between the
Detroit Lions and Dallas Cowboys at the Pontiac Silverdome in
Michigan, not far from the Elvis sighting capital, Kalamazoo, the
CBS cameras captured another fan with an Elvis sign. This one
read, "John Madden is Elvis." It was obvious network camera
mugging. The fan no doubt was aware that any poster bearing the
CBS announcer's name, not to mention Elvis's, was likely to draw
the director's eye. The sign could have also been read as a subtle
size reference connecting the rotund Madden with the late-model
Elvis. Whatever the intent or interpretation, the colorful commentator joined Glanville among the ranks of popular culture figures who
had been juxtaposed with Elvis.

These isolated incidents contain some whimsical implications.
First, the settings suggest Elvis prefers the National Football Conference to the American. And second, he likes the comforts of
indoor stadiums, such as the Silverdome and Superdome, a trend
which was perhaps established in the Houston Astrodome when
Glanville coached the AFC Oilers. And when Glanville resigned as

Houston's coach in 1990, did Elvis follow him to the NFC? And was it pure coincidence that an indoor stadium, the Georgia Dome, was built for Glanville's Falcons by 1992? The equation follows that if Elvis were an AFC fan, the Seattle Seahawks might be his logical team of choice. After all, its home field is The Kingdome, an appropriately named indoor domain for Elvis, that is, unless the Pacific Northwest is ruled by competing regional mythologies of local heros Jimi Hendrix and grunge god Kurt Cobain.

The placards also vicariously seat Elvis in the stands among spectators observing other heroic figures and gods. Elvis's poster presence merges not only with sports enthusiasts but religious followers as well. Another connection emerges when considering Elvis's primary poster competition—"Rock 'n' Rollen," a.k.a. Rollen Frederick Stewart. Stewart is the hybrid sports/religion fanatic with the rainbow-colored wig who has made a career of maneuvering the "John 3:16" scripture signs into camera view during televised sporting events. The rock and religion intersection is ironic, as Elvis and Jesus compete for equal time during sports broadcasts.

*Boston Globe* columnist Bob Ryan further muddled the "Elvis's team" question when he flippantly commented during ESPN's Sports Reporters (August 22, 1993) that the New England Patriots refashioned team logo resembled Elvis (Figure 5.1). An Elvis sighting in a sports emblem was reminiscent of claims of seeing Jesus' face in the Shroud of Turin or deciphering subliminal messages in advertisements such as the letters s-e-x in a photo layout for a product. A closer look reveals that Ryan's wry observation is arguably well founded. The Patriot image is just as much Elvis as it is Paul Revere or some other American hero in red, white, and blue. If the logo was designed to convey star-spangled spirit, then Elvis is certainly a worthy representative anyway. One need only consider how he initially symbolized freedom and the American Dream; and how patriotism was such an integral part of his later career, when "An American Trilogy" was the signature song of his Las Vegas shows.

The "New England Elvis's" notion becomes more fun when considering a Patriots' game against AFC rival, the San Diego Chargers. San Diego's lighting bolt emblem, combined with New England's Elvis look-alike, strangely synthesizes into Elvis's own "TCB" lighting bolt trademark. And in January 1997, the Patriots'

FIGURE 5.1. Does the New England Patriot resemble Elvis?

Source: NFL Properties.

appearance in Super Bowl XXXI in the New Orleans Superdome seemed an appropriate kickoff to the twentieth anniversary of Elvis's death.

## *PAGEANTRY, PARADES, AND SCHOOL SPIRIT*

Other "Elvis appearances" have checkered sporting events, whether the preseason or playoffs; in the stands and on the sidelines; during halftime, the historical, and hysterical.

As a grand-scale cultural event, the Super Bowl might be compared to Elvis as the mythic and commercial sprawl surrounding the game/event is ever expanding. The winter ritual annually attracts a record audience. They endure the two weeks of incomparable hype preceding Super Sunday, seemingly endless hours of pregame shows, predictions, and parties, and finally the game itself, which seldom lives up to its "ultimate game" billing.

By the 1990s, as the Super Bowl advertising rates approached $900,000 for a 30-second commercial spot, the networks and sponsors were intent on maximizing viewers and profits during each time period, including nongame slots. Programmers sought halftime extravaganzas and star attractions well beyond the Up With People axis. In January 1993, during halftime of Super Bowl XXVII, Michael Jackson's trademark crotch-grabbing, moon-walking performance provided more excitement than the lopsided game between Dallas and Buffalo.

Jackson's thrills weren't cheap, but proved to be a worthwhile investment for NBC and the NFL. The King of Pop's appearance, which earned an impressive 45.5 rating, contributed to Super Bowl XXVII's 45.1 overall mark, making it one of the highest rated commercial programs ever broadcast. The NFL signed Jackson as a preventive counter-programming move against the upstart Fox network, whose *In Living Color Halftime Show* drew away audiences the previous year, causing CBS' halftime numbers for Super Bowl XXVI to temporarily drop by about 20 percent.

One of *USA Today*'s sports columnists, Michael Hiestand, assessed the networks' halftime current and future strategies:

> Other than getting, say, Madonna or maybe Elvis, for next year's game, it's hard to see how the NFL can find another heavyweight [presumably no Elvis reference intended] capable of keeping network foxes out of its halftime chicken coop. (1993)

Although once again returning to Elvis as a point of origin for all of popular culture, Wiestand overlooked Elvis' halftime appearance in January 1989 at Super Bowl XXIV in Pasadena, California. The Coca-Cola-sponsored intermission marked a "new dimension" in Elvis impersonation, as the extravaganza featured "Elvis Presto, in 3-D."

The spectacle was a near debacle, as Coke failed to distribute enough 3-D glasses to Spectrums, 7-Elevens, and other stop' n' go markets for viewers to obtain for Sunday's gala. These locations represented an amusing marketing strategy as they were frequently cited as locations where Elvis had been sighted.

The 3-D image of Elvis was predictably accompanied by rounds of ridicule. "What's next?" one critic wondered, "A Geraldo [Rivera] graveside investigation of the King's resurrection?" (He may or may not have been aware that Rivera was among the first to probe various Elvis dead or alive conspiracy and cover-up theories on ABC's *20/20*, on September 13, 1979. One could imagine planners brainstorming to devise in a way Elvis had not yet been presented. Their 3-D concept represented further Elvis exhaustion. What could have easily been the impersonator zenith occurred a few years earlier, in 1986, during the Statue of Liberty ceremonies, when hundreds of "Elvii" bumped hips together on stage. The aerial view which captured the El-mass was, as one critic remarked, "Elvis's best angle."

The Presley impersonation pageantry persists. Elvis is clearly an "automatic for the people" attraction, one who has become as commonplace as shriners, marching bands, flags, and fireworks. The King reigns in parades. A regular at holiday, as well as regional events from Mardi Gras to small-town Midwestern harvest festivals, Elvis is also part of Aladdin's Royal Caravan that marches through Disney's MGM Studios Theme Park. Among the colorful cavalcade of characters that includes acrobats, magicians, snake charmers, a Genie, and Jasmine, is "Elvis" wearing a turban, reclining as royalty on a bed of nails.

Elvis "status" was elevated even higher in January 1993. The Clinton presidential inauguration, an extravaganza that threatened to reach the kind of excessive proportions usually associated with the Presley Estate, fittingly included in its parade an "Elvis Is Alive" float overflowing with Elvis look-alikes.

Several months later, in April, an Elvis impersonator sang the national anthem at the historical first meeting between baseball's expansion teams, The Florida Marlins and Colorado Rockies, in Denver's Mile-High Stadium. "You know it's an event when Elvis shows up at the gate," said Rockies' shortstop Walt Weiss. "Either that or you're in a 7-Eleven."

Though Elvis's image frequently triggers a predictable round of sarcasm, his seemingly mandatory inclusion at such grand nationalistic, commercial, and cultural events and ceremonies reaffirms that more than any hero, icon, ritual, or event, from baseball to the Super Bowl, Coca-Cola to Disney, the Statue of Liberty to the President of the United States, Elvis is the King of American Culture.

Another Elvis halftime appearance, this one during the 1991 Sugar Bowl on New Year's Day in New Orleans, might be considered by many more hysterical than historical. While the main attraction was the College football game between Tennessee and Virginia, an entertaining subplot also developed between Elfans and the Award-Winning Virginia Fighting Cavalier Indoor/Outdoor Precision (?) Marching Pep Band and Chowder Society, Unlimited!!

The rag-tag pep band has been marching to the beat of a different drummer since its founding 19 years ago. Uniformed in orange vests and painter's pants, the group scrambles onto the field at halftime while a student announcer provides commentary over the public address system. Known not only for being offbeat and off key, but also off-color, the outfit has frequently orchestrated complaints and controversies. A "contra band" as much as a pep band, administrative officials routinely conduct pregame checks of tubas and snare drums for prohibited items such as alcohol. Although considered one of the tamer groups of the small fraternity of "rogue" college pep bands—a list that includes numerous Ivy League schools, Rice, and Stanford—Virginia's bawdy and barbed routines got the band banned in West Virginia and Maryland.

Tennessee joined the list of those offended following the Sugar Bowl halftime show. The Chowder Society's irreverent presentation titled "Elvis Presley Is Dead," concluded with band members piling on top of an Elvis impersonator. Though approved in advance, as required, by a review of administrators, faculty, and band members, the skit struck a chord. What became known as "the Elvis Incident" placed Elvis squarely in the political correct climate of the 1990s. It was a true "Blue Suede Shoes" scenario; the band could "do what they wanted," but "lay off" Elvis, he was clearly someone they should not have stepped on, or in this case, piled on. Virginia's athletic department received a resentful letter from The Elvis Presley Fan Club, and numerous other complaints from irate fans, many who were so insulted they left their seats during the halftime festivities, or in their view, atrocities.

Elvis was a big man on other campuses as well. While he may have been a twisted part of Virginia's school spirit, he appeared as more of *a* School Spirit elsewhere. Perhaps one of the most unusual Elvis likenesses was pointed out during the 1992 NCAA Men's

College basketball tournament by *Atlanta Journal Constitution* "Sportscene" columnist Norman Arey. Arey's sighting rivals fellow journalist Bob Ryan's impressionistic view of Elvis in The New England Patriots logo, only a shade darker. Covering the Southeast regional game between St. John's and Tulane, Arey observed, "Tulane's 'Gumby' looks like Elvis Presley might if they dug him up today—green with a huge pompadour. . . ."

Other Elvis sports sightings occurred with considerably less fanfare, controversy, and quirkiness. During the second inning of a June 8, 1992 baseball game between the Chicago Cubs and St. Louis Cardinals at Busch Stadium in St. Louis, television director Arnie Harris, whose WGN-Chicago camera crew routinely pans the crowd for women, children, and "the unusual," spotted an Elvis look-alike dressed in black in the bleachers. The Where's Waldo?-like identification that had become so commonplace and routine led to a rather unusual exchange between color commentator Steve Stone and Hall of Fame announcer Harry Carey. Stone insisted to his partner that the face in the crowd *was* Elvis. "Cub fan, Bud man" Carey did not recognize his partner's tongue-in-cheek chiding and grew defensive. "That man is *not* Elvis. I knew Elvis Presley and that is not him!" An uncomfortable silence followed Carey's slurred statement, and the broadcasters quickly shifted their attention back to play-by-play of the game.

In 1996, Elvis was the center of another baseball broadcasting incident. Cincinnati Reds' announcer Marty Brennaman was ordered by Reds management to remove an Elvis shrine he had assembled in his radio booth. One night after the order, a plane pulled a streamer over Riverfront Stadium that read, "21-31! (the Reds' record at the time) It's not my fault! Elvis."

Penn State head football coach Joe Paterno voiced similar sighting skepticism while preparing for the 1995 Rose Bowl. When asked about his heavily favored Nittany Lions' Pacific-10 opponents, the Oregon Ducks, he said. "If I see Elvis down the street tomorrow, I'll believe they (the Ducks) are not very good."

Another reported Elvis encounter further suggested the King's favorite sport to be football. In August 1990, Detroit Lions punter, Jim Arnold, told the *Detroit Free Press*' sports columnist Mitch Albom he had met Elvis at a Krispy Kreme donut shop in Memphis.

"Been friends ever since," said the kicker. "He loves football." Moreover, the two tossed the ball around in Arnold's backyard. "He can throw the ball pretty good, too." Arnold also claims that Elvis gave him one of his trademark gold TCB necklaces. When asked if he was borrowing a page from Jerry Glanville's Elvis-worshiping playbook, or suffering from some similar delusion caused by a hard hit, the punter replied that unlike Glanville, he did not have to leave tickets for Elvis at the will-call window, "I'll give him the tickets myself." The skeptical sportswriter and playful punter's exchanges sounded like a comedy team. "He won't be coming in a UFO will he?" probed Albom. "Come on," replied Arnold, sensing his straight-man's set up. "I don't believe in that UFO stuff!"

### ELVIS HAS LEFT THE STADIUM

Just as Elvis impersonators have frequented sports events across the country, the postconcert signature, "Elvis has left the building," has also been occasionally drawn into the jock jargon of the three major sports—football, basketball, and baseball. When Elfan Jerry Glanville resigned as Houston Oilers coach in 1990, and was fired by the Atlanta Falcons in January 1994, the media could not resist convenient "Elvis has left the building" leads and farewells in their coverage.

It is worth noting that even when removed from football, Glanville relied on his "King connection." With hopes of starting a broadcasting career, the ex-coach chose Ed Hookstratten to represent him, only because Hookstratten was Elvis's agent for 23 years. (Hookstratten was actually the Presley family's attorney, best known for representing Elvis during his and Priscilla's divorce proceedings.) "He told me I was the easiest sell with the networks since Elvis," boasts Glanville (Martzke, 1994).

During a February 23, 1992 broadcast of an NBA game from Market Square Arena in Indianapolis, the site of Elvis's final concert performance, June 26, 1977, NBC courtside reporter Ahmad Rashad reminisced, "When I closed my eyes, I heard the PA announcer say, 'Elvis has left the building.'" In *USA Today*'s weekend television sports summary, watchful columnist Hiestand cited

Rashad's "Best Elvis Mention," adding, "And when he [Rashad] opened his eyes, Elvis really was gone" (1992).

In 1996, Indianapolis city planners proposed building a new sports complex and destroying Market Square Arena. A classic "evil developer versus passionate preservationists" conflict unfolded. While Elvis devotees were furious, Indiana Pacers team officials were clueless. They offered to move a commemorative plaque into the new building, hoping that would suffice as a replacement to the sacred site. "Elvis didn't sing in that new building," one fan said. "If they want to build another one, that would be like tearing Graceland down and rebuilding a house." The standoff continues.

Fellow NBC broadcaster and pop culture junkie Bob Costas also used the phrase at the end of the January 10, 1993 *NFL Live* telecast. When promoting the network's Sunday evening schedule, which included the made-for-TV movie, *Elvis and the Colonel: The Untold Story* Costas' cynicism surfaced. "Believe it or not, something you did *not* already know about Elvis." He then signed off, "As for us, we're out of the building."

One of the most humorous adaptations came, not surprisingly, from David Letterman. In an effort to coin a new phrase for baseball announcers to use when describing home runs, Letterman and his late-night lampooners suggested "Elvis has left the building" replace the worn litany "Going, going, gone," "It's outta here," and "way back . . ." Letterman's voice-over demonstration apparently was contagious as sports anchors across the country adopted the Presley postconcert announcement for narration during home run highlights on their nightly sports reports.

## COMEBACKS, CROSSOVERS, AND NONCONFORMISTS

The "comeback" might also be viewed as a connecting point common to both sports and Elvis mythology. Sports comebacks include both individual and collective accomplishments. Each professional sport has an annual "Comeback Award" in recognition of an athlete who has successfully recovered from an injury or sub-par season. In addition, sports histories and special features document accounts of teams' turnarounds and come-from-behind victories.

Elvis's own comeback has been commonly acknowledged to have begun on July 31, 1969, when he returned to Las Vegas for the first time since 1956, with the first of 51 performances at the International Hotel. His more remarkable comeback, of course, began in August 1977, and has sustained for the past 20 years. Zombie Elvis's "return from the dead," a latter-day Lazarus is a resurrection routine usually reserved for Biblical characters, science fiction, and horror sequels starring Jason and Freddy.

It is on this larger-than-life level that Elvis might be linked with athletes. Just as disbelief accompanies Elvis's death, there is a similar collective expression of shock when an athlete dies because of the widespread perception of invincibility. Elvis's "immortality" and "resurrection" have become a cultural standard, a reference point, often analogous with comebacks, including those in sports. If indeed Elvis's Second Coming occurs, it is a memorable sports line that might best characterize the triumphant event–Al Michaels' "Do you believe in miracles?!" exclamation during the 1981 Olympic hockey victory over the heavily favored Soviet Union.

During NBC's broadcast of an 1989 American League Playoff game between the Oakland A's and Toronto Blue Jays, it was Bob Costas again who was an Elvis name-dropper. With the A's holding a big lead in the late innings, baseball's premier relief pitcher, Dennis Eckersley, entered the game for the save opportunity. "Elvis has a better chance of coming back than the Blue Jays," predicted Costas. Scarred Toronto fans never forgave Costas for his lack of faith in the Blue Jays. Three years later, during game five of the 1992 World Series between Toronto and Atlanta, CBS' Pat O'Brien spotted a sign that read "Costas, you're banned for life," presumably in reference to his 1989 comment.

Along with Bo Jackson's rehabilitation from hip replacement surgery, another athletic comeback which received considerable attention during the early 1990s involved one of professional football's all-time greatest quarterbacks, Joe Montana of the San Francisco 49ers. As Montana's two-year rehabilitation from elbow surgery progressed, and the 1992 playoffs approached, there was much speculation as to whether the 49ers would replace starting quarterback and league most valuable player, Steve Young, with the recov-

ered Montana, who had led them to four Super Bowl championships during the previous decade.

In a *USA Today* front page story which appeared, ironically, on
Elvis's birthday (January 8), columnist Tom Weir assesses the mere
mortal magnitude of a Montana comeback in 1993 within a social
Elvisian context:

> . . . one need only look at how the two-year tale of rehabilitat-
> ing Montana's elbow has been followed. San Francisco has
> stayed even-keeled even while surveying a monstrous earth-
> quake, being hit as hard as any city by the AIDS epidemic, and
> losing a mayor to assassination.
>
> But every time Montana takes 50 warmup tosses at practice,
> its as if not only has Elvis come back, but he's brought John
> Lennon with him. (1993a)

Another Elvis subplot developed with the 49ers in 1993 after
Montana departed for the Kansas City Chiefs. When San Francisco's starting and back up quarterback Steves—Young and Bono—
were injured in preseason games, rookie Elvis Grbac out of the
University of Michigan was forced into the starting role. Throughout his career, Grbac was more successful at eluding rushing de-
fenders than the comparison curse brought on by his first name.
Even when he did not play, Grbac "lived up to his name" and the
irresistible association. When he missed a Michigan game on September 19, 1992 due to an injury, sportscasters and writers covering
the game conveniently labeled his replacement, sophomore Todd
Collins, an "Elvis Impersonator."

Grbac's Elvis "birthmark" was just as noticeable in the pros. In
appraising the 49er preseason quarterback dilemma, *USA Today*'s
Weir chose an Elvis point of view, rather than focusing on Young,
or Bono, whose own name contains rock references that span from
Sonny and Cher to U2. Weir's musings suggest spiritual underpin-
nings of a familiar Elvis savior scenario:

> That the San Francisco 49ers had to turn to Elvis Grbac as
> their exhibition-game quarterback on the anniversary of that
> other Elvis' death was just too good a coincidence. Maybe it's

time to quit lamenting the departure of Joe Montana and get some sideburns growing on this kid. (1993b)

Like Grbac, Canadian figure skater Elvis Stojko also received similar "first-name basis" treatment when CBS packaged the promos for its 1994 Winter Olympic coverage around the silver medal skater. One montage highlighting champion skaters Scott Davis, Brian Boitano, Viktor Petrenko, and Kurt Browning climaxes with Stojko, whom the voice-over dramatically bills as "an upstart named Elvis." Another 30-second spot showcases Stojko exclusively. The segment is shaped into an American Dream minisaga which abandons the traditional skating string music scores for a rockabilly backbeat, show business fanfare, and an introduction that boldly proclaims, "His name is Elvis . . ." A convenient marketing ploy likely to attract the attention of viewers, the name "Elvis" transcends the accomplishments of Stojko and his fellow world-class skaters. And, like the image of Elvis running a marathon or competing in other athletic events, the Olympic promos register an intriguing Elvis fantasy on ice.

Though not obsessive, Tom Weir frequently and casually mentions Elvis in his sports page commentaries. In a consoling column directed at the three cities who lost out to Jacksonville and Charlotte for an NFL expansion franchise, Weir punctuates his thoughts with a comforting, iconic, and hopeful Elvis.

> So take heart, losers. With or without the NFL, St. Louis will still have its arch and Mississippi River lore. Baltimore has its revamped harbor and its crab cakes. And Memphis has the grave of Elvis, occupied or empty. Like the King, you ain't really dead. (1993c)

Weir is not the only *USA Today* staffer who keeps an Elvis vigil in column space. It is fitting that references to the King routinely appear in every section of America's national newspaper (except for the colorful weather map), as if it was an unwritten gatekeeping policy for its pages. While Weir has established himself as leader among the sports scribes, Joe Urschel serves a similar role in the national newspaper's Section A editorial pages. And during the late 1980s, the designated Elvis editor of the "Life" section spelled Elvis's name in mock honor with all capital letters whenever it appeared among the fragments in the quick-read "Lifeline" column.

In addition to Joe Montana, Elvis has demonstrated a knack for being mentioned with some of the most outstanding athletes of other sports. When "The Great One"–hockey's Wayne Gretzky– hosted *Saturday Night Live* (May 13, 1989), one of the sketches he was featured in was called "Waikiki Hockey," an icy parody of the Elvis movie *Blue Hawaii*.

Prominent sportswriter/author Frank DeFord provides a more reverent treatment of Elvis and a superstar in a *Newsweek* essay, "A Rare Bird Bows Out." (1992) On the occasion of Boston Celtic Larry Bird's retirement, DeFord makes an unusual, but perceptive connection between the basketball legend and Elvis. In DeFord's view, both shared common ground as history-changing "cross-overs," in this case poor white boys who crossed color boundaries and distinguished themselves while reshaping predominantly black forms of expression–basketball and blues. DeFord was not the first to color Bird black. In the mid-1990s, *Inside Sports* published a survey of NBA players, and Bird unanimously topped the list in the category "White Players who play 'Black.'" DeFord's black-and-white perspective on Bird's basketball and American Dream fable arrives at a curious intersection:

> In 1979, when Bird at Indiana State (where ?) and [Magic] Johnson at Michigan State met in the NCAA championship, basketball was already accepted as a black game. The old snapshot of the freckle-faced farm boy hurling set shots at the barnyard hoop had been replaced by ghetto boyz dunking at the playground. The '70's had produced some white players who were pre-eminent for a while–West, Havlicek, and Barry at their peaks, Walton for his whole comet career–but Bird, from French Lick, Ind. (where?), loomed up out of wherever, make-believe, a cross between the Devil's own Shoeless Joe from Hannibal, Mo. in *Damn Yankees* and Elvis, taking rhythm-and-blues crossover. (DeFord in *Newsweek*, August 31, 1992)

In a quirky chronology of his personal experiences, Arkansas head basketball coach Nolan Richardson combines 4-H, rodeo routines, and Elvis, into an analogy for basketball standards of excellence when describing the speed, jumping ability, and ball handling of Georgetown University freshman guard Allen Iverson. "I've been through three calf shows, nine horse ropings, and I saw Elvis once, but I've never seen anything like that Iverson boy. It was almost like he had a string on it," said Richardson.

In another hardcourt comparison during the 1993 NCAA Final Four, Elvis's name surfaced, not as a crossover, but in a nonconforming context, as a symbol of rebellion and antiestablishment values. On an *ABC Evening News* segment which aired a few hours before the championship game between North Carolina and Michigan, *Detroit Free Press* columnist and frequent ESPN *Sports Reporter* panelist, Mitch Albom, along with *USA Today*'s Bryan Burwell, both alluded to Elvis when discussing the Michigan squad.

For the second consecutive year, the Wolverines were playing for the basketball title. In 1992, they had accomplished the unthinkable by reaching the championship game versus Duke with an all-freshman starting lineup. Juwan Howard, Chris Webber, Jalen Rose, Roy Jackson, Jimmy King–dubbed the "Fab Five"–captured the imaginations of sports fans and the media. However, amidst high expectations and careful scrutiny during their second season, the super sophomores became more widely known as the "Terrible Twos" than the "Fab Five."

Michigan's court cockiness, a collective presence characterized by baggy shorts, shaved heads, and trash talking, often attracted more attention from fans, the media, and opposing players, and coaches than their impressive athleticism. Critics routinely questioned their lack of sportsmanship and discipline. Many considered their style of play more appropriate for inner city playgrounds (which, of course, is where it originated) than the prestigious Final Four arena with the clean cut kids from Kansas, Kentucky, and Carolina.

Although the brief news segment did not allow for Albom and Burwell to elaborate on the Elvis analogy, their point is a valid connection. Further comparison of gestures, appearances, energy and enthusiasm, raises numerous Presley parallels. The Fab Five's in-your-face demeanor was the equivalent of an Elvis sneer; their shaved heads an Elvis ducktail; their hip-hop style up and down the court reminiscent of an Elvis hip shake across the stage. Not surprisingly, many of the same terms used to describe Elvis's threatening persona also surfaced in characterizations of the Michigan players–menace, defiant, punks, rebel, antiestablishment.

In both cases, there are generational as well as racial subtexts present. Elvis and the Fab Five personified youthful exuberance and alternative expressions which threatened the order of the status quo. Elvis's gyrations sent vibrations through 1950s America, while, at the same time, the black community resented his uprooting appropriation and self-serving integration of their rhythm and blues into the mainstream.

And despite being representatives of a prestigious Big Ten institution, and excelling in what was considered to be a "socially acceptable" setting for African-American youth–the basketball court–the Fab Five remained ominous 1990s figures. Their aggressive style, intimidation, and posturing was narrowly viewed by many as a rim-rattling version of rap music, which had, by the 1990s, surpassed other fear-striking forms of expression, such as rock and roll and heavy metal, as public enemy number one.

*Sports Illustrated*'s Ralph Wiley characterizes the win-at-all-costs world of college athletics as a "plantation system" whose predominant mode of operation exploits student athletes, particularly minorities. The Fab Five were new antiestablishment symbols who rebelled against the slave system of the NCAA structure. Their alternative expressions on the basketball court did not conform to the values, norms, and ideals of the intercollegiate athletic establishment. To many sportswriters such as Albom and Burwell, The Fab Five owed a small debt to Elvis as a standard of nonconformity.

## COMMERCIALS, CARDS, COLLECTIBLES, AND KARATE

One of the most vital dimensions of the Presley myth–commercialism–accompanies Elvis in sports settings through numerous marketing and merchandising linkages.

A commercial parallel might be drawn between Elvis and one of sports' all-time greatest figures, Michael Jordan. While both bear royal titles–"The King" and "His Airness"–they also share another distinction. Both are among American consumer and celebrity cultures' Chosen Few whose images are officially "possessions" and "properties." Just as Elvis is a registered trademark, Jordan's likeness became officially licensed in November 1992, when he, the NBA, and Nike sports apparel resolved a year-long dispute over Jordan's image for merchandising purposes. The financial tug of wars and commodification of the basketball superstar resembled Elvis's situation throughout his career. NBA deputy commissioner Russell Granik's postsettlement statement, that "the three parties are finding a way to live together and prosper," was an eerie echo, Colonel Tom Parker paraphrasing *Star Trek.*

Along those lines, there lies another Elvis-Jordan connection in the Jordanaires, not Michael's Chicago Bulls three-peat teammates, but the gospel/country band often referred to early in his career as "the music behind Elvis." Though an undeniably obscure link, it nonetheless triggers some intriguing possibilities with familiar advertising images. Rather than Hare Jordan, (Bugs Bunny basketball), the Jordanaires could play the Air Jordans in a gym pickup game. And instead of a Jordan shootout with Larry Bird for a McDonald's meal, match His Airness against the King in a royal court one-on-one showdown. Despite the playful potential, most advertisers preferred Jordan to blast off to cartoon planets, among other settings, for his multimillion dollar endorsements.

In February 1994, the Jordan-Presley commercial connection became a 60-second reality, brought to you by Nike. During the annual advertising showcase that the Super Bowl provides, the athletic wear company introduced a long-form commercial featuring Michael Jordan disguised as a character named "Kilroy." The campaign's concept was not a Madison Avenue original. Based on the Is Elvis Alive? phenomenon, and borrowing heavily from *The Elvis Files*, the tabloid-style investigative documentary narrated by Bill Bixby, the commercial integrates Jordan's retirement from professional basketball in 1993 with numerous Elvis-sighting conventions. Comedian/actor Steve Martin is cast as an *Unsolved Mysteries*-style narrator who presents fragments of evidence such as files, documents, audiotapes, video clips, and reports of Kilroy sightings, both on and off the basketball court.

Beneath the ad's spoof-like surface lies a connection and premise that contain considerable validity. Obviously, both Elvis and Jordan were kings of their professional domains. Jordan's departure from the game nonetheless sent shock waves beyond the world of sports. Though not quite the same magnitude of the Presley postmortem response, there was a similar sense of surprise, denial, and disbelief that followed Jordan's decision to retire at the peak of his career and following three consecutive world championships. The situation became more Elvisian in nature as skeptical sportswriters and fans echoed the Elvis faithful's second coming cries with predictions that their god, too, would soon return.

In March 1995, the second coming predictions were close to becoming a prophecy fulfilled. As the baseball strike lingered into threatening a new season, Jordan left the minor league ballpark behind and returned to practice sessions with his former team, the Bulls, as the NBA playoffs approached. The possibility stirred widespread expectations among frenzied fans and nonfans. Historical parallels emerged amidst the wave of top-story, front-page focus. Many considered it the most eagerly awaited sports comeback since Muhammed Ali reentered the ring following a three-year exile from boxing for resisting Army service during the Vietnam War. And others went beyond sports to made iconic King connections, citing Elvis's comebacks from the late 1960s–the NBC television special (December 3, 1968) that marked his first appearance before an audience in seven years, and his first Las Vegas performances (July-August 1969) since 1956–as well as the more recent reported returns from the dead. "I'm amused," said Jordan's agent, David Falk. "This is like the Elvis watch." And during one of his endless postcomeback interviews, Jordan himself acknowledged his royal predecessor. "I'm embarrassed that people treated [my comeback] as if I was Elvis or a god," he told TNT's Craig Sager.

Along other advertising avenues, the sporting goods chain, Champs, ran a television commercial that begins with the proverbial "fat lady singing" opera in a Wagner outfit, and ends with similarly overweight Elvi in costume snarling, "Thank you; thank you very much." The images provide unlikely bookends for the 30-second spot. In between, two channel-surfing teens remote from opera to sports to Elvis. While pausing on one station long enough to catch a glimpse of a professional basketball game, the two notice that NBA stars Don Majerle and Harold Miner are wearing the same shoes that they just bought at Champs. Moving on to another channel, four Vegas-style Elvis impersonators appear on their television screen. Off-camera, the TV-entranced teens' comment sounds like the teen spirit of MTV's adolescent bad boys, Beavis and Butthead, as they don't recognize the impersonator uniforms, "Who's this guy?"

Other by-products have been spawned from the Elvis-sports connection. By the late 1980s, trading cards had evolved from being a hobby to a thriving industry. Specialty shops, card shows, and conventions were havens for collectors. What was once the exclusive domain of sports, particularly baseball, had dramatically expanded its parameters. The one-time king company, Topps, competed with Fleer, Donruss, Upper Deck, and countless others for a share of the card market. With this growth also came specialization as companies tried to translate a plethora of popular culture images, events and icons into 2" × 5" color cardboard reproductions. Among the seemingly endless list of limited edition series were Desert Storm soldiers, Disney characters, serial killers, Playboy playmates, and television shows. A surprisingly late entry, Elvis joined the ranks in October 1992, when Major League Marketing, the Newport, Connecticut, company which distributes Score and Pinnacle brand trading cards, introduced a legend line of Elvis Presley cards. The set features 600 pictures spanning Elvis's entire career (12 cards per park, no gum, $1.49). The edition further connected Elvis to sports as the cards were frequently advertised during commercials of baseball telecasts. And the following year, a Martial Arts Masters 50-card set, which featured a "Fighting Star" card of Elvis, previewed at the National Sports Collectors Convention in Chicago.

The trading cards filled a noticeable El-void in the glutted Presley memorabilia mart. Though such a blank souvenir spot seems unimaginable, other collectibles soon followed. In October 1993, the Elvis Empire's expansion continued beyond sports and into toy territory. Hasbro announced a series of limited edition Elvis dolls. The fully poseable, authentically detailed 12-inch figures depict Elvis at various stages of his career. In keeping with the King's commemorative marketing strategy, the teen idol (1955), *Jailhouse Rock* (1957), and comeback television special (1968) dolls were available January 8—Elvis's birthday; and the gold lamé suit (1957), military (1960), and *Aloha from Hawaii* TV special (1973) available August 16, the anniversary of Elvis's death.

Miniature Elvises staking their claim down toy store aisles and on shelves was not action-figure foreshadowing of a corporate Toy's 'R Us takeover by Presley Enterprises. The gift shops that line the boulevard outside Graceland form their own Elv Is Us. And although the Elvis Kingdom may not quite match the magnitude of Disney's merchandising magic, the recently issued trading cards and line of collectibles are further affirmation of Elvis's endlessness, a set that will never be complete.

Elvis's image has also been exploited in sports as a promotional gimmick, particularly in venues outside the major league mainstream that frequently resort to unusual marketing and promotions to distract from an inferior product and level of competition. *Baseball Weekly* editor Paul White (1994) reported on such an instance eleven weeks into the 1994 major league baseball strike. In his column entitled, "Elvis Has Left the Park," (with a subtitle, "In Maine, you ain't nothin' but a Sea Dog"), White provides a Class A road trip travelogue through the minor league stops in the Northeast corridor.

Corresponding from "Somewhere near Woodstock, NY," White's lead is not the typical baseball-beat writer's first thoughts, even if minor league ball was the only game in any town that summer. "I knew I was in trouble when I saw Elvis," begins White, admittedly suffering from baseball depression. "Pumping gas or on a velvet background at some street corner, I could have handled. But Elvis at a minor league baseball game in Frederick, MD, convinced me it was time for drastic action."

During the initial stages of the strike, White found that escapes such as theme parks and television provided little comfort coping with the reality of life without the majors. Desperately seeking baseball, he embarked on a minor league therapeutical tour. Seeing "Elvis"–"Honest. They told us it was Elvis"–in Class A "amidst the bowling atop the dugout and trash collectors in Beanie-copter hats" was more a source of inspiration than a minor league marketing gimmick for the sportswriter. "Heck, I wouldn't have stayed in Memphis either if Michael [Jordan of the Birmingham Barons minor league team] wasn't going to play," reasons White.

White's playful, but passionate account of the experience suggests divine intervention and guidance at work. It is a familiar role for Elvis. He again is "The Mentor," just as he was in the film, *True Romance* (1993), lurking in the bathroom shadows, offering advice to Christian Slater's character. Only here, his presence more closely echoes the whispering voice in *Field of Dreams* (1989). Elvis's appearance provides a sign for White to continue "down the road and go on faith, the faith that every day I'll find more people who love baseball enough to keep playing."

White's minor league encounter provides further evidence of Elvis's omnipresence, as an intruder or riding the bus on the backroads reminder, no matter the nature or magnitude of the cultural event. One sportswriter's account of an obscure Class A appearance connected Elvis to the prolonged major league baseball strike that marked, if not scarred, the summer of 1994. And, it was part of the Presley living legacy, rather than health care reform or any other issue, that was the only thing capable of distracting the collective consciousness, if momentarily, from the summer's strongest siren—the O.J. Simpson murder case. The similarly strange July marriage of the King's daughter, Lisa Marie Presley, and the King of Pop, Michael Jackson, captured the headlines as well as our collective curiosity, again demonstrating the Presley power.

Elvis analogies became more common as the baseball strike lingered perilously close to Opening Day of the 1995 season. During the March 20, 1995 edition of ESPN's *Sports Center,* baseball correspondent Peter Gammons cites Elvis in his commentary comparing the skills of the striking professionals to those of the "replacement" players. "That's why they paid Elvis millions for a show in Vegas, and pass the hat for impersonators."

Presley promotions persist at minor league parks. In August 1995, the Flying Elvises lighted jumpsuit freefall into L.P. Frans Stadium following a Class A game between the Hickory (NC) Crawdads and Savannah (GA) Cardinals, received "Promotion of the Week" recognition in *USA Today*'s sports section (Ruibal, August 25, 1995:4C).

On a less inspirational level, the Tulsa Ambush sponsored an Elvis look-alike contest for one of its Indoor Soccer League matches. Team General Manager Vernon Riggs upped the incentive from Jerry Glanville's two seats on the 50-yard-line by offering one million dollars for "the real Elvis" to show up. As "bait," the concession stands served jelly doughnuts.

Other events and activities employed similar ridicule while using Elvis's image for promotional purposes. Pedal Power, an Atlanta-based bicycle shop, began its 1992 cycling schedule with a "Legend Lives" ride. The sponsors also used Elvis's eating habits as a focal point, as they set up an Elvisual in, of all places, a bakery window along the 42-mile route. In what could have been considered an allusion to the Mardi Gras' "King Cake" tradition, participants who spotted the hidden King were eligible to win prizes. "Elvis was seen taking out the trash at the Basket Bakery in Stone Mountain–smiling, singing, and sweating," reported bike shop owner Margaret Joffre. According to Joffre, the intent of the "Search for Elvis" ride was not as a tribute from fans, but simply to attract business, as well as riders for Pedal Power's cycling season.

In May 1992, a Schenectady, New York radio station used the Elvis stamp election as a model for its own sports poll. The station asked its listeners whether a statue being erected to honor Los Angeles Dodger manager Tommy LaSorda should depict the heavy LaSorda of several years ago, or the Ultra Slim-Fast version. Under the bold-type heading, "No Elvis Here," the *Atlanta Journal Constitution*'s "Sportscene" (1992) column reported that unlike the Elvis election, fans preferred the chubby LaSorda to the thinner, dieting one.

Another radio station attempted to redefine, or perhaps reduce, a classic world athletic competition to Elvis terms. In January 1988, WTVN in Columbus, Ohio, chose 15 Elvis impersonators for its Elvis Olympic Games, held on the eve of Elvis's birthday. The competition included categories such as pelvis-shaking, singing, and appearance, with the winner receiving $1,000 and a trip to Graceland for two. Although the event transcended the overweight jokes of other Elvents, pelvis shaking as a measure of athletic skill contained a similar irreverent tone.

Though such derision has become commonplace as the Presley myth has evolved, it is particularly convenient in sports. Elvis's martial arts training provides another example. His interest in the various forms began during his Army tour of duty in Germany, and developed into a passionate hobby for 18 years. During that time, Elvis diligently studied tae kwon do and kempo, earning an eighth-degree black belt in the process. He even suffered a broken wrist while practicing in September 1974.

But despite his proven proficiency, the King's martial arts mastery is frequently scoffed at. As recently as February 1992, hip-flip comedian Dennis Miller drew a political analogy to the Karate King. "Yeah, [Dan] Quayle deserves vice president like Elvis deserved a black belt." And in *Spin* magazine's "Dear Elvis" column (August 1993, p. 24), "Elvis" cites "that foreign boy Van Damme" in his "kick or be kicked" reply to a reader's kickboxing query. Perhaps Elvis himself contributed to the mockery by using karate in scenes of his movies, or integrating tae kwon do routines into his stage performances late in his career. While he may have been honored on a karate card, a sweating, overweight Elvis working out kung-fu style in a rhinestone jumpsuit does not exactly conjure images of homage to Bruce Lee or other Masters of the ancient art.

## THE ATHLETIC AND AESTHETIC

Greg Amenoff's sand-trap critique of Elvis's life, *King's Hole,* the cutout installation that is part of *Putt Modernism*'s 18-hole miniature golf touring art exhibit (see Chapter Four) places Elvis in an astroturf intersection of the athletic and aesthetic. Both represent comparatively awkward settings where Elvis has struggled for serious consideration and acceptance. Whether in galleries or grandstands, Elvis's presence in these realms is more frequently accompanied by scoffing, skepticism, and rejection than in other cultural arenas. He is an incongruous intruder. The widespread perception of Elvis "artlessness" mirrors the "lack of athleticism" which likewise deems him inappropriate or unqualified for inclusion in sports.

Sports is indeed a peculiar and demystifying place for Elvis, with its physical focus making the incompatibility more striking. Perhaps more than other prominent political, religious, cultural, and celebrity figures in American popular culture, athletes may be a mythical match for Elvis. They are larger than life heroes, gods and goddesses, with an aura of invincibility that extends beyond the fields of competition to the collective consciousness. Consider how, in 1986, Boston Celtics' first round draft pick (second overall selection), University of Maryland star Len Bias' cocaine-related death shortly after the draft set off a national alarm on drug awareness more potent than the later adopted simplified slogan, "Just Say No," coined by Nancy Reagan. Similarly, after a decade of AIDS, basketball's Magic Johnson tested HIV positive in 1991 and tennis star Arthur Ashe died the following year from the disease. This appeared to magnify the "it can happen to anyone" seriousness more so than others who had contracted the deadly virus.

Despite his own larger-than-life aura of invincibility, Elvis's image does not convey the physical prowess or meet the skillful standards required for "serious" consideration in an athletic context. Nonetheless, as he has managed to do in other unlikely settings such as art, Elvis has surfaced metaphorically and mysteriously in sports, connecting on numerous levels and in valid reference points that transcend the physical.

## THE FAMILY TREE
## AND FALLOUT FRAGMENTS

In the June 1, 1992 issue of *Sports Illustrated*, a two-column feature entitled, "The Pitcher King," appeared among the patchwork of fragments and quotes assembled in the weekly magazine's "Scorecard" section. An obvious reference to the mythical story and Terry Gilliam's film, *The Fisher King*, the title was appropriate as its subject was Elvis's third cousin, Kirk Presley, a high school sports star in Tupelo, Mississippi.

In between charting the family tree–Kirk's granddad and Elvis' granddad were brothers–reporter Sally Guard could not resist sprinkling the brief profile with her own sports-music wordplay such as "making records," "share of hits," and "more like (Denver Bronco quarterback John) Elway than Elvis."

Kirk innocently acknowledged that other than occasional name dropping during a family dinner conversation, or a "phone call from a guy who said he was Elvis," his famous cousin has not affected his life significantly. Yet no matter how minor or distant the connection, the genealogical link is certain to shadow the teenager as a blessing and a curse throughout his career. In the June 1993, amateur baseball draft, when the New York Mets selected Kirk as the eighth overall pick, the media profiles of the pitcher highlighted his Elvis connection as much as his personal baseball statistics. It was just the beginning of Kirk having to deal with fame, not so much his own, but rather to carry his cousin's cross.

With Kirk Presley, a branch of the Presley family tree becomes part of the accumulation of Elvis images and references scattered throughout the wide world of sports. The young Presley represents a biological link, which in some small, and perhaps strange way, legitimizes Elvis's presence in sports. At the same time, cousin Kirk also provides an odd assurance that Elvis's name will likely surface on occasion in sports for as long Kirk's baseball career continues; perhaps at his minor league pitching debut through his progress to the big leagues; in ballpark promotions and questions from reporters during interviews; in newspaper clippings and headlines; and whispers in the stands.

Kirk is family fallout from the Elvis Big Bang. He is one of the many Presley particles that have landed in the world of sports—major and minor, professional and amateur, fringe and novel; from the preseason to the playoffs, in domed stadiums, in the stands and on the sidelines; in bike rides and broadcasts; as family, fan, and phantom, emblem, mascot, and school spirit; in cards, collectibles, and columns; next to the Jordans, Montanas, Gretzkys, and Birds. Altogether, these floating fragments stand as further reminders of how the Presley roots feed every cultural branch.

# Chapter 6

# Elvision: The Presley Panorama

Television has also been a vehicle for perpetuating the Presley myth, with perhaps enough portrayals and performances to program The Elvis Channel, cable television's answer to radio's All-Elvis format.

Elvis himself might be considered an anachronistic television fanatic. Decades before couch potatoes and the eight-hour-per day household viewing average, Graceland was equipped with 14 TV sets, including the infamous three RCAs mounted side-by-side on the wall of The TV Room, which also served as an occasional pistol range for the discriminating viewer King. Just as songwriters interpret the shootout, television's creators have also responded. MTV's Itchy & Scratchy provide a cartoon reenactment of the incident; and "Shoots out the TV every time Robert Goulet comes on" is number one on David Letterman's *Top Ten List*, "Signs That Gorbachev Is on the Verge of a Nervous Breakdown."

Historically, the Elvis-television time line originates in the 1950s, when the infant medium boldly announced the King's arrival via his controversial and legendary hip-shaking, establishment-rattling performances on the period's popular variety programs–Tommy and Jerry Dorsey's *Stage Show*, and the *Milton Berle, Steve Allen*, and *Ed Sullivan Show*s.

Following Elvis's death in 1977, Elvis biographical dramatizations have checkered the network's prime-time schedules, including Kurt Russell's portrayal of Elvis in the Emmy Award-winning made-for-TV movie, *Elvis* (1979, ABC), which beat *Gone with the Wind* and *One Flew Over the Cuckoo's Nest* in the ratings when first telecast, February 11, 1979; Don Johnson's bloated King in *Elvis and the Beauty Queen* (1981, NBC); the highly rated mini-series *Elvis and Me* (1988, ABC); and a short-lived (ten episodes) docudrama series, *Elvis* (1990, ABC); Elvis and the Colonel: The Untold Story (1993, NBC); and the gastro-biography *The Burger and the King: The Life and Cuisine of Elvis Presley* (1996, Cinemax).

Elvision has not been limited to bios, the syndicated talk show circuit, or annual Elvis film festivals, a common cable commemoration of the King's August death. Elvis motifs, references, one-liners, characterizations, and story lines have appeared in a variety of televisual presentations and genres—specials, game show questions and columns, infotainment features, commercials, news, sports, children's shows, situation comedies, dramas, and even promos; and viewing environments—early morning and late-night fringe, prime-time, syndication, cable, network, and independent.

Many of the same Elvis themes and images that songwriters responded to are also popular reference points in characters, conflicts, and story lines of television scripts—impersonators, souvenirs, sightings, stories, deification, and demystification. But what may be most striking about Elvis as a small screen subject is the *comprehensiveness* of the representations. David Marc's view of television's landscape as "demographic vistas," becomes the "Presley Panorama," an Elvis expanse that embraces a broad spectrum of social classes, character types, ages, races, religions, regions, settings, and professions.

## ELFAN EXCESS: SACRED SCHLOCK

That's no hubcap, that's a beltbuckle.

—Alf, commenting on an Elvis souvenir (NBC)

A common postmortem and postmodern critique of Elvis views him as "a cynical commodity to such a point of excess, hysteria, and exhaustion that he actually disappeared into his own promotional culture" (Kroker, Kroker, and Cook, 1989). The adoring fans and commercialization are among the more obvious dimensions of the Presley universe, from Graceland visitors to the Elvisabilia that has been transformed into permanent images in the American consciousness and experience. Numerous sitcom characters, scenes, sets, and settings reflect the commodification, fanaticism, and objectification, both sacred and souvenir, that define the Elvis myth. From the network's prime-time "Must See TV" lineup to Nickelodeon's snickering kid/

adult cable connection, Elvisabilia is a prevalent part of television's iconography, from the obvious Elvis lamp as decor in Joe's apartment on *Friends* (NBC) or pets named "Elvis"–an alligator–on *Clarissa Explains It All*, and a dog on *Are You Afraid of the Dark?* to the quietly cute *Rugrats* pasting Elvis stamps on a toddler, to the subtle license plate slogan–"The Sideburn State"–in the "King of the Road" episode of *The Adventures of Pete and Pete*.

The sacred and souvenir dimensions intersect in a *Designing Women* (CBS) episode in which Mary Jo finds a shovel with the face of Elvis on it in her garage. The Shroud of Turin image solicits a wide range of responses from the ensemble. The requisite over-weight Elvis, Joey Buttafuco, and Jimmy Hoffa jokes are subordinate to the round of characterizations of the artifact–"a freak accident of nature, creepy, bad, amazing, strange reflection, and a sign from God." When Charlene insists Mary Jo has "been chosen," a theological debate over miracle and coincidence ensues. A curious crowd of shovel worshipers, a "paraspectacular paraphernalia" marketing manipulator ready to exploit the find into a profit, and a talk show appearance by "faith healer" Mary Jo parade through scenes before Elvis's image mysteriously disappears at the climax.

Visible in early episodes, but never referred to, Elvis's image on a commemorative Presley plate is part of the living room decor of the Conner's Midwestern home on *Roseanne* (ABC). While the *Jailhouse Rock* illustration is hardly a Norman Rockwellian slice of Americana, the plate's prominent place suggests its value to the blue-collar family.

Such an investment value may be minimal according to an episode of *Blossom* (NBC). Hip teenager Blossom Russo's college trust fund is part Presley portfolio, consisting of "10 shares of IBM and a commemorative Elvis plate." According to her boyfriend's appraisal, Blossom may have to settle for some community college rather than Vassar because she owns the Vegas version rather than more valuable Young Elvis edition of the dish.

An Elvis item is worth nothing to Paul's parents during an iconic face-off in *Mad About You*. Jamie offers an Elvis silver spoon to her in-laws as a replacement for their commemorative JFK utensil that she lost. The Buchmans flat-out refuse.

Although the resale and flea market value of Elvisabilia may be high, there are some collectible items money cannot buy. Blanche, the Southern senior citizen on *The Golden Girls* (NBC), refuses to contribute her Elvis salt and pepper shakers for a garage sale. "The cherished things he left behind—movies, songs, and seasonings," chides Dorothy, the anti-Elvis of the golden group. (On the animated series *Bobby's World* [Fox], the mother also owns a set of the spice shakers.) In other episodes, she characterizes an unauthorized Elvis fan club as a "support group" for Blanche, and ridicules another of her genuine Elvis artifacts—a partially-eaten pork chop in a glass container. "Didn't he have beautiful teeth?" boasts Blanche. "Elvis would have never left this much meat on it," replies Dorothy with the requisite fat joke.

On a larger scale, Davey, the Irish doorman in *The Days and Nights of Molly Dodd* (NBC, Lifetime), is the proud owner of one of the Cadillacs from the King's fleet. When he shows his building tenant Molly the prize possession "he bought from one of the King's bodyguards in '72," she appears bewildered by Davey's casual royalty reference. "The King?" a doubting Dodd asks. "Elvis," replies Davey, bluntly in a "who-else?" manner.

Elvisabilia is also a popular gift item. On *Grace Under Fire* (ABC), a single-parent sitcom with a Southern nasal accent, homeowners present the Neighborhood Watch captain with an $8 \times 10$ photo of Elvis in the Army.

On *Doogie Howser, M.D.* (ABC), teen doctor Doogie and his best friend Vinnie visit spiritual adviser Madame Maureena to inquire about Vinnie's film school future. As the prophetess gazes into her crystal ball, Elvis gazes down from a poster behind her. The image on the wall transcends the souvenir. Hanging like a cross or other religious icon, the poster has a deifying aura of omnipresence and divine guidance more mystical than the Madame's.

While many Elvis artifacts contain meanings as symbols of spirituality and salvation, a darker side is presented in the Oregon woods "sap opera," *Twin Peaks* (ABC), created by David Lynch and Mark Frost. Jack-of-all-sleaze Benjamin Horne rises from bed with his mistress, clutching what appears to be a small Elvis bottle or doll. "Going to give Little Elvis a shower," says the villainous Horne. Though the miniature object only appears in one episode, and its form, function, and contents remain vague, it nonetheless becomes an evil accomplice with Horne; guilt by association as he commits seven deadly sins. The object is also fitting as a token tribute that juxtaposes one mystery–Who Killed Laura Palmer?–with the cultural mystery of mysteries–Elvis.[1]

Elvis references are routinely included in episodes of *Full House* (ABC) and *Coach* (ABC), primarily because the characters Jesse Katsopolous and Luther Van Dam are die-hard Elfans. Together with Blanche, Carla from *Cheers* (NBC), and Charlene from *Designing Women* (CBS), they comprise an Elvis Fan Club of television characters.

Jesse, an aspiring rock musician, is among the members of the extended family unit that fills the San Francisco house on this cute sitcom. Jesse's Elvis devotion has been a staple of the long-running show's scripts. His name itself may be derived from Elvis's stillborn twin, Jesse Garon. The King is a part of every big event in Jesse's life. Standing beneath the Elvis poster in his room, he lobbies for an Elvis wedding rather than a traditional ceremony and reception preferred by his fiancé. The couple engage in a similar debate when choosing names and a nursery theme for their twins (another sibling subtlety?). Although Elvis loses out to "Fun at the Circus," Dad provides a consolation prize–a mobile with little jumpsuited Elvii to dangle over the crib. Throughout the show's eight seasons, friends and relatives routinely call attention to Jesse's impressive inventory of Elvisabilia, including car wax, "Love Me Tender" underwear, a Colonel Parker pepper grinder he received as a gift to go with his Elvis spice rack. "I couldn't imagine him happier, unless he found out he is related to Elvis," says his wife following a joyous family moment. Cousin Joey reveals that Jesse "spent more time voting for the Elvis stamp than the last three presidents."

Jesse is also determined to pass the royal legacy down to future generations. He works on an Elvis jigsaw puzzles with his twins, and teaches his niece singing and karate "the Elvis way" for her school play. And when Jesse enters a contest, it is not surprising he performs an Elvis medley.

Fumbling assistant football coach Luther Van Dam is the Big Elvis Fanatic on Campus at Minnesota State. He and his best friend, Head Coach Hayden Fox, frequently engage in Elvis believer/nonbeliever debates. One such incident involves Luther's missing Elvis towel. "Do you know how much it's worth!" asks a panicked Luther. When Coach suggests his friend invest in something more conservative, such as real estate, Luther defends the value of his souvenir. "It is conservative; it's the cheapest thing in the Elvis catalog," he says. "I could've bought the bag of Elvis hair from a barber in Memphis but they couldn't guarantee it." As a custodian pushes a cart with a bundle of dirty towels past Coach's office door, a hopeful Luther gives chase, becoming a metaphor for the broader cultural Presley pursuit. Luther's "condition" only worsens. In a 1997 February sweeps episode, the fanatic further forsakes Coach's financial advice and blows his $50,000 life savings on an Elvis suit at an auction in Las Vegas.

Perhaps the most inventive presentation of Elvisabilia could be found in the pay-all-your-bills cable game show *Debt* (Lifetime), hosted by icon Wink Martindale. In one challenge, contestants could win cash and a trip to Graceland if they could throw an inflatable Elvis off a building into a Cadillac convertible several stories below.

## DISGRACELAND OR AMAZING GRACELAND?

Elvis's house has *balls*.

–Michael St. Gerard,
who played Elvis in *Elvis* (ABC)

. . . Graceland strains and bulges with that kind of secret stuff. It's like looking at your own living room through the eyes of the Avon lady. . . . Ghosts walk through [the mansion] alongside every tourist, whispering softly about the places we call home.

–Karal Ann Marling,
*Graceland: Going Home with Elvis* (1996)

Graceland, whether viewed as a symbol of redemption, a royalty reaping ripoff, or gathering place for necrophiliac jamborees, provides an attractive mid-South source for television scriptwriters. Instead of characters interacting within the usual sitcom settings such as the office, living room, or kitchen, they escape to Memphis where they stand before the iron music notes of Graceland's gates, and are surrounded by the kitsch and commercialism of the Jungle Room and boulevard gift shops. The setting is inherently rich with reference points and comic one-liners, enough for numerous shows to structure entire episodes around.

One of the more unusual references to the Elvis estate appears in the opening montage of the reality show *Cops* (FOX). A shot of a green "Graceland" sign with an arrow seems slightly out of place among the urban nightscapes and crime and punishment camcorder images which appear on the screen as Ziggy Marley's "Bad Boys" bounces on the soundtrack.

*Murphy Brown* spins the mansion and its excess into a political analogy, characterizing the White House as a "Republican Graceland without Elvis."

The site is more commonly used as a backdrop in gags and as a destination for characters in sitcom story lines. Carla, the feisty waitress at *Cheers*, hopes a change in the Boston bar's management will result in a "real vacation" for her—six weeks at Graceland instead of just one. Likewise, when the Winslows lobby for vacation spots on *Family Matters* (ABC), Grandma prefers Memphis to Disneyworld, Lake Geneva, or Las Vegas.

A weekend in Memphis is a dream come true for both Hayden and Luther on *Coach*. For Hayden, it is a chance to mingle with the elite of his profession at the national coaches convention, and for Luther it means just one thing—Graceland. Anticipating a souvenir spree, Luther takes an empty trunk with him for Presley purchases. When they arrive at their hotel lobby, Coach expresses his relief that they did not spend their entire weekend at the airport gift shop. "Thanks for rescuing me from there," says Luther, already sporting an Elvis cap, "The King Lives" button, and chewing Elvis gum. In two days and two visits to the mansion, Luther's trunk becomes Elvis excess baggage, filled with a wig, sideburns, blue suede bathroom slippers, sequined robe with "The King—Love Me Tender" on back, and silk, bell-bottom, collar-up pajamas. To make the visit even more complete, he goes on the Elvis Impersonator Riverboat Cruise.

Hayden further experiences Luther's fanaticism when his reservations get mixed up and he is forced to share a room with his assistant. Things get worse for the whiny head coach. He forgot to pack pajamas, so he has no choice but to wear Luther's Elvis sleepwear, a fashion fate comparable to cross-dressing for the macho Elvisphobic. Luther's sour serenade of "Heartbreak Hotel" as a lullaby does little to comfort his humiliated friend lying next to him.

Graceland is also the setting for a *Designing Women* episode titled "E.P. Phone Home." This script presents a tender view of Elvis devotion as the partners of Atlanta's Sugarbaker Interior Design Firm travel to Memphis. Charlene is the Elfan among the associates. Her devotion is established during the show's first season opening titles and credits, as a framed Elvis photo is a part of her montage of still shots assembled to introduce each character.

In this episode, a client gives Charlene four tickets for a V.I.P. tour of Graceland during Elvis Club's Nostalgia Weekend. She enthusiastically tries to convince her uninterested partners to do Memphis and the King's place. The familiar Elvis "believer/nonbeliever" struggle emerges. "You get to see rooms nobody sees!" begs Charlene, who also gets free hotel accommodations because she owns an authentic piece of Elvisabilia–an autographed hand towel that Elvis actually wiped his face with. The incentives cannot initially sway Mary Jo, Suzanne, and Julia, who is the most hostile resister. "I'd rather be tied buck naked to the town clock," she exclaims.

The story line's souvenir emphasis and stereotypical characterization of Elfans parallels the *Coach* episodes, with Luther and Charlene kindred spirits. Charlene, too, defends the value of her towel, which she keeps frozen in Tupperware to preserve its original sweaty state. "Listen, this is an authentic, not like all that other worthless junk people spend their money on," the helplessly devoted Charlene blindly rationalizes, adding that she "just couldn't resist" and "only buys the tasteful ones."

In addition to the souvenir saturation, the episode is filled with other familiar Elvis reference points and character types framed within a believer/nonbeliever context. Among the Presley paraders whom Charlene and her accompanying design skeptics encounter at a Graceland coffee shop are Del and six-year-old Ricky, a father-son Elvis impersonator duo whose costumes are made out of his wife's wedding dress from her previous marriage; a condescending tabloid reporter doing a feature on hard-core Elfans, whom he reduces to "geeks, weirdos, losers;" and Vern, a truck driver from Mississippi, whose son died of leukemia at age eleven and was buried with a "TCB" beltbuckle.

Though an obvious synthesis of Elvis's father, twin brother who died at birth, and occupational roots, Vern represents Elvis incarnate, a holy man destined to reach even the most ardent disbelievers such as Julia. Vern's "Elvis story" contains religious elements such as healing, universality, revelation, mysteries of faith, and conversion. Elvis's songs were serenades of salvation for Vern as he coped with his son's death. His testimony is familiar filled-with-the-spirit fare: "I don't know what it is that Elvis gives people. But whatever it is, I felt it. It picked me up. Kept me going. Got me through."

Meeting Vern becomes Julia's "Elvis experience." Her rescue of him from becoming another print victim of the tabloid reporter is fate. Julia is touched by Vern's story and recognizes a common ground; her son is the same age as Vern's son. The experience reveals part of the deeper spiritual meaning of the Presley myth as it marks a transformation of the biggest doubter among the Sugarbaker Elvis dissenters.

The visit has not converted Mary Jo and Suzanne. On the ride home, they complain about the cheap hotel, Elvis kooks, and "weirdest weekend," and nag Charlene about her need for a 9' × 12' Elvis rug. "I can't explain it," she says. "It's a sickness."

A call-in song dedication on the radio for Julia from Vern interrupts the backseat psychoanalysis. As "Are You Lonesome Tonight?" plays, Julia rests her head against the window and gazes contentedly out. The closing shot reveals their car driving into the darkness with an "E.P. Phone Home" bumper sticker affixed to the rear. The sticker is presumably the same one Charlene bought when they first arrived at Graceland. Embarrassed at the time, Julia refused to have the souvenir placed on the car, and stuffed it in her purse. As they leave Memphis, Charlene asks for the sticker and Julia lies, saying she lost it. Julia's secretly placing the souvenir on the car is a religious rite, an affirmation of her conversion and newfound understanding of Elvis Presley.

Religiosity is also implied in an episode of *Newhart* (CBS), as Vermont's backwoods brothers Larry, Darryl, and Darryl participate in a walkathon. Fourteen hundred miles later they phone Dick at The Stratford Inn to tell him they have arrived at their destination—

Graceland. There is a sense of fate and an inevitable journey to the promised land in the scene. The brothers are foot soldiers on a spiritual quest; they are the three wise men following a distant star; they are the "poorboys and pilgrims" of Paul Simon's song who arrive at the gates with "reason to believe they shall be received."

*Grace Under Fire*'s (ABC) Graceland episode features the familiar diner scenes, encounters with mysterious strangers who embody Elvis, a mansion montage using actual stills, and a wedding bouquet-catching fantasy about marrying a seed salesman whom Grace mistakes for the immortal Elvis. While it may not contain the rapid-fire references of the *Coach* and *Designing Women* Memphis meccas, there are two lines that linger. Looking around during the tour, Grace remarks, "Elvis just didn't have enough stuff, did he?" And, following the visit, Grace appears moved. The mansion was not the museum she expected. "It's like they took a piece of Elvis's life and freeze-framed it," she says. "Now I know why everybody comes here." While the comments may be quite simple and accurate in their characterization, they serve as a poignant parenthesis for Grace's Graceland experience. They are playful and prayerful points connecting Disgraceland and Amazing Graceland. And in between there lies more. You can hear it in the tone of Grace's nasal voice. The sound is similar to the expression on Julia's face gazing out the car window following her visit. There is reflection in Grace's words; they don't surprise, solicit, or even seduce laughter like standard sitcom lines. Instead, they speak for many visitors at Graceland. They whisper, they wonder, and they wish.

## *"I DID NOT SEE ELVIS . . .": GHOSTS, GODS, AND (IF I COULD) DREAM SEQUENCES*

*Charlie:*  He's back.
*Sydney:*  Who's back?
*Charlie:*  Elvis . . . Who do you think?

*—Civil Wars* (ABC)

The faith and doubt, fanaticism and skepticism, ghosts and gods, dreams and reality, and dead or alive debate that connect points along the Elvis sightings spectrum provide dramatic elements, conflict, and comic relief easily adapted into television narratives.

Although the titles of the reality shows *Unsolved Mysteries* (NBC) and the syndicated *In Search Of . . .* may best characterize the posthumous Presley fascination, these documentary-style programs have avoided Elvis in their investigations. A sketch on the comedy/ variety series, *In Living Color* (FOX), provides a parodied glimpse of what a typical tabloid inquiry might find–a grossly overweight Elvis trying to hide behind a tree from a reporter and videographer.

The Canadian comedy troupe, The Kids in the Hall, present a more unusual, but memorable meditation on Elvis being alive with a sketch entitled, "If Elvis Was My Landlord." The fantasy is a visual version of "Jesus Was Way Cool," the metaphysical musical mono-toned musings of another Hall, John S., of the New York band, King Missile. According to the Kids' landlord litany, tenant "life would be a *Roustabout*"; Elvis "could have my key, would let friends come up, let us play music loud, eat cheese curls instead of pills, sweep my halls, and tie your garbage bags." The sketch closes with the apartment dweller paying rent to Elvis, who is wearing a toolbelt over his jumpsuit. "Elvis has left the building" punctuates the routine. (The same line also closes an episode of *Frasier* [NBC] and is para-phrased into a classroom entrance announcement for a teacher on *Mr. Rhodes* [NBC].)

Elvis updates are more frequently found in syndicated infotain-ment fare such as *A Current Affair* and *Hard Copy*, and occasionally the soft focus of prime-time magazines, such as *48 Hours* (CBS), which produced a "Crazy About Elvis" edition in 1992.

Advertisers have also adapted the sightings phenomenon into commercial campaigns. "Now do you believe in Elves?" says a Keebler elf to a skeptic. "For another cookie, honey, I'd believe you were Elvis," she replies. One of the commercials in Anheuser-Busch's Bud Dry's "Why Ask Why?" series attempts to explain "why rock and roll will never die," with images that include Elvis as a gas station attendant, and in an elevator with an exiting passen-ger doing the familiar double take. "While legends may come and go, cool refreshment is here to stay," the announcer states in the tag, failing to mention that "so is Elvis."

It should not be surprising that Elvis's name is dropped frequently on *The X-Files* (FOX), television's most intelligent dramatic series, a creep show which blends government conspiracies, hoaxes, cover-ups, paranormal and psychic activity, and inexplicable phenomena. Dour FBI agent, Fox Mulder, whose obsession–"The truth is out there"–serves as the show's premise, integrates Elvis into his personal and professional outlook as a standard on the belief scale. Mulder's training appears to have included sociologists Eric Hoffer and Leon Festinger's concepts of "true believers" and "cognitive dissonance." "This is the part where they bring Elvis out," Mulder tells his partner Scully while sitting at a faith healer's revival, a miracle ministry under investigation. "People looking hard for miracles make themselves see what they want to see." Mulder refers to another agent who is closed minded to anything "strange" as "the type of person who thinks Elvis is dead." And his lament for the lack of leads in another case includes Rodney King and the King. "People videotape police beatings on dark streets; there are sightings of Elvis in three cities everyday. Yet nobody saw a pretty woman being run off the road in a rental car." And while searching for deep, dark family secrets in the incestuous Peacock clan's decrepit house, Mulder sighs, "Oh no!" as his flashlight illuminates an old newspaper with the headline "Elvis Presley Dead at 42." Mulder's moan is mocking, yet self-conscious, as he is too aware of his own obsessive pursuits of elusive phenomena.

An episode during *The X-files* fourth season provides a seemingly inevitable revelation about the suspicious-minded agent. Mulder uses his vacation time for what he calls a "spiritual journey" to a "special place" he has always wanted to go to. When Scully asks how she can get in touch with him, Mulder refuses to reveal his destination. When he later calls to check in, Mulder is in Memphis at Graceland. The droll Mulder displays a childlike, candy store exhuberance. He wears Elvis-style sunglasses and imitates the King's karate routine after he hangs up his cell-phone, never disclosing his location to Scully.

Agent Mulder's skepticism standard has been used by others as a measure of credibility, or lack of it, in numerous television exchanges:

> She and I believe it just like we believe you believe Elvis is performing at Radio City tonight.
> > —attorney, *Law and Order* (NBC)

> The one [car] with Elvis in it.
> > —doubting detective, *Law and Order* (NBC)

Yeah, she thought she saw Elvis's face in a package of beef jerky.

—a neighbor, *The Trouble with Larry* (NBC)

That's a good theory; did you come up with that one the last time you sighted Elvis?

—husband to wife, *Step By Step* (ABC)

Yeah, and Billy's Mom thought she saw Elvis at the gas station yesterday.

—Tim to his son, *Home Improvement* (ABC)

Is Elvis there, too?

—Bart Simpson asks Homer, who has called home from a mental institution and tells the family about a delusional patient who thinks he is Michael Jackson, *The Simpsons* (FOX)

The surreal setting of *Eerie, Indiana* (NBC) (Fox), a *Wonder Years* in *The Twilight Zone*, similar to the *X-File* environment, is an ideal place for Elvis to take up permanent residency. In the show's opening titles, a montage establishing Eerie as "the weird center of the planet," includes "Elvis" strolling out in his sunglasses, bathrobe, and slippers to pick up the morning paper on his front lawn. There is a Cadillac in the driveway and an American flag draped in his window. The image suggests one of the popular post-Presley theories, that Elvis remains alive as part of the government's witness protection program, a theory which grew out of his honorary, and ironic, appointment as a federal drug agent during the Nixon administration. The Midwestern location is illogically logical for Elvis; what better place to hide out inconspicuously than in a neighborhood where Big Foot goes through the trash, UFOs land in cornfields, and a coven of zombie housewives host Tupperware parties. No doubt, the Loch Ness monster swims at the local quarry.

The only person who notices the strangeness in the placid town is the paperboy, 13-year-old Marshall Teller, a transplant from New Jersey. Marshall eventually runs into the "weird fat guy" from his paper route while at his favorite hangout, World of Stuff, a one-stop antique shop, arcade, and diner. "Say, aren't you . . . ?" says Marshall, a familiar verse to the familiar face in sunglasses and a white jumpsuit eating a burger at the counter. Marshall needs advice about how to handle the competition for the new girl in town, whom he wants to ask to the seventh grade dance. "Get her something tender and nice, like a Cadillac," offers the man. "I'm fresh out. Love's a heartbreaker." When Marshall's coming-of-age counterpart Kevin Arnold finds himself in a similar dating dilemma in the 1960s suburbia of *The Wonder Years* (ABC), he too, looks to the wise King for guidance, as he wonders to himself, "Now, what would Elvis do?" Though the King clone cameo in *Eerie* is brief, Marshall's revision of the "live fast, die young" adage to "living on the frontier between life and death," is fit for the 1990s King.

Marshall's *Eerie* Elvis encounter mirrors Jesse's on *Full House*, when he loses sight of his family values while pursuing a record deal. A familiar formula, or Presley pattern, is evident: The diner setting is convenient for fat jokes (Elvis pours gravy on his salad); the character (Jesse) delivers an initial "familiar face" response ("You look like someone . . .") to a heavy-set, sideburned guy in fashionable Elviswear (scarf), who responds with a clue ("Thank you; thank you very much"), but the confounded character still cannot place the face ("looked exactly like Wayne Newton"), but nonetheless pours his heart out to the stranger, who, like a guardian angel, offers Elvisian wisdom ("Take care of business"). Elvis episode script complete.

"Spotting Elvis," an episode of the short-lived, hour-long series *Johnny Bago* (CBS), is an unusual environmental encounter with Elvis in a Pacific Northwest forest. The cast of characters includes overzealous eco-warriors, territorial lumberjacks, tabloid reporters, the endangered spotted owl, and the on-the-lam con man Johnny Tenuti. When Johnny's Winnebago is forced off the road by a logging truck, he winds up in Mystery Trees R.V. Park and Campground where his "weird neighbor" is a potbellied, sunglassed, gun-happy Elvis "layin' low" in a trailer hitched to a pink Cadillac. Although cast as the familiar guardian angel, mystical mentor, and shadow figure who twice rescues Johnny from hostile deep forest surroundings, Elvis is vulnerable, and hungry. Explaining to Johnny why he went "the RV route," Elvis refutes the various conspiracy theories that have circulated regarding his "disappearance," slipping in Jimmy Hoffa, Lee Harvey Oswald, and Richard Nixon references in the process. "I just wanted to eat," he tells Johnny while preparing a stack of deep-fried fluffer nutter sandwiches with banana. "I lost *it!*"

Johnny attempts to mend the King's damaged self-esteem. He encourages a royal return to splendor, but must first give Elvis a refresher course on how to be Elvis, an instructional sequence that has become commonplace, particularly in presentations involving retro time travelers or impersonators. Elvis's comeback trail begins in the forest, where his live performance unites the loggers and eco-activists in a magical musical production number reminiscent of one of his films. Elvis then "leaves the forest" for the Wacky Wee-chie Water Show. Johnny's encounter with Elvis and nature causes him to reflect upon "greening" from both commercial and conservation contexts. In a concluding moral of the tale, Johnny explains to his mother why he did not "cash in" on Elvis or his fake photograph of a spotted owl. "See, Ma, we gotta take care of our legends; everybody's always trying to chop 'em down to size."

In addition to being staples of tabloid television inquiries, sightings, story lines, and references have fit naturally into dramatic presentations with professional broadcast and journalist settings. On *Good Sports* (CBS), a short-lived series featuring Ryan O'Neil and Farrah Fawcett as co-anchors, the staff socializes at a local comedy club where stand-up comedian Richard Belzer tells an Elvis fast-food sighting joke. Belzer's routine is a microcosm of the comedy circuit, where Elvis has been a running gag for years. Though its broadcast life was even shorter than *Good Sports*, *WIOU* (CBS) managed to pass a sightings story through the gatekeeping process at WNDY. At the financially troubled station, one editor's soft news is another's front page headline, especially if the story involves Elvis.

WPIG radio resorts to an Elvis Impersonator contest to boost it's ratings, a ploy which prompts a Les Nessman editorial at *WKRP in Cincinnati* (first run syndication). The nerdy Nessman accuses the competing station of "sinking to the lowest depths of sensationalism for its own selfish purposes," saying they should be ashamed and allow Elvis to rest in peace. Nessman's sincere words result in a call from Elvis himself. WKRP management, in turn, want to "bring Elvis in alive" and broadcast his comeback, a story line derived from actual radio station promotional gimmickry during the late-1980s. An Elvis stampede, in which the real Elvis escapes ("Run Elvis, you're in danger!" cries a staffer) leads to some final on-air thoughts from Les and late-night DJ Mona Loveland. "If you're out there somewhere, please, stay out there somewhere," pleads Les. Mona follows, "Elvis is alive. He has to be. There's just too many people that need him." Lurking outside their studio window is Elvis in his familiar ghost and god guise to punctuate and perpetuate the episode.

An Elvis look-alike named Elwood Pressler joins the FYI staff as a temp out of *Murphy Brown*'s endless secretary pool. When introduced to Elwood, members of the news team respond with "Where do I know you from?" puzzlement. Miles swears Elwood is Jay Leno; others mistake him for Roy Orbison. During the last scene of the running gag, Murphy walks by Elwood's desk where he is in the middle of a hushed phone conversation. "No, I said the *jumbo* chicken box!" he raises his voice. Murphy stops, does a double take with a "No, it couldn't be" frown that expresses both doubt and reassurance.

Sensational journalistic settings are secure settings for Elvis. The *TV Guide* ad for the premiere of *Naked Truth* (ABC) inquires about its lead character, a tabloid reporter, "Is Nora having Elvis's baby?" In "Heartbreak Hotel," an episode of the syndicated horror antholo- gy *Freddy's Nightmares*, hack Roger Ditano is assigned to investi- gate an Elvis sighting at a hotel in sleepy Springwood. Wry dialogue regarding Elvis's whereabouts between Ditano and the hotel clerk threads the scenes. "Nope, left this morning to do a concert with John Lennon," the quirky clerk responds when first asked about the hotel guest. Later, Ditano inquires, "Is Elvis back?" "Nope, not yet," says the clerk. "Of course not," says Ditano. Days later, the frustrated reporter, now pursuing a different story, storms past the front desk. "Just thought you'd want to know . . . Elvis is dead," confirms the clerk. "Thanks for the news flash," says Ditano. Nei- ther man really believes Elvis is alive; their deadbeat discourse are mere formalities and part of their mundane jobs.

Elvis does eventually appear in Springwood, but at the hospital rather than the hotel. Editor Ellen arrives to make arrangements for reporter Roger, who has choked to death on a jawbreaker. As she waits at the nurses' station, an orderly pushing an appliance dolly with a corpse on it wheels by. The stiff passenger is a male, in his 50s, with a jet black bouffant, bright blue satin bell-bottom rhinestone jumpsuit, eyes frozen open, upper lip in snarl. "Who's that?" asks a fixated Ellen. "Elvis," Dr. Coppage firmly answers. "Is he dead?" asks Ellen. "Of course, everyone knows that," he reassures the unconvinced

*The World Enquirer* editor who races after her story as it rolls down the corridor.

The final scene neatly captures our continuing cultural curiosity and faithful fanaticism. Contrary to Dr. Coppage's belief, not everyone knows, or accepts that Elvis is dead. The whispers of faith and doubt linger and many continue to chase the ghost.

The ghost characterization has been a common televisual response to the posthumous Presley sightings. Elvis "ghosts" have appeared in the cartoon spook spinoff *Beetlejuice*; at a costume party and Halloween haunted house on *Roseanne* episodes; and been the basis for a legal case on *L.A. Law* (NBC). In the dramatic series, a defendant claims a real estate contract should be void because the house he bought is haunted. According to the testimony, the paranormal nuisance is not rattling chains, but faintly singing. When probed further, the witness swears the crooning spirit is Elvis.

There is no magical mystery, according to the supernatural spirit on *Ghostwriter* (PBS). When a group of children pose the Nietzchean-like question, "Is Elvis dead?" the magic letters reply, "Who's Elvis?"

The uncertainty of spotting Elvis also translates into dreams. In the off-key, piano-manufacturing small town series, *Grand* (NBC), an evil Elvis standing amidst flames appears to a woman who has dreamed she is dead. The musical messenger escorts the dreamer to her judgment in a disco inferno (Hellvis?) rather than rock and roll heaven. To their credit, the writers resist the obvious use of "Hunka Burnin' Love."

In the middle of an undefeated season on *Coach*, Luther, so convinced that his plane crash dream is an omen, cancels the team flight to a big game. "It was so real I could've touched Elvis. He was across the aisle from me; I gave him my dessert," he explains, trying to convince the ever-doubting Coach Fox that train travel is safer. What Coach dismisses as a "stupid dream" is for true believer Luther a bona fide religious revelation. The same faith and doubt surfaces in another episode when Luther looks for evidence in an *In Search of Elvis* documentary (a fictional variation of the Bill Bixby-narrated *The Elvis Files* [1990]), a tabloid trail from the desert near Las Vegas to Sea World that includes Howard Hughes, fishermen, and a large wooly bear in a Rhinestone jumpsuit. When Coach returns later to find his friend still mesmerized by the videotape, he

smugly asks, "They find Elvis?" An unwavering Luther enthusiastically replies, "Nope, but they're close!"

Like Luther, Russell on *Grace Under Fire* has never even considered the possibility that Elvis might actually be dead. "I'd love to go
to Memphis and see Graceland before Elvis dies," he says, accepting
Grace's invitation to accompany her to Tennessee for the weekend.

Bartender Sam Malone and the alien Alf also experience Elvisitations in their dreams. In the show's 1990-91 season finale of *Cheers*,
womanizer Sam decides he would like to settle down and be a father.
While baby-sitting for Frasier and Lilith's son, Sam falls asleep
while watching the Saturday night late movie, *Blue Hawaii*. He is
awakened by Elvis's voice from the bar TV screen mounted above
him. The juxtaposition is both ghostly and godly. As Sam looks up
and listens to Elvis offer advice on parenting from his film set, it is as
if he is worshiping at an altar or mountaintop. There is also simultaneous irreverence as Elvis reveals a human side; he is slightly offended when Sam refers to Lisa Marie as "a real babe."

When Frasier returns to pick up their son, Sam relates his Elvis
encounter to his psychologist friend and that he is not sure if it was a
dream or if Elvis actually appeared. Frasier listens as if engaged in a
therapy session, then calmly begins his analysis, "I have four or five
patients who have sworn the same thing, Sam. I'll tell you what I've
told them . . ." There is a pause, followed by Frasier's frustration in a
final emphatic phrase that shouts to all the Elvis sightseers, ". . . *The
man is dead!*"

The same belief and doubt conflict is well illustrated in an *Alf*
(NBC) episode, as the alien from the blown-up planet Melmac and
his earth guardian, Willie Tanner, debate the likelihood of Elvis
moving in on their block. With a tabloid tone—"Elvis Meets Creature from Space"—the "Alfis" script may be one of the more comprehensive Elvis televisual treatments, as it blends popular culture
and rock and roll references with a barrage of Elvis jokes.

When nosey neighbor Raquel reports to the Tanners that a man
named Aaron King—in his early fifties, sings in the shower, Southern accent—is renting the house two doors down, Alf, already under
the influence of his Legend of the Month book, *Elvis Is Alive*,
proclaims, "We found Elvis!" (Alf is established as an Elvis fan in

an earlier episode when he suggests the Elvis ceremonial package to Neal for his Las Vegas wedding.)

Determined to prove the doubting Willie that he is not "grasping at straws," the obsessive Alf gathers evidence: a tape of a 3 a.m. phone conversation with Aaron King, which played backwards, sounds just like early Elvis; red corduroy slippers he salvaged from King's trash ("He changed the fabric and color to protect himself from garbage-scavenging fans," theorizes Alf.); hidden messages in song lyrics such as "I found a new place to dwell;" and rearranged letters in Elvis's name.

Alf then invites the neighbor over, using a plate of peanut butter and banana sandwiches as bait, and instructs Willie to "monitor him for Elvis-like behavior."(He more closely resembles syndicated *Healthline* host Dr. Red Duke than Elvis.) King eats one of the sandwiches, says Elvis's trademark "Thank you very much," and leaves, which is a cue for Alf to announce, "Elvis has left the building." The Elvis one-liners are virtually nonstop.

Despite Alf's persistent Presley probing, with a reminder that "Elvis was a brilliant actor," the Tanners are not converted. Finally an exasperated Willie shouts, *"Leave the man alone!"* Willie's rebuke is an echo of Frasier's at the Cheers bar. Their comments reverberate beyond Sam and Alf. They are scolding Elfanatics for their undying fixation. Neither Willie or Frasier's chastising chips away at the Presley myth; they are defending the dignity of a dead Elvis. To counter, Alf's response is equally revealing in its characterization of the fervent believer. "I won't rest until I prove this man is Elvis Presley," says Alf as he dozes off to sleep.

A dream sequence follows in which Alf sneaks into the neighbor's house, which inside "looks like Priscilla had a heckuva lawn sale." The man explains apologetically that his real name is Clarence Williams III, and a that he is truck driver from Tupelo and an Elvisabilia collector. Alf insists the man is a "fugitive from fame."

As Alf awakens, he repeats, "In my heart, I'll always know you *are* Elvis." Once awake, he says, "You mean I was just dreaming Elvis is alive?" Together, the comments succinctly capture the unwavering faith of the true believers as well as the doubt, denial, and disappointment that have characterized the sightings phenomenon.

Bart Simpson also has an Elvis mantra. The animated image of bad Bart standing at the school blackboard repeatedly writing "I did not see Elvis" provides a glimpse into the surface of our cultural subconscious and the range of responses to the sightings phenomenon. The phrase and its repetition contains both belief and doubt. If Bart is a true believer being persecuted, his faith will not likely sway no matter how many times he must write the denial. The phrase might also be interpreted as an expression of doubt, an "I do not believe in ghosts" chant that will hopefully remove any uncertainty or "what-if?" possibility that teases the imagination. Bart could be Murphy Brown, the FYI news crew, Alf, or any Elvis sightseer trying to decide whether the newsroom gofer, new neighbor, or look-alike at the fast-food restaurant is the famous singer.

## IN THE NAME OF ELVIS: IMPERSONATORS AND IMPERSONAS

Lotta people look like Elvis.

–Johnny Tenuti, *Johnny Bago* (CBS)

On the popular drama series, *E.R.* (NBC), Dr. Susan Lewis (Sherry Stringfield) waits to transport a patient to the operating room on another floor. The elevator door opens, and a procession of Elvis Impersonators inexplicably exits, prompting the frustrated doctor to remark, "What is this, a convention?" The scene could easily substitute a television screen for the elevator, with Dr. Lewis channel surfing across the wave of Elvii that is the Presley Pipeline. These mirror reflections rival the more transparent ghost-like images of Elvis for frequent small screen appearances.

The genre distribution is equally widespread, with talk and tabloid shows particular havens for the King clones. *Good News'* (TNT) profile of an Elvis Impersonator in New York's Washington Square rising from a coffin to perform Elvis standards, and *A Current Affair*'s interpretation of what a contemporary Elvis music video would look like–an Impersonator standing by a river at night singing Bruce Springsteen's "I'm On Fire"–represent typical treatments. (Although singer Chris Isaak's music videos may provide a better projection of Elvis in the age of MTV.)

AT&T cleverly adapts Elvis Impersonators as "spokespersons" for a series of television commercials for the Yellow Pages. In an "objects in mirror appear closer" situation, two Elvis Impersonators are involved with a fender bender on their tail-finned cars. "Who do you think you are?" confronts one clone to another. "Who do *you* think I think I am?" smugly replies the look-alike. Looking skyward, as if for divine guidance, they wonder "what *he* would do." A glimpse of the tow truck driver reveals another Elvis look-alike. In another in the company's series of ads, James Earl Jones lectures before a classroom filled with Elvis Impersonators. "That's how you tell a genuine article from mere imitation," smoothly bellows the instructor's unmistakable voice.[2]

Whether examining room and courtroom cameos on *Doctor, Doctor* (CBS) and *Night Court* (NBC), Halloween costumes on *Bobby's World* and the *Jeff Foxworthy Show* (NBC), a predictable performance (and Wayne Newton joke) on a *Roseanne* Las Vegas episode, or as a one-liner on *Evening Shade* (CBS), Elvis Impersonators have provided situation comedies with a rich source of laughter and a recognizable character type who needed no exposition. Blue collar, white collar, or cop collars are easily transformed into upturned jumpsuit collars. The references are so instantaneously identifiable that program packagers have frequently incorporated Elvis into 15-second promos for new episodes and shows. For example, hyping its 1995 fall lineup entry, *Brotherly Love*, featuring Joey, Matt, and Andy Lawrence, NBC's promo punchline lists a "little Elvis" as a long-lost Lawrence sibling. And *NewsRadio*'s Phil Hartman does an NBC "Must See TV" promo as a young, gyrating Elvis.

Such promos often misrepresent the Elvis emphasis of the particular episode, often exploiting his image only for the trailer itself, and thus, generate viewer interest. For example, the promos—both broadcast and those printed in newspaper TV listings—for an installment of the reality series, *Rescue 911*, states, "Elvis's birthday burdens trauma center." The phrase suggests the emergency may be related to an overzealous Elfan celebration. Predictably, the Presley premise of the promos proves misleading. While the dramatized events presented in the show take place in Memphis on January 8, there is no mention of Elvis or his birthday. The only reference appears in a shot of a family in the hospital waiting room sitting beneath a sign "Elvis Presley Room."

The string of Impersonator sitcom scenarios is exhaustive. On a sweeps episode of *Blossom*, desperate Dad, a struggling musician, takes a job at Disneyland as an Elvis Impersonator. The closing scene is a particularly striking iconic juxtaposition as the costumed Impersonator stands beside *Beauty and the Beast's* Belle with the Magic Kingdom's trademark fireworks and castle in the background. In another episode of the series, the teenagers return early from a night out because a Chuck Berry Impersonator and Elvis Impersonator got into a fight at the club they were at. Historically, Jerry Lee Lewis might have been a more appropriate reference.

The writers for *Perfect Strangers* (ABC) and *Sledge Hammer!* (ABC) demonstrate that there are easily enough Impersonator gags and references for entire sitcom episodes. In "The King and I," immigrant Balki is hypnotized into Elvis. The premise blends Presley and Pavlov, as any ringing bell, whether an elevator, telephone, alarm clock, or coffee cart, triggers Balki in and out of the familiar and formulaic Elvis traits—turned up collar, unbuttoned shirt, curled lip, swivel hips. His condition gets complicated when he and roommate Larry meet for a tax audit. Following a Las Vegas-type introduction, Balki says he wants to "go over a little number of my own," and breaks into a spirited *Jailhouse Rock* choreography. The rapid-fire references include his version of "Heartbreak Hotel," an offer to buy the auditor a Cadillac, and the mandatory "Thank you; thank you very much" conclusion.

In "All Shook Up," an episode of the sitcop *Sledge Hammer!* (that was also distributed on home video), someone is trying to control the Elvis Impersonator overpopulation by murdering 15 of the King's men in three weeks. Detective Hammer, a hair-trigger, hair-brain (cro)Magnum-packing Dirty Harry clone is assigned to the case. Skeptical from the start, he winces, "I guess I just have a suspicious mind."

In addition to Presley puns, much of the humor in the episode is derived from Elvisuals adapted into the conventions of the police genre. In the opening sequence a low-angle shot follows someone in blue suede shoes stalking an impersonator competition winner. Hitchcockian shrill shower scene strings play as a gold microphone repeatedly strikes the victim. A chalk outline of the homicide traces an Elvis pose in the cement. The camera slowly pans a row of corpses lying on morgue slabs, each with an exaggerated Elvis pompadour peeking from beneath the sheets. At a police lineup of impersonators, suspects are asked to step forward and perform an Elvis routine. "Too bad *That's Incredible* isn't on anymore," says Hammer.

Hammer decides the easiest way to solve the "whodunit?" is to be "be one of them," so he enrolls in the local School of Elvis Impersonators. "I know how to imitate Elvis," he says confidently. "Move your hips, shake your hips, and look bloated." Although all of the Presley pupils "act strange" in Hammer's view, his primary suspect is the school's custodian, a Japanese man who also cleans at the nightclub where the Elvis competition is held. Hammer's instincts prove correct. The custodian is a closet King clone whose personal Presley pathology is that he "is largely superior and can do Elvis more efficiently than any of the [other impersonators]."

The case marks a conversion for Hammer. The detective evolves from a skeptical nonbeliever, to acting in and out of the image of Elvis, to showing signs of being a believer by listening to Elvis on his Walkman and planning a Graceland vacation.

Although the hit series, *Seinfeld* (NBC) has not contributed an Elvis episode, Jerry is cast as The King (of Comedy) by *Rolling Stone*. Inspired by the dual images of the Elvis stamp election, the publication printed two different cover shots for the September 22, 1994 issue. In one, the comedian poses in gold lamé, in another he snarls in a jumpsuit while holding an oversized drumstick.

Impersonator appearances and references have surfaced in some unusual locations. In the mythical Cicely, Alaska, on *Northern Exposure* (CBS), Adam, a mountain man who is a gourmet chef, resorts to an Elvis analogy when his culinary art is contaminated by the wrong ingredients. "This is not pancheta, Dave. This is bacon!" he chastises his apprentice. "These ingredients are modulated to create a perfect harmony and you waltz in here like some tone-deaf, low-life Elvis Impersonator throwing a B-flat into the middle of my A-sharp major concerto . . . Ugh!"

Elvis Impersonator images have also checkered children's programs, from Public Broadcasting fare to cartoon channels. An Elvis look-alike appears in the opening montage of kid's math show, *Square One* (PBS), while a young Elvis with "King Repair" embroidered on the back of his jacket services a jukebox on *Shining Time Station* (PBS). The *Muppets Classic Theater* presents the story of the Shoemakers and the Elvi–three Elvises who make blue suede shoes. The Shoemaker repays them by designing gold-encrusted Las Vegas-style jumpsuits. And following a chorus line of tropical fruit singing his show's opening theme, Garfield the cat wisecracks, "I'm sick of these singers. Can we get something like Elvis Impersonators next time?" Such Elvis references are more likely to connect with older audiences, or simply amuse the writers themselves, rather than the shows' youthful target audience.

The African-American community is also another unlikely setting, due to lingering hostility toward the rip-off King. Yet Steve Urkel, the prototype nerd in the middle-class black family sitcom, *Family Matters*, "does" Elvis in three separate episodes–as a hip-hop Elvis rapping a tune; as "Robo Dork," whose functions include swiveling its mechanical hips and vocoding "All Shook Up;" and as an Elvis/Einstein hybrid that evolves from wearing a cardigan sweater to a Vegas version in a jumpsuit. The transformation, similar to Balki's hypnosis into Elvis, is the result of a basement DNA experiment gone awry. Preparing for an interview for MIT, Steve accidentally crosses Einstein elixir with an Elvis strand from his celebrity hair collection and comes out of his chamber Albert Presley. Urkel's black Elvii are reminiscent of an Eddie Murphy reincarnation routine as Elvis during a *Saturday Night Live* sketch.

The tone is slightly more reverent on *The Cosby Show* (NBC), where Grandfather Huxtable reflects on Elvis's *Ed Sullivan Show* appearance, and in another episode offers wisdom, "Crazy world; hasn't been the same since Elvis and Priscilla broke up."

Elvis's likeness and name have been implied or presented in forms which vary slightly from the Impersonator blueprint, but nonetheless provide identity, or mistaken identity. On *Home Improvement*, Tim fashions "His and Her" mannequins which unintentionally resemble Elvis. Toonces, the cat who could drive a car, is shown grooming his rebellious Elvis-like hairdo during its prime time special on NBC. Once behind the wheel, the cat paws the car radio tuning knob as "You Ain't Nothing but a Hound Dog" begins. Sonny Crockett's pet gator on *Miami Vice* (NBC) is named "Elvis." On *Growing Pains* (ABC), Mike uses Elvis's name while trying to impress an older woman. The teenager tells the woman his sister Chrissy is a boy named Chris E., and the "E" stands for Elvis.

*Saturday Night Live*'s writers present a similar mistaken identity gag when *Beverly Hills 90210* heartthrob Jason Priestley hosted the show, February 15, 1992. As part of the opening monologue, the teen idol answered scripted questions from the studio audience about fellow 90210ers Luke Perry and Shannen Doherty. Planted in the crowd, cast member Rob Schneider rises from his seat and asks with a straight face, "Are you any relation to Elvis Priestley?" Beyond the surname subtleties, the question seemed strangely plausible considering the sideburned Priestley's young-Elvis aura.

*Lois and Clark*'s (ABC) Perry White is a fatherly Colonel Parker-type persona to Clark Kent's young Elvis and the rest of his newspaper staff. The editor has a photo of Elvis on his wall and one on his desk, as if his own child or grandchild. When he is elected Mayor of Metropolis, Elvis shows up at the victory party. Elvis is very ingrained into White's worldview and vocabulary. He explains to a young reporter how Elvis got the cape idea from Superman and philosophizes on how Elvis bridges generations. White replaces the phrase "Great Caesar's ghost!" with "Great shades of Elvis!" And when commenting on current events, he editorializes about "terrorists blasting us to Elvis and back."

Although such Elvis/death synonyms have been more frequently expressed in film scripts, a few have surfaced in television as well. *Larroquette's* (NBC) Hemingway waxes eternal, "He's dead; he's stiff; he's boxing with Elvis." And on the syndicated children's show *Xuxa,* a puppet covers its eyes, says it sees Elvis and a message about being "dead meat."

Elvira, horror hostess for the syndicated spook spoof *Movie Macabre,* is an Elvis persona more than an Impersonator. In her jet black hair, tight black gown, and vamp sexuality, she is at once Mistress of the Dark and the King's Queen, the daughter Elvis and Morticia Adams might have conceived. The connection contains some authenticity. Cassandra Peterson, the former Las Vegas showgirl who plays Elvira, met Elvis when she was 17 and credits him with changing the direction of her career.

While Impersonator and impersonas have been a staple of comedy presentations, the more complex social, psychological, and religious subtexts of Elvis Impersonation are explored in the pilot episode of

*Civil Wars* (ABC), producer Steven Bochco's dramatic marriage of *Divorce Court* and *L.A. Law* set in New York.

Elvis, or delusions of Elvis, are grounds for divorce between Murray and Natalie Seidelman. During the court proceedings, Murray explains that during a visit to Graceland he experienced a convulsing conversion in The Jungle Room. "The spirit of Elvis Presley entered my mortal flesh, sir. It's in my body and soul and won't go away," testifies the sneering, Southern-drawling, jumpsuited husband.

Dr. Zelnick, a credible psychiatrist whose patients include delusional types who believe they are celebrities such as Florence Henderson and Slappy White, is called upon to render a mental evaluation of Murray. The doctor avoids rendering a clinical diagnosis of Murray's condition. Instead, his perspective on the multiple personality disorder is simple and sympathetic. He considers Murray to be "thriving" as someone who has discovered an alternate way of being in the world. The behavior that Natalie's lawyer labels as "bizarre" or "aberrant fantasies" is in Dr. Zelnick's view simply a "choice," one person's response to the "desperately alienated times when people latch onto whatever sense of identity they can latch onto."

Murray's testimony is equally insightful as it places Elvis imitation along the religious spectrum that includes cult of personality, conversion, possession, and oneness.

> . . . you understand, that throughout all revealed time there's always been an Elvis. Call him Buddha. Call him Jesus. Call him the Bal Sham Toh. Call him Johnny Carson. You see, figures emerge. People recognize who they are and they gather around them just like they gather around me.
>
> You see, there's been a visitation. Murray Seidelman has left the building and the King has moved in. This is *not* acting.
>
> You know how much a suit like this weighs? Thirty-seven pounds. The Aztec Sundial model weighs even more. Now, sir, there are times when I may not feel like going through the bother of putting one on. I'm not up to it. Maybe I think it'd be easier just not being the King. And that's when I say to myself, "El, take care of business." So, I put on the suit, the belt, the rings, chains, because this is what Elvis wears. And *I am Elvis*!

The writers' intelligent sociopsychological perspective, along with Dennis Franz's characterization, are unlike other dramatic portrayals of Elvis Impersonation which emphasize the comic. Though the inherent impersonator humor emerges in Murray's excesses, he is ultimately sympathetic, a character in need of compassion more so than a caricature created for laughs. Even when the judge grants Natalie the divorce due to "cruel and inhuman treatment," the writers avoid a convenient opportunity for a "don't be cruel" line, which would have been automatic in other presentations.

Outside the courtroom, Murray attempts to reconcile, by asking his "Queen" to go on the same date Elvis went on with Ann-Margret in *Viva Las Vegas*. When Natalie explains that she wants Murray, not Elvis, her now ex-husband explains who he is: "I'll give you a 43-year-old overweight appliance salesman with a heart condition. Murray Seidelman wears a 44 portly, and no matter how much money he makes or what he does with his life, no one is going to care if he lives or dies."

Clearly, Elvis, or the image of Elvis, fills Murray's midlife, providing meaning and identity. After Natalie rejects his final offer to renew their vows at the Aladdin Hotel in Las Vegas, the scene fades with Murray/Elvis singing the anthem fit for a King, "I Did It My Way."

## *RETURN TO SPLENDOR?*
## *ELVIS, OUT OF TIME*

No matter what you do, you can not, not, not, not mess up for Elvis; or change anything, 'cause you'll change history. Big time.

—Al to Sam (as Elvis), *Quantum Leap* (NBC)

I don't want Elvis to go down in history as a guy who was overweight in a white jumpsuit looking for a peanut butter sandwich.

—Jerry Schilling, Coproducer, *Elvis* (ABC)

Numerous representations have provided a historical context by placing Elvis in, out, and along various points of the time line. In a commercial from its retro campaign, McDonald's presents a 1950s slice of Americana as two school-age sisters sit in front of the family's black and white television, eagerly anticipating Elvis's *Ed Sullivan* appearance.

The scene utilizes the *Wonder Years*-style nostalgic narration. "Those sideburns. And the way he moved made us weak in the knees," says the voice-over, looking back with a hint of adolescent longing. Sitting through the other acts–circus dogs, the talking mouse–are foreplay building to the Elvis climax. Just as Ed Sullivan begins to introduce Elvis to the screaming studio audience, the TV screen goes black. Looming behind the set is the embodiment of 1950s pelvis Presley parental paranoia, the father, who smugly smiles, "Aw, must've been a blackout."

To ease the frustration, and perhaps his guilt, Dad takes his daughters to McDonald's for their first visit to the fledgling fast-food franchise. "Now, isn't this better than old what's-his-name?" a relieved mom offers her own anti-Presley propaganda. The tactic works; even the young girls are satisfied with the substitute. "We may have missed part of rock and roll history, but somehow we didn't mind just then," adding how they didn't hold a grudge years later when they found out it was their diabolical dad who actually pulled the plug on the TV set.

The juxtaposition of these two cultural icons in 30 seconds presents a moral dichotomy between the sexuality, desire, and rebelliousness associated with Elvis, as opposed to the conservative family values presented by McDonald's. Clearly, the parental preference for their daughters' "first time" is for the "billions" beneath the golden arches rather than in view of Elvis.

In a revisionist history episode of *The X-Files*, the Act Two subtitle appearing on the screen–"Just down the road a ways from Graceland"–links the King figures Martin Luther King and Elvis. There is no mention of Elvis or Graceland in the dramatic narrative about the assassination of the Reverend King on the balcony of the Lorraine Hotel in Memphis in 1968. The subtitle subtley suggests a Presley proximity to significant historical events.

The notion of "creating your own past" and Elvis links a trilogy of television episodes with such literary works as Jack Womack's *Elvissey*, and Michael Moorcock's *Behold the Man* (1970), the story of a man who goes back to Biblical times and "takes over" for Jesus after discovering the would-be Savior is actually a moron. Moorcock's premise is adapted into an episode of *The New Twilight Zone* (CBS), substituting an Elvis Impersonator who goes back in time to meet Elvis. When he finds Elvis dead, he replaces the King.

The time travelers on *Bill and Ted's Excellent Adventure* (FOX) and *Quantum Leap* (NBC) both make stops in the mid-1950s to visit Elvis and tinker with history in the process. The episodes echo Robert Rankin's back-to-the-future novel *Armageddon: The Musical* (1991) about alien television producers who travel back in time to prevent the young Elvis from entering the Army. Fed up with rejection after they lose in the "Battle of the Elvises" contest that they were hoping would land them a recording contract, Bill and Ted recruit a (dead) ringer–"Elvis dude"–for the next competition. Having the benefit of historical hindsight, Bill and Ted first get "the future of rock and roll" fired from his truckdriving job at Crown, then instruct him how to be a singing, shaking, snarling Elvis. Playing "All Shook Up" on the diner's jukebox confuses, rather than inspires, Elvis. "Somebody stole my voice," he says.

The plan backfires. The time bandits' authentic transport loses at his own contest because he sings "most un-Elvis like;" his young voice does not sound like "Elvis" yet. The moral of the adventure comes from father (time) figure Rufus, who explains to Bill and Ted that imitating Elvis is a meaningful, reverent act. He questions the two dudes' motivation for entering the contest, and suggests that they committed sacrilege because they were more interested in receiving a record deal than honoring the King.

The more imaginative and socially conscious series, *Quantum Leap*, features Dr. Sam Beckett, a physicist being bounced around into strangers' bodies between the 1950s and 1980s as the result of a flawed experiment. Sam does not travel alone; he is accompanied by Al, a holographic observer. Using Ziggy, a portable computer that provides odds and reasons for Sam's situations, Al "coaches" Sam, making sure his traveler follows the "rules of the road." Unlike the time (dis)honored traditions of television time travel that allowed for tinkering, Beckett is not "allowed" to alter major historical events. He may, however, slightly modify the course of "ordinary people's" lives. As a result, Sam's adventures often re-

semble the earthly goodwill missions of Michael Landon's proba-
tionary angel on *Highway to Heaven* (NBC).

Sam's diverse "leap" list includes unknowns and a roster of famous figures such as Marilyn Monroe, Jackie and John F. Kennedy,
Lee Harvey Oswald and Elvis. Sam's Elvis encounter is similar to
Bill and Ted's, especially the requisite diner scenes with musical
production numbers. Sam also arrives "pre-Elvis," in July 1954,
during what Al calls "a very important time in Elvis's life"–two
days before he is discovered. Sam's compassionate purpose as Elvis
is to help Sue Ann, a local singing waitress with Opry aspirations,
stagefright, and an oppressive fiancée, Frank. "Nothing wrong with
being a dreamer. Everybody should be a dreamer," Sam/Elvis tells
her in follow-that-dream fashion. In the process, Sam almost revises
Elvis's story. When Sam/Elvis accidentally arranges to have Sue Ann
sing a duet with him at what would be his legendary Sun Session, Al
materializes with some modern-day reminders. "Sam, you're turning
the King of Rock and Roll into Donnie and Marie," he corrects. "In
1954, the world was not ready for Sonny and Cher."

The intersection of past, present, and future within the account of
Elvis's beginnings and the Sue Ann subplot provides texture to the
historical narrative. Sam's experience as "King for a day," combined with his awareness of how the Elvis story actually evolves,
provide a panoramic perspective of the time line. "Walking a mile
in Elvis's blue suede shoes before he became the idol of millions
made me realize he was just a normal person," reflects Sam on his
rocking role. "I kept wondering if he would've been happier had he
stayed that way."

One of the most respectful and respectable presentations of Elvis's life, *Elvis* (ABC), premiered on Sunday night, February 6,
1990. Produced in alliance with the Presley estate, the docudrama
marked the first time a famous life had been dramatized as a weekly
prime-time series. The show's focus was on Elvis's early years,
from 1954 when he recorded his first singles, to 1958, when he
joined the Army. The intimate portrait starred Michael St. Gerard,
who also appeared as Elvis in the Jerry Lee Lewis bio film, *Great
Balls of Fire!* "The name [Elvis] can get so big that it becomes a
joke at points," says the show's coproducer Jerry Schilling. "I think
this series brings it back down to a very human level."

Despite having highly rated lead-in shows such as *Roseanne* and *America's Funniest Videos*, the producers' noble historical and human aims, critical praise and Elfan approval, *Elvis* failed to attract the network's twenty- and thirtysomething target audience. That demographic appeared hopelessly locked into tabloid sensationalism, sightings, and the overweight, overglitzed Vegas version of the King. After 10 of its 13 episodes aired, *Elvis* was "out of time;" ABC canceled the show on May 26, 1990, replacing it with repeats of *Mission: Impossible*. Since its demise, *Elvis* has frequently aired in its entirety on programming blocks in syndication and independent outlets such as TNT and WTBS during Elvents (such as the stamp celebration) held in January and August.

In 1991, there were other signs of Elvis being "out of time" on television. The original TV tabloid, *A Current Affair*, and its progeny, *Hard Copy*, were enjoying their highest ratings since the late 1980s, and not because of their long-time sensational scoop, Elvis. "We're kind of tired of Elvis Presley," admitted *Hard Copy* anchors Terry Murphy and Barry Nolan. Supplanting the King as "favorite subjects" were Madonna, Liz Taylor, Marilyn Monroe, Cher, and Michael Jackson, "in that order." Although *A Current Affair*'s producers said they were "tired of Madonna," Elvis did not make their "hot" list, which included Jackson, Taylor, Ted Kennedy and Marlon Brando (Graham, 1991).

Despite the failed docudrama series and the tabloid's "old news" attitude toward Elvis, the Presley presence continued to be widely transmitted in programming. Comedy has emerged as the Presley vehicle, from sitcom scenes, episodes, one liners, props, and characters to a slogan for margarine ("Elvis ate it; why don't you?") on David Letterman's "Top Ten List." Elvis is a compatible and convenient King of Comedy, an ideal and endless resource for assembly line writers who must daily or weekly provide 30 to 60 "jokes" for their shows. His songs, souvenirs, and sayings ("Thank you; thank you very much," "Elvis has left the building"), his gyrations and gestures, sideburns and sneer, sightings and stories, the costumes and clones, are Kingdom conventions easily identifiable and laughable.

The demographic appeal is also far reaching, if not a universal embrace of age, race and ethnic origins, social class, region, and profession. Broadcasters, reporters, animated characters, doctors, detectives, lawyers, judges, cops, coaches, blue collar, white collar, small town, urban, aliens, immigrants, back woods brothers from Vermont, Southern metropolitan designers, senior citizens, teens, toddlers, and pets are among the types who have paraded through the Presley Panorama that is Elvision.

## NOTES

1. "Little Elvis," according to Albert Goldman, was what Elvis called his penis. In *Dead Elvis* (1991, pp. 183-185), Greil Marcus writes that Benjamin Horne presumably used the bottle as a dildo. As for the contents, the author lists whiskey, sperm, and homunculi as possibilities. Artist Joni Mabe corrects Marcus, claiming the bottle was actually a doll stuffed with cotton from the King's belly button.

2. Jones also appears in another Elvis scenario as an ex-con turned detective in *Gabriel's Fire* (ABC). While investigating leads at a local pawn shop, the store owner tries to interest Bird in a guitar by mentioning that Elvis got his first instrument at a pawn shop. Historically, the reference is inaccurate, as Elvis's mother Gladys purchased her son's first guitar at the Tupelo Hardware Company, even though Elvis wanted a rifle.

# Chapter 7

# Elvis II, The Sequel:
# The Never-Ending Story

Brad: Dad, what's *The King and I?*
Tim: Aw, some singing film with Elvis.

*—Home Improvement* (ABC) 1993

Elvis was a brilliant actor. He could play anything from a singing race car driver to a singing deep sea diver.

*—Alf,* Alf (NBC) 1988

Among the anniversary activities and common commemorations of Elvis' birth and death are film festivals. Like some biannual seasonal rite, die-hard Elfans, B-movie buffs, and syndicated television programmers are among those who eagerly anticipate early January and mid-August block scheduling of Elvis movies. While such Elfests tend to mark the extent of American culture's recognition of Elvis's acting career, some of the more interesting ricochets from the Presley filmography are imports. Although foreign film critics have yet to go as far as to regard Elvis as an auteur the same way they have Jerry Lewis, there are other indications of Elvis movies' broad appeal abroad, as several countries have paid homage in various ways to Elvis the actor.

The Republic of Central Africa recently issued a series of stamps which honor five of Elvis's most popular movies—*Heartbreak Hotel, Love Me Tender, Jailhouse Rock, Harem Scarum,* and *Blue Hawaii* (Figure 7.1). The London-based music magazine, *New Musical Express,* produced *The Last Temptation of Elvis* (1990), an all-star cover compilation tribute record featuring 26 songs from Elvis movies.

One of the more unusual and engaging homages to Elvis movies can be found in a movie, *Eat the Peach* (1986), an obscure Irish film

FIGURE 7.1. Stamps from the Republic of Central Africa honoring Elvis movies.

which had a very limited theatrical and video rental distribution in the United States. Based on a true story, the offbeat film is about two hard-luck friends, Arthur and Vinnie, who suddenly find themselves unemployed. While watching television at a local tavern, they are so inspired by a "roving, restless, reckless" Elvis in the movie, *Roust-about* (1964), that they construct their own "Wall of Death," a huge wooden cylinder in which the two dreamers perform daredevil stunts on their motorbikes. The barrier represents hope and freedom to Arthur and Vinnie, who believe it is their ticket to fame, fortune, and the big time that lies beyond the boundaries of their rural Irish border village.

Such real life, enthusiastic expressions of devotion, and by-products have usually been more commonly inspired by an Elvis serenade, sighting, sweaty scarf, or other sacred artifacts, than by one of his big screen adventures. However, that certainly does not diminish the significance of the movie mark on Elvis's time line. For Elvis, movies were both a preoccupation and occupation, dating from his youth, and continuing to the point of almost exclusively defining his career for more than a decade. According to most biographical accounts, it was a career in acting Elvis longed for more than anything, including singing. He wanted to be a James Dean more than he wanted to be the next Dean Martin. After completing his first feature film, *Love Me Tender* (1956), Elvis told disc jockey Charlie Walker during an interview in San Antonio that making movies was a "dream come true, the biggest thing that had happened."

Despite starring in 31 feature films between the years 1956 and 1969 (*Elvis–That's the Way It Is* (1970) and *Elvis on Tour* (1972) were concert performance documentaries), Elvis struggled for respect as an actor. Although his performances were filled with hope and energy, and the movies were very popular, they were also very formulaic, and never received much critical acclaim or recognition for artistic merit. "There is something sad about the futility of his [Elvis's] actions, for despite his dedication, the feature films in which he starred never really rise above dreary predictability," writes Patsy Guy Hammontree (1985, p. 240).

The guaranteed box-office success of each release ironically contributed to the second-rate status of Elvis's films. Studios were aware of the loyalty of Elvis fans. It did not matter how shallow the story lines, how silly the songs, or repetitious the roles; a larger-than-life

Elvis energized on a big screen in a dark theater was enough. And if that satisfied the audience, which it did, there was no incentive for the studios or producers to vary from the formula and interrupt the assembly-line operation.

A key ingredient of the Elvis film formula was, of course, the music. In the liner notes to *The Last Temptation of Elvis* soundtrack tribute, "EAP" writes, "You know the best thing about those movies anyway? It wasn't the scripts for sure; it was the music." Decades after the fact, the ghostwriter may have recognized that about the movies he starred in, but not while he was alive. Perhaps naive, Elvis did not consider a singing role "acting." Regardless, the musical performances were obligatory. No producer or investor would financially support a movie with a nonsinging Elvis. As a result, Elvis became a musical hybrid of his two Dean idols—James and Martin—on the silver screen. And years later, the furry, wisecracking, alien Alf's sitcom summary of Elvis's range (as in singing) of roles as a "brilliant actor" is quite poignant. Whether behind the wheel of a sports car, hanging from the mast of a tuna boat coming into port, in prison or at poolside, Arabia or Appalachia, there was a song and dance for every setting, situation, and role Elvis was in.

Elvis's abilities as an actor are often debated. Some argue that he was hopelessly inept, while others believe he had potential that was left untapped. Ludicrous scripts, stereotyped roles, and in many cases, working with second-rate directors, were stifling factors which allowed him little opportunity to develop his acting skills. Film critic Renata Adler acknowledged as much in her review of *Speedway* (1968):

> This is . . . another Presley movie—which makes no use at all of one of the most talented performers of our time. Music, youth, and customs were much changed by Elvis Presley twelve years ago; from the twenty-six movies he has made since he sang "Heartbreak Hotel," you would never guess.

Even "Elvis" himself expresses frustration with his situation as he steps out of character on location from a film set and appears to Sam Malone in a dream during an episode of NBC's *Cheers.* "I don't know what they got me doing in this one, frolicking on the beach or jumping into some stock car," he laments to the sleeping bar owner. The comments from this Elvis and the "EAP" who wrote the liner notes in the *Last Temptation* compilation provide hindsight views of how Elvis more than likely might assess his film career.

Death has not elevated Elvis's acting career above B-movie status. There has been no postmortem groundswell for a reassessment of Elvis's film contributions; the critical disclaim for the most part remains. Elvis's movies have joined his other trademarks–sideburns, lip snarl, jumpsuit, overweight, et al.–as referents routinely ridiculed.

At times, such movie mentions appear accidental. Actor Tom Hanks, for example, has shown a tendency to drift into Elvis tangents during talk show conversations. During an appearance on David Letterman's show in the late 1980s, Hanks pointed out how Elvis appeared to have lost his rhythm sometime in between his early films such as *Jailhouse Rock* (1957), and those he starred in during the 1960s. Hanks rose from his seat to demonstrate the tight, less animated Elvis–hands at his side, slightly swaying with feet in place–singing "Clambake." As it turns out, the routine was a warm-up for Hanks's Elvis wiggle as Forrest Gump in 1994.

Though comic tinged, Hanks's critique echoes critic Adler's view, and no doubt others, from years earlier. They were asking a familiar question, "Elvis, what happened?", only in a different context. Something had been noticeably "lost" in between Elvis's first four films in the 1950s and the 27 that followed during the next decade. Many, most notably John Lennon, conveniently pointed to the personal "military intervention" from 1958 to 1960 as an interruption that affected Elvis's career continuity in film as well as music, and marked the beginning of his demise.

Despite the lingering indifference and irreverence toward Elvis's film career, his Hollywood years are noteworthy. While Elvis might not have been the brilliant actor Alf considers him, there are scenes, performances, and, as "EAP" himself insists, music from the movies which remain memorable. Certainly, Elvis's classic *Jailhouse Rock* routine withstands the test of time through decades of song and dance, from swinging sock hops to boppin' in *Bandstand's* spotlight, to the *Saturday Night Fever* disco inferno of the 1970s, to the contemporary choreography of MTV's landscape. Elvis's rhythmic movements do not appear the least bit dated or out of place next to Prince or Paula Abdul, Michael Jackson's moonwalk, or his sister

Janet's gyrations of the Rhythm Nation, or Madonna's Blonde Ambition expressions in vogue and vulgar videos and stage musicals.

Elvis bio-bibliographer Patsy Guy Hammontree argues that measuring the significance of Elvis's film career does not rest exclusively in considerations of quality and quantity. She gives Elvis the benefit of the many doubts, pointing to his perseverance and popularity through that period.

> [He] artistically survived a decade of mediocrity. It is remarkable that he overcame that experience to become an even greater success in personal appearances, both in Las Vegas and on concert tours around the country. Further, his economic success in films is not to be slighted. Only a rare individual could have escaped being buried forever by bad films. Elvis triumphed over them for his renaissance in another entertainment genre. (p. 245)

## *ELVIS A.D.:*
## *REEL REPRISE*

That renaissance evolved into a resurrection. Elvis's active afterlife featured "appearances" in every entertainment genre, including film. Like literature, television, art, and music, Elvis's reel reprise contains a complete range of conventions, as Elvis references and representations can be found in dialogue, characters, themes, iconography, motifs, and settings. The film frame fragments and "appearances" range from the striking to the subliminal, scenes to behind the scenes, special effects to soundtracks, titles to trailers, and major studio to independent releases in virtually every film genre and subgenre—musicals, fantasy, romance, comedy, action, adventure, mystery, biography, thriller, horror, animation, road pictures, and period pieces.

## *EVIL TWINS:*
## *THE UNBEARABLE LIKENESS OF BEING?*

*Fan Mag Reporter*:     Who would you like to be?
*Mishima*:              Elvis Presley.

—Mishima (1985)

While most of the Elvis sightings and citings in film are as obvious as the boy named "Elvis" in *Free Willy 2* (1994), or Andrew Dice Clay's black leather persona, costarring with Priscilla Presley, in *The Adventures of Ford Fairlane* (1990), there are other illusory and loose-linked connections which can be deciphered. For example, perhaps the most fitting title for an Elvis Presley biography comes from a film, *The Never-Ending Story* (1984). The title became even more appropriate for Elvis's life and afterlife when an oxymoronic sequel to the magical timeless fantasy was released in 1990. Likewise, the title, story, and setting of the South Seas shipwrecked remake in 1980 of the British film, *The Blue Lagoon* (1949), starring child actor Brooke Shields, invites comparison to *Blue Hawaii*.

Elvis analogies are readily decipherable on and beneath the surfaces of various film narratives. *Melvin and Howard* (1980) might be subtitled, "Melvis and Howard," as the slice-of-Middle American-life film loosely links Elvis with another mysterious millionaire–Howard Hughes–and the ordinary Melvin Dummar, who was named beneficiary of Hughes's $156 million dollar fortune in a Mormon will following his death in April 1976. Based on the reported true story of Dummar's chance encounter with the hitchhiking Hughes in the desert between Utah and Nevada, director Jonathan Demme shapes Bo Goldman's Academy Award-winning screenplay into a bittersweet fable about the elusiveness of the American Dream.

Despite being at opposite ends of the socioeconomic spectrum, there is a little bit of Elvis in each of the film's title characters. When Dumars stops in the desert night to urinate, he finds Hughes (Jason Robards) lying injured in the sagebrush, and gives him a lift in his pickup. Their trip into Reno resembles an old Elvis hitching a ride with young Elvis, with much of their front seat conversation (and the story's premise) foreshadowing of the belief and doubt that would accompany the Elvis sightings later in the decade. "I'm Howard Hughes," says the grizzled tycoon. Though leery of his passenger's tabloid headline introduction, Dummar respectfully replies, "I believe anybody can call themselves whatever name they want."

Dummar is not as obvious an Elvis look-alike as the driver of a catfish farm truck in the film adaptation of John Grisham's best-selling law firm formula, *The Firm* (1993). But in the dark shadows of the Nevada night, Melvin's behind-the-wheel, sideburn profile bears a striking resemblance to a young Elvis, perhaps driving a Crown Electric truck on the Mississippi backroads. (In other scenes, particularly when Melvin sings at the office Christmas party, his chops are more young Neil Young, circa Buffalo Springfield, than young Elvis.) The Elvis image becomes even more fanciful when Melvin prods Hughes to sing, suggesting "Love Me Tender" or "Don't Be Cruel," as possible tunes. Hughes, a cantankerous old coot with fading memories of happiness, chooses "Bye, Bye Blackbird," perhaps for its appropriate opening verse, "Got no one to love and understand me . . ."

Other Presley parallels, such as consumerism, excess, and exploitation, unfold with Melvin's life. He struggles to cope with marriage, his job, family, friends, finances, and fame. Just as his service station is on the brink of going out of business, a stranger arrives in a limo and drops what appears to be Hughes's last will and testament into Dummar's life. The reclusive Hughes leaving his fortune for the nobody who picked him up in the desert and loaned him a quarter, was analogous with Elvis giving strangers and waitresses Cadillacs. The results are similar as well. Skepticism, jealousy, chaos, exploitation, and loss of anonymity follow for the contemporary proletariat, who finds himself in a no-win situation. Dummar's Tires becomes a Graceland, a small-town spectacle with press conferences, lawyers, long-lost relatives and newfound friends smothering the Hughes heir. And just as most Elvis sightings and encounters are routinely questioned or shrugged off with tabloid indifference, most people doubted the authenticity and origin of the will, or that Melvin Dummar ever met Howard Hughes.

The royal and resurrection references in Disney's animated feature film *The Lion King* (1994) also fit the Elvisian myth narrative. "Simba, everyone thinks you're dead!" says a startled Nala upon discovering her best friend in the jungle. "You're alive! And that means you're the King." Young Simba is reluctant royalty. "No, I'm not the King! Maybe I was gonna be, but that was a long time ago. Things change." A similar exchange could easily be constructed from the resurrection rhetoric that has been a doctrine for the true believers of the "Elvis is Alive" movement. This Disney-Presley mythical Kingdom coincidence was further expressed in April 1996 in a *USA Today* advertisement for *Lion King* postage stamps boldly stating, "Move over Elvis . . . Collectors Proclaim Simba The New King."

*The Atlanta Journal/Constitution* film critic, Eleanor Ringel, appears to be stricken with the similar sighting symptom that Mojo Nixon, Molly Ivins, and others have shown, seeing and believing that there is a little bit of Elvis in everything and everyone. After looking closely and reading between the lines, frames, and images of *Honey, I Blew Up the Kid* (1992), the engaging critic suggests that the formula-reversing sequel to the Disney hit, *Honey, I Shrunk the Kids* (1989), is actually an Elvis parable. In the story, absent-minded inventor Wayne Szalinski (Rick Moranis) accidentally zaps his two-year-old son with an enlarging ray. The toddler grows into a giant and heads to Las Vegas where he stalks the strip.

Similar "Elvis in disguise" analogies might then be made for other larger-than-life characters in other movies. Mr. Sta-Puff, the giant marshmallow monster in the paranormal comedy *Ghostbusters* (1984), is a playful embodiment of what an exhumed or reincarnated Elvis might look like. A sticky white mass rather than decaying dust and ashes, the fluffy fellow is a psychic nuisance towering 20 stories tall that resembles an overinflated floating figure in the Macy's Thanksgiving Day parade in New York City.

Other special effects have also attracted Elvis. John Carpenter's *In the Mouth of Madness* (1995) borrows a prop page from *Prehysteria*'s (1993) Tyrannosaurus Rex "Elvis," affectionately referring to their mechanical monster by the same name.

Perhaps one of the more obvious Elvis character comparisons lies with Jason, the slashing star of the endless sequence of *Friday the 13th* films from Camp Run Amok. Next to Elvis, perhaps no figure in American culture has embodied, or disembodied, a greater immunity to death for such a long period of time than Jason. Following the initial *Friday the 13th* (1980), Jason returned for seven subsequent sequels that span an entire decade. His is a never-ending story; there were four *Friday the 13th*'s which followed *Friday the 13th: The Final Chapter* (1984)! During the 1980s, moviegoers were conditioned to Jason anticipation every summer in much the same manner Elfans celebrate Elvis anniversaries. And just as audiences grew weary of the invincibility and exploitation, wondering when, or if, the Jason saga would end, similar tired curiosity is expressed toward an Elvis.

Another frightfully fanciful script adaptation possibility is that the person behind the mask is not Elvis, but his twin brother, Jesse Garon, who was stillborn at birth. That story line holds numerous comic and horrific possibilities, ranging from Jesse's being alive all along, to a return from the dead to either inherit his brother's throne or wreak revenge.

In addition to the shared quality of imperishability, Jason's trademark hockey mask which concealed his identity also bears some significance in relation to Elvis. In 1978, singer Jimmy Ellis, a vocal dead ringer for Elvis, recorded a number of songs under the alter ego, "Orion." Producer Shelby Singleton, who bought Sun Records from Sam Phillips in 1969, decided to disguise Ellis's identity on his first Sun single, "That's All Right (Mama)"/"Blue Moon of Kentucky"– Elvis's first hit and flip side recorded in 1954–leaving listeners to speculate that the songs might actually be alternate Elvis takes. Instead of listing Ellis on the label, only a question mark appeared. In 1978, Ellis/Orion also appeared as an unidentified singer performing with Jerry Lee Lewis on the album *Duets*, raising further speculation that it was actually Elvis singing, particularly on "Save the Last Dance for Me." That same year, Gail Brewer-Giorgio's novel, *Orion*, the story of a rock and roll singer who faked his own death, was published, further fueling the fervor of followers who believed Elvis was alive and singing. Two years later, perhaps it was Elvis, or evil twin Jesse Garon, who donned the mask to begin his postmortem movie career in disguise as alter ego Jason. Actor Michael Madsen reinforces the possibility of such a preposterous premise. In discussing the strangest role he had been asked to play, Madsen said, "Helvis. It was about an illegitimate son of Elvis Presley who is a psychopathic killer by day and an Elvis Impersonator at night."

## DEATH BECOMES HIM

Though many of the Elvis citings and connections are admittedly abstract, the free associations with Elvis and death are quite appropriate. Elvis's name has been conveniently substituted, and used synonymously, symbolically, and metaphorically with a wide spectrum of concepts, with death, religion, drugs, guns, food, fame, and fortune, among the most common.

Many of these themes are expressed variously as Elvis synonyms in slices of film dialogue. For example, Elvis is equated with wealth, among other pleasures, in *Shakes the Clown* (1991). In a "morning after" scene, a hungover Shakes (Bobcat Goldthwait) stumbles out of the bathroom to find the young son of the woman (wholesome Florence Henderson invertedly cast from her Brady Bunch mom days) whom he has just spent the night with. Dutifully, or to save (clown) face, Shakes slips the kid some change "to go out and buy something real nice." Unimpressed at the Big Spender's gesture of generosity or pittance of a bribe, the young boy, rolling his eyes, replies, "Thanks, Elvis. This'll go a long way in the toy store." While the youthful sarcasm can be read as reference to Elvis's propensity to share his wealth and present total strangers with Cadillac gifts, the name calling also fits Shakes's various indulgences.

In the film *Undercover Blues* (1993), Elvis is an unalienable right of every citizen in the law according to agent Jefferson Blue (Dennis Quaid). As Blue drags away a suspect for questioning, he modifies the familiar legal litany: "You have the right to remain silent. If you give up that right, you may talk, sing, dance, impersonate Elvis, or anything you like . . ."

More than any other death has perhaps been the one theme most frequently connected with Elvis in film. Like other expressions of popular art, films have concretely and abstractly reflected the widespread cultural haunting, "I thought I saw a ghost, and it looked like Elvis."

The interchangeability of "Elvis" and "ghost" is illustrated in, among other places, an exchange between two friends in the low budget, made-for-video, erotic thriller *Sexual Malice* (1993). "By the look on your face, I thought you were going to say you saw Elvis," responds one woman after her shocked friend relates how she accidentally witnessed her boss having sex with a caterer at a party.

A similar ghost-like "mistaken identity" exchange involves Elvis name dropping in the South American film, *A Very Old Man with Enormous Wings* (1988). While walking on the beach following a cyclone, two villagers are confounded as they discover an old man with wet wings emerging from the water and climbing onto shoreline rock. They wonder if the man is the devil, a martian, or even a bird of paradise blown off course during the high winds. One overwhelmed observer believes the unidentified fallen or floating object may be an angel. "If that's an angel, then I'm Elvis Presley," counters his disbelieving friend. The mention of Elvis seems appropriate in the scene as he is routinely juxtaposed with or identified as an angel, devil, alien, ghost, or fallen Icarus figure. At the same time, the response substitutes Elvis for the more commonly used standards of belief and doubt such as the Easter Bunny and Santa Claus. As the surreal story line evolves into an ironic allegory, the film becomes even more analogous with Elvis. The saviorlike title character possesses a mysterious, magical demeanor that attracts onlookers and tourists who wonder about the man's identity, origin, and "heavenly message."

Belief and make believe are also presented in the "Return to Sender" iconography of *Dear God* (1996). The postal service's dead letter office has a row of sorting bins for its "most misdirected mail," featuring Superman, the Tooth Fairy, the Easter Bunny, God, and Elvis.

Predictably, an Elvis sighting is mentioned in *Blink* (1994), a thriller about an eye transplant recipient who witnesses a murder. The film's premise features familiar shadowy Elvisian dichotomies of belief and doubt, the real and imaginary. The police are skeptical of Emma Brody's (Madeline Stowe) eyewitness account because of her unreliable vision; her new eyes are still adjusting to their new home. When John Hallstrom (Aidan Quinn), the investigator assigned to the case, describes to Brody, some of unsubstantiated information he has received during his career his litany of lousy leads is punctuated with Elvis. "One guy even told me he saw Elvis Presley at his brother's bar mitzvah," says the doubting detective, his voice rising as if he is stating the ultimate dead-end lead. In *The Frighteners* (1996), an Elvis statue is among the poltergeist participants floating through a playfully possessed house. "He's alive!" exclaims the haunted homeowner.

In *A Million to Juan* (1993), a son tells his mother that she has a better chance of seeing Elvis than getting the house's broken heater fixed.

Sometimes the ghost actually is Elvis, as is the case in "A Ghost," the second of three interconnected vignettes that comprise independent filmmaker Jim Jarmusch's *Mystery Train* (1989). Luisa, a young Italian widow, has a close encounter of the Elvis kind when she checks into the decrepit Arcade Hotel in Memphis. The woman is not in the Bluff City on a Presley pilgrimage, but waiting overnight before flying her deceased husband's body back to Rome for burial. She is, however, amused when a coffee shop wacko announces that a year ago he picked up the King hitchhiking. Moreover, it seems that Elvis had a comb he wanted the driver to pass on to Luisa. Ironically, it is not the widow's husband's departing soul that appears to her as a spirit in the night, but Elvis, once again displaying his mystic knack in a strange, but appropriately enchanting and haunting manner. "The idea for the ghost came in before all the Elvis-sighting stuff," explains Jarmusch. "Although I'm sure some people will think it was a conscious attempt to be au courant."

The Elvis-death film context is expansive, a virtual celluloid necropolis that extends beyond ghosts. George Romero's apocalyptic horrors—*Night of the Living Dead* (1968), *Dawn of the Dead* (1978), and *Day of the Dead* (1985)—are a touchstone trilogy that could be adapted to the Presley afterlife line where Elvis has become an archetypal zombie. That is why he could easily be a stand-in for the vengeful slasher behind Jason's mask; a kindred spirit with Freddy Krueger infiltrating our subconscious; or a sliming, slovenly spirit being pursued by Dr. Venkman (Bill Murray) and his merry band of freelance ghostbusters. Or why the disturbing "buried alive" premise of the French psychological thriller, *The Vanishing* (1988) (and its American remake by the same director, George Sluizer in 1993) is also a fitting metaphor for Elvis A.D. To paraphrase from the title of Richard Zemeckis' black comedy, *Death Becomes Her* (1992), death has become Elvis.

It appears to be an unwritten rule of the Hollywood screenwriting trade that if a film, no matter the genre, has any kind of six-feet-undertones—be it plot, subplot, setting or scene—an Elvis reference or cameo is a convenient necessity.

In yet another Halloween setting, "Elvis" is used as a death synonym in the horror spoof, *Ernest Scared Stupid* (1991). The film is the fourth Jim Varney "Vern" vehicle for his country bumpkin character, Ernest P. Worrell. Popularized in television commercials, Ernest P. has since gone to camp (1987), jail (1990) (the result of a switch set up by an evil inmate look-alike), saved Christmas (1988), and ridden again (1994) on the big screen. In the aptly titled trick-or-treat sequel, he inadvertently releases a villainous troll from its tomb. As the dimwitted hero is about to triumph over the dwarf demon, Ernest P. sneers, "You're history . . . You're Elvis." A more profane, but slightly less fatalistic version is used by Tony in *Wildside* (1995): "You're past it. You know you're past your fucking time. You're fucking Elvis."

Action hero Jean Claude Van Damme echoes Ernest P.'s utterance during a similar good-versus-evil confrontation in John Woo's *Hard Target* (1993). "Look at it this way; at least you're going to get to meet Elvis," he consoles his enemy before disposing of him. In addition to its obvious death connotation, the line also contains a subtext of deification. Instead of the common eulogistic phrase, "meeting your Maker," it is Elvis who is presented as a divine figure waiting to greet us in the afterlife. What may be the most interesting point about Van Damme's line is its commercial connection to Elvis as well. Whether due to editing or only intended as a marketing ploy, the scene never appears in the movie, only in the film's trailers preceding its theatrical release.

In the Hollywood version of *The Vanishing* (1993), an observant elderly black woman, Mrs. Charmichael, also substitutes "Elvis" for "the dead." "What's all the ruckus?" she scolds the noisy neighbors pounding at her apartment door. "You're gonna wake Elvis!" The line may be another subtle example of the cliched Americanization process during the film's adaptation from its foreign original. Such Elvis homage is unusual from the African-American community; it is particularly unlikely from an elder spokesperson such as the one Mrs. Charmichael embodied. But a shot of the inside of Mrs. Charmichael's living room that reveals an Elvis commemorative plate hanging on the wall next to one of Martin Luther King, lends some credibility to Elvis being a meaningful part of her folksy wisdom and heritage.

In the similarly sinister setting of *Bad Influence* (1990), the secretly depraved Alex (Rob Lowe) utters an Elvis catchphrase to pronounce a person dead. Standing over the still-warm body, the creepy character casually intones, "Elvis has left the building," as if administering his victim's last rites. The same phrase punctuates a triumphant strike in a battle against earth invaders in *Independence Day* (1996).

Unlike Alex's murder murmur, or the exclamatory alien death knell, Nick Holloway's (Chevy Chase) Elvis death notice comes in the form of a toast in *Memoirs of an Invisible Man* (1992). "No they're sane. A beautiful blonde and a dead man," he lifts his glass during a dinner conversation. "Here's to Elvis." Holloway's indistinguishable, fleeting character might be viewed as an invisible embodiment the illusory Elvis.

## HEAVEN AND HELLVIS

"Being" Elvis results in death in *Elvis' Grave* (1990), a film which presents the tragic, rather than the common comic context of Elvis Impersonation. The conventions and stylings of the Elvii form—gestures, gyrations, costume—are inherently comic, and readily invite parody. No matter how serious the intentions of the performers may be, would-be Kings tend to align at the lighter end of the dramatic spectrum, and struggle to transcend caricature. They are instantly identifiable, if not intrusive, on a scene; subtlety is not possible. Recent films offer some examples. Cheech Marin does Elvis singing "Love Me Tender," in *Cheech and Chong's Next Movie* (1980). One of the supporting characters in John Landis's offbeat, insomniac comedy, *Into the Night* (1985) is an Elvis Impersonator who drives a 1959 Cadillac with the custom-painted "The King Lives" on the side. Not to be upstaged by Bo Diddley's presence in *Rockula* (1990), an Elvis Impersonator performs among the teenage vampires and virgins. In the comic book film that was a 1994 summer smash, *The Mask*, special effects transform Stanley Ipkiss (Jim Carrey), from zero to hero in a spinning array of familiar figures on a nightclub stage, including Elvis, who mumbles his slogan, "Thank you very much." And an Impersonator crawls off a gurney looking for his guitar in the emergency room of a Memphis hospital in another Grisham adaptation—*The Client* (1994). (The film also features an Elvis pez candy dispenser and Susan Sarandon's attorney character saying, "Elvis has left the building.")

Steven King hints at the tragic consequences of oneness with the King in *Needful Things* (1993), yet another of the prolific author's novels with a typically more horrible than horrifying screen adaptation. The sell-your-soul scenario involves a devilish small-town shop owner in Maine who provides objects of desire in exchange for pranks. A woman who barters for a pair of Elvis's sunglasses experiences the King's curse instead of a blessing. Likewise, in the musical remake, *Little Shop of Horrors* (1986), Steve Martin's sadistic dentist, Orin Scirvello is a leather-clad, motorcycling, nitric oxide-inhaling Presley punk persona who eventually becomes plant food.

Formal gatherings of Elvis Impersonators, whether club competitions or conventions, have become a frequent backdrop for narratives. Like the Henderson and Buffet literary entries, the film, *Honeymoon in Vegas* (1992) features a setting that is saturated with imitative imagery. Writer-director Andrew Bergman casts dozens of Elvis Impersonators to drift in and out of scenes, in foregrounds, backgrounds, and to the ground from the sky in the climax.

The corps of 34 skydivers, known as "the Flying Elvises, Utah Chapter," represents perhaps one of the most memorable presentations of Elvis impersonators. The group and its scene were a central component in the marketing strategy for the film. Not only were they featured in the advanced billing of trailers, promos, and posters—"a comedy about one bride, two grooms, and 34 flying Elvises"—but "34 Flying Elvises, Utah Chapter" became the film's descriptive catchphrase in the word-of-mouth reviews among movie audiences.

The lasting image of the sky raining Elvises over the Las Vegas neon night is richly metaphorical as it is memorable. The floating figures are aliens—invasion of the Elvii—a tabloid prophecy fulfilled; they are jumpsuited saviors descending from the heavens, falling stars; they are the businessmen in black bowler derbies portrayed in similar sky-falling fashion in Rene Magritte's painting *Golconde* (1953); they are fallout from the Elvis Big Bang that has become American popular culture.

In contrast to these playful Presley portrayals, *Elvis' Grave* is an unsuccessful attempt to present the evils of Elvis imitation. The film never progressed beyond a special preview screening in selected Southeastern theaters. Just as the project's distribution was limited, so was the production itself, which leaned closer to no-budget than low-budget. The story line never advances much farther beyond the typical cheap thriller billing of its promotional poster—"Impersonation is the highest form of flattery. Unless you're caught dead in the act." Above the phrase, an oval cloud encircles the film title in chiseled tombstone type; below is an imitation Elvis lightning bolt logo in red. The combined result of the poster's design suggests divinity and duality—heaven and hell, good and evil, god and devil, life and death—all familiar opposites and linkages all along the Elvis axis. These points, and the distance between, may, in large part, help account for the Presley prevalence in the death context.

Numerous other references have appeared in films with supernatural subtexts and afterlife themes. In the teenage horror spoof, *Buffy the Vampire Slayer* (1992), and live-action cartoon *Beetlejuice* (1988), Buffy (Kristy Swanson) and Betelgeuse (Michael Keaton) both drop Elvis's name. When Merrick (Donald Sutherland) corners Buffy in her high school gymnasium to recruit her as "the chosen one" of her generation to kill roaming vampires, the disbelieving Valley Girl sasses, "Does Elvis talk to you? Does he tell you to do things?"

Free-spirit Betelgeuse (Michael Keaton) uses Elvis's name as a decoy after a successful exorcism of the living for some newly-deads. While sitting in a crowded afterlife waiting room, the rene-gade ghoul attempts to trick a tribal head shrinker to look the other way so he can switch numbers with him. "Hey, look—there's Elvis! Yo, King," exclaims the ghost groupie.

In the thriller *Flatliners* (1990), a group of daring young medical students sample the afterlife experience through a series of danger-ous experiments conducted on each other. Seduced by death and driven by their egos, the students aim to break through to the other side and look God himself in the eye. The project escalates to a from-hero-to-eternity competition to "flatline" (the lack of vital signs that produces a flat line on EKG and EEG monitors) the long-est. Nelson (Kiefer Sutherland) discovers that the curtain of death, once penetrated, does not close behind, and he is haunted by an aggressive demon from another world.

The film's life and death manipulating premise provides another Presley parallel, if not parable. Not surprisingly, Elvis's name sur-faces as an automatic resurrection reference point. During a late-night, post-op group gathering at a coffee shop, the students boast to the waitress, "We just came back from the dead!" Unimpressed, she shrugs off their accomplishment and continues to pour coffee. "I'm not surprised. We had Elvis in here last night." The waitress serves as a droll reminder that Elvis may be the champion flatliner, continually traveling back and forth across the life and death border in our collective cultural consciousness.

Elvis's eternal presence is also made known in Albert Brooks's *Defending Your Life* (1991), as well as Richard Zemeckis's *Death Becomes Her* (1992). Brooks's comedy is set in Judgment City, an afterlife way station where individuals have the opportunity to account for their activities from their most recent lifetime before proceeding to their final destination. Though an ideal setting for Elvis, it may have been too obvious a gag for Brooks to emphasize in his intelligent, insecure strand of humor. Nonetheless, he acknowledges the icon of death, using Elvis's name as a time-line touchstone. In a scene at a club where waiting souls frequent while waiting for their tribunal hearing, a stand-up comedian approaches Dan Miller, robed at his table, and tries to find out the visitor's age in Twenty Questions fashion. "Let's play a little game," the comedian begins. "Elvis. Dead or alive?"

*Death Becomes Her* takes our cultural obsession with anti-aging cremes and cosmetic surgery to surreal and special-effect extremes. The film's age-old vanity-and-vengeance narrative of the quest for eternal youth provides another appropriate perpetual Presley premise. Elvis even lands a cameo appearance. He stands in a ballroom filled with the select group of beautiful people who have swallowed the longevity potion. Among the other famous faces mingling in the crowd are his fellow cultural icons, Marilyn Monroe and Andy Warhol. An emcee, presiding over the gathering from a balcony above, admonishes the immortals about their terms of endurement, particularly the stipulation that after ten years, participants are required to fake their death. "First, I must remind all of you who have staged your own deaths of our very strict policy against popping up in public to grab a few headlines," he scolds. "I won't name names; you know who you are." An incriminating cut to Elvis shows him casually confessing to his entourage, "I was just trying to have some fun; that's all I was doing." Of course, the death hoax, witness relocation program, government conspiracy, wax dummy in the casket, and accompanying sightings have been among the prevalent Presley postmortem theories disseminated and embraced throughout the network of Elvis true believers and disbelievers. This familiar death mythology echoes *Is Elvis Alive?* guru and gatekeeper Gail Brewer-Giorgio's novel *Orion* and *The Elvis Files: Was His Death Faked?* (1990).

Elvis goes from cameo to cadaver conversation piece, as his name surfaces in death-related dialogue in other comedies. In *Casual Sex?* (1988), Nick proclaims, "I'm gonna be huge! I am gonna have more fans than Elvis! And I won't even be dead! Think about it!" Elvis is also a reference point in a discussion in the fantasy-comedy, *Drop Dead Fred* (1991), named after a mischievous and repulsive imaginary childhood friend. "Pain makes you interesting; look at Elvis," says Janie. "But didn't he kill himself?" asks Liz. "Yes, but before that he was very interesting." And perhaps more interesting after that.

## *1950s FIXTURE AND MUSICAL MONUMENT*

Elvis has been well represented as a historic and iconic touchstone in period pieces, musicals, and biographies. This cross section of narratives spans several decades and musical genres, and portrays real and fictional characters at various stages of their careers—from wanna-bes, to stars, to has-beens.

Although Elvis's life, legacy, and landscapes appear timeless and limitless, the period and place he may be most attached to is the 1950s South. Several films set in that era and region include Elvis as the obvious child of the birth of rock and roll backdrop. An Elvis fairgrounds performance and racism are among the experiences which mark an Alabama college sorority member's social awakening in *Heart of Dixie* (1989). The generation gap and tense undercurrents resulting from the new musical forms of expression of the times surface during a scene in the made-for-cable movie, *Memphis* (1992). The story, based on Shelby Foote's *September, September*, and cowritten by novelist Larry McMurtry, is about three white-trash drifters who kidnap the grandson of a wealthy black family in Tennessee in 1957. While paging through a newspaper, Cybil Shepherd's character enthusiastically proclaims to her older partner-in-crime that Elvis is back from his tour of duty in the Army. Brother, seated with his back turned to her, mutters an indifferent, "Who?" and continues to polish his wing tips, a foot fashion statement of his age and ideology. "Elvis," she says, as if that should be enough. "Elvis who?" and "Oh" are the only responses he can manage as she explains further. His clueless state confounds and frustrates the young woman. "How can you be so dumb?" she asks. "We all got our blind spots. Mine just happens to be this fella named Elvis," Brother replies. "He is a fella, isn't he?" After she defends Elvis masculinity and further scolds Brother for "not keeping up better with what's going on in the world and taking more pride" in the Mississippi boy, the scene ends with Brother, still hunched over brushing his shoes in his hand, rolling his eyes and sighing a muffled, "Elvis." The scene, particularly Shepherd's disbelief toward Brother's Elvis ignorance, is not locked into the 1950s South. Not knowing of or about Elvis is just as, if not more, unthinkable, and perhaps even laughable, in contemporary culture and the high-tech times of the information age as it was 40 years ago. The question "Elvis who?" suggests extreme isolationism and a monastic existence, and would no doubt trigger similar expressions of bewilderment today as in *Memphis*.

The origin of Elvis's hip-shake is one of the events Tom Hanks' wise-fool Forrest Gump encounters while skimming through the last half of the twentieth century and colliding Zelig-like with history. In the fable, young Elvis is a tenant at the Gump's boarding house. Forrest, despite his cumbersome leg braces, is doing his best to teach Elvis how to "wiggle." No sooner does Elvis ask, "Show me that step again," than he is shown shaking on television during one of his early variety show appearances.

Such Elvis encounters, and their frequent revisionist results, have been requisite stops along numerous time travelers treks, whether in film, television, or literary narratives. Nor are Elviscenes exclusive to box office smashes and mainstream entertainment. Independent filmmaker Randy Clower's *My Adventures in the Time Spiral*, one of the short films featured in the *Best of the N.Y. Underground Film and Video Festival*, is an alternative *Forrest Gump* with a cynical subtext. The computer-animated journey, described by one critic as "some Carmen Santiago hipster educational video," places the hero in various significant historical moments, including a scene with Elvis. However, a disturbing pattern materializes. At each stop, antagonists verbally and physically abuse the hero for having a ponytail and wearing an earring.

Elvis period presence is also represented in the teenage musical *Grease* (1978), biographies of rock and roll pioneers Buddy Holly and Jerry Lee Lewis, and in the starmaking machinery movie, *The Idolmaker* (1980), based on the life of Philadelphia producer Bob Marucci, who discovered, manufactured, and managed Fabian and Frankie Avalon. Though the appearances are brief and the references often mere mentions, they pay mandatory historical homage. For example, in *Grease*, while Stockard Channing sings, "Look at Me, I'm Sandra Dee," Elvis is mentioned and his photograph is shown.

A much more compelling subtext and rock and roll relevant representation can be found in *Great Balls of Fire!* (1989), an inexplicably tame PG-13 version of Jerry Lee Lewis's dark-rated life, starring Dennis Quaid as the Pentecostal, pistol-packing, piano-pumping pariah. Most of the scenes featuring Elvis (played by Michael St. Gerard, who later played the singer in the ABC television series, *Elvis*) are forgettable. During a montage sequence, a sneering Elvis and his bedmate watch Lewis's televised performance on *The Steve Allen Show*. In another scene (when Lewis torches his piano on stage to spite Berry, the show's closing act, and then allegedly uttered a racial slur to Berry as he came backstage), both Elvis and Chuck Berry appear ready to accompany an equally caricatured Killer to a 1950s retro masquerade party. Seeing these imitation rock deities is comparable to watching Charlton Heston play Biblical characters, and at times feels more appropriate for Jerry Lewis rather than Jerry Lee Lewis.

The film features other Elvis ironies and quirky casting connections. Mojo Nixon and ex-X member, John Doe, have roles as Lewis's drummer and cousin, J.R. Both musicians have written songs about Elvis. Quaid himself, perhaps forgetting which character he was portraying, slips into speaking Elvese with a patented, "Thank you; thank you very much," when his cousins let him stay at their house. Behind the scenes reports indicated that late in the production, Quaid, like many Elvis Impersonators, may have gone too far into his role and became afflicted with an identity crisis, actually believing he was Lewis and could perform his songs better than the Killer. In the subsequent wave of interviews in the film and rock presses and talk show circuit, Quaid said he would not do another film until a record label signed him.

Buried beneath Jack Baran's sanitized script, and director Jim McBride's bubble gum flash, there is a shot of Lewis's reflection in a Sun Studio window, peeking out to see Elvis arriving. The composition subtly frames Lewis's life, a *Paradise Lost* saga with a backbeat and redneck drawl. Striking and sympathetic, the solitary image is a soulful chronicle of the years 1956 through 1958. That narrow, but event-filled period saw the poor, God-fearing boy from Ferriday, Louisiana, arrive at the Memphis home of his cousin, J.W., fall in love with his 13-year-old daughter, Myra Gayle Brown, and rise from oblivion to the top of the pop, country, and R&B charts all at once, as the hottest sensation at Sun Records, where producer Sam Phillips was eager to find a new Elvis to replace the one the Army borrowed for a few years.

It was Lewis's romance with Myra that led to his professional demise in 1958 during what was to be a triumphant tour in England. It did not take the Fleet Street press long to discover that Myra was Lewis's 13-year-old (not 15 as Lewis claimed) cousin bride and that Lewis had not even divorced his second wife. Scandal erupted and the man who would be king was dubbed nothing more than an incestuous cradle snatcher. Promoters canceled the tour and Lewis's career tumbled off the charts and into the backroad dives and honky-tonks.

Those three years are compressed into Lewis's looking-glass gaze toward the omnipresent Elvis. He sees a god, as well as a ghost who will haunt him. The reflection frames a portrait of the hell-bent and heaven-sent singer, foreshadowing his life. The meteoric rise and fall by the age of 23. The contradictions and struggles, demons and darkness, tragedy and turmoil, sin and salvation, hard livin' and almost dyin', kissin' and crusadin' cousins, and six wives, two of them suspiciously dead. Later in the film, when a uniformed Elvis appears at the studio late at night before leaving for duty, and concedes to Lewis, "Go on take it; take the whole thing." Yet, the crown proves thorny and elusive. The rock rumor persists that it was Elvis's shadow in the form of Colonel Parker, lurking in London who encouraged the Lewis press probe to ensure that the challengers to the King's throne keep their distance while Elvis played Army.

## GENERATIONS, LOCATIONS, AND MUSICAL VARIATIONS

You're either an Elvis person or a Beatles person.

—Uma Thurman, *Pulp Fiction* (1994)

Elvis's shadow is cast well beyond rock and roll's roots and pioneering performers. Just as he is identified as an historical 1950s fixture, Elvis is also widely represented in film as a monument among musicians of many generations, styles, social classes, and regions. As a reference point, he is a common thread connecting aspiring singers and bands in many geographical locations, from the children's world of animation, Nashville and the American South, to Japan, Ireland, Finland, and back to Graceland.

One of the more colorful settings with an Elvis subtext is in the animated animal feature *Rock-a-Doodle* (1992). Directed by Don Bluth, a former Disney artist whose film credits include *An American Tale* (1986), *The Land Before Time* (1988), and *All Dogs Go to Heaven* (1989), the feature-length cartoon (briefly intercut with brief live-action stock) is a Presley parable with a barnyard backdrop. Chanticleer is a singing rooster who thinks his crowing makes the sun rise each morning. When proven wrong, the proud cock is brokenhearted. He leaves his farm and friends and heads for the bright lights and Big City, where he finds success as a nightclub singer.

The Presley parallels abound: pink 1950s-style graphics for the title; the rooster's appearance, voice and gestures; adoring hens and chicks; musical numbers and cartoon choreography which critics readily compared to Elvis's movies; and a career transition to a Vegas-type entertainer known as "The King," managed by a Colonel Parker-type fox named Pinky.

Like Elvis, Chanticleer also becomes a sought-after savior. When darkness and torrential rain threaten to hide the sun forever, the farm critters, led by Edmond, a little boy turned kitten, head to town to find Chanticleer. They believe that only their rooster friend's crowing can send away the clouds and save everyone from an evil owl, the Grand Duke.

Another familiar figure in the film from the Elvis file is singer Glen Campbell, who provides the voice of Chanticleer. The Elvis/Campbell connection dates back to the 1960s, when the two singer's musical paths frequently crossed. Campbell played guitar and sang backup on the *Viva Las Vegas* soundtrack, and Elvis covered a number of Campbell's compositions in concert and on record. These included "Turn Around, Look At Me," "By the Time I Get To Phoenix," "Gentle on My Mind" and in addition, both recorded versions of the Bobby George/Vern Stovall tune, "Long Black Limousine." In 1970 a special edition magazine devoted an entire issue exclusively to Campbell and Elvis.

Both singers were also known to occasionally do brief, but accurate, imitations of each other during their live shows. It was Campbell's

Elvis impersonation that significantly shaped the direction of *Rock-a-Doodle*. According to Bluth, his original intentions were not necessarily to relate a Presley parable. "Glen went in and did the initial thrust of the character," he explains. "When we animated a little bit of it, we said, 'Wait a minute, that's turning out differently than we thought,' so we called him back."

What evolved was another "accidental Elvis" occurrence. Blum explains,

> Originally, he wasn't going to mimic him [Elvis]. In fact, we were very shy about asking him to do that. But once he heard the music, he started laughing, and we didn't know how he was going to take this, but he stepped to the mike. He suddenly did Elvis. I think he did it just because it was a hoot. And then he said, "The Jordanaires are in town; let's bring them in and have them sing backup." ("Bluth," 1992)

Perhaps best known for being River Phoenix's last film, *The Thing Called Love* (1993) is a story with a steel-pedal soundtrack and a struggling songwriter named Presley. Miranda Presley (Samantha Mathis) is a fledgling songwriter from New York City who heads straight for the Bluebird Cafe, Music City's mecca. Like the other prominent Presley women before her–Gladys, Priscilla, and Lisa Marie–Miranda experiences how the Presley name can be more of a burden than a blessing. Though determined to succeed, Miranda resists the temptation of fabricating some career-enhancing, distant-cousin connection. Instead, she wears the name as a middle name disclaimer, rather than a royal title. She is quick to insert, "No relation to Elvis," before the curious can ask about her lineage.

Across the continent, two band members dream of fame and fortune, citing their respective role models in *Living on Tokyo Time* (1987), a Japanese-American *Odd Couple*. "When I get famous, I'm gonna buy a limo and jacuzzi like Isaac Hayes," says one musician. His partner adds, "I'm gonna buy a lotta drugs, like Elvis."

British director Alan Parker uses the same energetic "Hey kids! Let's put on a show" spirit he presented in his *Fame* (1980) fantasy to chronicle the irresistible rise and inevitable fall of a North Dublin soul band made up of Irish working class kids in *The Commitments* (1991). The fictional biography is sprinkled with Elvis references, even though his name is never mentioned in Roddy Doyle's slim, dialogue-heavy cult novel from which the film is adapted. Elvis is a subtle reminder, if not an occasional intruder, on the sacred souls of the Motown legends, who are the band's inspiration. The group initially appears puzzled when their flinty, ingenious manager, Jimmy Rabbitte, suggests their staple be 1960s-style soul music. While the recruits all like the sound, they do not particularly identify with it. Rabbitte's ethno(il)logic class equation proves persuasive: "The Irish are the blacks of Europe. Dubliners are the blacks of Ireland. North Dubliners are the blacks of Dublin."

Elvis is revered in the Rabbitte household, where his picture hangs above a Pope John Paul portrait and Virgin Mary statues in the living room's hallowed hierarchy. The King, nonetheless, is a source of tension between godfather James Brown disciple Jimmy and his Elvis-worshiping father. When Jimmy tells his family about organizing a band, Dad rises from the dinner table. "You need a singer?" he playfully asks. Grabbing a sauce-bottle microphone, he begins to sing. "Wise men say, only fools rush in."

It is not what Jimmy had in mind. "Elvis is not soul," he says emphatically. "Elvis is God!" counters the elder Rabbitte, with father-to-son, and-don't-you-forget-it sternness. Jimmy offers an irreverent counter-theology. "I never pictured God with a fat gut and a corset singing "My Way" at Caesar's Palace."

Mr. Rabbitte witnesses further sacrilege during the auditions that Jimmy holds at the house. Among the fiddlers and folkies, acappella singers and bag pipers, punks and rockers hoping to prove they have the soul to join "the world's hardest working band" is a group singing an accordion-driven stomp called "Elvis was a Cajun." Looking in, Jimmy's father cannot believe his ears. "It's fookin' blasphemy!" he exclaims. "Elvis wasn't a Cajun." Though such lively Louisiana roots are among the few musical styles that do not commonly appear on Elvis' list of influences, singer John Hiatt entertained similar notions during the 1987 New Orleans Jazz and Heritage Festival by wearing an "Elvis Zydeco" T-shirt while performing.

Jimmy's father finally receives some affirmation of his faith in Elvis from Joey "the Lips" Fagan, the oldest Commitment, an accomplished session musician who claims to have toured with all the greats. Like everyone, Joey has an Elvis story to tell. He mesmerizes the Rabbittes with his tale about how one night at Graceland, Vernon Presley "wasn't drinkin' lemonade" and picked up Lips' trumpet, "Gina," and "puked right into her." Joey went upstairs to find Elvis. "Elvis, me man. Look what your daddy's done to Gina and who's gonna pay to have her cleaned." According to Lips, Elvis took the instrument to the bathroom, "ran it under the tap and gave her a good wipe," and returned it saying, "Please forgive my daddy." An awestruck Mr. Rabbitte falls back into his chair, then cautiously, almost devoutly asks, "Tell me something, Joey, all the time you were at Graceland, did you ever see Elvis use any drugs?" "No, brother," replies Joey without hesitation. The testimony triggers a chain reaction from the Rabbitte family. "I knew it!" exclaims the father, then turning to Jimmy with an I-told-you-so tone, "I always said . . ." Then Mrs. Rabbitte's "My God Almighty!" punctuates the scene like an "Amen!" during an emotional church service.

Proven to be effective in America and Ireland, the familiar *Fame* formula has an Elfinnish flavor with a *Stranger Than Paradise* sensibility in Aki Kaurismaki's *Leningrad Cowboys Go America* (1989). Less talented than the Commitments, the Leningrad Cowboys are an offbeat combo of Sha Na Na, the Pogues, and Blues Brothers. The eight-piece outfit's most distinctive trait is not its musical fusion, but its fashion—a uniform appearance highlighted by jet-black pointed pompadours extending unicorn-like from their foreheads. Combined with equally exaggerated elflike shoes to match, and sunglasses, the look creates a kitschy Elvis Orbison feel similar to that of rockabilly alternative act Hillbilly Frankenstein.

The Cowboys' modern wasteland tour is a *Lost in America* journey with Elvis nuances that include cover songs; a Cadillac (sold to them by a used car dealer played by independent filmmaker Jim Jarmusch); a stop in Memphis; and a controlling Colonel-like manager named Vladimir. In addition, one of the musicians, Pekka, stands as an Elvis metaphor. The night before the struggling band departs the tundra for the U.S.—a place where "they'll put up with anything"—Pekka stays out too long in the cold rehearsing and is frozen stiff. Declared neither dead or alive, Pekka nonetheless makes the trip, transported by his fellow Cowboys in a coffinlike wooden box secured to the top of the car. They ice him down at each stop during the trek between New York City and Mexico, where they are headed to play a wedding gig.

The popsicle Pekka as a Presley parallel becomes more noticeable when a police officer interrupts the refugees' mock jazz funeral procession down a New Orleans sidestreet. Climbing onto the roof of their "hearse," the cop examines the possible corpse lying in the oversized cooler filled with beers. Uncertain of its condition, he turns to the band members and asks, "How do you know this guy's dead?" The doubting inquiry is the familiar expression of Elvisian ambiguity. Pekka on parade is a preserved Presley–freeze-dried, embalmed, refrigerated, mummified, and immortalized. The accompanying implications of resurrection follow when Pekka thaws South of the border, his return aided by a bottle of Tequila.

Johnny Suede's (Brad Pitt) quest to be a hip pop singing success is a pompadour and circumstance saga reminiscent of the Fab Finnish combo. In *Johnny Suede* (1991), a *Wizard of Oz* meets *Pee Wee's Big Adventure*, the lead character sports an exaggerated coif that might prompt Stray Cat Brian Setzer, Cosmo Kramer, and Lyle Lovett, or Don King to ask enviously, "Who does your hair?" A narrator explains how "Johnny has it all"–the look, the hair, the clothes–everything except one thing that would make him feel complete. Suddenly, a pair of black suede shoes drops out of the night sky like Florsheim manna onto the phone booth in the alley where Johnny walks. Though the color may be a shade off, the pair of patented Presleys are a falling famous footwear fashion statement. Like Dorothy's ruby slippers, and Cinderella's glass slippers, the suede shoes contain a mythical and magical nature for Johnny.

Johnny has a split persona. Although he views himself as a Ricky Nelson-type, Elvis is clearly part of his being as well. Standing on a stage in front of an audience of screaming teens, Johnny adapts the Elvis stance into Beat Poet posturing. He holds one of his sacred suedes up to the microphone, combs it with a toothbrush, and cooly begins his recitation:

> Suede is a funny thing. It's rough, but soft. It's strong, but quiet. And it don't wrinkle and it don't crack. And it don't stand out so much in a world of leather and vinyl. (He whispers, then pushes the mike stand.) You don't notice it at first. But once you do, you can't take your eyes off it and you wonder how the hell you ever overlooked it in the first place.

As Johnny points to the crowd, all that is missing is the Elvis sneer.

Johnny Suede's half-Nelson hold on Elvis is a rarity. Sort of. Even though Elvis's and Ricky's careers briefly intersected, similarities between the two singer/actors seldom have been cited. While Peter Guralnick is among those who recognize Nelson's appropriation of the Elvis sneer, stance, and repertoire, Nelson was perhaps more often compared to Pat Boone.

One of the more intriguing and obscure connections surfaces in *True Dylan*, Sam Shepard's one-act play based on an actual California conversation he had one afternoon with Bob Dylan. During the play-wright-songwriter discourse, Dylan links Elvis's idol, James Dean, with his famous contemporaries of the 1950s. The free-wheeling, six-pack chat on a brick patio overlooking the Pacific Ocean begins with Dylan's preoccupation with James Dean. He has just returned from the spot on the Paso Robles highway where the rebel hero was killed in 1955. "You know what Elvis said?" asks Dylan. "He said that if James Dean had sang he'd've been Ricky Nelson." Shepard responds curiously, "Is that right?"

Dylan then exits stage right to "make a couple phone calls." Upon returning, he asks Shepard a question, but the playwright is too distracted digesting Dylan's Elvis quote. Shepard acts as if he was caught off guard, perhaps expecting to ease into the conversation rather than being greeted with such a striking statement. "If James Dean sang he'd've been Ricky Nelson?'" repeats the entranced Shepard. "Elvis said that?"

Published in *Esquire* magazine (July 1987, pp. 60-68), the script does not indicate the tone or expression in Shepard's voice, thus making his response imaginatively ambiguous and difficult to decipher. Is Shepard overwhelmed by the union of such a fantastic four-some in one phrase? Is he shocked that such a nugget emerged so quickly in their conversation? Is he sorting through the arrangement and its iconic intricacies? Or is he bewildered by the anonymity of the quote; why hasn't he read or heard it before? Perhaps he doubts Dylan's translation or its authenticity and origins? Or is he surprised that Elvis could make such a profound analogy?

By any interpretation or reading, Elvis's line is a remarkably rich, if not haunting text, striking in its characterization, obscurity, and im-probability, and its essence further enhanced by Dylan's nasal citation.

One would expect to find such a connection in the writings of a Marcus or Guralnick, rather than in an observation attributed to a poor white trash truck driver from Tupelo, Mississippi, named Elvis. The quote may read like some elementary popular culture assignment—use four famous figures in the same sentence—but its significance and impact transcends words. Bob Dylan quoting Elvis comparing Jimmy Dean to Ricky Nelson is a mythical mouthful.

That moment from Dylan's conversation with Shepard might be compared to four-and-a-half musical minutes of the god-like gathering for Dylan's thirtieth anniversary celebration at New York's Madison Square Garden, October 16, 1992. The collective Grammy-nominated performance of "My Back Pages" represented a monumental nexus, a rock formation of recitation, rosary and religion, communion and chronology, legend and lineage. Aging gracefully, gleefully, grungefully—Byrds' founder Roger McGuinn, Tom Petty, Neil Young, Eric Clapton, George Harrison, and Dylan, backed by a band that included G.E. Smith, Al Kooper, Steve Cropper, and "Duck" Dunn, alternated verses as if swearing some solemn oath.

Whether play, page, or performance, the effect of these two tableau expressions is similar. There is a strong sense of something sacred or special being spoken and sung, even if experienced indirectly through reading Shepard's one-act play, viewing the Bobfest concert video, or listening to its accompanying recording. They are defining moments and events in themselves. Bob Dylan citing Elvis; Elvis comparing James Dean and Ricky Nelson; and some of rock's most important musicians singing Dylan is mythmaking at its best—myth magnifying myth.

Elvis has not only been a prevalent reference point in films about aspiring musicians, he also merits multiple mentions in *One-Trick Pony* (1980), the story of a 1960s folk-singing has-been. Paul Simon stars as Jonah Levin, an aging rock star trying to salvage his marriage and adapt to the changing music industry and audience. Although his career is fading, Jonah, too, was initially inspired by Elvis. His wife (Blair Brown), however, never had much faith in Jonah's elusive Elvis dream. In a "grow up" speech, she bluntly assesses his lingering adolescence and career. "You have wanted to be Elvis Presley since you were thirteen. Now that's a goal you're not likely to achieve. He didn't do so well with it himself," she says. "Don't you think it's time you give up that illusion?"

Jonah nonetheless continues to travel the country by van, playing the small club circuit with his little band. While on the road, the musicians engage in a lively round of "Rock and Roll Deaths," a simple game of trivia that involves naming deceased singers, whether from natural causes, overdoses, suicides, or plane crashes. The bored band members compile an extensive necrology that ranges from the obvious qualifiers—Hendrix, Joplin, Valens, Holly, Croce—to lesser knowns such as Tim Hardin, Terry Kath of the group Chicago, and the drummer of the Average White Band. The game abruptly dead end's when someone from the back seat of the van says, "Elvis." Although their list is incomplete, the utterance of Elvis's name is a climactic punctuation mark that reverberates with reverence reserved for the King. Underneath the hush in the van with nothing apparently left to be added, Jonah quietly confirms, "Yeah, he's dead."

## *FETISH AND FASHION STATEMENTS*

Another reverent Elvis death acknowledgment appears later in a bathroom scene while Jonah shaves and his young son watches. A reflection in the mirror reveals Jonah's T-shirt as a 100 percent cotton obituary that reads, "Elvis Presley 1935-1977."

Such Elvis memorabilia has been sparse as film iconography. The T-shirts, scarves, velvet portraits, decanters, and such are most commonly found scattered throughout films such as *One-Trick Pony* and others that feature Presley premises and characters who are Elfans.

The attention to the Elvis's artifacts and images varies. Some shots linger, such as the pan to Elvis's portrait beneath the Pope in the Rabbitte living room, or the zoom to a troubled teenager's Elvis poster in her bedroom in *Out of the Blue* (1980). Others provide only a glimpse. Standing in the doorway of Mrs. Charmichael's dwelling, we peek inside to see portraits of Elvis and Martin Luther King Jr. hanging side by side on her wall. An Elvis Pez candy dispenser in *The Client* is inconspicuous. In *Into the Night* (1985), singer Carl Perkins, who plays a hood, is leaning against a car reading a copy of *Elvis, What Happened?* In the made-for-video thriller, *Liar's Edge* (1992), an "I (♥/

Love) Elvis" bumper sticker attached to a car blends unobtrusively with the film's Niagara Falls misty tourist atmosphere.

Elvis is also a hotel fixture. Not only does his presence pervade the halls and walls of Memphis's rundown Arcade Hotel in *Mystery Train*, his image also appears at another sleazy boarding joint in *The Indian Runner* (1991), actor Sean Penn's impressive directorial debut, inspired by Bruce Springsteen's song, "Highway Patrolman," from his dark *Nebraska* (1982) record.

Elvis's likeness is part of a late-night conflict between a shacked-up guest and management. The scene and its characters exhibit a Midwestern decadence that is restrained *Twin Peaks*. The hotel manager, an obese carnival candidate, confronts a hard-luck loser, Frank, about the excessive noise in his room. The temperamental veteran with a criminal nature is controlled, but uncooperative. Standing in the doorway, Frank pays little attention to the manager, and instead looks down at Elvis's face floating on the innkeeper's orange tent of a T-shirt.

The image is not the tragic Elvis memorialized on Jonah's shirt in *One-Trick Pony*. Nor is it the same Elvis Neil Young wore on September 30, 1989 while performing "Rockin' in the Free World" on *Saturday Night Live*, a face characterized, if not dissected, by Greil Marcus as

> distant, detached, crudely sculpted, very dead, and as Young sang, the face seemed to take on the casts of busts of Abraham Lincoln that dot the interiors of *The Manchurian Candidate*: saddened, betrayed, forced to witness every treason. (1991, p. 196)

Elvis may be a forced witness again standing in the doorway of the rowdy hotel room. But he is also a mediator situated between the manager and guest. He is a bouncer, a big brother, a parent, a police officer, there to restore order. He is as alive as the innkeeper. Frank appears to be reacting to, and rejecting, Elvis, as much as he, is the manager. He is drawn to Elvis. He looks him in the eye, rather than acknowledging the timid night clerk, then pulls the Beefy-T over the manager's head, symbolically smothering the voice of authority in black-on-orange Elvis. Frank's in-your-silkscreen-face act of defiance renders both Elvis and his messenger powerless.

Film references and visits to the Memphis memorabilia mecca, Graceland, have been minimal compared to those presented in other cultural fare. In the comedy, *Ace Ventura, Pet Detective* (1994), Ace (Jim Carrey) follows a lead to a football hero's parent's home while investigating a case involving a missing dolphin. The inside is a wall-to-wall homage to their son's athletic accomplishments. Hoping to gain access and a clue, the charming pet detective feigns reverence, saying, "This is my Graceland."

A similar proclamation by a suburban Atlanta family is the basis for independent filmmaker George King's wry 30-minute documentary, *Ten Thousand Points of Light* (1991). Every yuletide season from 1982 until 1990, the Townsends transformed their Stone Mountain, Georgia, brick ranch house into their own Winter Wonder Graceland. Their decorating frenzy, known as the "Elvis Christmas House," is a crafty collision of King, King of Kings, and Claus. "Christmas and Elvis go together. Nothing will take the place of Christ. But Elvis was a good man; he was good to everybody," says Granny Margaret Townsend, the family's obsessive matriarch who originated the tradition 23 years ago.

The visual extravaganza is a meteoric blaze of twinkling lights illuminating an array of Elvis memorabilia, rampant reindeer, Santas, and angels. Interspersed among the earthly icons are traditional and nontraditional Nativity scenes, including one created from white and dark chocolates, graham crackers, and a baby Jesus molded out of marshmallows. The site also features its own version of "The Jungle Room," called "Fantasy Room," and a soundtrack with strains of Tennessee Ernie Ford crooning, "How Great Thou Art." Further mirroring its Memphis model, the fabled attraction drew an estimated 4,000 visitors annually during its eight-year holiday existence before the family moved to North Carolina in 1990.

The tinsel Townsend excess is a familiar kitsch aesthetic that checkers the American cultural landscape, beginning in Memphis at Graceland and stretching down the road to Paul MacLeod's 24-hour, seven days a week, 365 days a year "Graceland Too" in Holly Springs, Mississippi; to Stephanie Pierce's installations at Where's the Art? in Portland, Oregon; to Eddie Fadal's Waco, Texas home converted into a mini-museum; to the altar in Val's Halla record shop in Oak Park, Illinois; and on to an endless number of points and accidental destinations in between and beyond.

*Ten Thousand Points of Light* does not succumb to convenient Lettermanesque mockery apparent in other 30-minute Elvideos. Among them are those distributed by Rhino Home Video–the tall and tell tale tabloid and comic sketch collection, *Elvis Stories* (1990), featuring among other items, burger king Corkey whose patties transmit messages from Elvis; and *Mondo Elvis* (1990), an account of the "real-life" rites and rituals, dreams and devotions of Elfanatics. Instead, King's sympathetic portrayal of the talkative Townsends as mainstream eccentrics, with a strict television regimen and a generous community spirit, aligns more comfortably along the slice of Americana axis with the pseudohip Texas crazies in David Byrne's film *True Stories* (1986), Jonathan Demme's Melvin Dummar, and even Michael Moore's angst-ridden working-class in *Roger and Me* (1989). *Ten Thousand Points of Light* is gently ironic and affectionate in its observance of working-class values, rituals, quirks, and obsessions.

Whether a souvenir stop or sacred shrine, Graceland is seemingly a mandatory mission for most musicians. In the concert documentary, *U2: Rattle and Hum* (1988), the Memphis mansion is among the attractions and activities the band members find themselves engaged in. Through the emigrant view of the Irish rockers, American director Phil Joanou captures what Karen Woods describes in Marshall Crenshaw's film guide, *Hollywood Rock* (1994), as a "distinctly European fascination with Americana [that is] part awe, part contempt" (p. 238).

The stop at Graceland is but one essential element in the composite. Bono and band also perform "Still Haven't Found What I'm Looking For," in Harlem with the gospel choir Voices of Freedom; watch the mighty Mississippi River roll; record at Sun Studios; and deface the Embarcadero in San Francisco. "The only scenes really missing are trips to the Grand Canyon and Mount Rushmore," writes Woods. "To an outsider, America is brash, adolescent, and dangerous, and that's the way we see the country here."

### OUT OF THE BLUE SUEDE
### AND INTO THE BLACK:
### THE 1960s ELVOID

When tracing Elvis representations and references in film, there is a striking gap between the fertile 1950s, where Elvis is a fixture, and more recent settings that begin with the 1970s. The 1960s are barren. Whereas the 1950s is a renowned Presley Period, the decade that followed is barren, as Elvis is notably absent from films with distinct 1960s backdrops. Filmmakers chose to portray the turbulent sociopolitical currents of the era and collective consciousness with the likes of Mrs. Robinson and easy riders in search of the real America; post-Army Elvis appeared detached from the pulse of the times. The Elvoid might further be explained by the fact that the 1960s was the period when Elvis was most involved with his own movie career. As a result, the number of references were reduced, or limited to Elvis the actor, which apparently has been a considerably different identity to harness and represent than the polarized Presleys predominantly portrayed—the young 1950s punk and the later model—Las Vegas jumpsuited King.

Small-town Ohio in 1972 is the setting for one of the ultimate Elfantasies—kidnapping the King (whether dead or alive)—in *Heartbreak Hotel* (1988). Ironically, the film's release, and its premise, coincided with the wave of sightings that swept the country during the late 1980s. Written and directed by Steven Spielberg disciple, Chris Columbus, the story is about a teenager named Johnny Wolfe who kidnaps Elvis and brings him home to cheer up his mother (ex-Elvis costar Tuesday Weld), an Elvis devotee who is recovering from a car accident.

The movie substitutes Elvis as the otherworldly figure that arrives to touch the lives of a troubled suburban family without a father figure. "Think E.T. with a Southern drawl," characterizes *Atlanta-Journal Constitution* (September 30, 1988, p. 5C) film critic, Steve Dollar. (Bumper stickers parodying Spielberg's lovable extraterrestrial with the substitute message, "E.P. Phone Home," coincided with the film's release and sightings phenomenon.) Johnny and his afraid-of-the-dark kid sister, Pam, live upstairs over the family business, The Flaming Star, a fleabag motel run by the mother, a divorced alcoholic with a junkyard boyfriend. Johnny is a Michael J. Fox type, who prefers the Stones and the Dead to Elvis. He has his own rock band that was banned from the high school talent show. To make matters worse, his working-class status prohibits him from dating his dream girl.

Universally panned by critics, *Heartbreak Hotel* is packed with B-grade cliches, tongue-in-cheek lines, and pure Elvis shtick. "[It] plays more like *That Darn Elvis.* . . . A thin idea gets stretched thinner," writes Dollar. For example, Johnny and his pals desperate kidnapping plot involves Rosie, the local pizza matron, who resembles Elvis's mother, Gladys. They travel to Cleveland where Rosie, in makeup and wig, convinces Elvis she is his beloved mother returning from her grave for one last visit with her son. She lures Elvis outside his hotel at 3 a.m. and the high schoolers chloroform the King and whisk him away in—what else—a pink Cadillac.

Once Elvis is abducted in the plot, the fantasy descends to absurd levels. Johnny jumps on the 1970s Elvis critical bandwagon, telling his hostage he has lost his sense of danger. As the two bond, Elvis shares tips about picking up women, offers instruction in pelvis-grinding, and agrees to make an appearance at the high school talent show. Johnny is converted, as is his bedroom; it becomes a Jungle Room replica. Elvis also helps redecorate the rest of the rundown motel's interiors in vintage Graceland kitsch. Columbus also includes the requisite Elvis fat joke when Elvis pines for the grease and glory of a cheeseburger. Even tender scenes, such as the bedside moments when Elvis comforts young Pam, are smirking reminders of the widespread revelations of sensationalists such as Albert Goldman about the King's fondness for pubescent adolescents.

Other Elvis fantasies appear in more recent films. In the pyrokinetic comedy, *Wilder Napalm* (1993), Debra Winger's character relates a less fanciful Elvis scenario from her subconscious sleepscape. "Last night I dreamt we were Elvis and Ann-Margret in Las Vegas," she announces to her husband at breakfast. "Again?" he says nonchalantly without looking up from working a newspaper crossword puzzle. The indifference is almost identical to Brother's immunity to Cybil Sheppard's attempt to draw him into an Elvis discussion in *Memphis*. Winger explains that this episode was different; they were booked in a hotel lounge that was reminiscent of Sartre's *No Exit:*

> We were like prisoners held captive unless, or until you could sing. And I mean, you were Elvis, so it wasn't like you couldn't sing. But you wouldn't do it!
> "Come on King."
> "No thanks, ma'am. I think I'll just stick with this valet parking thing, uh, uh."
> Think that means something?

As the plot evolves, it becomes clear that her recurring dream, particularly "Elvis's" refusal to sing, is foreshadowing of Winger's reformed husband's refusal to use his pyrokinetic skills, even when prodded by his antagonistic brother.

Elvis's image also surfaces in the context of a sexual fantasy in the S&M comedy, *Exit to Eden* (1994), the adaptation of Ann Rice's story of a young man who goes to a pleasure resort to work out his kinks. Upon seeing a pudgy Dan Aykroyd in a bondage outfit, wicked whipster quipster Rosie O'Donnell denounces the captivating sex-slave fashion as style, "Elvis goes to hell."

Elvis is also an object of affection to another troubled family's teenage daughter in *Out of the Blue* (1980), an independent film directed by Dennis Hopper. Hopper plays Don, an alcoholic truck driver who serves a six-year prison term after his semi-trailer rig rams a school bus, killing six children. His ex-wife is a drug addict and small-town waitress.

Their daughter, CeBe (Linda Manz), an Elvis-worshiping, leather-jacketed, cigarette-smoking, streetwise 15-year-old, is the film's centerpiece. Elvis is her imaginary friend who helps her escape and cope with her pathetic parents. "I'm gonna be like you; you'll see," says the aspiring rock star to her ghost hero, as she sings along to his tunes. (In addition to CeBe's shoe-polish-hair Elvis routines while barricaded in her room, freak street musicians cover Elvis in another scene.)

CeBe frequently displays an Elvisian androgyny; beneath her punk bravado is a vulnerable child. A camera shot tilts up from CeBe sucking her thumb while clutching her stuffed teddy bear, to a cross-shaped collage of Elvis images on her bedroom wall. Her father, also a hero to her, recognizes that Elvis is a means of communicating and relating to his daughter. "Am I as sexy as Elvis?" Don asks. And in another scene, he says, almost exasperated with his daughter's obsession, "Elvis, Elvis, Elvis. Man, I know about Elvis."

Though the families in *Out of the Blue* and *Heartbreak Hotel* both are located on lonely street and share similar states of disorder and dysfunction, there is a stark contrast in the narrative tones. Hopper chooses fatalism over fantasy. He has shaped a bitter tragedy about adolescent alienation and its accessories–rebellion, heartbreak, and loneliness–that escalates to a nihilistic conclusion.

*Out of the Blue* is also a post-Punk period marker that appeared on the decade cusp a short time after Elvis's death. Hopper, originally hired only to act, took over as director two weeks into production and rewrote the script. Initially screened at Cannes Film Festival in 1980, the film's widespread release was hindered by distribution deal difficulties.

The title is inspired by the Neil Young song, "My My, Hey Hey (Out of the Blue)," a punk anthem to Johnny Rotten from Young's *Rust Never Sleeps* (1979) album. Hopper has listened to the record; his direction places Presley and punk rock alongside each other. In the opening sequence, CeBe is hitchhiking, wearing her denim jacket with an embroidered "Elvis" on the back, as Young's acoustic whine plays on the soundtrack. The lyrics that proclaim "rock and roll will never die," and that "it's better to burn out than to fade away" foreshadow the film's fiery finale. CeBe and her family join Presley, Rotten, Cobain and other flaming fatalities, while Hopper, Young, and less tortured souls remain as survivors struggling to interpret their stories.

The Presley Punk union surfaces again during a linear conversation between CeBe and a taxi driver. "Elvis . . ." says the driver, identifying the tune coming from the backseat. "Elvis is with me forever. Punk is here to stay. Disco sucks," recites CeBe in a programmed monotone, her litany spanning several musical eras. "Elvis . . . he was one of the first punks," responds the driver, hoping to enlighten the 15-year old passenger.

While *Out of the Blue* may be Post-Punk, it is also Post-Presley. The Kings–Elvis and Johnny Rotten–are "gone but not forgotten" as the spirits of '76 and '77 are alive in CeBe. It is one of the few films which expresses a genuine sense of mourning for Elvis, rather than using his image in a comic context. Through CeBe, and the well-placed montages with Young's songs, "My My, Hey Hey" and "The Thrasher," Hopper captures the lingering grief and collective cultural coping in the first three years following Elvis's death.

## KING OF THE ROAD:
## CONVERTIBLE ODYSSEYS AND GHOST RIDES

One of the most popular film subgenres for Elvis citings since the late 1980s and early 1990s has been the road (and roadkillers) picture.

Not only has a Presley persona defined several leading characters on their cross country journeys, the King has also been cast as a mentor, an anti-Elvis, a dog, devil, and ghost. The settings and stops, scenery and scenarios the Presley passenger is thrust into along the way comprise a familiar landscape of sex, drugs, violence, and rock and roll.

*True Romance* (1993), *Wild at Heart* (1990), *Kalifornia* (1993) and *Highway 61* (1991) all travel the backroads, mining the junk-white trash-popular culture which Elvis has fashionably and comfortably settled into as a patron saint figure. The cross country cruising companions in these films are a combination of Bonnie and Clyde, Sid and Nancy, and Elvis and Marilyn, who joy-ride in their coffin-carrying cruiser convertibles–Cadillacs, Continentals, T-Birds, and Galaxie 500s.

In *True Romance*, stylishly directed by *Top Gun's* Tony Scott from another torturous, bullet-riddled screenplay by writer Quentin Tarantino, Elvis's credit is as "The Mentor" (Val Kilmer), a guardian angel figure who regularly appears in the bathroom shadows and mirrors to offer advice to Clarence Worley (Christian Slater), an Elvis worshiper who works in a Detroit comic book store.

In the opening scene, as Charlie Sexton's "Graceland" rockabilly-bye-babies on the soundtrack, Clarence sits at a bar discussing his hero Elvis with a woman. It is clear that Clarence has considered the King on many levels. His barstool treatise reveals how deep rooted his admiration is, as he drifts into a confessional psychosexual view of the androgyny and beauty of Elvis.

> He [Elvis] *is* rockabilly. Mean, surly, nasty . . . In that movie, he couldn't give a fuck about nothin' . . . except rockin' and rollin', livin' fast, dyin' young, and leavin' a good-lookin' corpse. I watch that hillbilly and I want to be him so bad.
>
> Elvis looked good. I ain't no fag, but Elvis was prettier than most women. Most women. You know, I always said, if I *had* to fuck a guy, I mean *had to*; if my life depended on it; I'd fuck Elvis.

The woman listening to Clarence replies that she would do the same. "Really?" enthuses Clarence. "Well, when he was alive, not now," she corrects dizzily. "I don't blame you," he replies. "So, we'd both fuck Elvis. Nice to meet people with common interests."

Although Clarence is unable to convince the woman to accompany him to a Kung Fu triple feature, that same night at the movie theater he meets the girl of his dreams, Alabama Whitman (Patricia Arquette), a sweet, polyester and peroxide gal from the Deep South. Although a novice call girl, she could very easily be the "good girl" Tom Petty sings about in "Free Fallin'." "I never had as much fun with a girl my whole life," Clarence tells her. "You like Elvis; you like Janis; you like Kung Fu movie; you like the Partridge Family." The two marry the next day in a two-tattoo ceremony at City Hall.

The romance becomes a love and let die travelogue as the honeymooners head for California with a suitcase filled with cocaine after nobly slaying Alabama's pimp. Hot in pursuit of their purple Cadillac, and leaving a blood-on-the-tracks trail are trigger-happy Hollywood movie execs, cops, and Mafia mobsters, all claiming possession of the lost luggage.

Amidst the carnage and chaos, Clarence routinely slips into the bathroom to communicate with the higher power, Elvis. As The Mentor, he advises Clarence as Bogart advises Woody Allen in *Play It Again, Sam*, only Kilmer's shadowy figure is more like the antagonistic devilish angel perched on the left shoulder delivering cool pep talks. The Mentor likes Clarence's macho. "Can you live with it? Are you haunted? Kill him," advises Elvis regarding Alabama's pimp. Those phrases are strikingly ironic coming from Elvis. It also marks the second time Kilmer has been cast as a rock deity, having played Jim Morrison in Oliver Stone's *The Doors* (1991).

Beyond Elvis's bathroom role, other references thread the narrative. "Elvis" rescues Alabama during a savage struggle as she smashes an Elvis whiskey decanter over her assailant's head. He surfaces again at a hamburger joint on the cover of *Newsweek* that someone is looking through. Clarence recognizes the issue, and stops to offer his critique, saying it is probably the second-best piece he's ever read on Elvis Presley, "It covers the whole spectrum." (The anniversary article, "Forever Elvis," was written by Jim Miller for *Newsweek*, August 3, 1987.) And in the final scene, Alabama's narration reflects on her relationship with Clarence, as she watches him and a little boy frolic on the beach, "Things be much as they are now, except maybe I wouldn't have named our son Elvis." Patricia Arquette's role in the film strangely foreshadows her own "true romance" in real life as she eventually married actor Nicholas Cage, who has been cast in numerous Elvisian roles.

## *KING CAGE*

*Wild at Heart* follows a very similar road map. Based on Barry Gifford's novel (1990), director David Lynch transforms the story into a Southern Gothic heart of darkness odyssey through hell, Hot Tuna, Texas, and Oz. Behind the wheel winding through this weird and wild world are ex-con Sailor (Nicholas Cage) and Lula (Laura Dern), an Elvis and Marilyn on a roller coaster ride to redemption.

Lynch's adaptation features a Presley persona and point of view not found in Gifford's original story. The only mention of Elvis in the novel is as a fat red dog. "Don't look like Elvis ever missed a meal, Red," says a man kneeling next to the dog (p. 112). The Presley pet reference not only ricochets to alligators named "Elvis" (*Miami Vice's* (NBC) Sonny Crockett and Nickelodeon network's Clarissa each are proud owners on their shows), but more specifically connects with another violent, white-trash road trip, *Kalifornia*. This nightmarish, cross-cultural double date fetures a bored yuppie couple, one of whom is writing a book on serial killers. They are traveling companions with a redneck Sid and Nancy duo, Early Grace (Brad Pitt), who is a serial killer, and Adele Corners (Juliette Lewis). At a trailer park scene that closely resembles the passage in Gifford's novel, the landlord yells to his pit bull humping another dog, "Elvis, get the fuck off him."

Like Clarence in *True Romance*, Sailor is an Elvis acolyte. He speaks the Presley language, and even croons a few Elvis tunes throughout the film, including "Love Me Tender" from the hood of a car in the climax. His jacket, which he proudly proclaims as his "personal symbol of duality and individuality," is a snakeskin version of Elvis's famous gold lamé designed by Nudie's Rodeo Tailors in Hollywood.

Like the T-shirts, scarves, shoes, and jumpsuits, the jacket is among numerous Elvis clothing conventions with its share of interconnections in other cultural texts. Among other linkages, the jacket triggers a fatalistic fashion flashback to the circa 1978 *Saturday Night Live* body's-still-warm sketch, "Elvis Presley's Coat," in which the gold lamé hangs by itself on a stand, shaking and rotating on a stage "in concert." "Hear the hits; see the coat," hypes the announcer. The sketch is out of the K-Tel tour mold, complete with Elvis on the soundtrack, cutaways to a screaming audience, and raves in the lobby following the premiere. "I've seen all the imitation coat shows and they don't compare," gushes one "concert goer." "Simply mindboggling," adds another. The tag concludes, "The King may be dead, but the coat lives on."

The iconic gold lamé suit is displayed in a more reverent fashion in an Albert Watson photograph on the cover of one of *Rolling Stone*'s three twenty-fifth anniversary special issues (November 12, 1992), this one devoted to "Portraits: The History of Rock and Roll in Photography."

Sailor's jacket is sacred and symbolic, just as Byron Bluford's jumpsuit was worn as a source of power in *Stark Raving Elvis*, or Johnny Suede's shoes that completed his cool ensemble. Two years later in *Honeymoon in Vegas*, Cage would make a similar Elvis fashion statement with a jumpsuit. When Cage's character, gambling gumshoe Jack Singer and his fiancé Betsy (Sarah Jessica Parker) first arrive in Las Vegas for a wedding weekend, they are standing in a hotel lobby congested with Elvis Impersonator conventioneers. "I gotta get one of those suits," he says half-seriously. At the climax, he is forced to don one of the flared rhinestone costumes that literally becomes a jumpsuit when he desperately enlists as a parachuting Presley by joining the earthbound "Flying Elvises." Only after the commitment-shy Jack "becomes Elvis" by wearing the suit is he empowered and confident enough to "win back" his girl whom he lost in a poker game. During the finale, Betsy is cast into a *Bye, Bye, Birdie* role, wearing a showgirl outfit while awaiting her descending hero. The film becomes *Viva (Honeymoon in) Las Vegas* with the reunited couple becoming a latter-day Elvis and Ann-Margret. Two years later, a similar scenario involving floating Elvis impersonators and showgirls strutting on a desert highway appears in the music video for Sheryl Crow's, "Leaving Las Vegas" (1994).

The character Sailor marks a baptism for Cage as Elvis. *Honeymoon*'s Jack Singer followed, then *Saturday Night Live*'s writers recognized the typecast and wrote a sketch called "'Lil Elvis," (an Elvis penis subreference) which featured guest host Cage as a miniature King. In addition, it does not take a close examination of Andy

Kauffman's Elvis Impersonation routine to recognize the striking separated-at-birth similarity between Cage and Kauffman; Cage could easily pass as the late comedian's evil twin, or Andy incarnate.

American Culture scholar Greg Metcalf suggests Cage may be more appropriately viewed as an "anti-Elvis" than as Elvis. "Between *Wild at Heart* and *Honeymoon in Vegas*, Cage's characters are clearly defined in the context of Elvis, but he is someone who is clearly not Elvis," writes Metcalf in a personal correspondence. Years after these films, the anti-Elvis in Cage subtly surfaces again as he and the King are reunited and juxtaposed as symbolic opposites in *It Could Happen to You* (1994). In the romantic comedy, Cage plays good guy, Charlie Lang, a New York City cop who splits his winning lottery ticket with a hard-luck waitress (Bridget Fonda). When Charlie's free-spending wife Luisa (Rosie Perez) has their place remodeled, a gold Elvis bust is part of the decor. The camera shot does not emphasize the King's presence. The sculpture sits silently in the background, eavesdropping as Charlie and Luisa clash and unravel over their financial philosophies. While the statue stands as an appropriate symbol of excess, it is also a shadow following Cage throughout his career.

Cage's own perspective on his series of roles reinforces, to a degree, the "anti-Elvis" postulate. He rejects any "one with the King" connection, whether as Elvis himself or an impersonator. Instead he seems to place himself in some "accidental Elvis" category:

It's amazing to me how they [Elvis Impersonators] actually can do that, just commit their entire lives to being somebody else. . . . Elvis people are wonderful people, what they're doing is noble, it's faithful and loyal, but they're Elvis. I mean, you talk to them, and they will talk Elvis to you as Elvis. They never drop the accent.

One guy's name was Dale Elvis. And he would say (Cage in Elvis mode) "Hey Nicky, I'd like to talk with you a little about E, I thought you did a mean E in *Wild at Heart*. Let's have a beer and talk about E.

I like him and everything, but I just didn't have anything to say about Elvis. It's kind of crazy that I have these two movies back to back, *Wild at Heart* and *Honeymoon in Vegas*, and they both have something to do with Elvis. (Sandberg-Wright, 1992, p. 57)

## *ROADKILL*

Elvis is also a roadside attraction and friend of the devil on a trip from Northern Ontario to Louisiana in *Highway 61*, directed by Canadian independent filmmaker Bruce McDonald. A journey more tame than its across-the-border counterparts and more closely aligned with the Leningrad Cowboys trek, *Highway 61* is a sardonic, idiosyncratic rock and road meditation featuring an odd couple with a coffin strapped to their Galaxie 500 traveling down the legendary highway immortalized in the Bob Dylan song.

Pokey Jones (Don McKellar, who co-wrote the screenplay), a barber and frustrated trumpet player, finds a frozen stiff in his backyard. Pretending to be the dead man's sister, tough-talking Jackie Bangs (Valerie Buhagier)–(a homage to the late rock critic, Lester Bangs?)–"a fugitive from a heavy metal road crew," stashes a load of heroine in the corpse and convinces the introverted Pokey to transport her and her pine-boxed brother across the border, all the way from Thunder Bay to Louisiana for a New Orleans jazz funeral.

There are numerous quirky, music-related encounters during their southbound trek along the infamous two-lane blacktop, including a stop at Dylan's home in Hibbing, Minnesota (actually 60 miles off Highway 61). At another exit, a father is grooming his three daughters to be the next Wilson Phillips, singing their "own unique blend of feel-good pop." After stopping at the gates of Graceland, Pokey and Jackie visit a reclusive rock and roll couple who are in a drugged stupor shooting at chickens inside their own Memphis mansion.

Hot on the odd couple's heels is a hellhound named Mr. Skin, a Satanic figure who barters for people's souls. His itemization of what souls have cost him include $20, a pint of alcohol, and Elvis memorabilia. Elvis has marked Mr. Skin's time line beyond soul exchanges. When the sallow "Satan" explains his recognition of his power, he lists significant cause-and-effect events, notably the fact that the night he lost his virginity, Elvis died. (A similar tale is told in the Odds' song "Wendy Under the Stars.")

Beyond Mr. Skin's experiences, Elvis's presence in *Highway 61* is implicit. Though the narrative does not make him a focal point of the journey, being the King of rock and roll, he can be viewed as the highway itself, or a metaphorical map connecting all musical points. Director McDonald, widely regarded as the quintessential outlaw of the new Canadian cinema, sees *Highway 61* as an extension of his previous film, *Roadkill* (1990), although the treatment for *Highway 61* was written first.

*Roadkill* is another rock and road movie about a woman named Ramona who is sent into the wilds of northern Ontario to cut short the mangled tour of his renegade rock band, The Children of Paradise. Arriving at a similar latitude as folkie Michelle Shocked's "Anchored in Anchorage," Ramona is stranded in Sudbury and her search for the band becomes a search for herself. The film has been diametrically described by Canadian critics as ". . . maybe the best-ever rock and roll movie" and "One of the worst pieces of trash ever committed to celluloid."

"If *Roadkill* was about the death of rock and roll, *Highway 61* is its funeral," offers McDonald. Rock and roll is obviously an integral part of his vision as a filmmaker. Yet, McDonald's focus is not as much on the music as it is the attitude and spirit. Between the lines of McDonald's film genre and elementary rock geography lessons lie a character composite of Elvis, and a perspective that at the same time reflects the Punk premise and the Youngian "Out of the Blue" view:

> But a rock and roll movie should contain elements of rock and roll within its structure, within its story, within its execution. It's a sort of attitude, a sort of go for it. . . . The elements of rock and roll would be sex, a hint of violence, a good back beat, a bit of "Fuck You," you know, drive all the way until the wheels fall off and burn kind of thing.

And to McDonald, the highway represents miles of musical lineage.

> Highway 61 ends in Thunder Bay—the cold Canadian North . . . If you trace it from Thunder Bay, it passes across the border in Hibbing, Minnesota, where Bob Dylan was from; through Minneapolis where Prince is from; to Saint Louis

which hooks up with the Mississippi, home of Miles Davis and Chuck Berry and then it goes through Memphis.

So you know it's more than just a highway; it's like a song-line, you get a history of pop music. You start with the top and you've got Zeppelin and the Cult, you know, white-boy-blues-based rock and roll. If you trace that down to the Delta you've got people like Muddy Waters and Robert Johnson; you know it ends up in a barber shop in New Orleans. (Owen, 1990)

## THE ELUSIVE ELVIS: LONG MAY YOU RUN

American independent filmmaker Jim Jarmusch rides the rails rather than the road, with his *Mystery Train* streaking into and stopping in the birthplace of rock and roll–Memphis. While Elvis may not be a dashboard saint or represent the freedom of the open road in the film, he embodies the spirit of rock and roll, both figuratively and literally. He is a mystery train *and* a runaway train. "[The movie] is like going on a road trip with no destination. You're there just to enjoy the ride," writes Sarah B. Weir in *Hollywood Rock* (Crenshaw, 1994, p. 163).

Like his previous critically acclaimed and idiosyncratic films, *Stranger Than Paradise* (1984) and *Down By Law* (1986), *Mystery Train* is a lyrical comedy with the usual (or unusual) Jarmusch trademarks–a sparse look, deadpan dialogue, archetypal American settings and music, and marginal characters who are variously immigrants, tourists, vagrants, amiable lowlifes, drifters, and dropouts. "Just listening in a bus station is more valuable than watching mainstream films," says the indie-film avant guardian about his inspiration. The most noticeable distinction in *Mystery Train* is that it is Jarmusch's first color feature, which in itself is a strange ricochet from the underwater adventure, *The Abyss* (1989), in which a hippie character says, "Elvis is in color even when the rest of us are in black and white."

*Rolling Stone*'s Peter Travers describes Jarmusch's films as "cinematic tone poems." Jarmusch considers himself a "minor poet who writes fairly small poems" and does not "try to make epic-scale things." Quoted in *Interview* magazine he says, "I'd rather make a movie about a guy walking his dog than about the emperor of China" (Sante, 1989, p. 148).

While Elvis is easily epic, the idea of telling three stories, none of which initially had anything to do with Elvis or Memphis, came first for Jarmusch. He resists the Elvis exploitation to the point of demystification.

> I think it's unfortunate when people just buy a myth. [Elvis was] somebody who was in the right place at the right time [and] just a guy and he got elevated to the status of almost a saint, like the Pope or something because people can make money off that. (p. 148)

Like so many other artists who admit to not being big Elvis fans but end up using him as subject matter, Jarmusch's "creative involvement" with the King was unintentional. He, too, seemed seduced by the sound of the cultural siren Elvis has come to represent, and nearly drowned in the Presley deluge.

> Music leads me to location, and it gives me all kinds of excuses to do research. I can search for rare records and study the history of these cities.
> He [Elvis] snuck in there; you got to watch out for him . . . When I first came to Memphis I went to Graceland immediately. By the time I left Memphis, I was so sick of Elvis I never wanted to hear about him again. (p. 148)

*Mystery Train* is a collection of three "fairly small poems" involving the overlapping activities of people whose only intersections are missed connections on the outskirts of Memphis at the rundown Arcade Hotel; the hovering presence and prenatural energy of Elvis; and an all-night blues station. (The Arcade, which was recently demolished, also appears in the background of a shot in the TBS film, *Memphis*, as one of the characters leans against his car listening to Elvis on the radio.) While the premise and hotel setting resemble Neil Simon's Beverly Hills *California Suite* (1978), (Jarmusch uses the approach again in *Night on Earth* [1991], with five different stories unraveling at the same time in taxis across the world), *Mystery Train's* unconventional, open-ended narrative is far more hip, with more neon, noir, and night. Camouflaged in the small, well-observed moments, circumstances, and relationships of the interweaved trilogy is a minimalist meditation on nocturnal existence: the fringes, transience, rhythm and blues, Memphis, legends such as Elvis, and the people who believe in them.

Bracketing "A Ghost," the story of an Elvisitation to a young Italian widow, are "Far from Yokohama" and "Lost in Space," vignettes involving innocent teenage Japanese tourists, Jun and Mitzuko, checking out the legendary Sun Records; and Johnny (former Clash member Joe Strummer), a hood nicknamed "Elvis" (even though he more closely resembles Bruce Springsteen) and his fellow fugitives, holed up after a liquor store heist. The three episodes are linked by site—the Arcade Hotel, where there are no TVs, but garish portraits of the impassive King looking down from the walls in every tacky room; sounds—an offscreen gunshot and a train whistle (subtle Elvis references?); and soundtrack—Elvis crooning "Blue Moon" on the radio. Further connecting the distinct situations and their characters as they pass through the Arcade's linoleum lobby are the hotel clerk (Screamin' Jay Hawkins) and his bellboy sidekick (Spike Lee's younger brother Cinque). The two exchange Elvis trivia and ponder such factoids as "At the time of his death, if he were on Jupiter, Elvis would have weighed 648 pounds."

Jarmusch deftly captures Elvis's elusiveness; "as the film goes on, Elvis keeps moving, no one can keep up with him, no one can pin him down" (Marcus, 1991, p. 196). Elvis proves as pervasive as he is evasive. "There he is again," points out a worshiping Mitzuko to Jun upon seeing the King's framed image on the wall as they arrive in their room in the opening episode. In the final story, the leaning portrait in Room 22 triggers the same response from Johnny, only he finds the King's omnipresence more disturbing than fascinating. "Christ, there he is again! They ought to get rid of that fucking guy," complains Johnny. "Turn it around; it gives me the creeps . . ."

Jarmusch romanticizes, rather than satirizes, Elvis and Memphis, and avoids the easy rock mockery. His impressions are those of an outsider, similar to that of the Leningrad Cowboys immigrant outlook. The visitor view is apparent in all of the characters. Mitzuno and Jun's entire image of America is formed out of popular culture, and Elvis is the centerpiece. (Their tour also includes a stop at Fats Domino's house in New Orleans after they do Memphis.) "This is America and the city of Elvis," says Mitzuno to Jun as they sit beneath a public Elvis statue, debating who is the real King, Elvis or Carl Perkins. In their room at the Arcade, Mitzuno offers visual aids to support her argument. "Study his face carefully," she urges Jun while reverently staring at the Elvis portrait hanging in front of them. She then removes a photo album from their suitcase and opens it. On each page, she has placed an image of Elvis opposite his "look-alikes"–an ancient Middle East King, the Buddha, the Statue of Liberty ("She's Elvis, too"), and Madonna. "Elvis was more influential than I thought," concedes the Perkins fan Jun.

The grieving Italian widow Luisa does not fully understand the widespread fascination with a dead singer in America, but she, too, is quietly intrigued after her coffee shop encounter with an Elfanatic and his hitchhiking tale. Even after her talkative roommate for the night, DeeDee, discredits the source and story as nothing more than an urban folk legend–"I think everyone in Memphis has picked up Elvis's ghost hitchhiking"–Luisa appears charmed by the possibility.

Johnny, the English thug, struggles to relate to American popular culture. While his drunken roommates, Will and Charlie, engage in a slurred discussion about the 1960s television series, *Lost in Space*, Johnny remains indifferent. "I guess I missed that bit of American culture," he says while urinating in the bathroom. Elvis, however, strikes a chord with him. Unlike fellow foreigners Jun and Luisa who eventually "accept" Elvis, Johnny resists conversion. He is puzzled and pissed by the Presley presence. It is an intrusion, especially in "a black hotel, in a black neighborhood, with black dudes working at the desk." "Why is he [Elvis] fucking everywhere?" lashes Johnny. "Why don't they have a portrait of Otis Redding or Martin Luther King, huh?"

In a particularly perceptive and poetic review of *Mystery Train*, film critic Roger Ebert (1993) writes:

> He (Jarmusch) is a romantic who sees America as a foreigner might–as a strange, haunting country where the urban landscapes are painted by Edward Hopper and the all-night blues stations provide a soundtrack for a life.

The best thing about *Mystery Train* is that it takes you to an America you feel you ought to be able to find for yourself, if only you knew where to look. (p. 443)

"Mystery Train," the song and *Mystery Train*, the movie, are loosely linked with Highway 61, the road and movie. The traveling companions from each film—the Japanese couple, Jun and Mitzuko, and the Canadians Pokey and Jackie—are kindred spirits. Their journeys cross the American cultural landscape, with the displaced persons experiencing sights and sounds along the way that eventually intersect at Elvis. Jarmusch offers some context on the outsider view of American culture and answers, in part, the "where to look."

> What I like about the idea of Japanese kids in Memphis is, if you think about tourists visiting Italy, the way the romantic poets went to Italy to visit the remnants of a past culture, and then if you imagine America in the future, when people from the East or wherever visit our culture after the decline of the American empire—which is certainly in progress—all they'll really have to visit will be the homes of rock and roll and movie stars. That's all our culture ultimately represents. So going to Memphis is a kind of pilgrimage to the birthplace of a certain part of our culture. (Sante, p. 148)

Bruce McDonald's view of Highway 61 and its sites is similar. The more specific spirit of the legendary highway's miles lies in its song line, a lineage that contains the history of American popular music. And it was that same music that Jarmusch followed to New Orleans to film *Down By Law*, and then led him to Memphis as a location for *Mystery Train*.

Just as Highway 61 is a musical time line, the song "Mystery Train" embodies a lineage that can be traced back to the Carter Family's 1930 folk song that was passed between races, "Worried Man Blues." When Little Junior Parker and Sam Phillips co-wrote "Mystery Train," they based it on the Carter tune. Parker and his band The Blue Flames were the first to record the song in 1953, although Elvis's appropriation two years later—his last record made at Sun Studio—popularized the song as one of his early signature songs. Over the years a number of musicians have hopped aboard and rode the "train . . . sixteen coaches long" with covers, including the Turtles with Hugo Winterhalter and His Orchestra in the mid-1950s, and more recently, the Band, and Neil Young.

Jarmusch bookends *Mystery Train* with the Presley and Parker, black and white, exquisite originals on the soundtrack. The energetic Elversion opens the title sequence, while Parker moans a somber, blues rendition over the closing credits. Although Jarmusch does not like using songs specifically as soundtrack, "Mystery Train's" appropriateness travels well beyond inspiring the movie's title.

"To me, it ["Mystery Train"] tells the best tale of all," writes Greil Marcus in his own masterpiece *Mystery Train* (1982, pp. 203-207). Marcus's musicology of the song is loaded with the author's trademark insights, many which mix metaphors with Elvis's life, as well as Jarmusch's film years later.

Marcus explores Elvis's Carter cultural connection:

> The Carter Family was completely real to Elvis; the white gospel culture they represented was implicitly *his* in a way that no other culture, be it Hollywood or the blues, could ever quite be. This was his inheritance and his birthright; the blues and the movies were something he made real for himself. On the earlier Sun records, Elvis had left home with the blues and come back on the flipside; "Mystery Train" gave him a blues that was rooted in his own community. (p. 205)

The Carters' "Worried Man Blues," about a man who lays down to sleep by a river and wakes up in chains, is analogous with the Presley narrative. "You would have to go a long way to match that as an image of the devil in a dream, or as a plain symbol of a land whose profound optimism insures that disaster must be incomprehensible," writes Marcus (p. 204). The mood of the song, and its "supernatural loneliness," ruminates in the distant gaze of the Elvis portraits hanging throughout The Arcade's rooms. Those faces, trapped inside their frames, are better preserved than any of the decaying building's other fixtures.

Elvis's "Mystery Train" vocal over vivid opening Amtrak, kudzu, and train station images announces his "Gothic story, driving forward against invisible doomsters to triumph, victory, and a laugh," while Parker's punctuates the film with a sense of defeat and departure. Because Elvis proves so elusive throughout the missed connections among the Arcadian guests, "the only way they can end the movie is to cut it off, to end it with Junior Parker's version." (Marcus, 1991, p. 196)

Marcus's adroit weaving of the Carters, Parker, Presley, and the "fate on wheels" that the song "Mystery Train" symbolizes is ideal for Jarmusch's characters and their circumstances.

> With "Mystery Train," both originals were brilliant. They took the train as far as it could go–in one direction–and the hard meaning Junior Parker and the Carter Family gave to the song was also part of Elvis's inheritance. If that meaning was forcefully obscure, that uncertainty was the song's point: the uselessness of action, the helplessness of a man who cannot understand his world, let alone master it. The singer was to enter this world, suffer it, make the world real, and thus redeem it. Elvis had his job cut out for him if he was to make the song his own. (1982, p. 206)

There is a subtle sense of uselessness of action and uncertainty in what Jarmusch describes as "the inconsequential little things and minor differences in perception and circumstance" among *Mystery Train*'s characters, whether they are asking for a fuck or forgiveness. The decrepit Arcade Hotel is transformed into the Heartbreak Hotel. And when Elvis's ghost appears to Luisa, he reveals a wearisome misunderstanding of his earthly world and its obsession with him. Like the Arcade visitors, Elvis doesn't understand his place. He is disoriented; it's the "wrong address." "Excuse me," he politely apologizes. Elvis's ghost is a spectral preview of the final episode; he is the one "lost in space."

The mystery train metaphor evolves beyond the song and film. "The train is the perfect metaphor in this movie," writes Ebert. "It's not where it's been that's important, or even where it's going. It's the sound of that whistle as it finds its way through the night."

Ebert's assessment of *Mystery Train*'s unresolved narrative, that "it is not how the story ends that is important, but how it continues," also applies to Elvis, and to some degree all of us. There is no resolution; the story is open-ended. We continue to look through the

Presley prism; we attempt to solve the puzzle; we hear the siren's seductive song; we chase the elusive ghost.

The train that began as a mystery remains a mystery; it has also become a runaway train and a train of thought. It does not stop in Tennessee, nor is it, to borrow the Guralnick title, the "last train to Memphis." Its 16 coaches roll on, past Sun Studios and Graceland, across Union Avenue and the King's Boulevard, between Presley's rhythm and Parker's blues, down Highway 61, across the American cultural landscape, connecting all points and destinations, known and unknown. Elvis is the sound of the whistle and the place "where to look." Elvis is the song and the movie; the train and the terrain. He is the ghost that haunts us, he is trapped in time and lost in space. Elvis is not only the King, but the Siren of American culture.

# Chapter 8

# From Post Office to Oval Office: Idolatry and Ideology in the 1992 Presleydential Elections

He thought he was the King of America

> —MacManus (Elvis Costello)
> "Brilliant Mistake" © 1986
> Plangent Visions Music Inc. (ASCAP)

This is America, Alf. We don't have a King.

> —Eight-year-old Brian Tanner
> *Alf* (NBC), October 1988

In Howard Waldrop's "Ike at the Mike," (1982), a short story from his collection *Strange Things in Close Up*, General Dwight D. Eisenhower abandons politics and the military for music, becoming a jazz master good enough to play with Louis Armstrong. Sitting in the audience watching the Ike and Satchmo duet is Elvis Presley, a young Senator whose political pursuits include Presidential ambitions.

Waldrop's fictional flip-flop is a rather intriguing foreshadowing of Elvis' political activity in 1992. While his adopted anthem, "The American Trilogy," and his quiet acceptance of an ill-timed draft notice to serve his country in the Army in December 1957 painted a patriotic portrait of Elvis, there are very few purely political pieces of the mythical Presley puzzle. The three RCA television sets mounted

A different version of this chapter was published in *Popular Music and Society*, Vol. 18(1), Spring, pp. 19-50.

side by side on a wall in the yellow and black TV room of the Graceland mansion have a political connection. The idea for the multiple sets reportedly was inspired by Lyndon Baines Johnson, who watched three separate network news broadcasts at the same time while in the White House. Elvis, however, preferred tuning in to sports programming. Perhaps the most notable "political involvement" for Elvis occurred in December 1970, when he visited the oval office and was named honorary federal narcotics agent by President Richard Nixon. The mythical meeting has been the subject of poems, songs, cartoons, and is the most requested photograph from the Library of Congress.

By 1992–Elvis 15 A.D.–and an election year–the lines between politics, culture, and religion grew increasingly and intensively entangled. Among the cast of real and fictional candidates and characters who appeared, disappeared, and reappeared were femme fatales Gennifer Flowers and Jennifer Fitzgerald, radical right(eous) persecuting Pats–Buchanan and Robertson, Murphy Brown and Sister Souljah, and of course, Texas billionaire H. Ross Perot. Also emerging within the sociocultural mileau and ideological muddle was King Elvis, appearing both postal and presidential, an omnipresent embodiment of power and imagination.

In fit-for-a-King fashion, the unprecedented and extravagant sequence of events surrounding the Elvis stamp both parallel and intersect with the 1992 presidential political process, complete with candidates and campaigns, primaries and polls, debates and discourse, media coverage and character questions, and an election–only in this one, Perot would not be a factor.

### ALONG THE ELVIS STAMPAIGN TRAIL: THE POSTAL PROCESS

Forget all these guys who want to be president. Next week, Americans will start voting on something they really care about. The King.

–Joe Urschel, "A Winning Candidate: Elvis"
*USA Today* (April 2, 1992, p. 11A)

Everyone wants to be on a postage stamp/
But nobody wants to die

—Pat MacDonald of Timbuk 3
"Standard White Jesus" © 1989
Mambadadi/I.R.S. Music Inc. (BMI)

Although there are striking similarities, second comings, and prophecy to parody parallels between Presley and Perot, the Elvis stampaign had been in the works for nearly 15 years, compared to the spur-of-the-moment messiah Perot's Warholian 15 minutes.

The push for Presley postage began almost immediately following Elvis's death in 1977. Since then, the United States Postal Service (USPS) has reportedly received more than 60,000 letters lobbying for a representation of Elvis. The requests from the philatelic and faithful fans could not be considered until 1987 because postal rules specify that a candidate for stampdom must be dead at least ten years before being considered.

While Elvis waited in U.S. postal purgatory, at least six other countries issued their own stamps honoring the American icon, many commemorating the tenth anniversary of Elvis's death. The foreign Presley postage portrayals represent an eclectic, and at times peculiar, stamp collection. The Elvis on West Germany's stamp displays a game show host likeness; Madagascar's (Malagasy Republic) resembles Ritchie Valens as well as Native American similarities; Republic of Islam's features Elvis in James Dean and motorcycle poses; and Central African Republic's is a Blue Hawaiian crooner under a rainbow. St. Vincent, the tiny island of the British West Indies, included dual images of Elvis in its Leaders of the World series, the younger portrait described in a *Musician* "No Such Zone" layout as "middle-era-Elvis-as-homicidal-maniac (the striped-shirt one)" (1992). The island also appropriated the East African nation Tanzania's ambitious nine-stamp set depicting Elvis in various stages of his musical and acting career, which resembles the Lakeside Graphics T-shirt with multiple Elvises. Similar nine-stamp editions of John Lennon and Madonna followed, as well as an eight-stamp entertainer block which included Elvis, Madonna, George Michael, Mick Jagger, Michael Jackson, David Bowie, Prince, and Frank Sinatra.

In July 1988, the USPS 13-member Citizens' Stamp Advisory Committee (CSAC) met to review proposals for new stamps to be issued during the next four years. The committee—which includes such celebrities as Karl Malden and former Notre Dame basketball coach Richard "Digger" Phelps, but no musicians or popular music writers/critics—meets approximately six times a year to develop and consider stamp ideas. Of the 2,000 proposals reviewed, between 25 to 35 a year are recommended to the Postmaster General, who makes the final decision.

The proposals are not limited to presidents and pioneers. They have included the American outhouse, hog callers, Bonnie and Clyde, and a pretzel stamp with beer-flavored glue. Vying with Elvis in 1988's postage primary was a diverse field that included etiquette arbiter Emily Post, Annie Oakley, boxers Joe Louis and Rocky Marciano, John Wayne, Nat King Cole, Zane Gray, the Three Stooges, Marilyn Monroe, and Thomas Wolfe. In a 1-900 phone poll conducted by *USA Today* in July, Elvis was a clear favorite with more than 2,000 votes.

Later that year, Elvis's candidacy again came into question with the publication of Gail Brewer-Giorgio's *Is Elvis Alive?* (1988) which placed an asterisk by his death in the minds of many as it evolved from a grass-roots series of UFO-like sightings at Burger Kings in Kalamazoo, Michigan to a national phenomenon and best-seller. If the claims were true, Elvis was highly visible during 1988's election year. His presence might be viewed as a symbolic and strategic part of the Presley political plan. With Gail Brewer-Giorgio the Presley Party publicist and answer to Democratic, Republican, and Independent strategists, communication, and campaign directors, the groundwork appeared to be laid for Elvis for the next election year in 1992.

In the fall 1990, the CSAC announced plans for a Legends of American Music Series which would feature approximately 14 rock and roll and rhythm and blues artists in a 20-page stamp booklet to be issued in 1993. Among those being considered with Elvis on the "eligibly dead list" were Buddy Holly, Ritchie Valens, Bill Haley, Janis Joplin, Jimi Hendrix, Mama Cass Elliot, Jim Morrison, Sam Cooke, and Otis Redding. According to CSAC chairperson Jack

Rosenthal, there was considerable committee debate as to who among these musicians merited such a tribute.

> There are conflicting views among committee members on these people. Some feel that some of them are not the most wonderful examples to hold up to young people. We've had to agonize about this.

> Of course, all the deceased presidents have a stamp. And we don't have to dig too deep to find some presidents who were not exactly Boy Scouts.

Whether leftover lifestyle scrutiny from Gary Hart's 1988 demise, or a portend of the moral highground facade of future campaigns, character was as much a criteria as contributions for even stamp candidates. In Elvis's case, Rosenthal rationalized his overdose the same way many others have—that it was from prescription drugs, while others such as Hendrix and Joplin died from illegal drugs. To Postmaster General Anthony M. Frank, Elvis was an obvious and necessary choice; a rock and roll series without him "would be unthinkable."

The possibility of an Elvis stamp triggered widespread reaction and generated discussion in forum-like fashion. The divergent views were perhaps best represented in "Face-Off," the 250-words-or-less point-counterpoint column of *USA Today*'s June 9, 1989 editorial page. Priscilla Parker (a fanatical pseudonym?), president of the We Remember Elvis Fan Club, argued that a stamp honoring Elvis was long overdue, and that collectors and fans worldwide were waiting for "the most wanted stamp in history." In her editorial, Parker rejects the "bad influence on youth" rap from Elvis detractors. She recognizes, as well as rationalizes, Elvis's lifestyle. "Yes, he did have a dependency on prescription drugs, as do millions of Americans," writes Parker. She even suggests the selection committee is guilty of a double standard, citing author Jack London who died of drug and alcohol abuse but was honored on a stamp.

Writer/entertainer Steve Marcel points to Elvis's lifestyle and deathstyle, as well as the cultural and commercial overkill, as reasons an Elvis stamp should not be issue. Marcel's counterpoint commentary rings with the familiar 1950s fears of Elvis as a threat to the traditional values embodied in the establishment. Marcel's lofty view is as derogatory as Parker's is devoted. His tone is casually condescending; referring to Elfans as "these fanatics," and Elvis as "just a musician." To Marcel, Presley's postal presence represents another popular culture contaminant, one that "would dilute the importance of everyone else who has been so honored."

Had Parker or any of "these fanatics" written a rebuttal, they probably would have agreed with Marcel on one point—that Elvis's death was disappointing. Then they might have responded to Marcel's negative interpretation of the myth, arguing that Elvis was more than "just a musician" and that Marcel's comparisons to Batman and Tiffany are inappropriate. Dissecting Marcel's argument further, one might point out that Elvis is already immortalized; that he served his country, (and in the view of John Lennon, "died when he went in the Army"); and he certainly followed his dream. Nonetheless, Marcel, like many others, concludes that "in this kennel of society's champion pedigrees, there just ain't no room for a houn' dawg."

In January 1992, the USPS made official what had long been a foregone conclusion—a 29-cent Elvis stamp would be issued both alone in a single-subject sheet, and in a booklet with other musicians early in 1993. The stamp approval was met with further disapproval, this time from some surprising sources. Many in the Presley Party preferred a solo stamp to a series, and resented their candidate's inclusion with other musicians. "This is not what I've worked nine years for," said disappointed stampaign director Pat Geiger. "He's not one of a group. He's one of a kind." Peacemaker Postmaster Frank diplomatically painted Elvis as a postage pioneer. "What we've done is translate this push for an Elvis stamp into a whole series," said Frank.

The announcement marked the next stage in the postage political process. The "Indecision '92" theme used by the Comedy Channel during its presidential convention and campaign coverage seemed to fit the Presley stampaign as well. Because Elvis's career has been commonly divided and defined in two distinct periods—the early and late—there arose the confounding question regarding the stamp—"Which Elvis?"

After reviewing 65 renderings submitted by eight artists, the Postmaster and CSAC selected two Elvis finalists. On February 24, at what might be considered the Presley Party's convention, held appropriately at the Las Vegas Hilton, Postmaster Frank presented the "Elvis ticket" as he unveiled the two-stamp designs which had been nominated during the portrait primary. The USPS provided satellite coverage of the novel news conference from the Showroom stage, site of 839 sold-out performances by Elvis. "Delegates" present at the ceremony included a parade of personalities from the Presley past. Among them were Milton Berle, on whose television show Elvis made several mid-1950s appearances; Barbara Eden, costar of *Double Trouble*; Nicky Blair, who appeared in *Viva Las Vegas*; and Kathy Westmoreland, a former backup singer.

The event was historical as Frank announced that for the first time in the 152 years since the United States issued its first stamp, the public would select a stamp. Recognizing the widespread interest in the Elvis stamp, Frank was willing to allow fans to have an active role, and surrender his authority to pick the winning design to a national postcard poll.

Frank outlined the election guidelines. Five million unstamped, pre-addressed ballots would be produced and distributed; another 4.5 million inserted and attached to a keepsake page in the April 13 issue of *People Magazine*. Voters were to mark their Presley preference beneath one of the portraits represented in black and white on the reverse side of the polling cards and include 19 cents in postage. Ballots were to reach the Memphis post office box destination between April 6 and midnight April 24. And, in the spirit of any election, color posters of the Elvying candidates appropriately joined the "Most Wanted" posters on display in the lobbies in most of the nations's 40,000 post offices (Figure 8.1).

The stamp runoff resembled the recent magazine publishing trend of printing two separate covers of the same issue for readers to choose from at newsstands. At the post office, voters could choose between Mountain Lake, Maryland designer Mark Stutzman's "young Elvis," and an "older Elvis" drawn by John Berkey of Excelsior, Minnesota. Descriptions of the contrasting depictions ranged from "early, rebellious, hip-pumping, rock and roll menace, smooth, 1950s, Memphis, slick-haired, swivel-hipped, Elvis the younger;" to "mature, late-model, latter-day, older, sequined, jumpsuited, Vegas, chunky, extra crispy, bloated, pill-popping,

FIGURE 8.1. Posters were used to advertise the campaign to choose which picture of Elvis would adorn a stamp.

paranoid, lounge singer, concert, with chins, rhinestone encrusted, Elvis the elder." The Postmaster General characterized the two Elvises on Larry King's radio show as "the thin one" and "the later, somewhat heavier one." USPS spokesperson Jim Adams officially amended that to "young Elvis" and the "more contemporary Elvis."

Although such weighty distinctions have become collective cultural characterizations of Elvis, both stamp designs are more flattering than they are fattening. Even Berkey's older Elvis is a love-me-slender version that does not reflect the overweight King of later years. Both portrayals are relatively tame–waist-up only, head shots over a microphone, with one word–"Elvis"–appearing in a torn ticket stub design in the lower left corner. The style is conservative–airbrushed rather than black velvet–and the images rather caricatured. "Both are a little too cartoonist," critiqued Mark Kellner of *Stamp Collector* newspaper. "A better image could be found by going to any K-Mart in the south or getting a black velvet portrait of Elvis."

Before balloting began, oddsmakers, perhaps swayed by the Hilton home field advantage, made the older Elvis the favorite. With *USA Today*'s sports analyst Danny Sheridan, the Vegas version was 8:5; and with an admittedly biased Art Manteris, vice president of race and sporting operations at the Las Vegas Hilton, he rated 6:5.

A microcosm of the larger political process, the three-week stamp election generated its share of enthusiasm and cynicism, controversy and comedy, from participants and observers. Many had obviously listened to the Postmaster's encouragement to "vote early, vote often." At the election's midway point, there were scattered reports of ballot shortages. The national post office announced it would not print additional ones, but authorized divisional branches to do so if they chose. In addition, plain postcards indicating an Elvis preference would be permitted.

Although there was no obsessive daily poll tracking, some sampling of voters was conducted (Figure 8.2). One poll of "experts"–22 Elvis impersonators, including "Elvez," the Mexican Elvis, and the mayor of Jasonville, Indiana–reinforced initial oddsmaker as the older Elvis had a 12-10 edge over the younger. A pre-election survey in *USA Today* offered different results. The poll drew 5,317 responses, including one written on the stationery of the late Speaker of the Pennsylvania House of Representatives, James

FIGURE 8.2. Polling voters.

Source: Bob Rogers, reprinted by permission of United Features Syndicate, Inc.

Manderino. "Speaking as the authority from that great velvet paint-ing in the sky, I must opt for the youthful photo," the letter said. The readers expressed a return-to-slender preference by a 3:1 ratio: the younger 3,848 (72.4 percent) to older 1,339 (25.2 percent); 130 said neither.

The media attention the stamp received dating from its pre-ap-proval days continued during and after the 1992 election. Readers, viewers, and listeners routinely responded with their preferences, suggestions, and views—both serious and sarcastic—during call-in shows, in newspaper editorial pages, and 1-900 phone surveys. For example, one respondent felt a more fitting postal tribute would be a rubber-stamp Elvis in a swivel-hip pose with one of three phrases—"Return to Sender," "Address Unknown," or "No Such Zone"—to replace the current "pointing finger and hand" image used for misdirected mail.

Both popular culture and political pundits, press, and panelists from print and broadcast media frequently provided campaign commentaries, tidbits, reports, and references that often sought cosmic, comic, and cultural connections with the presidential race. On the day of the Elvis election announcement (February 24), *CBS Evening News* coverage provided what turned out to be a bizarre broadcast baptism for the campaign. Following anchor Dan's rather skeptical lead—"You'd think the post office would have better things to think about than Elvis . . . Well, they don't . . ."—a feature summarized the Las Vegas press conference, then explored other angles to the unprecedented election story. The segment was not subtle in pointing out the profit the USPS stood to make, an estimated $20 million through postage required for the postcard ballots and philatelic financing from the stamp collecting community.

Because of the "dead for a decade" stamp eligibility law, the "Elvis lives" angle seemed convenient to work into the report. That editorial decision perhaps became regrettable, thanks to confirmed Elvis fanatic Joe Lee, who was asked to comment on the forthcoming stamp. Lee was interviewed in his Washington, DC record store as an adjacent television set ran a video-verite clip of the King slipping into a getaway car in a strip-mall parking lot. "I think they should bend the rules a bit because he's [Elvis] still alive. But he still deserves a stamp," commented Lee using his best hick accent.

The skillful prank, unrecognized by the *Evening News* staff, had its origins in a February 1991 *Washington City Paper* feature on Elvis sightings by Sean Piccoli. In the "true believer" profile, Lee describes the contents of his sighting videotape: Elvis at suburban eateries and ducking into a Dodge with Maryland "TCB 1" license plates. After seeing the article, producers from the CBS news magazine, *48 Hours*, contacted Lee with hopes of looking at the "exclusive" footage. Before sending the tape (which Lee confessed he made with filmmaker Jeff Mentges), Lee re-edited scenes to give it a "herky-jerky Zapruder feel." *48 Hours* never aired the tape, but Lee's reputation as a leader among the "Elvis lives" legions eventually reached the *CBS Evening News* team, who contacted Lee while assembling the stamp feature.

"I immediately sensed the idea that they were looking for someone to say he's alive," said Lee, who gladly accommodated the CBS crew. Lee described the reporter as "the most steely-eyed person [he'd] ever seen;" she never winked, nodded, or doubted his testimony. However, when she left Lee's store, the hip CBS cameraman, apparently aware of Lee's game, burst into laughter (Piccoli, 1991).

*USA Today's* Joe Urschel appeared to be a self-appointed campaign publicist among print journalists, as Elvis was frequently a topic of his biweekly columns. In "A Winning Candidate: Elvis" (April 2, 1992), Urshel's view echoes the *CBS Evening News* report, as he hints at the USPS' underlying greed motive. He accuses Postmaster Frank of "using" Elvis to get "widespread positive publicity for his moribund organization," and parlaying the Presley image into profit. In Urschel's view, it was another example of one American metaphor–Elvis–feeding another–money.

Even some of the most celebritized journalists, could not resist ruminations. Satirist Andy Rooney of *60 Minutes* (CBS) offered his stamp of disapproval during the show's April 12, 1992 broadcast. Rooney whines that the USPS did not ask the public if "it was right to have someone like Elvis" on a stamp; nor did the USPS offer enough Elvises to choose from. While pointing out, like others, the expected stamp sale success, Rooney suggests other "great Americans" to honor, with appropriate pictures the public could choose from. Rooney's roll resembles a criminal line up, which no doubt reflects how he feels about Elvis being stamped. Included are: Richard Nixon, as President or the day he was forced to resign; boxer Mike Tyson, in his prime as heavyweight champion or handcuffed as a convicted rapist; Leona Helmsley, happy or imprisoned for tax fraud. Rooney follows the lead of fellow journalists who treated the stamp election as a convenient opportunity to criticize the USPS. Rooney's final "nominee" is Fred Smith, president of Federal Express. "If you care to vote . . . don't mail in his name," advises Rooney. "Send it Federal Express. It'll probably get there quicker that way."

Larry King, writing on the King in his *USA Today* "People: News and Views" (April 20, 1992), wonders, "The next thing they'll ask the presidential candidates is which Elvis stamp they support. (They already asked Bill Clinton this. He chose the young Elvis.)"

Likewise, in "Fat Elvis, Sticking to the Issue," (May 14, 1992), arch conservative Art Buchwald playfully ponders parallels between 1992's elections. He reviews the "bitter election"–from the charges and questions of credibility and qualifications raised by both the Thin and Fat Elvis camps during the campaign to post office exit polls. Rather than use Elvis to snipe at the USPS, Buchwald targets Ross Perot, who at the time was in the first act of his three-act presidential play. Buchwald (1992) concludes:

> Pundits are predicting that if it [the Elvis stamp election] is a tie, just one person is worthy of appearing on the stamp and that's Ross Perot. He may not be the most qualified to be President of the United States, but the public believes that Perot, with all his money, is the only one who will stick once you lick him on the back.

Even Elvis offered his editorial view in the monthly "Dear Elvis" column of *Spin* (May 1992), responding to a reader's question, "Do you like the idea of the post office putting you on a stamp?" He ghostwrites:

> . . . I really don't give a damn, to tell you the truth. I ain't getting no cut out of the profits or nothing, but then again it don't hurt nobody and it's right flattering. I don't mean no offense, but seems like a lot of people out there spend half their time licking my rear end anyway, so might as well go to some use. I'd rather have my picture on a stamp than on the back of a damn milk carton or a two-dollar bill, that's for sure.

While many treated the stamp election with one-liners and levity, others sought a more serious angle. The African-American community, in particular, continued to express what has long been a "blacklash" to Elvis homage. By the 1990s, rap was well established as a hip-hop topic. While discussions frequently centered on the music's popularity, message, fears, or violence, Elvis's name often surfaced as a familiar 1950s rebellion reference point.

In his June 9, 1992 *USA Today* column, Urschel responds to Public Enemy Chuck D.'s comment–"My heroes don't appear on no stamps"–by placing rap, rock, rebellion, and generation gaps within a Presley perspective. "And that [Chuck D.'s comment] may be true. But it is equally true there was a time when people thought Elvis Presley was threatening. The young one."

Denver writer J. Elyse Singleton, an African American, views the widespread fear of rap in a similar context of "reincarnations for those long-departed souls who used to pray for Elvis's hips to stop moving."

One of the more thoughtful commentaries triggered by the Elvis stamp was written by Gannett News Service columnist DeWayne Wickham, who advocates similar recognition for the Buffalo Soldiers, black troops who were sent into the American West during the late 1800s to protect wagon trains and safeguard settlements. Among its accomplishments, the infantry is credited with capturing Geronimo, hunting down Billy the Kid, and rescuing Teddy Roosevelt from disaster during his famous charge up San Juan Hill during the Spanish-American War. Wickham laments that Elvis and Laurel and Hardy have been honored on stamps, while the exploits of this African-American military unit have largely gone unnoticed, except for a recently dedicated monument in Fort Leavenworth.[1]

In honor of the final day of Elvis balloting on April 24, and perhaps to boost its Friday night ratings, CBS aired a two-hour prime-time special, *Elvis: The Great Performances*, compiled from the video documentary series of the same title. The election results were announced at Graceland early Thursday morning, June 4. The 6:30 CDT was to accommodate the network morning shows. (The same three networks which provided live coverage, along with CNN, of the Elvis event chose *not* to broadcast a presidential news conference that same night.) Among those gathered at the ceremony were postal officials, the two artists who designed the stamp finalists, and many fans, including long-time Elvis stamp advocate, Pat Geiger, who was flown in from her Vermont home. Priscilla Presley opened the Express Mail envelope and revealed the winning portrait—the "young Elvis" in a 3:1 landslide. "Of all the awards and honors he received, this probably would be the most special for him," said Elvis's ex-wife. E-mail had arrived.

The campaign aftermath featured characteristic postelection analysis of facts and figures. Young Elvis received 851,200 (75 percent) votes to 277,723 (25 percent) for the older. The 1.1 million ballots cast appeared to indicate an impressive voter turnout. However, that number represented only about 12 percent of the 9.5 million official ballots printed and distributed by the USPS and *People Magazine*. "The ballots are going to be more rare than the stamps," says USPS spokesperson Robin Minard. "People probably mailed one in and kept one or more." Minard said she expects many will paste the stamp to the ballot and send it to Memphis to be cancelled on the first day of issue.

Postal officials braced for an Elvis stamp-ede. The USPS Philatelic and Retail Services Department confirmed earlier estimates of $20 million profits from the Elvis stamp and booklet sales. Associate Postmaster General Edward Horgan announced that 300 million stamps would be printed, nearly twice the 160 million printed for a typical commemorative stamp. According to Carl Burcham, general manager of the Stamp Marketing Division, nearly one-half the 1.1 million customers who mailed in Elvis ballots used 29-cent stamps instead of the required 19 cents for postcards. According to figures published in the USPS newsletter, *Postal Leader* ("Elvis Stamp," June 16, 1992) the difference yielded $50,000 in additional revenue, which was a portion of the $268,000 total earnings generated by the balloting. The stamp design was also licensed for nearly 100 products, from jackets to jewelry, that would flood the market with a Yule-tidal wave. Despite the numerous criticisms leveled at the USPS during the campaign, officials believed the Elvis promotion marked one of its most successful public relations efforts ever conducted. A two-page print advertisement promoting a "Buy America" agenda–"Only One Stamp Outsells Elvis . . . Made In the U.S.A."–provided an ideal caption, not only for the stampaign, but the Elvis myth.

True to Postmaster Frank's suggestions of Elvis as a postage pioneer, the January 1993 issuing of Elvis's solo stamp would precede the Presidential inauguration by a few days and the first "Legends of American Music" series: Rock and Roll, Rhythm and Blues (Bill Haley, Buddy Holly, Clyde McPhatter, Ritchie Valens, Otis Redding, Dinah Washington, and Elvis) in June; Country and Western (Hank Williams, the Carter Family, Patsy Cline, Bob Willis) in September, with separate Hank Williams in August; Broadway Musicals (*Oklahoma!*, *My Fair Lady*, *Showboat*, *Porgy and Bess*) in March. Fourteen other genres, including folk, blues, and jazz remain under consideration.

At the October 1992, announcement of the Music Series selections from the Hard Rock Cafe in Washington, DC, discussion centered around noticeable rock omissions Jimi Hendrix and Janis Joplin, and fashionable questions of character. When asked about whether the choice of legend Hank Williams, who succumbed to liquor and pills, was consistent with "family values," new Postmaster General Marvin Runyon, presumably punning, answered, "I don't think any of us is letter-perfect." The comment seemed an appropriate summary of the Elvis stampaign, and segue into the presidential campaign.

### FROM POSTAGE TO PARTY PLATFORMS, PEROT, AND POP POLITICS: "THE ELVIS FACTOR"

The year 1992 marked the political awakening of the Elvis Presley myth. While Americans were preoccupied with choosing an Elvis stamp, the late King reportedly was casting a ballot in the April 9 parliamentary election in Britain. He was among historic personages contacted by a psychic for a beyond-the-grave newspaper poll. The *Sun* reported that Elvis, Queen Victoria, and Winston Churchill lined up behind Prime Minister John Major's Conservative Party; while Josef Stalin, Mao Tse-tung, Karl Marx, and John Lennon supported Neil Kinnock's Labor Party.

In addition to his "interest" in British politics and his own dual candidacy for stampdom, Elvis was drawn into the year's other significant election. Though not with the impact of the populist puppeteer Perot, Elvis's peculiar presence could be traced from the post office to the presidential primaries, through conventions and campaigns, to the White House.

Elvis's initial appearance in the presidential race was during the Democratic primaries as somewhat of an alter ego, or kindred spirit, to the party's eventual nominee, Arkansas Governor Bill Clinton. After learning of the presidential candidate's admiration for the King, the press began to occasionally refer to Clinton as "Elvis." (Other accounts claim the nickname originated as a Secret Service joke.) In a *Newsweek* (March 9, 1992) interview the week before Super Tuesday, reporter Eleanor Clift's lead question to Clinton was not about issues, other candidates, qualifications, or character. She begins, "I want to start with the Elvis connection. What is your feeling toward him?" Clinton explained how he experienced Elvis as a cultural rage growing up across the river from Mississippi, in the storybook-sounding "place called Hope." He also considered the political impact the Elvis connection and moniker might have with voters. "I could do worse," he tells Clift. "[If elected] then all the Elvis fans could say, 'Well, Elvis *is* alive. It's just another thing I could do for the country."

Clinton's connection with Elvis transcends admiration. Among other "Aw, shucks" similarities, both were Southern, white, poor boys from families with strong mother figures. While successfully pursuing their dreams, both represented multiplicity and the possibility of being all things to all people, and were eager to prove it. They attracted diverse classes and races, and displayed particular appeal to young audiences. And both symbolized energy. A relentless campaigner, Clinton seemed to embrace the Warren Zevon philosophy, "I'll sleep when I'm dead." Reporters and aides, struggling to keep pace with his work-around-the-clock schedule, came to rue the notion of the sleepless world they referred to as "Elvis time."

Elvis became a memorable musical and mythical marker along the Clinton campaign trail. During the New York primary, Clinton sang "Don't Be Cruel" on a radio talk show in response to the barrage of allegations about his personal life and character assassination attempts which would escalate until November. Clinton's cover rendition resembled a hymn or prayerful recitation to protective power, Guardian Elvis, for divine guidance through tribulation.

During the previous two presidential elections, there were similar efforts to integrate popular music into the political vernacular. In 1984, Ronald Reagan joined the legions who misinterpreted Bruce Springsteen's "Born in the USA" as he attempted to conveniently adopt the song as a patriotic anthem. Four years later, George Bush cited Bobby McFerrin's "Don't Worry, Be Happy," and the late Republican Party campaign guru Lee Atwater frequently engaged in supper-club style blues jams with B.B. King.

"Politicians spend all their time trying to get elected. They don't have time to watch TV or listen to music," offers *USA Today's* pop culture monitor, Joe Urschel (June 23, 1992, p. 11A). "So when they try to be hip, they look stupid." That is, unless it's Bill Clinton. This was somewhat different. This was Elvis. And the Clinton-Elvis bond appeared to be, at least on the surface, more credible, more sincere, and a more acceptable "of the people" linkage. The Reagan-Springsteen symbiosis was not. Democratic opponent Walter Mondale quickly refuted the association when he delivered perhaps his best line before the landslide loss: "Bruce may have been 'born to run', but he wasn't born yesterday." Wisconsin Democratic campaign director Bob Decheine provided a "common folk" spin on the Clinton-Elvis connection. "Politics has become nasty. People see politicians as phony," says Decheine. "Liking Elvis makes Clinton seem more real."

Clinton's hip and music competency quotas received boosts when he did his best "Slick Willie," in sunglassed bluesman guise, delivering a strikingly soulful saxophone rendition of "Heartbreak Hotel" on *The Arsenio Hall Show*, June 3. While Clinton's talent might not have been worthy of a record deal, he did not come across as a second-rate talent show contestant. Clinton's musical moonlighting on the talk show circuit stirred haunting parallels to Elvis's 1950s television variety show performances, as his late-night *Arsenio* appearance seemed destined for legendary status in pop politics. A video clip or reference to Clinton's sax solo would be included as a campaign highlight in virtually every media postelection review. When considering all the allegations against Clinton during the campaign, it might be somewhat surprising that opponents did not raise Milli Vanilli-type, saxophone-sync, audio authenticity questions about his *Arsenio* performance. In 1996, Clinton's "sax appeal" was iconized alongside Elvis on a limited edition of postage stamps issued in the Central African Republic of Chad.

Elvis's role during the 1992 election approached a level of exaltation in July at the Democratic Convention in New York City. The party seemed determined not to repeat the misjudgments they had made with its previous presidential candidates. Someone in the camp apparently had paid close attention to colorful columnist Molly Ivins assessment of Michael Dukakis following the 1988 convention: "The man has got no Elvis." Clearly, the same could not be said of this year's model. With a Thursday night prime-time, pre-*Must See TV* audience witnessing, Bill Clinton's running mate, Senator Al Gore, was introduced to the sounds of Paul Simon's "You Can Call Me Al." The vice presidential nominee began his acceptance speech: "I've dreamed of this since growing up in Tennessee. Coming here to Madison Square Garden, and being the warm-up act for Elvis."

Gore's opening line, though presumably an ice breaker designed, in part, to convey humor and Southern charm, was as fertile as it was folksy. The comment was a captivating combination of power, imagination, and divine implications that seemed to verify, or make official, Elvis's presence. The words resonated like an opening benediction to the party's patron saint–Elvis–symbol of all things possible. In this case, the goal was the White House, after a 12-year Republican reign. One could almost hear Elvis's whispering "If I Can Dream" in between the blaring notes of the Dem-anthem, the Fleetwood Mac 1970s hit, "Don't Stop." Or imagine an appropriate follow-up to Gore's musical intro with another Simon song, "Graceland," to christen candidate Clinton's presidential journey. Gore's invocation seemed to elevate the Clinton-Elvis relationship to a higher level, one that was perhaps spiritual in nature and suggested rebirth, reincarnation, or possession. Earlier that same day, Ross Perot's surprising withdrawal from the race further fed the fantasy. Was Perot's announcement in recognition of Elvis, an acknowledgment of his power and political presence; and that the Democratic Party, and the country, were headed in the right direction because, to borrow a John Hiatt verse, they were "riding with the King?"

That direction, at least in the convention's immediate afterglow, was the open road. Clinton and Gore became a ticket to ride, as they adapted a Kerouac or Ken Kesey chapter into a road movie, and became the boys on the bus embarking on a cross-country trek spreading their message of change.

Considering that the Republican Party's convention was hardly a "Hooray for Hollywood" atmosphere, it was ironic that the Grand Old Party countered the newly anointed Democratic deity, Elvis, with its own grand old god and Hollywood heavy, Ronald Reagan, who was resurrected as a reminder of the party's 1980s glory days. The mythical meeting of Elvis and Reagan, two of American culture's most prominent and powerful figures, bridged both conventions and framed the 1992 campaign.

With television, film, and the evils of popular culture under attack, it was no surprise to hear Elvis's name uttered at the Republican convention, although the context was surprisingly different. President Bush's first reference was a familiar "sighting" allusion that came while accusing Clinton of shifting positions. "He's been spotted in more places than Elvis Presley," said Bush. Then, during his acceptance speech, Bush introduced the American public to a new financial phrase to file alongside "Reagan," Voodoo," and "Trickle Down" economics. He labeled the Clinton recovery plan for the country "Elvis economics," and claimed that it would "lead the nation into the Heartbreak Hotel." "We should be so lucky," writes *USA Today*'s Urschel, quick to point out that "Heartbreak Hotel" was the top selling song in 1956, and when Elvis sang it on *The Milton Berle Show*, the 25 percent of the nation that tuned in represented a higher percentage than viewers who watched the Republican convention, which was carried on four networks, C-Span, and the Comedy Channel.

"Elvis Economics" provided instant material for monologues and columns. "You know what the difference is between Elvis and Bush's economic plan?" asked Arsenio Hall. "Some people actually claim they've seen Elvis recently." And Urschel, in "Does Elvis Live in Economics, of All Places?" (*USA Today*, August 25, 1992), considered Elvis the perfect metaphor for what the President had turned the economy into—"a bloated enigma that had to be pumped up with a lot of artificial stimulants." Ironically, just four days before the election, in its October 30 editorial page, *The Atlanta Journal/Constitution* ran a quarter-page graphic that compared the national debt to "that other American institution, Elvis," charting the amount from Elvis's birth in 1935, to his death in 1977, and on to the present, when "the Elvis legend looms just as large as, well, the debt . . . $4 trillion the amount America now owes in love-me-(legal)-tender."

Urschel explains why Bush should embrace "Elvis Economics:"

> Even without a new record or concert, Elvis is still earning $15 million a year. Now, *that's* a record you can run on. Elvis didn't mortgage his children's future. Lisa Marie will inherit $100 million on her 30th birthday. And, talk about the trickle-down theory, he *gave* Cadillacs to his friends.

We should not have to explain Elvis to the president of the United States. But in terms any politician should understand: People *paid* to vote for Elvis–even when it was just for a stamp.

Actually there was some precedence for "Elvis Economics" beyond the post-mortem millions of his estate. In September 1988, Leader Federal Savings and Loan of Memphis (not involved in the S & L scandal) issued an Elvis Mastercard, making the King the first person ever featured on plastic. Although John Love, publisher of *Credit Card News*, viewed it as a joke, Leader received 1,112 phone calls about the card during the two days following the announcement; and, after mailing out 200,000 applications, the response was three times what a regular card solicitation would have drawn. Leader added a toll-free Elvis line to accommodate the overwhelming number of inquiries. The idea of Leader's senior vice president Brad Champlain, the card has a $36 annual fee, 17.8 percent interest rate, with part of the profits donated to the Elvis Presley Memorial Foundation designed to help children and fund music scholarships. Robert McKinley, publisher of *RAM Bankcard Update* declared the card a "hit." Others wondered if the Elvis Gold (Record) Card would soon follow.

While Bush may not have been predicting an "In Elvis We Trust" revision destined to be imprinted by Democrats on currency and coin, there was a subtext of prophecy fulfilled in his cautionary remarks about Elvis. In 1987, Mojo Nixon and Skid Roper's "Elvis Is Everywhere" warned of the evil opposite of Elvis–"the anti-Elvis." The duo suspected actor Michael J. Fox, because "he has no Elvis in him." In the popular 1980s television series, *Family Ties* (NBC), Fox starred as Alex Keaton, prototype young Republican (an autographed picture of Richard Nixon framed on a wall in his room) and the son of aged-hippie parents. The equation–though subtly twisted and vicarious–playfully suggests that if loyalist Alex, who in real life is the anti-Elvis Fox, is the embodiment of Republican ideals, then it would seem to follow that his party's platform which he so enthusiastically embraces is essentially anti-Elvis. Bush's "Elvis Economics" statement further recognized and reinforced that the Republican Party, like Fox, "has (nor wants) no Elvis in it." And just as Elvis and Reagan represent two-party polarity, Fox's character Alex, if nothing else, provides a fitting fictional and political counterpart to Candace Bergen's 1990s, liberal, female, single-parent, broadcast professional, and Dan Quayle target, Murphy Brown.

Elvis's "equal time" appearances at both party conventions established him as factor to be figured in with the countless other demographic data and voter variables. "Obviously, no one on the Bush speechwriting team understands the power of pop culture; otherwise, they'd never have conceded the Elvis vote to the Democrats," writes the insightful Urschel.

Elvis events continued to checker the campaign trail following the conventions. In a strange series of late-August "King of the Road" confrontations, Texas Republicans interrupted the Clinton bus tour across the state with Elvis impersonators following his route, singing, and serving bologna sandwiches, in what GOP spokesperson Mark Sanders called, "The Don't Be Fooled Tour." "Bill Clinton thinks he's Elvis, but we've got the real thing," claimed the Victory '92 Texas GOP headquarters. The statement almost sounded like a thin-veiled convention retraction, with the Republicans sensing, if not acknowledging, that there actually was an "Elvis vote," and attempting to win back any of the Presley population who might have been swayed during either convention.

Elvis was also a key figure, along with serial killer Jeffrey Dahmer, in the weird Wisconsin Senate race between Russ Feingold and two-term incumbent Bob Kasten. The relatively unknown, underfunded Feingold defeated two opponents in the Democratic primary using a homespun ad with a mock-tabloid headline—"Elvis Endorses Feingold!" Bob Decheine, Feingold's campaign director, says the ad was intended to say to voters, "You're too smart to believe everything you read." The ad apparently struck a chord and soon Feingold was being greeted with "Where's Elvis?" chants. Posing under a giant Elvis beach towel, Feingold thanked the King for his primary victory and did an Elvis impersonation. His Republican rival, who suggested Feingold supported legislation that would allow the cannibal Dahmer parole, offered an Elvis clock as congratulations for the primary victory. Feingold, following Clinton's cue, urged his opponent, "don't be cruel" during the election. His campaign considered adopting an Elvis theme song, but couldn't afford the rights. Decheine explored other avenues, such as appropriating Ann-Margret's *Viva Las Vegas* character's name–"Rusty"–which is also Feingold's nickname. However, as the diligent King-tracking columnist Urschel points out, another Feingold tabloid spoof headline "Elvis Marries Rusty!" would not play well on the "family values" front.

In an endorsement of his fellow Rhodes scholar and Elvis devotee (and eventual winner in the senate selection), Clinton said,

> The real reason I so deeply support him [Feingold] is Elvis Presley is for him. It's well known that I commune with his [Elvis] spirit. I can tell you this, as I walked in here today, he said, "I am for Russ Feingold. I am not for Bob Kasten."

"There's something really weird about it," said Decheine. "Elvis is inherently funny, but not in a bad way. People love him. He's a mythic character. A tragic figure. Ultimately, the Republican tactic of using Elvis to bash Clinton will backfire. You must use Elvis positively."

As the presidential campaign progressed toward election day, much of the Elvis political subplot was drowned out by the repeated party mantras–"Change and the economy" versus "Trust and character"–the so-called debates, town meetings, rallies, spinning and stumping, advertisements and infomercials, talk shows, polls and Perot II. Yet Elvis appeared to be unwilling to surrender the spotlight completely to politicians, especially during the fifteenth anniversary of his death. Whether business as usual for the Presley estate, or a brilliant subtle strategy bordering on the subliminal by the Democrats, Elvis's name and image were just as visible in the cultural landscape as those on campaign bumper stickers, buttons, billboards, and slogans.

In August, RCA released *Elvis: The King of Rock and Roll–The Complete '50s Masters*, a five-CD, 140-song collection of rare early recordings. *Honeymoon in Vegas*, a film billed as "The story of one bride, two grooms, and 34 flying Elvises" (Utah chapter) was a late-summer box office hit. The movie's soundtrack, an eclectic compilation of Elvis covers, was a crossover success, charting well on both country and pop categories. The Elvisynergy also included Billy Joel's "All Shook Up" video, which was in heavy rotation on the music channels, while Elvis himself was the featured artist for September on VH-1. The CBS news magazine show, *48 Hours* assembled five separate features into a one-hour "Crazy About Elvis" presentation which aired on August 12. Made-for-quick-cash publications appeared instantly in bookstores. Crown's flimsy 60-page, *Elvis for President*, authored by "The Committee to Elect the King," lays out the TCB Party's campaign strategies and slogans ("Read My Hips"), the Presley Platform, suggestions for a running mate as well as a Queen for the King, and the Elvis Presidency, including the first 100 days and cabinet appointees. As the committee sees it, the only factors that could derail the campaign are drug testing and an autopsy. Another notable book on the "shelvis" was *In Search of the King* (Gelfand, 1992), a colorful ripoff of the popular search game book series, *Where's Waldo?*, that featured finding Elvis among the faces in the crowd at his various familiar haunts, including Graceland, Hawaii, and Las Vegas. And one month before the November election, Major League Marketing, the Westport, Connecticut, company which markets and distributes Score and Pinnacle brand sports trading cards, introduced a line of Elvis Presley cards featuring 660 pictures spanning Elvis's entire career.

### THE MEN WHO WOULD BE KING:
### THE MYSTERY (TRAIN) OF DEMOCRACY

The message may be that if you want to get elected in America, it doesn't hurt to pay homage to the King.

—Joe Urschel, "In This Democracy, Don't Knock the King," *USA Today*, September 15, 1992, p. 12A

elvis was made by america,
so america could remake itself

—Bono, "Elvis: An American David" (1994)

The dynamic between the 1992 Elvis stamp and presidential elections represent metaphorical jewels in the King's cultural crown, missing links of his gold chain connecting the American landscape that is his domain. With the addition of missing political pieces of the Presley puzzle, the Elvis myth becomes more complete.

The Presley postal-political relationship is filled with playful parallels and intriguing possibilities, beyond the obvious "democracy at work." Much of the richness is expressed in the miniature dimensions of the young Elvis stamp-elect. Like most recent candidates, Elvis encountered, and endured, questions about his character. Upon winning his postal primary for stamp approval, he became his own ticket, running in his own election. Though representing different person and periods, Elvis/Elvis was a can't-lose candidate.

In a year when Ross Perot's grass-roots movement revealed voter discontent with the political system, the Presley party's "duplicate candidacy" for stampdom also reflected the evolvement of the two major parties in 1992–that is, at times, indiscernible. While their ideologies and agendas remained clearly different, there was a noticeable shift in the Democratic platform from the liberal left toward the middle of the road, and a slight Republican resemblance (before they embraced the far right). Actress Susan Sarandon declined an invitation to speak at the Democratic national convention because "the party was no longer liberal enough." (She and Tim Robbins, whose timely political satire about a power-abusing, right-wing, folksinging Senator *Bob Roberts* appeared in theaters during the campaign, still qualified for the Hollywood elite/family values blacklist as an unmarried couple who are parents of two children together.)

Similarly, *Rolling Stone*'s Anthony DeCurtis (1992) labeled the "new Democrats" "fake Republicans." He argued the party sent the wrong message to freedom of expressionists, especially in music, when nominating Al Gore because it raised the "Tipper Question." Tipper Gore was proof that Democrats, too, had family values. She, along with Susan Baker, Secretary of State James Baker's wife, cofounded the Parents Music Resource Center in 1985. DeCurtis accuses of Gore of "masquerading as a moderate," and fears her "readiness to align with conservative forces, proximity to power to advance her own cultural agenda, and most disturbing of all, to create a McCarthyite spectacle of artists testifying before Congressional hearings to justify their works."

Others expressed similar reservations about Tipper, albeit in different voices. Ice T's "KKK Bitch" describes falling in love with young nieces of Tipper Gore. Of course, the free speech issue was further magnified by his controversial "Cop Killer." Following hostile reactions—including bomb and death threats—widespread criticism from police groups, Congress, Oliver North and the president, among others; and Charlton Heston's biblical baritone recitation of lines from Ice T's songs before Time-Warner stockholders and executives, Ice T voluntarily dropped "Cop Killer" from his *Body Count* record, and reinforced fears of self-censorship.

The PMRC premise of the need to "protect" children from the supposedly harmful content of popular music, and the same fears which engulfed the Ice T controversy, have their roots in 1950s Elvis. The postal image of Elvis leaning over a 1950s microphone served as a reminder of cultural liberation, waist-up television appearances, rows of screaming teenagers, panicked parents and a rattled establishment.

In addition to the stamp, Elvis appears as a messenger for freedom of expression in Billy Joel's black and white video of "All Shook Up" from the *Honeymoon in Vegas* soundtrack. A strong anti-censorship message is conveyed through footage of Elvis hipshaking, leg wobbling across stages, Beatles bashing, record burning, and condemning statements against popular music.

A two-party interpretation of the Elvis stamp also translates fear, but through generational and philosophical distinctions. The Democratic call for "change" was inherently accompanied by fear. People, by nature, are apprehensive about new approaches and often find it easier to remain with the comforts of the familiar, even in the most trying circumstances. In this sense, Clinton appears analogous with the early Elvis. He represented change, and to some degree, risk, to voters. In addition, there was the youth, energy, and a rock the vote attitude that threatened to rattle the White House walls. Were voters ready for a new generation of leadership with baby boomer baggage? A junk food/junk culture prez who eats at McDonald's, watches *American Gladiators*, jogs in a *Rolling Stone* t-shirt, and associates "B-52's" with the band before the bombers? A vice president who wears Grateful Dead daddy Jerry Garcia-designed ties? Resurrecting a Fleetwood Mac hit for an anthem? Rallies featuring a Demo-listen derby of U2, John Mellencamp, and R.E.M., a band whose name even Dan Quayle should have no trouble spelling? And introductions by R.E.M.'s Michael Stipe whenever in Georgia, either Athens or Atlanta? Clearly, this new boss was not the same as the old boss.

In contrast, the Republicans were indeed grand and old, a reflection of the late model Elvis—bloated, safe, mainstream. Their neopuritan platform was largely founded on fear. Diversity, choice, alternative lifestyles, career women, opportunities for minorities, the middle class and poor, ideas and knowledge from the culturally elite, nontraditional families, and many views deemed "politically correct," were considered threats to "family values" and society's status quo, striking the same panic button 1950s Elvis did.

There was also a more subtle subtext of fear toward the Clinton-Gore Southern accent. Throughout the campaign, the Republicans frequently expressed "Remember what the country was like the last time a Southerner was in the White House" admonitions, characterizing Clinton as a Jimmy Carter country-clone. In his August 1987 *LA Weekly* article, "The Elvis in You," Michael Ventura's synthesis of Elvis's political effect with Jesus, the South, and youth, seems particularly relevant to Clinton, his own religious and political roots (in particular as a student in the 1960)s his new approach, and the accompanying Republican fears in 1992. Ventura writes:

> . . . especially in the South, they talk about Elvis and Jesus in the same breath. There's a good reason for that. Elvis was the first public figure since Jesus that couldn't be ignored by any segment of his civilization, yet that foretold and embodied a new mode of being that would eventually dismantle the very society that was so fascinated by his presence.
>
> Which is perhaps, the final, and most significant, of Elvis' paradoxes. In his early years Elvis was virtually apolitical, yet no one else in the '50s except Martin Luther King had as huge a political effect in the United States. Elvis singlehandedly created what came to be known as the "youth" market, the demand for the form of music he made popular. Through being united as a market, that particular wave of youth felt the cohesion of community that became the '60s upheaval, an upheaval that all our politics since have been in reaction to, for or against.

In discussing the work of feminist and cultural critic, Camille Paglia, Greil Marcus (1991) writes that "culture today has so completely replaced government that there are no politics, and culture itself has lost its border and domain." Examples have become plentiful, from Ronald Reagan himself to 1992's media-saturated campaign culture; and even Poland, where Prime Minister Tadeusz Mazowiecki vowed that, if elected, he would bring the Rolling Stones to his country. The desperate promise resembled George Bush's last-minute, 15-minute appearance on MTV two days before the election, after months of declining, (and virtually ignoring the youth audience) not "wanting to become a teenybopper at 68."

As the parameters of the Elvis myth expanded to include political dimensions, two familiar keystones appear which lock the Presley puzzle pieces in place–power and imagination. Presidentially, both John F. Kennedy and Ronald Reagan can be credited with replacing politics with culture. While Kennedy's charisma captured the public imagination, Reagan dominated, owned, and controlled it (Marcus, 1991). In 1992, it was Ross Perot who approached the cultural throne. As a ringmaster of a three-ring circus, complete with sideshows, a writer-director-star of his own three-act political power play, or simply the spoiler in a three person race, Perot captivated the American public with his flawed, but feisty, folksy presence. A revision of Dr. Hunter S. Thompson's gonzo adage often seemed appropriate: "When the going gets weird, the weird turn to Perot." Largely defined by control and domination, Perot at times appeared to be running for Owner, rather than President, of the nation. Unconventional in his exclusive reliance on a television campaign, he dominated the airwaves, spending his reported yearly interest–$100 million–on infomercials and advertising. In the process, he alone single (cash-in) handedly represented a national economic recovery, and stood as a living, spending testimony to Bob Dylan's remark from years ago, "Money doesn't talk–it swears."

Yet the "Elvis Factor" outweighed (no pun intended) the "Perot Factor." The omnipresent, omnipotent, and now political Presley met Perot's challenge to his reign over the collective imagination of America as he always has–surfacing, in often mysterious ways or whispers that are reminders of his ruling royalty. One need only recall one year ago, on November 7, 1991, when professional basketball star Magic Johnson announced his (first) retirement because he had tested positive for the HIV virus. While ABC and CBS concluded their evening news broadcasts in rather eulogizing tones, the *NBC Nightly News'* final segment reported on Graceland being added to the historical register as a national landmark. Compared to the magnitude of the day's startling top story, and the AIDS crisis itself, the Graceland feature was strikingly insignificant—except that it was Elvis. And in a perverse way, the juxtaposition seemed to momentarily make him analogous with the AIDS disease. Though the results were less tragic, many had contracted and tested positive for the contagious Elvirus. And one could almost imagine anchor Tom Brokaw signing off that evening by saying, "Long live the King."

In 1992, it was the Elvis stamp, Elvis Clinton, Elvis economics, "Elvis endorses Feingold," along with a new wave of commemorative memorabilia. Fifteen years after his death, Elvis again demonstrated he was more invincible than Superman (who died in the DC comics in November), better than Madonna's *SEX* photo album, and could capture, control, and dominate the public imagination like nothing else could, be it a president or politician, entertainer or event. Even Madonna, whose multimedia manipulations many believed would result in her being an heir apparent Queen of Culture, with an entrepreneurial empire exceeding Elvis's Kingdom, recognized that Elvis was King of Kings in American culture. Closing the last show of her 1990 *Blond Ambition Tour*, she left the stage proclaiming, "I love you, too, Elvis—without Elvis, you're nothing!"[2] And it is Greil Marcus's timeless comment written in 1976 which best characterizes our enduring fascination with Elvis, and the difference between him and other "challengers," from Madonna to Perot: "And of course we respond: a self-made man is rather boring, but a self-made king is something else."

The myths of the Elvis-Kennedy-Reagan trinity intersect for comparison at a Clinton crossroad. In the November 2, 1992 issue of *Newsweek* Joe Klein observes, "There are screamers, shirkers, and jumpers now; they react with a fervor that hasn't been seen in American politics since the Kennedy days. (Ronald Reagan was better loved; perhaps—but that was Lawrence Welk music; this is Elvis.)" Whether ironic or intentional, the title for the piece—"Prisoner of the People"—is fitting for Elvis' career, and now perhaps Clinton's term as president.

Clinton himself contributed to the Elvis-Kennedy dynamic. Just before the election, he recalled the JFK statement at the end of the 1960 campaign—that "the mystery of democracy was about to re-express itself." The phrase resonated with distant familiarity; it was the link that eventually connected with Elvis. Woodrow Wilson used those words—"mystery of democracy"—when dedicating the log cabin where Abraham Lincoln was born, and passed the phrase on to the mayor of Tupelo, Mississippi when dedicating Elvis Presley's two-room, wood frame birthplace on Old Saltillo Road. In 1992, as well as the "mystery of democracy" about to re-express itself, the mystery train. Elvis, who himself had been the focus of a democratic process during the stamp elections, had repositioned himself into a new setting—the political realm—where he would express himself through Bill Clinton and the White House during the next four years. Perhaps that is what took Elvis such a long time to "actively" pursue politics; he was waiting to find the appropriate "running mate." Clinton fit the bill and became that vehicle. He had some Elvis in him.

The union placed both the King and President in a new context, with endless reference points waiting to be connected. A newspaper ad for Capitol Hill's Trover Shop, read "As the spirit of Elvis prepares to move into the White House, it's time to read *When Elvis Died . . .*" a book by Neal and Janice Gregory.

"Have you noticed the Bill Clinton impression that I can't do sounds just like the Elvis Presley impression that I can't do?" remarked David Letterman during a routine. His late-night monologue is one tributary in the steady stream flowing to and from the Elvis wellspring. Other observations, jokes, images, and fancies were certain to follow during the Elvis-Clinton term. Would James Carville, the "ragin' Cajun" spin doctor who masterminded the Clinton campaign continue to evolve into a Colonel Parker figure? Would the Presley estate do a Disneyworld-style commercial similar to those immediately following world championship sporting events, when they ask the most valuable player, "What are you going to do?"; and the star gushes on cue, "I'm going to Disneyworld!", this version featuring the press asking Clinton at his election victory celebration the same questions, only his hoarse response would be, "I'm going to Graceland!"? Would a Clinton inauguration ceremony be an exercise in excess comparable to that surrounding Elvis? Would daughter Chelsea become the First Family's Lisa Marie, her name inscribed on the side on Air Force One? Would presidential press conferences end with the White House press secretary announcing, "Ladies and gentleman, Elvis has left the building"? Would President Clinton discuss his first 100 days in office in "Taking Care of Business with a flash" terms?

It was not difficult to imagine the speechwriting staff shaping Presley passages into reflective, relevant, rhetoric to be delivered as Clinton oration. Citing Dave Marsh was just one possibility:

> Elvis Presley was an explorer of vast new landscapes of dream and illusion. He was a man who refused to be told that the best of his dreams would not come true, who refused to be defined by anyone else's conceptions.
>
> This is the goal of democracy, the journey on which every prospective American hero sets out. That Elvis made so much of the journey on his own is reason enough to remember him with the honor and love we reserve for the bravest among us. Such men made the only maps we can trust. (1992, p. 234)

Perhaps the most defining and consolidating moment of the Elvis-Clinton fusion could be seen the day after the election (November 4) during Ted Koppel's ABC prime-time, behind-the-scenes documentary that followed the Clinton campaign during its final 72 hours leading up to the November 3 election. Shortly before the party plane landed in Arkansas following a frenzied, whirlwind, cross-country campaign wrap-up, a confident Clinton reached for the cabin's loudspeaker system to address his devoted traveling entourage. The camera shot framing Clinton as he held the palm-sized intercom bore a strange and striking resemblance to the Presley postage pose with a 1950s microphone. Then at the end of his brief message, Clinton declared, "Elvis lives!"

Perhaps never before had that often-uttered phrase echoed with such clarity and fancy. A more powerful and imaginative reverberation than the Madonna post-tour Elvis affirmation—"Without Elvis, you're nothing!"—Clinton's "Elvis Lives!" was a declaration of victory that brought candidate Elvis full circle, from conception, to convention, to campaign climax. Clinton's words were spoken with more conviction than when he told *Newsweek*'s Eleanor Clift eight months earlier during the primaries, "If I am elected, then all the Elvis fans could say, 'Well, Elvis *is* alive . . .'" Now it was President-elect Clinton who was saying—and had he not been so hoarse, probably shouting—"Elvis lives!", as if he had been converted into a true believer or possessed along the campaign trail to the White House. The statement was also a paradoxical expression; at once a punctuation mark as well as proclamation of perpetuity and profuse possibility: Was it mere coincidence, cosmic connection, or fate, that Elvis was 42 years old when he died, and Bill Clinton was about to become the 42nd President of the United States?

On January 8, 1993, the fifty-eighth anniversary of Elvis Presley's birthday, the Elvis stamp was officially issued as a postage stamp during a ceremony at Graceland. Two weeks later, on January 20, President-elect Bill Clinton was sworn in as President of the United States during a ceremony at the White House. A coronation and an inauguration, honoring the King of Rock and Roll aboard the mystery train, and the King from Little Rock riding the rails of the mystery of democracy across the mystery terrain; both men about to re-express themselves as King of America.

## NOTES

1. The USPS issued a stamp honoring the Buffalo Soldiers, April 22, 1994, in Dallas, Texas.

2. In Steve Pond's interview with Jeff Ayeroff, co-president of Virgin America ("The Industry in the Eighties, *Rolling Stone,* November 15, 1990:113-17), Ayeroff scratches the surface of the Elvis-Madonna myth connection. Among other points, Ayeroff views Madonna as "better than Elvis was, because Elvis was manipulated, as opposed to being a manipulator. . . . She is politically correct where Elvis was politically incorrect."

# Epilogue

He keeps going... and going... and going....

Source: Courtesy Greg Metcalf.

# Bibliography

Adams, Douglas. 1992. *Mostly Harmless.* New York: Ballantine.

Antonen, Mel, and Rod Beaton. 1993. "Behind the Seams: Base-ball's Odds and Offbeat." *USA Today.* May 13, p. 3C.

Arey, Norman. 1992. "Sports 2: Norman Arey's Sportscene." *Atlanta Journal Constitution.* March 21, p. D2.

Atwood, Margaret. 1986. *The Handmaid's Tale.* New York: Houghton Mifflin.

Bangs, Lester. 1977. "Where Were You When Elvis Died?" in Greil Marcus, (ed.). 1987. *Psychotic Reactions and Carburetur Dung.* New York: Knopf.

Banney, Howard F. 1987. *Return to Sender: The First Complete Discography of Elvis Tribute and Novelty Records, 1956-1986.* Ann Arbor, MI: Pierian Press.

Barry, Dave. 1993. "Dead Reckoning." *The Washington Post Magazine.* September 5, p. 36.

Barson, Michael (comp.). *Rip It Up! Postcards from the Hey Day of Rock 'n' Roll.* New York: Pantheon.

Barth, Jack. 1991. *Roadside Elvis: The Complete State-by-State Travel Guide for Elvis Presley Fans.* Chicago: Contemporary Books.

Bennetts, Leslie. 1993. "k.d. lang Cuts It Close." *Vanity Fair,* August, pp. 94-98, 142-146.

Blount, Roy Jr. 1983. "Elvis! The King Is Dead But That Thing Still Shakes." *Esquire.* December, pp. 172-176.

"Bluth Finds Animation Something to Crow About." 1992. *Atlanta Journal/Constitution.* April 3, p. D7.

Bono (Hewson of U2). 1994. "Elvis: An American David." In Geri DePaoli (ed.), *Elvis + Marilyn 2 x Immortal.* New York: Rizzoli.

Bordowitz, Hank. 1988. "Elvis Doesn't Live Here Anymore," *Spin,* October, p. 22.

Brewer-Giorgio, Gail. 1988. *Is Elvis Alive?* New York: Tudor.

Brewer-Giorgio, Gail. 1989. *Orion.* New York: Tudor.

Brewer-Giorgio, Gail. 1990. *The Elvis Files: Was His Death Faked?* New York: Shapalsky Publishers, Inc.

Brooks, Tim, and Earle Marsh. 1992. *The Complete Directory to Prime Time Network TV Shows, 1946-Present* (fifth edition). New York: Ballantine.

Buchwald, Art. 1992. "Fat Elvis: Sticking to the Issue." *Washington Post.* May 14, p. C1.

Buffett, Jimmy. 1989. *Tales From Margaritaville: Fictional Facts and Factual Fictions.* New York: Fawcett Crest.

Butler, Brenda Arlene. 1993. *Are You Hungry Tonight?* New York: Gramercy.

Byron, Ellen. 1989. *"Graceland"* (play).

Cameron, Dan. 1989. "Joni Mabe at Sandler Hudson: Glop Art." *(Atlanta) Creative Loafing.* December 30, pp. 23-24B.

Carlson, Thomas C. 1994. "Ad Hoc Rock: Elvis and the Aesthetics of Postmodernism." *Studies in Popular Culture.* XVI:2. 1994. pp. 39-50.

Cauchon, Dennis. 1988. "Buying All the Time: Fans Hound Bank for Elvis Card." *USA Today.* September 20, p. 2B.

Cauchon, Dennis. 1992. "Elvis Sighted on Stamp." *USA Today.* January 8, p. 1D.

Chadwick, Vernon (ed.). 1997. *In Search of Elvis: Music, Race, Art, Religion.* Boulder, CO: Westview Press.

Chaplin, Julia. 1994. "Myth Thing." *Spin.* December. p. 44.

Charters, Samuel. 1992. *Elvis Presley Calls His Mother After The Ed Sullivan Show.* Minneapolis: Coffeehouse Press.

Childress, Mark. 1990. *Tender.* New York: Ballantine.

Choron, Sandra and Bob Oskam. 1991. *Elvis! The Last Word.* New York: Citadel Press.

Clift, Eleanor. 1992. "Political Ambitions, Personal Choices." *Newsweek.* March 9, p. 36.

Cocks, Jay. 1977. "Last Stop on the Mystery Train." *Time.* August 29, pp. 56-59.

Cohen, Scott. 1988. "Forever Young." *Spin.* June, pp. 37-40.

Crawford, John. 1988. "Baboon Dooley Rock Critic Consults the Deity!" (cartoon) *Spin,* June, p. 32.

Crenshaw, Marshall. 1994. *Hollywood Rock.* New York: Agincourt Press/Harper Collins.

Crowe, Cameron. 1982. "Neil Young: Still Expecting to Fly." *Musician*. November, pp. 54-62, 96-99.

Committee to Elect the King, The (comp.). 1992. *Elvis for President*. New York: Crown.

Corliss, Richard. 1989. "The King is Dead—or Is He?" *Newsweek*. October 10.

"Dear Elvis" (column). October 1988-May 1994. *Spin*.

DeCurtis, Anthony. 1992. "Tipper: Dems Send Wrong Message." *Rolling Stone*. September 3, p. 17.

DeFord, Frank. 1992. "A Rare Bird Bows Out." *Newsweek*. August 31.

Denisoff, R. Serge and George Plasketes. 1995. *True Disbelievers: The Elvis Contagion*. New Brunswick, NJ: Transaction Books.

Desauliniers, Marcel, and Nancy Gardner Thomas (illustrator). 1996. *An Alphabet of Sweets*. New York: Rizzoli.

DePaoli, Geri (ed.). 1994. *Elvis + Marilyn: 2 x Immortal*. New York: Rizzoli.

Doll, Susan (contributing writer). 1989. *Elvis: A Tribute to His Life*. Lincolnwood, IL: Publications International, Ltd.

Dollar, Steve. 1988. "It's Hard to Get All Shook Up Over Silly *Heartbreak Hotel*." *Atlanta Journal/Constitution*. September 30, p. 5C.

Dollar, Steve. 1991. " 'Elvis Christmas House's Alive and Well On Video." *Atlanta Journal Constitution*. December 20, 1991, D8.

Dubler, Linda. 1991. "All The King's Men." *Creative Loafing* (Atlanta). July 27, pp. 61-62.

Duff, Gerald. 1995. *That's All Right Mama: The Unauthorized Life of Elvis's Twin*. Dallas: Baskerville.

Dundy, Elaine. 1985. *Elvis and Gladys*. New York: Macmillan.

Dunn, Jancee. 1993. "Art Garfunkel" (interview). *Rolling Stone*. November 24, p. 28.

Earle, Joe. 1993. "Fan Has Elvis Stamp Stuck on Her," *Atlanta Journal Constitution*. January 8, p. A3.

Ebersole, Lucinda, and Richard Peabody (eds.). 1994. *Mondo Elvis*. New York: St. Martin's.

Ebert, Roger. *Roger Ebert's Movie Home Companion* (1993 ed.). Kansas City, MO: Andrews and McMeel.

"Elvis Dead at 58." 1993. *Weekly World News*. June 15.

"Elvis Stamp: Good Business." 1992. *Postal Leader* (USPS Newsletter). Vol. 22, no. 11, June 16, p. 3.

Farber, Manny. 1962. "White Elephant and Termite Art." in *Negative Space: Manny Farber on the Movies.* New York: Praeger.

Flanagan, Bill. 1986. *Written in My Soul: Rock's Great Songwriters Talk About Creating Their Music.* Chicago: Contemporary Books.

Flippo, Chet. 1989. "Burning Love." *Tennessee Illustrated.* July/ August, pp. 15-18.

Flippo, Chet. 1993. *Graceland: The Living Legacy of Elvis Presley.* San Francisco: Collins.

Fowler, Christopher. 1984. *How to Impersonate Famous People.* New York: Prince Paperbacks/Crown.

Fox, William Price. 1981. *Dixiana Moon.* New York: Viking.

Fox, Les, and Sue Fox. 1996. *Return to Sender: The Secret Son of Elvis Presley.* Orlando, FL: West Highland.

Friedman, Kinky. 1993. *Elvis, Jesus, and Coca-Cola.* New York: Bantam.

Frew, Timothy. 1992. *Elvis.* New York: Mallard.

Gable, Donna. 1993. "Elvis, Special Delivery." *USA Today.* January 5, p. 3D.

Gelfand, Craig, and Lynn Blocker-Krantz. 1992. *In Search of the King.* New York: Perigee/Putnam.

Geller, Larry, and Joel Spector, with Patricia Romanowski. 1989. *If I Can Dream.* New York: Simon and Schuster.

Gibson, William. 1984. *Neuromancer.* London: Gollancz.

Gifford, Barry. 1990. *Wild at Heart: The Story of Sailor and Lula.* New York: Vintage.

Glanville, Jerry, with J. David Williams. 1990. *Elvis Don't Like Football: The Life and Raucous Times of the NFL's Most Outspoken Coach.* New York: Macmillan.

Glen, Scott. 1988. "Forever Young" *Spin.* June, pp. 37-40.

Goldberg, Michael. 1992. "Elvis's Stamp of Approval." *Rolling Stone.* March 19, p. 18.

Goldman, Albert. 1981. *Elvis.* New York: McGraw-Hill.

Graham, Jefferson. 1991. "Scandal Is All in a Day's Work." *USA Today.* December 9, p. 3D.

Graham, Jefferson. 1992. "In Sweeps Month, Elvis Sighted on Tabloid Shows." *USA Today.* May 4, p. 3D.

Green, Tom. 1990. "Series Won't Sugarcoat 'Rebel' Elvis." *USA Today.* February 6, pp. 1-2D.

Greer, Jim. 1990. "Ten Best." *Spin.* April, p. 60.

Greer, Jim. 1994. "A Year in the Life of Rock 'N' Roll: Part Ten." *Spin.* August, pp. 76-77.

Gregory, Neal, and Janice Gregory. 1992. *When Elvis Died: Media Overload and the Origins of the Elvis Cult* (second edition). New York: Pharos Books.

Grizzard, Lewis. 1984. *Elvis Is Dead and I'm Not Feeling So Good Myself.* Atlanta: Peachtree.

Guard, Sally. 1992. "The Pitcher King." *Sports Illustrated.* June 1, pp. 9-10.

Gunderson, Edna. 1994a. "To Remember the Best of Rock's King." *USA Today.* October 7, pp. 1-2D.

Gunderson, Edna. 1994b. "No Backing Down From Rock's Edge." *USA Today.* November 15, pp. 1-2D.

Gunderson, Edna, and David Zimmerman. 1994. "Today's Stars Hail the King of Rock 'n' Roll." *USA Today.* October 10, p. 4D.

Guralnick, Peter. 1989. *Lost Highway: Journeys and Arrivals of American Musicians* (revised edition). New York: Harper and Row.

Guralnick, Peter. 1994. *Last Train to Memphis: The Rise of Elvis Presley.* Boston: Little, Brown.

Hammontree, Patsy Guy. 1985. *Elvis Presley: A Bio-Bibliography.* Westport, CT: Greenwood Press.

Handleman, David. 1989. "Holy Art!" *Rolling Stone.* April 20, pp. 65-68.

Hannah, Barry. 1993. "Mother Mouth," in *Bats Out of Hell.* Boston: Houghton Mifflin, pp. 153-154.

Hardy, Lawrence. 1995. "Lifeline: All Shook Up." *USA Today.* August 7, p. 1D.

Haring, Bruce. 1996. "'Virtual Graceland' Brings Wonder of Elvis to CD-ROM." *USA Today.* August 7, p. 3D.

Harrison, Ted. 1992. *Elvis People: The Cult of the King.* London: Fount Paperbacks.

Hasson, Judi. 1992. "A Weird, Wacky Wisconsin Senate Race." *USA Today.* October 28, p. 8A.

Henderson, William McCranor. 1984. *Stark Raving Elvis*. New York: E.P. Dutton.

Hiestand, Michael. 1993a. "TV Sports." *USA Today.* February 3, p. 3C.

Hiestand, Michael. 1993b. "TV Sports." *USA Today.* February 24, p. 3C.

Hiestand, Michael. 1992. "TV Sports: ABC's Three-Men Booth That's a Lot of Talking." *USA Today.* February 24, p. 3C.

Hoffer, Eric. 1951. *True Believers*. New York: Harper and Row.

Hopkins, Jerry. 1971. *Elvis: A Biography.* New York: Simon & Schuster.

*I Am Elvis: A Guide To Elvis Impersonators.* 1991. New York: Pocket Books/Simon & Schuster.

Jacobs, A.J. 1993. *The Two Kings: Jesus, Elvis*. New York: Bantam.

Janowitz, Tama. 1985. "You and the Boss." *Spin.* November; Reprinted in Clinton Heylin (ed.), *The Penguin Book of Rock and Roll Writing*. New York: Viking, pp. 439-444.

Johnson, T.R. 1992. "Stamping Out Elvis." Paper presented at Annual Conference of the Popular Culture/American Culture Association in the South Conference, Augusta, GA, October.

Kalpakian, Laura. 1992. *Graced Land*. New York: Grove Weidenfeld.

Kalpakian, Laura. 1992. "Spirit of Elvis: Why the King Holds Such Lasting Posthumous Power." *USA Today.* August 14, p. 4D.

Kelly, Katy. 1993. "The President and the King." *USA Today.* January 5, p. 1D.

Kelly, Tom. 1993. "Elvis II: A Question of Grace." *Christianity and Crisis.* February 15, pp. 28-29.

King, Larry. 1992. "People and Views." *USA Today.* April 20, p. 2D.

King, Stephen. 1991. *Needful Things*. New York: Penguin/Dutton.

Klein, Joe. 1992. "Prisoner of the People." *Newsweek.* November 2, p. 58.

Kluge, P.F. *Biggest Elvis*. New York: Viking.

Kroker, Arthur, Marilouise Kroker, and David Cook. (eds.) 1989. *Panic Encyclopedia: The Definitive Guide to the Postmodern Scene*. New York: St. Martin's.

Landis, David. 1992. Which Elvis Stamp Will Be Returned to Sender?" *USA Today.* February 25, p. 1D.

Landis, David. 1993. "The Artist Who Put His Stamp on Elvis." *USA Today*. February 22, p. 4D.

Landis, David and Dick Sproul. 1992. "Readers: Young Elvis Licks Old." *USA Today*. March 6-8, pp. 1,8A.

Larson, Gary. 1988. *The Far Side* (cartoon). "What Really Happend to Elvis." Universal Press Syndicate.

Lee, Spike. 1990. "Eddie" (interview with Eddie Murphy). *Spin*. October, p. 34.

Levine, Al. 1993. "It Ain't Nothin' But an Elvis Stamp, *Atlanta Journal Constitution*. January 9, p A3.

Levitt, Shelley. 1990. "The Man Who Would Be King," *US*. March 19, pp. 18-27.

Ludwig, Ken. 1994. *Lend Me a Tenor*. (play)

Mabe, Joni. 1988. *Joni Mabe's Museum Book*. Atlanta: Nexus.

Mabe, Joni. 1992. *A Classic Postcard Book*. Atlanta: Nexus.

Mabe, Joni. 1996. *Everything Elvis*. New York: Thunder's Mouth Press.

MacEnroe, Colin. 1992. Loss Weight Through Great Sex with Celebrities the Elvis Way. New York: Crown.

Maislen, Alan D. 1989. "In Search of Historic Elvis." *Rolling Stone*. December 14-28, pp. 196-201.

Malley, Jack D. and Warren Vaughn. 1993. *Elvis: The Messiah*. Mount Horeb, WI: TCB Publishing.

Maney, Kevin. 1994. "Theme Airfares the Latest Thriller." *USA Today*. January 13, p. 12B.

Marc, David. 1982. *Demographic Vistas: Television in American Culture*. Philadelphia: University of Pennsylvania Press.

Marc, David. 1984. *Demographic Vistas: Television in American Culture*. Philadelphia: University of Pennsylvania.

Marcus, Greil. 1982. *Mystery Train: Images of America in Rock 'n' Roll Music* (second edition). New York Dutton.

Marcus, Greil. 1987. "Antihero." *Spin*. August, pp. 65-66.

Marcus, Greil. 1991. *Dead Elvis: A Chronicle of a Cultural Obsession*. New York: Doubleday.

Marino, Jan. 1991. *The Day That Elvis Came to Town*. Boston: Little, Brown, & Company.

Marling, Karal Ann. 1996. *Graceland: Going Home with Elvis*. Cambridge, MA: Harvard University Press.

Marsh, Dave. 1985. *The First Rock and Roll Confidential*. New York: Pantheon.

Marsh, Dave. 1985. *Fortunate Son: The Best of Dave Marsh*. New York: Random House.

Marsh, Dave. 1987. *Glory Days: Bruce Springsteen in the 1980s*. New York: Pantheon.

Marsh, Dave. 1989. *The Heart of Rock and Roll*. New York: Penguin/Plume.

Marsh, Dave. 1992. *Elvis*. (second edition) New York: Thunder's Mouth Press.

Martzke, Rudy. 1994. "Sports on TV." *USA Today*. January 19, p. 3C.

Mason, Bobbi Ann. 1994. "Shouts and Murmurs: All Shook Up." *The New Yorker*. February, p. 96.

McCranor, William. 1996. "The Transformation from English Teacher/Writer into Elvis Impersonator." Paper presented at the Popular Culture/American Culture in the South Annual Conference, Savannah, GA, October.

McCray, Patrick. 1992. *The Secret Files* (two-issue series). San Diego, CA: Revolutionary Comics.

McCray, Patrick, and Dave Garcia (art). 1993. *Elvis Shrugged* (three-issue series). San Diego, CA: Revolutionary Comics.

McEwan, Ian. 1990. *The Innocent*. New York: Doubleday.

McKeon, Elizabeth, Ralph Gevirtz, and Julie Bandy. 1992. *Fit for a King: The Elvis Presley Cookbook*. Nashville: Rutledge Hill Press.

McNeil, Alex. 1996. *Total Television: The Comprehensive Guide to Programming from 1948 to the Present* (fourth edition). New York: Penguin.

McNeil, Legs. 1988. "Elvira: The Interview." *Spin*. October, p. 14.

Miller, Jim. 1987. "Forever Elvis." *Newsweek*. August 3, p. 46.

Moorcock, Michael. 1970. *Behold the Man*. New York: Avon.

Mooser, Steven. 1994. *Elvis Is Back and He's in the Sixth Grade*. New York: Bantam.

Moody, Raymond. 1987. *Elvis After Life: Unusual Psychic Experiences Surrounding the Death of a Superstar*. Atlanta, GA: Peachtree.

"No Such Zone." 1992. *Musician*. September, p. 114.

Nagourney, Adam. 1992. "If Bush Can't Win Here . . ." *USA Today*. August 27, p. 8A.

Orth, M. 1977. "All Shook Up: Heartbreak Kid." *Newsweek.* August 29, pp. 46-49.

Owen, David. 1990. "Bruce McDonald: Director as Rock 'n' Roll Hoser." *I.C.E.* March, pp. 7-9.

Paglia, Camille. 1990. *Sexual Personae: Art and Decadence from Nefertiti to Emily Dickinson.* New Haven and London: Yale.

Panta, Ilona. 1979. *Elvis Presley: King of Kings (Who Was the Real Elvis?).* Hicksville: Exposition press.

Panter, Gary. 1984. *Invasion of the Elvis Zombies.* New York: Raw Books.

Parker, Priscilla, and Steve Marmel. 1989. "Face-Off: Putting Elvis on a Stamp." *USA Today.* June 9, p. 10A.

Piccoli, Sean. 1992. "News Bites: Return to Sender." *Washington City Paper.* March 6, p. 12.

Pirarao, Dan. 1987. *Too Bizarro.* San Francisco: Chronicle Press, p. 40.

Plasketes, George. 1989. "The King is Gone But Not Forgotten: Songs Responding to the Life, Death, and Myth of Elvis Presley in the 1980s." *Studies in Popular Culture.* XII:1, pp. 58-74.

Plasketes, George. 1994. "From Post Office to Oval Office: Idolatry and Ideology in the 1992 Presleydential Elections." *Popular Music and Society.* Vol. 18(1) Spring, pp. 19-50.

Pond, Steve. 1990. "The Boy King." *Rolling Stone.* April 5, p. 41.

Pond, Steve. 1990. "The Industry in the Eighties" (interview with Jeff Ayeroff, CEO-Virgin America). *Rolling Stone.* November 15, pp. 113-117.

Pratt, Linda Ray. 1979. "Elvis, or the Ironies of a Southern Identity." In Jac Tharpe (ed.), 1979. *Elvis: Images and Fancies.* Jackson: University of Mississippi Press, pp. 40-51.

Presley, Priscilla Beaulieu with Sandra Harmon. 1985. *Elvis and Me.* New York: Putnam's.

Pritikin, Karen (text) and Kent Barker (photographs). 1992. *The King and I: A Little Gallery of Elvis Impersonators.* San Francisco: Chronicle Books.

Quain, Kevin (ed.). 1992. *The Elvis Reader: Texts and Sources on the King of Rock 'n' Roll.* New York: St. Martin's.

Rankin, Robert. 1991. *Armageddon: The Musical.* New York: Dell.

Ridgeway, Karen. 1988. "In Search of the King: Fans Say Elvis Is Popping Up All Over the Place." *USA Today.* August 16, p. 5D.

Robbins, Ira A. (ed). 1989. *Trouser Press Record Guide* (fourth edition). New York: Collier Books.

Robinson, Kim Stanley. 1996. "A Colony in the Sky." *Newsweek.* September 23, p. 59.

Rogan, Johnny. 1982. *Neil Young.* London: Proteus.

*Rolling Stone.* 1977. "Elvis." September 22, pp. 37-59.

*Rolling Stone.* 1992. (Elvis's gold lamé suit in "Portraits: The History of Rock and Roll in Photographs" cover). Issue 643. November 12.

*Rolling Stone.* 1994. (Beavis and Butthead Elvis, "5,000,000 Can't Be Wrong" parody cover.) Issue 678. March 24.

*Rolling Stone.* 1994. (Jerry Seinfeld as "King of Prime-Time Comedy" dressed in Elvis's gold lamé suit and his sequined jumpsuit poses, two covers.) Issue 691. September 24.

Ruibal, Sal. 1995. "Promotion of the Week." *USA Today.* August 25, p. 4C.

Sammon, Paul (ed.). 1994. *The King Is Dead: Tales of Elvis Postmortem.* New York: Delta.

Sandberg-Wright, Mercy. 1992. "Interview: Cage Dweller." *Creative Loafing* (Atlanta). August 29, pp. 57-58.

Sante, Luc. 1989. "Mystery Man" (interview with Jim Jarmusch). *Interview.* November, pp. 146-148, 207.

Scherman, Rowland. 1992. *Elvis is Everywhere.* New York: Clarkson Potter.

Sellers, Richard West. 1993. "Blue Suede Stars." *The Washington Post.* January 10, p. 21A.

Shapiro, Herbert, and Patrick McCray. 1992. *The Elvis Presley Experience* (seven-part series). San Diego, CA: Revolutionary Comics.

Shapiro, Herbert, and Patrick McCray, with Aaron Sowd (art). *The Elvis Presley Experience.* (seven-issue series). San Diego, CA: Revolutionary Comics.

Shepard, Sam. 1987. *True Dylan* (a one-act play). *Esquire.* July, pp. 59-68.

Shepard, Steve. 1991. *Elvis Hornbill: International Business Bird.* New York: Henry Holt and Company.

Singleton, Elyse. 1992. "Rapping Rap? Get Serious!" *USA Today.* June 9, p. 8A.

Sloan, Kay and Constance Pierce. 1993. *Elvis Rising: Stories on the King.* New York: Avon Books.

Snider, Mike. 1995. "Electronic Homage to Elvis." *USA Today.* January 15, p. 2D.

Spencer, T. M. 1989. *Christmas with Elvis.* (play)

"Sportscene: No Elvis Here." 1992. *Atlanta Journal Constitution.* May 16, p. D2.

Stankowicz, Tony, and Marie Jackson. 1996. *The Museum of Bad Art: Art Too Bad to Be Ignored.* Kansas City: Andrews and Mcmillan.

Stern, J. David. 1990. "The King is Back." *TV Guide.* February 17-23, pp. 4-10.

Stern, Jane and Michael. 1987. *Elvis World.* New York: Alfred A. Knopf.

Stewart, Doug. 1995. "Now Playing in Academe: The King of Rock 'N' Roll." *Smithsonian.* November, pp. 56-66.

Strausbaugh, John. 1995. *E: Reflections on the Birth of the Elvis Faith.* New York: Blast Books.

Stromberg, Peter. 1990. "Elvis Alive?: The Ideology of American Consumerism." *Journal of Popular Culture,* 24, pp. 11-19.

Taylor, Roger G. (comp.). 1987. *Elvis in Art.* New York: St. Martin's Press.

Tharpe, Jac L. (ed.). 1979. *Elvis: Images and Fancies.* Jackson: University of Mississippi Press.

Thompson, Charles C. II and James P. Cole. 1991. *The Death of Elvis Presley: What Really Happened.* New York: Delacorte.

Tosches, Nick. 1977. *Country: Living Legends and Dying Metaphors in America's Biggest Music.* New York: Stein and Day.

Travers, Peter. 1989. "An Elvis Ghost Ride." *Rolling Stone.* November 30, p. 48.

Trebbe, Ann. 1992. "Writer Takes a Shrine to Elvis." *USA Today.* May 28, p. 2D.

Urschel, Joe. 1992a. "A Winning Candidate: Elvis." *USA Today.* April 2, p. 11A.

Urschel, Joe. 1992b. "Rock Hits the Other Side of the Generation Gap." *USA Today.* June 9, p. 10A.

Urschel, Joe. 1992c. "Does Elvis Live in Economics, of All Places?" *USA Today.* August 25, p. 10A.

Urschel, Joe. 1992d. "In This Democracy, Don't Knock the King." *USA Today.* September 15, p. 12A.

Urschel, Joe. 1992d. "Candidates Need to Whistle a Happy Tune." *USA Today.* June 23, p. 11A.

Ventura, Michael. 1987. "The Elvis in You," *LA Weekly.* August 14-20, p. 20.

"Viewpoints: King Size Debt Nears Legendary Status." 1992. *Atlanta Journal Constitution.* October 30, p. A15.

Vigoda, Arlene. 1996. "Lifeline: And Speaking of." November 26, p. 1D.

Vigoda, Arlene. 1996. "Lifeline: Blue Suede Toe Shoes." *USA Today.* May 29, p. 1D.

Waldrop. Howard. 1982. "Ike at the Mike," in *Strange Things in Close Up: The Nearly Complete Howard Waldrop.* London: Legend/Arrow, pp. 49-64.

Walken, Christopher. 1995. *Him.* (play)

Walker, Alice. 1981. "Nineteen Fifty-Five," in *You Can't Keep a Good Woman Down.* New York: Harcourt Brace Jovanovich, pp. 3-20.

Walker, Alice. 1990. *The Temple of My Familiar.* New York: Pocket Books.

Wayne, Carl. 1990. "Film's Avant-Guardian." *Rolling Stone.* March 22, p. 38.

Weir, Tom. 1993a. "Montana's Magic Melts Young Hearts." *USA Today.* January 8-10, pp. 1-2A.

Weir, Tom. 1993b. "Auburn Gets Reprise From NCAA." *USA Today.* August 20, p. 3C.

Weir, Tom. 1993c. "Sometimes Losers Really Win." *USA Today.* January 9, pp. 1-2A.

West, Red, Sonny West, Dave Hebler (as told to Steve Dunleavy). 1977. *Elvis: What Happened?* New York: Ballantine.

White, Gail. 1996. "Elvis Worship." *Atlanta Journal Constitution.* February 24, p. H6.

White, Paul. 1994. "Elvis Has Left the Park." *USA Today.* August 22, p. 5C.

Whitmer, Peter. 1996. *The Inner Elvis: A Psychological Biography of Elvis Aaron Presley.* New York: Hyperion.

Wickham, DeWayne. 1992. "Honors, But No Stamp." *USA Today.* June 8, p. 8A.

Wojahn, David. 1990. "W.C.W. Watching Presley's Second appearance on 'The Ed Sullivan Show,' Mercy Hospital, Newark, 1956"; "The Assassination of Robert Goulet as Performed by Elvis Presley: Memphis, 1956"; "Nixon Names Elvis Honorary Federal Narcotics Agent at Oval Office Ceremony, 1973"; "Elvis Moving a Small Cloud: In the Desert Near Las Vegas"; "At Graceland With a Six-Year-Old, 1985"; "Pharoah's Palace (Memphis, 1988); in *Mystery Train*. Pittsburgh: University of Pittsburgh Press.

Womack, Jack. 1987. *Ambient*. New York: Doherty & Associates/ Tor Books.

Womack, Jack. 1988. *Terraplane*. New York: Weidenfeld & Nicolson.

Womack, Jack. 1990. *Heathern*. New York: Doherty & Associates.

Womack, Jack. 1993. *Elvissey*. New York: Tom Doherty Associates.

Worth, Fred L., and Steve D. Tamerius (comp.). 1990. *Elvis: His Life from A to Z*. New York: Wings Books.

Wright, Daniel. 1996. *Dear Elvis: Graffiti from Graceland*. Memphis, TN: Mustang Publishing.

# Discography

Adrenalin A.O.D. 1987. "Velvet Elvis." *Flomungus Fungus Amoung Us*.

Anderson, Laurie. 1989. "Hiawatha." Difficult Music (BMI). *Strange Angels* (Warner Bros. 25900-1).

Aztec Two Step. 1986. "Velvet Elvis." *Living in America* (Reflex REC 8601).

Balin, Marty. (L. Russell, K. Fowley, D. Diamond). 1981. "Elvis and Marilyn." Teddy Jack/Bad Boy/Rare Magnetism Music (BMI/ASCAP). *Balin* (EMI America SO-17054).

Blue Aeroplanes. 1991. "Colour Me." Dizzy Heights Music/ Chrysalis Music, Ltd. *Beatsongs* (Chrysalis CHEN 21 3218561).

Blue Nile, The. 1996. "God Bless You Kid." Buchanon/Coldstream (PRS)/WB Music (ASCAP). *Peace at Last* (Warner Bros. □9□45848-2).

Buckingham, Lindsey. 1992. *Out of the Cradle*. (Reprise □9□26182-2)

Burnett, T-Bone. 1983. "After All These Years." Arthur Buster Stahr Music (ASCAP). *Proof Through the Night* (Warner 23921-1).

Butthole Surfers. 1983. "The Revenge of Anus Parsley." *Butthole Surfers* (Alternative Tentacles).

Carnival Art. 1992. "Little Elvis." U.S. Momentum Inc./Virgin Songs, Inc. (BMI). *Welcome to Vas Llegas* (Beggars Banquet/ RCA 66101-2).

Carter Family, The. 1930. "Worried Man Blues." (Bluebird□G020).

Cave, Nick, and the Bad Seeds. 1985. "Tupelo." Dying Art Ltd./ Mute Song. *The Firstborn Is Dead* (Homestead).

Cohn, Marc. 1994. "Walking in Memphis." *Marc Cohn* (Atlantic 78478-2).

Cool It Reba. 1982. "Money Fall Out the Sky." Race Music (BMI). *Money Fall Out the Sky* (Hannibal).

Copeland, Greg. 1982. "At the Warfield." Nel Mezzo Music (ASCAP). *Revenge Will Come* (Geffen GHS 2010).

Costello, Elvis. 1977. *My Aim Is True* (Stiff Records Ltd./Columbia□JC□35037).

Costello, Elvis. 1984. "Worthless Thing" and "Sour Milk Cow-Blues." Plangent Visions Music (ASCAP). *Goodbye Cruel World* (Columbia FC39429).

Costello, Elvis (also MacManus or Lovable MacManus). 1986. "Brilliant Mistake," "I'll Wear It Proudly," and "Suit of Lights." Plangent Visions Music Inc. (ASCAP). *King of America* (Columbia FC 40173).

Costello, Elvis. 1995. *Kojak Variety* (Warner Bros. □45903-2).

Counting Crows. 1993. "Round Here." Blackwood Music/Jones Falls Music (BMI). *August and Everything After* (Geffen Records DGCD 24528).

DB's (Peter Holsapple). 1984. "Rendezvous." Misery Loves Company (BMI). *Like This* (Bearsville 1-25146).

Dead Milkmen. 1987. "Going to Graceland." Golf Pro Music (BMI). *Bucky Fellini* (Enigima ST-73260).

Death Ride '69 (Don Diego/Linda LaSaber). 1988. "Elvis Christ." *Elvis Christ* EP (Little Sister LS-01).

Del-Lords. 1986. "Saint Jake." *Johnny Comes Marching Home* (EMI ST-17183).

Dire Straits. 1991. "Calling Elvis." *On Every Street* (Warner Bros.).

Dread Zeppelin. 1990. *Un-Led-Ed* (I.R.S. IRSD-82048).

Dread Zeppelin. 1991. *5,000,000\** (I.R.S. X2-13092).

Dylan, Bob. 1990. "TV Talkin' Song." Special Rider (ASCAP). *Under the Red Sky* (Columbia 46794).

Dylan, Bob. 1993. "My Back Pages." Special Rider Music (ASCAP). *Bob Dylan: The 30th Anniversary Concert Celebration* (Columbia 474000 1).

El Vez. 1994. *Graciasland.* (Sympathy for the Record Industry).

Elvis Hitler. 1988. "Disgraceland," and "Elvis Ripoff Theme." *Disgraceland* (Restless 72330-1).

Eurythmics (A. Lennox/D. Stewart). 1989. "Angel." BMG Music Publishing, Inc. (BMI) *We Too Are One* (Ansta).

Forbert, Steve. 1995. "Lay Down Your Weary Tune Again." Rolling Tide Music (ASCAP). *Mission of the Crossroad Palms* (Giant/Paladin 9 24611-2).

Forgotten Rebels (M. DeSadist/C. Houston). 1988. "Elvis Is Dead." Rebel Music/LaRana Music (BMI). *Surfin on Heroin* (Restless 72258-1).

Fogerty, John. 1985. "Big Train (from Memphis)," and "I Saw It on TV." Wenaha Music (ASCAP). *Centerfield* (Warner Bros. 1-25203).

Generic Blue Band (S. Turner). 1986. "Elvis in Paraguay" (Hot Fudge HF012).

Gruschecky, Joe, and the Iron City Houserockers. 1992. "Talking to the King." *End of the Century* (Razor and Tie).

Henley, Don. 1989. "If Dirt Were Dollars" Cass Country/Kortchmar (ASCAP). *The End of the Innocence* (Geffen 24217-2).

Hiatt, John. 1983. "Riding With the King." Queen Isabella's Songs (ASCAP). *Riding with the King* (Geffen GHS 4017).

Hiatt, John. 1988. "Tennessee Plates." Lillybilly Music (BMI). *Slow Turning* (A & M 5206).

Hitchcock, Robin. 1990. "Queen Elvis." *Eye* (Twin/Tone) and 1995 (reissue) (Rhino R2 71841).

Human Radio (Ross Rice). 1990. "Me and Elvis." House Projects Music/Hook N'B Music (Sony Music Publishing). *Human Radio* (Columbia).

Jackson, Michael. 1995. *HIStory: Past, Present and Future, Book I.* (Epic□E2K59000).

Jason and the Scorchers (J. Ringenberg). 1984. "Broken Whiskey Glass." Coleman Music (BMI). *Lost and Found* (EMI America ST-17153).

Joel, Billy. 1982. "Elvis Presley Boulevard." (B-side to "Allentown" single). Family Productions (BMI).(Columbia 3803413).

Leroi Brothers. 1985. "Elvis in the Army." *The Leroi Brothers* (Profile PRO 1209).

Lewis, Jerry Lee. 1978. *Duets* (Sun 1011).

Living Colour (Vernon Reid). 1990. "Elvis is Dead." Famous Music Corporation/Dare to Dream Music (ASCAP). *Time's Up* (Epic 46202).

MacColl, Kirsty. 1993. "There's a Guy Works Down the Chip Shop (Swears He's Elvis)." *Essential Collection* (Stiff).

Mekons, The. 1989. "Memphis, Egypt." *The Mekons Rock 'n' Roll* (A & M/Twin Tone).

Mr. Bonus (Peter Holsapple). 1986. "Elvis What Happened?" Misery Loves Company Music (BMI). *Luxury Condos Coming to Your Neighborhood Soon* (Coyote TTC-8559).

Morrison, Van. 1990. "In the Days Before Rock 'n' Roll." Caledonia Productions Ltd. (ASCAP). *Enlightenment* (Mercury 847 100-1).

Myles, Alannah. 1989. "Black Velvet." *Alannah Myles.* (Atlantic).

Nightingales, The. 1981. "Elvis, the Last Ten Days" (Cherry Red, U.K.).

Nile, Willie. 1991. "Everybody Needs a Hammer," and "Don't Die." Watercolor Music (ASCAP). *Places I Have Never Been* (Columbia CK 44434).

Nile, Willie. 1992. "Heart of Wonder." Watercolor Music (ASCAP). *Hard Times in America* EP (Polaris Records PR-9200-2).

Nixon, Mojo, and Skid Roper. 1986. "Twilight's Last Gleaming." Tallywacker Tunes/LaRana Music (BMI). *Frenzy* (Restless 72127).

Nixon, Mojo, and Skid Roper. 1987. "Elvis Is Everywhere." Muffin Stuffin Music/LaRana Music (BMI). *Bo-Day-Shus!!!* (Enigma ST 73272).

Nixon, Mojo, and Skid Roper. 1989. "(619) 239-KING." Muffin Stuffin/LaRana Music (BMI). *Root Hog or Die* (Enigma 7-73335-1).

Odds, The. 1991. "Wendy Under the Stars." Virgin Music/Gymwork Music (ASCAP). *Neopolitan* (Zoo/BMG).

Parker, Graham. 1991. "Weeping Statues." Geep Music/Ellisclan Ltd. *Struck by Lightning* (Demon Fiend 201).

Parker, Graham. 1991. "Museum Piece." Ellisclan Ltd. (EP Demon Records) (France).

Parker, Graham. 1995. "Loverman." Ellisclan Ltd. *12 Haunted Episodes* (Razor & Tie RT 2817).

Petty, Tom, with Jeff Lynne. 1989. "Free Fallin'." Gone gator Music/SBK April Music (ASCAP). *Full Moon Fever* (MCA 6253).

Petty, Tom. 1994. "It's Good To Be King." Gone Gator Music (ASCAP). *Wildflowers* (Warner Bros. 9 45759-2).

Popinjays, The. 1992. "Vote Elvis." Sony Music Entertainment. *Flying Down to Mono Valley* (Epic/One Little Indian EK 52822).

Pink Lincolns (C. Barrows/D. Martin). 1987. "Velvet Elvis" Greedy Bastard Records (001).

Pink Slip Daddy (M. Cancer/R. Riprock). 1988. "Elvis Zombie." Cancerous Music/Asphalt Music (ASCAP). *Pink Slip Daddy* (Apex/Skyclad 18).

Public Enemy (C. Ridenhour, H. Shocklee, E. Sodler, K. Shocklee). 1989. "Fight the Power." (BMI) *Music from 'Do the Right Thing'* (Motown MOT 6272) and *Fear of a Black Planet* (Def Jam/Columbia).

Reed, Lou. 1982. "The Day John Kennedy Died." *The Blue Mask* (RCA□AYL1□4780).

R.E.M. 1994. *Reckoning.* (I.R.S.□SPy0044).

R.E.M. 1994. "What's the Frequency, Kenneth?" Night Garden Music/ Warner Tamerlane (BMI). Monster (Warner Bros. 9 45740-2).

R.E.M. 1992. "Man on the Moon." R.E.M./Athens Ltd. (BMI). *Automatic for the People* (Warner Bros 9 45055-2).

Replacements, The (Paul Westerberg). 1985. "Bastards of Young." NAH Music (ASCAP). *Tim* (Sire 25330).

Residents, The. 1989. *The King and Eye* (TORSO□33137) and 1990 (Enigma E PRO 240).

Ringling Sisters, The. 1990. "Velvet Crush." Labas Music/Bum 'em Up Music/Hollenbeck Music (BMI). *60 Watt Reality* (A & M Records 75021 5337 2).

Presley, Elvis. 1992. *Elvis-The King of Rock 'n' Roll, The Complete '50s Masters* (RCA□07863□66050-2).

Robertson, Robbie. 1987. "American Roulette." Medicine Hat Music (ASCAP). *Robbie Robertson* (Geffen GHS 24160).

Saint Etienne. 1993. "Hobart Paving." Warner Chappell Music (BMI). *So Tough* (Warner Bros. 9 45166-2).

Simon, Paul. 1986. "Graceland." Paul Simon Music (BMI). *Graceland* (Warner Bros. 25447-1).

Sonic Youth. 1990. "Tunic (Song for Karen)." Savage Conquest Music (ASCAP). *Goo* (DGC).

Sons of Elvis. 1995. *Glodean* (Priority).

Sons of Ishmael. 1987. "Elvis Incorporated." *P.M.D.A.S.* (EP Otto Records).

Springsteen, Bruce (with Chuck Berry). 1985. "Johnny Bye Bye" (B- side to "I'm On Fire" single) (Columbia 38-04772).

Springsteen, Bruce. 1984. "Pink Cadillac." B-side to "Dancing in the Dark." Bruce Springsteen (ASCAP) (Columbia 38-04463).

Springsteen, Bruce. 1992. "57 Channels" (and Nothin' on). Bruce Springsteen (ASCAP). *Human Touch* (Columbia□C5□3000).

Straw, Sid (S. Kempner). 1985. "Listening to Elvis." Prince of the Bronx (BMI). *Luxury Condos Coming to Your Neighborhood Soon* (Coyote TTC 8559).

Talking Heads, The. 1979. "Cities." Index Music/Bleu Disque Music Co. Inc. (ASCAP). *Fear of Music* (Sire Records SRK 6076).

Talking Heads, The. 1985. *Little Creatures* (Sire□9□25305-1).

Thompson, Richard. 1993. "From Galway to Graceland." *Watching the Dark: The History of Richard Thompson* (Hannibal HNCD 5303).

Thompson, Richard. 1994. *Mirror Blue* (Capitol□0777□7□81492□2 □4).

Timbuk 3 (Pat MacDonald). 1989. "Standard White Jesus." Mambadadi/I.R.S. Music (BMI). *Edge of Allegiance* (I.R.S. IRS-82015).

Transvision Vamp. 1988. "Born to be Sold." (ASCAP). *Velveteen* (UNI 605).

U2 (Bono Hewson). 1984. "Elvis Presley and America." Island Music Inc. (BMI). *Unforgettable Fire* (Island 90231-1).

Vandals (J. Escalante/R. Allen). 1988. "Elvis Decanter." Greco Roman (ASCAP). *Slippery When Ill* (Restless 72289-1).

Various Artists. 1992. *Honeymoon in Vegas: Music from the Original Motion Picture Soundtrack* (Epic Soundtrax EK 52845).

Various Artists. 1994. *It's Now or Never: The Elvis Presley Tribute* (Mercury).

Various Artists. 1990. *Last Temptation of Elvis, The: Songs from His Movies* (New Musical Express NME 038/039).

Wainwright, Loudon III. 1993. "Happy Birthday Elvis." *Career Moves* (Charisma/Virgin 0777 7).

Wall of Voodoo (A Prieboy/ M. Moreland). 1987. "Elvis Bought Dora a Cadillac." Skeek Music BMI. *Happy Planet* (IRS 5997).

Wonder Stuff, The. 1990. "Mission Drive." Polygram Music Publishing Ltd. *Never Loved Elvis* (Polydor 847252-1).

X (John Doe/Exene Cervanka). 1981. "Back 2 the Base." 812 Music (BMI). *Wild Gift* (Slash SR 107).

Young, Neil. 1979. "My My, Hey Hey (Out of the Blue)." Silver Fiddle Music (BMI). *Rust Never Sleeps* (Warner Reprise 0898).

Zappa, Frank. 1988. "Elvis Has Just Left the Building." Munchkin Music (ASCAP). *Broadway the Hard Way* (Barking Pumpkin D174218).

Zevon, Warren. 1982. "Jesus Mentioned." Zevon Music (BMI). *The Envoy* (Asylum 60159).

# Filmography/Videography

*The Abyss.* 1989. James Cameron. 20th Century Fox.

*Ace Ventura, Pet Detective.* 1994. Tom Shadyac. Morgan Creek/ Warner Bros.

*Adventures of Ford Fairlane, The.* 1990. Renny Harlin. 20th Century Fox.

*Adventures of Priscilla, Queen of the Desert, The.* 1994. (Australian). Stephen Elliott. Polygram.

*My Adventures in the Time Spiral.* 1994. Randy Clower. In *Best of The NY Underground Film and Video Festival, Year One.* (Home video). Film Threat Video.

*Bad Influence.* 1990. Curtis Hanson. Columbia Pictures.

*Beetlejuice.* 1988. Tim Burton. The Geffen Film Company/Warner Bros.

*Blink.* 1994. Michael Apted. New Line Cinema.

*Buffy the Vampire Slayer.* 1992. Fran Rubel Kuzui. 20th Century Fox.

*Burger and the King: The Life and Cuisine of Elvis Presley, The. 1996.* (Made for Cable, British). James Marsh. British Broadcasting Corporation.

*Casual Sex?* 1988. Genevieve Robert. Universal/MCA.

*Cheech and Chong's Next Movie.* 1980. Thomas Chong. Universal.

*Client, The.* 1994. Joel Schumacher. Warner Bros.

*Clive James Fame in the 20th Century.* 1993. (PBS series). Clive James and Beatrice Ballard. BBC-TV Productions/WQED Pittsburgh.

*Commitments, The.* 1991. (British). Alan Parker. 20th Century Fox.

*Dear God.* 1996. Garry Marshall. Paramount Pictures.

*Death Becomes Her.* 1992. Richard Zemeckis. Universal/MCA.

*Defending Your Life.* 1991. Albert Brooks. Warner Bros.

*Drop Dead Fred.* 1991. Ate De Jong. Polygram and Working Title Films.

*Eat the Peach.* 1986. (Irish). Peter Ormrod. Columbia Pictures.

*Elvis.* 1979. (Made for TV movie). John Carpenter. Dick Clark Motion Pictures.

*Elvis and the Beauty Queen.* 1981. (Made for TV movie). Gus Trikonis. Columbia Pictures Television.

*Elvis and the Colonel: The Untold Story.* 1993. (Made for cable movie). New World Television.

*Elvis Files, The.* 1990. (Home video). Laurette Healey. Media Home Entertainment.

*Elvis' Grave.* 1990. David Westbrook Hughens. Westbrook Productions I, Ltd.

*Elvis: The Great Performances, Vol. 1, Center Stage.* 1990. Buena Vista.

*Elvis: The Great Performances, Vol. 2., The Man and His Music.* 1990. Buena Vista.

*Elvis and Me.* 1988. (Made for TV movie). Larry Peerce. New World Television.

*Elvis Stories.* 1990. (Home video). Ben Stiller. Kingsley Celluloid Productions, Ltd. Rhino Home Video.

*Ernest Scared Stupid.* 1991. John Cherry. Touchstone Pictures/ Buena Vista.

*Exit to Eden.* 1994. Garry Marshall. Savoy Pictures.

*Firm, The.* 1993. Sidney Pollack. Paramount Pictures.

*Flatliners.* 1990. Joel Schumacher. RCA/Columbia Pictures.

*Forest Gump.* 1994. Robert Zemeckis. Paramount Pictures.

*Free Willy 2: The Adventure Home.* 1995. Dwight Little. Warner Bros.

*Friday the 13th.* 1980. Sean S. Cunningham. Paramount Pictures.

*Frighteners, The.* 1996. Robert Zemeckis. MCA/Universal.

*Ghostbusters.* 1984. Ivan Reitman. RCA/Columbia Pictures.

*Grease.* 1978. Randal Kleiser. Paramount Pictures.

*Great Balls of Fire!* 1989. Jim McBride. Orion Pictures.

*Hard Target.* 1993. John Woo. MCA/Universal.

*Heart of Dixie.* 1989. Martin Davidson. Orion Pictures.

*Heartbreak Hotel.* 1988. Chris Columbus. Touchstone Pictures.

*Highway 61.* 1991. (Canadian–British). Bruce MacDonald. Paramount Pictures.

*Honey, I Blew Up the Kid.* 1992. Randal Kleiser. Walt Disney Productions.

*Honeymoon in Vegas.* 1992. Andrew Bergman. Castle Rock Entertainment/New Line Cinema.

*Idolmaker, The.* 1980. Taylor Hackford. MGM/United Artists.

*In the Mouth of Madness.* 1995. John Carpenter. New Line Cinema.

*Independence Day.* 1996. Roland Emmerish. Centropolis Entertainment/20th Century Fox.

*Indian Runner, The.* 1991. Sean Penn. The Mount Film Group/ MICO/NHK Enterprises.

*Into the Night.* 1985. John Landis. Universal/MCA.

*It Could Happen to You.* 1994. Andrew Bergman. Columbia/Tri-Star.

*Johnny Suede.* 1991. Tom DiCillo. Paramount/Miramax.

*Kalifornia.* 1993. Dominic Sena. Polygram Film Entertainment/ Viacom/Propganda Films.

*Leningrad Cowboys Go America, The.* 1989. (Finnish). Aki Kaurismaki. Orion Pictures.

*Liar's Edge.* 1992. Ron Oliver.Tri-Star/Columbia New Line.

*Lion King, The.* 1994. Roger Allers, Rob Minkoff. Walt Disney Productions.

*Little Shop of Horrors.* 1986. Frank Oz. Warner Bros.

*Living on Tokyo Time.* 1987. Steven Okazaki. Charter Entertainment.

*Mask, The.* 1994. Charles Russell. New Line Cinema.

*Melvin and Howard.* 1980. Jonathan Demme. MCA.

*Memoirs of an Invisible Man.* 1992. John Carpenter. Warner Bros.

*Memphis.* 1992. (Made for TV movie). Yves Simoneau. Turner Entertainment.

*Million to Juan, A.* 1993. Paul Rodriguez. Columbia

*Mishima: A Life in Four Chapters.* 1985. Paul Schrader. Filmlink.

*Mondo Elvis.* 1990. (Home video). Tom Corboy. Monticello Productions/Rhino Home Video.

*Mystery Train.* 1989. Jim Jarmusch. Orion Classics.

*Natural-Born Killers.* 1994. Oliver Stone. Warner Bros.

*Needful Things.* 1993. Fraser C. Heston. Castle Rock Entertainment/New Line Cinema.

*Never-Ending Story, The.* 1984. Wolfgang Peterson. Neue Constantin Film Prods./Warner.

*One-Trick Pony.* 1980. Robert M. Young. Warner Bros.

*Out of the Blue.* 1980. Dennis Hopper. New Pacific Pictures.

*Paul Simon: Born at the Right Time.* 1992. Susan Lacy and Susan Steinberg. Thirteen/WNET and MTM Enterprises.
*Prehysteria.* 1993. Albert Band and Charles Band. Paramount.
*Pulp Fiction.* 1994. Quentin Tarantino. A Band Apart & Jersey Films/ Miramax.
*Rock-a-Doodle.* 1992. Don Bluth. Samuel Goldwyn/Goldcrest.
*Rockula.* 1990. Luca Bercovici. MGM/UA.
*Sexual Malice.* 1993. Jag Mundhra. Axis/Daris Joint Venture/ A-PIX Entertainment.
*Shakes the Clown.* 1991. Bobcat Goldthwait. I.R.S. Media/Columbia Tri-Star.
*Ten Thousand Points of Light.* 1991. (Home video). George King. Independent.
*Thing Called Love, The.* 1993. Peter Bogdanovich. Paramount.
*True Romance.* 1994. Tony Scott. Morgan Creek/Warner Bros.
*Undercover Blues.* 1993. Herbert Ross. MGM/United Artists.
*U2: Rattle and Hum.* 1988. Phil Joanou. Paramount.
*Vanishing, The.* 1988. (British). George Sluizer. 20th Century Fox.
*Vanishing, The.* 1993. George Sluizer. 20th Century Fox.
*Very Old Man with Enormous Wings, A.* 1988. (South American). Fernando Birri. Gabriel García Masquez Collection.
*Wild at Heart.* 1990. David Lynch. Heron Communications/Polygram/Propaganda Films.
*Wilder Napalm.* 1993. Glenn Gordon Caron. Baltimore Pictures/ Tri-Star.
*Wildside.* 1995. Franklin Brauner. Evergreen Entertainment.
*Woman Who Loved Elvis, The.* 1993. (Made for TV movie). Ronald M. Lautore. Napel Country Prods. Inc./Grossbart Barnett Prods./ HBO Worldwide.

# Television Programs

*Adventures of Pete and Pete, The.* (Nickelodeon). Will McRobb, Chris Viscardi.

*Alf.* (NBC). 1986-1990. Paul Fusco, Tom Patchett. Alien Productions.

*Are You Afraid of the Dark?* (Nickelodeon). D.J. MacHale. Cinar Productions.

*Arsenio Hall Show, The.* (Syndicated). June 3, 1992.

*Beetlejuice* (Syndicated). (Animated). Tim Burton, David Geffen.

*Bill and Ted's Excellent Adventures.* (FOX). 1992.

*Blossom.* (ABC). 1991-1995. Paul Junger Witt, Tony Thomas, Don Reo.

*Bobby's World.* (FOX). (Animated). Howie Mandel, Mitch Schauer. Levy Productions/Film Roman, Inc.

*CBS Evening News with Dan Rather.* (CBS). February 24, 1992.

*Civil Wars.* (ABC). 1991-1993. William Finkelstein. Steven Bochco Productions.

*Clarissa Explains It All.* (Nickelodeon). Mitchell Kriegman. Thunder Productions.

*Cheers.* (NBC). 1982-1993. Glen Charles, Les Charles, James Burrows.

*Coach.* (ABC). 1989-present. Barry Kemp, Judd Pilot, John Peaslee. Bungalo 78 Productions.

*Cops.* (FOX). 1985-present. Malcolm Barbour, John Langley.

*Cosby Show, The.* (NBC). 1984-1992. Bill Cosby, Ed Weinberger, and Michael Lesson. Carsey-Werner Co.

*Current Affair, A.* (Syndicated). 1987-1996. Ian Rae, Peter Brennan.

*Days and Nights of Molly Dodd, The.* (NBC) 1987; (Lifetime) 1988-1991. Jay Tarses, Bernie Brillstein.

*Debt.* 1996-present. (Lifetime). Dean Young. Lifetime Productions/ Faded Denim Productions.

*Designing Women.* (CBS). 1986-1993. Harry Thomason, Linda Bloodworth-Thomason. Mozark Productions.

*Doctor, Doctor.* (CBS). 1989-1991. Norman Steinberg.

*Doogie Howser, M.D.* (ABC). 1989-1993. Steven Bochco, David Kelley. Steven Bochco Productions.

*Eerie, Indiana.* (NBC). 1991-1992. (FOX) 1997-. Karl Schaefer, John Cosgrove, Terry Meurer, Jose Rivera. Unreality Productions.

*Elvis.* (ABC). 1990. James Parriott, Rick Huskey, Priscilla Presley. Navarone Productions.

*E.R.* (NBC). 1994-present. Michael Crichton, John Wells. Constant & Amblin Productions.

*ESPN Sports Center.* (ESPN). 1979-present.

*Evening Shade.* (CBS). 1990-1994. Linda Bloodworth-Thomason, Harry Thomason, Burt Reynolds. Mozark Productions.

*Family Matters.* (ABC). 1989-present. William Bickley, Michael Warren. Miller/Boyett Productions.

*48 Hours.* (CBS). 1988-present. Catherine Lasiewicz. CBS News Productions.

*Frasier.* (NBC). 1993-present. David Angell, Peter Casey, David Lee, Christopher Lloyd. Grub Street Productions.

*Friends.* (NBC). 1994-present. Kevin Bright, David Crane, Marta Kauffman.

*Freddy's Nightmares.* (Syndicated). 1988-1990.

*Full House.* (ABC). 1987-1995. Jeff Franklin. Miller/Boyett Productions.

*Golden Girls, The.* (NBC). 1985-1992. Susan Harris. Witt-Thomas-Harris Productions.

*Ghostwriter.* (PBS). 1992-present. Children's Television Workshop.

*Good Sports.* (CBS). 1991. Alan Zweibel.

*Grace Under Fire.* (ABC). 1993-present. Chuck Lorre. Carsey-Werner Co.

*Grand.* (NBC). 1990. Michael Luson.

*Growing Pains.* (ABC). 1985-1992. Miller/Boyett Productions.

*Hard Copy.* (Syndicated). 1989-present. Lisa Gregoisch. Paramount Domestic TV.

*Home Improvement.* (ABC). 1991-present. Carment Finestra, David McFadzean, Matt Williams. Wind Dancer Productions.

*Homicide: Life on the Street.* (NBC). 1993-present. Barry Levinson, Tom Fontana. Northern Entertainment/NBC Productions.

*In Living Color.* (FOX). 1990-1994. Keenen Ivory Wayans. Ivory Way Productions.

*Jeff Foxworthy Show, The.* (ABC). 1995; (NBC) 1996-present. Tom Anderson, Billstein-Grey Productions.

*John Larroquette Show, The.* (NBC). 1993-present. Paul Junger Witt, Tony Thomas, Don Reo. Impact Zone Productions.

*Johnny Bago.* (CBS). 1993. Robert Zemeckis, Peter S. Seaman, Jeffrey Price.

*Kids in the Hall, The.* (HBO) 1989-1992; (CBS) 1992-1995.

*L.A. Law.* (NBC). 1986-1994. Steven Bochco, Terry Louise Fisher.

*Late Night with David Letterman.* (NBC). 1982-1993. NBC Productions.

*Late Show with David Letterman.* (CBS). 1993-present. Rob Burnett. Worldwide Pants Inc.

*Law and Order.* (NBC). 1990-present. Dick Wolf, Joseph Stern. Wolf Films.

*Lois and Clark: The New Adventures of Superman.* (ABC). 1993-present. Robert Singer. December 3rd Productions.

*Mad About You.* (NBC). 1992 to present. Danny Jacobson, Paul Reiser. Nuance Productions.

*Miami Vice.* (NBC). 1984-1989. Michael Mann.

*Mr. Rhodes.* (ABC). 1996-present. Peter Noah. Universal Television.

*Murphy Brown.* (CBS). 1988-present. Diane English, Joel Shukovsky.

*NBC Nightly News.* (NBC). NBC News. November 7, 1991.

*New WKRP in Cincinnati, The.* (Syndicated). 1991-1993. Hugh Wilson. MTM Enterprises.

*Newhart.* (CBS). 1982-1990. Doug Wyman, David Mirkin. MTM Enterprises.

*NewsRadio.* (NBC). 1995-present. Paul Simms. Brillstein-Grey Productions.

*Nightcourt.* (NBC). 1984-1992. Stuart Kreisman, Chris Clueff.

*Nightline.* (ABC). ABC News. April 27, 1993.

*Northern Exposure.* (CBS). 1990-1995. John Falsey, Joshua Brand, Finnegan/Pinchuk Productions.

*Perfect Strangers.* (ABC). 1986-1993. Miller/Boyett Productions.

*Quantum Leap.* (NBC). 1989-1993. Donald Bellisarius, Deborah Pratt.

*Roseanne.* (ABC). 1988-present. Roseanne Arnold, Tom Arnold, Rob Ulin. Carsey-Werner Co.

*Rugrats.* (Nickelodeon). Klasky/Csupo, Inc.

*Saturday Night Live.* (NBC). 1975-present. Lorne Michaels. NBC Productions.

*Second Noah.* (ABC). 1995-present. Pamela K. Long. Longfeather Productions. MT2 Services Inc.

*Shining Time Station.* (PBS). 1989-present. WNET/Quality Family Viewing.

*Simpsons, The.* (FOX). (Animated). 1990-present. James L. Brooks, Matt Groening. Gracie Films.

*60 Minutes.* (CBS). 1968-present. Don Hewitt. CBS News. April 12, 1992.

*Sledge Hammer!* (ABC). 1986-1988. Alan Spencer. New World Productions.

*Square One TV.* (PBS). 1987-1994. Children's Television Workshop.

*Step by Step.* (ABC). 1991-present. Miller/Boyett Productions.

*Toonces and Friends.* (NBC special). 1991. Jack Handey, John Fortenberry. Broadway Video/NBC Productions.

*Twilight Zone, The (New).* (CBS). 1986-1996; (Syndicated) 1988. Philip DeGuere.

*Twin Peaks.* (ABC). 1990-1991. Mark Frost, David Lynch. Propaganda Productions.

*Wings.* (NBC). 1990-present. David Angell, Peter Casey, David Lee. Grub Street Productions.

*X-Files, The.* (FOX). 1993-present. Chris Carter. Ten Thirteen Productions.

*Xuza.* (Syndicated). 1993-1995. Sami Rami.

# Song Title Index

# Subject Index

Titles of books, films, television shows, record albums, and art work are printed in italics; chapters, episodes, and slogans are enclosed by quotation marks. The letter "i" indicates an illustration reference; "n" indicates a footnote reference.

## Order Your Own Copy of
## This Important Book for Your Personal Library!

## IMAGES OF ELVIS PRESLEY IN AMERICAN CULTURE, 1977-1997

### The Mystery Terrain

_____ in hardbound at $39.95 (ISBN: 1-56024-910-2)

_____ in softbound at $24.95 (ISBN: 1-56023-861-5)

COST OF BOOKS_____

OUTSIDE USA/CANADA/
MEXICO: ADD 20%_____

POSTAGE & HANDLING_____
*(US: $3.00 for first book & $1.25*
*for each additional book)*
*Outside US: $4.75 for first book*
*& $1.75 for each additional book)*

SUBTOTAL_____

IN CANADA: ADD 7% GST_____

STATE TAX_____
*(NY, OH & MN residents, please*
*add appropriate local sales tax)*

**FINAL TOTAL**_____
*(If paying in Canadian funds,*
*convert using the current*
*exchange rate. UNESCO*
*coupons welcome.)*

☐ **BILL ME LATER:** ($5 service charge will be added)
(Bill-me option is good on US/Canada/Mexico orders only;
not good to jobbers, wholesalers, or subscription agencies.)

☐ Check here if billing address is different from
shipping address and attach purchase order and
billing address information.

Signature_____

☐ **PAYMENT ENCLOSED: $**_____

☐ **PLEASE CHARGE TO MY CREDIT CARD.**

☐ Visa  ☐ MasterCard  ☐ AmEx  ☐ Discover
☐ Diners Club
Account # _____

Exp. Date _____

Signature _____

Prices in US dollars and subject to change without notice.

NAME _____

INSTITUTION _____

ADDRESS _____

CITY _____

STATE/ZIP _____

COUNTRY _____ COUNTY (NY residents only) _____

TEL _____ FAX _____

E-MAIL_____
May we use your e-mail address for confirmations and other types of information? ☐ Yes    ☐ No

*Order From Your Local Bookstore or Directly From*
**The Haworth Press, Inc.**
10 Alice Street, Binghamton, New York 13904-1580 • USA
TELEPHONE: 1-800-HAWORTH (1-800-429-6784) / Outside US/Canada: (607) 722-5857
FAX: 1-800-895-0582 / Outside US/Canada: (607) 772-6362
E-mail: getinfo@haworth.com
PLEASE PHOTOCOPY THIS FORM FOR YOUR PERSONAL USE.

BOF96